Russia
and the
Russians

Also by Kevin Klose

Surprise! Surprise! (with Ron Shaffer)
The Typhoon Shipments (with Philip A. McCombs)
I Will Survive (with Sala Pawlowicz)

Russia
and the
Russians

Inside the Closed
Society

Kevin Klose

W· W· Norton & Company
New York   London

The text of this book is composed in Janson, with
display type set in Times Roman Bold and Avanta Garde. Composition and
Manufacturing by Haddon Craftsmen, Inc.
Book design by Bernard Klein

First Edition

Library of Congress Cataloging in Publication Data

Klose, Kevin
Russia and the Russians.

Bibliography: p.
Includes index.
1. Soviet Union—Politics and government—1953
2. Dissenters—Soviet Union. 3. Soviet Union—Description
and travel—1970 . 4. Klose, Kevin I. Title.
DK274.K58 1984   947.085   83-23745

ISBN 0-393-01786-9

W. W. Norton & Company, Inc., 500 Fifth Avenue, New York, N. Y. 10110
W. W. Norton & Company Ltd. 37 Great Russell Street, London WC1B 3NU
1 2 3 4 5 6 7 8 9 0

For Eliza

Contents

The Way In

AFTER a long flight from London Heathrow that carried us high over Denmark, the North Sea, Poland, and White Russia, the British Airways jet bearing my wife, Eliza, and me to our new home in Moscow began to descend through broken cloudtops. Sun streamed around the plane and fell in shafts across unkempt green meadows. Below, we could see clusters of dark gray and brown hamlets scattered across the landscape. Stands of dark pines broke the pattern of large fields. We were too high to make out humans, but there were cattle, farm trucks, tractors, and even some horse-drawn wagons slowly making their way along dusty byways and two-lane roads. There were few automobiles, but as we approached the outskirts of the Soviet capital we could see plenty of fat, dingy gray buses lumbering along major highways. In the distance we could see darker shadings and shapes that suggested the apartment blocks and factories of a great metropolis rising above this undulating rural counterpane.

On that day in late June of 1977, we felt no urgency to reach the ground. The view from a few thousand feet was beguiling, and we knew we would have at least three years in the Soviet Union, where I was to be Moscow bureau chief for *The Washington Post*, to try to understand details that we could never see from the air. As we peered through our tiny window in the aircraft, we wondered what lay ahead. We had tried to prepare ourselves and our three children by imagining that the Moscow assignment might be like a long voyage on a small sloop. We would need to rely on each other to a degree previously unknown in our Washington lives. We knew we would need patience, fortitude, and a sense of humor. But would this really help us live in so strange a place, and what could we— Americans from the most powerful, pampered, and open society in the world—really hope to learn of the inner nature of a totalitarian state? What was Soviet reality? What would the Russians have to teach us?

Now we could see the most spectacular sight of all: the Moscow River winding across the plain, a brownish industrial thoroughfare carrying barges, small inland oilers, dredges, and scows of various types. Flashing around these slow-moving craft, like swallows or waterbugs, were white-hulled hydrofoils. They darted up and down the curving river, carrying sightseers bound for the countryside. The scene looked so joyous and exhilarating that suddenly I didn't want the journey from America to end: whatever the reality would be down there on the ground, it could never match the illusion created by seeing Moscow from this safe distance. The sharpness of that regret remains today, six years later. For, close up, the truth of Russia was far more painful than I ever could have imagined. In the first year, there were separate pieces of reality, a mosaic of experiences and impressions that contradicted and confounded. But they helped form the lens within me.

Eliza stayed in Moscow for ten days to see what was needed to make our lives work and then returned to Vermont to finish the summer with her parents and family. She would return in mid-August with the children. Meanwhile, I began to feel my way around. I traveled by train to Kiev and spent the weekend with Robin Porter, an American diplomat who headed a small U.S. contingent preparing to open a consulate in the Ukrainian capital. The effort was canceled after the Soviets invaded Afghanistan, but when Porter played host to a neophyte Moscow correspondent that event was still more than two years in the future. My companion in the train compartment on the way down was a heavyset civil engineer who had lost his left leg at mid-thigh in the defense of Moscow in the autumn of 1941. His prosthesis looked as if it weighed twenty pounds and it squeaked and protested when he unstrapped it and stood it by his bunk.

In Kiev, I discovered that Alexander the Great had preceded me to the same spot. Gold coins, necklaces, and rings from his times had been found in various places in the southern Ukraine and were preserved in a special museum of Scythian gold at the Peschora Lavra, an ancient monastery on a bluff above the Dnieper River, with an extensive catacomb deep beneath the cliffs. Without hesitation, I descended into the musty maze of narrow, dimly lit tunnels, lined with urns and reliquaries containing the skulls and bleached bones of saints long dead and forgotten. I have discovered since that my tolerance for confined places like the catacombs has vanished. The years in Moscow left me with a strong case of claustrophobia.

Later in July I went to Sochi on the Black Sea with Robin Knight of *U. S. News & World Report* and David Satter of the *Financial Times* of London, an American acquaintance from Washington who became my closest friend in Moscow. We stayed at the Pearl Hotel, a high-rise just off the beach. Warm breezes wafted through my fourteenth-floor bedroom, and, in the morning, the unmistakable damp rasping of hoe through wet cement rose from the weedy, rubble-strewn courtyard behind the hotel. Looking down, I saw a *babushka* mixing cement by hand in a large, square, wooden tub. All alone, she was building an Olympic-sized swimming pool in the backyard of the Pearl Hotel. It had taken seven years of intermittent labor to build the hotel. I was astonished that the crews could even keep the blueprints straight from year to year.

We sunned on the shingle beach, resting on rented slat pallets, and swam in the Black Sea's warm, brownish water. The hotel had buoyed off a swimming area about a hundred yards from shore. I would swim out there and lie on my back with my heels hooked over the buoy line. The sky was not much different from the one over summertime Washington—low, puffy clouds in a heavy, humid atmosphere that made them seem even lower. Small picket boats moved on the horizon. I wondered if a person could escape the country by slipping down the coast to Turkey by boat.

In Sochi Harbor, a larger patrol craft with sparkling trim lay moored to a pier. Years later, someone in Moscow claimed that it was the personal boat of Yuri Andropov, the KGB chief who succeeded Leonid Brezhnev as party leader in 1982. It could have been; the vessel had that spit-and-polish look of being owned by someone with great wealth or great power. In Andropov's case, maybe both.

Back in Moscow, Malcolm Browne, then with *The New York Times,* and I went to visit Benjamin Levich, a corresponding member of the Soviet Academy of Sciences who was the highest-ranking

of the privileged scientific elite ever to apply for emigration. Levich
and his wife, Tatiana, lived in a handsome building on Leninski
Prospekt that carried a huge sign on its roof hailing the gains of the
Socialist Revolution. "Don't speak in the lobby or in the corridors,"
Mal cautioned. Why give up even one crumb of information with-
out making the secret police go to some effort?

Like dozens of other Jewish scientists, the Leviches had been
refused permission to leave Russia even though their children had
been allowed to emigrate to Israel several years before. Under the
Helsinki Agreement, which Leonid Brezhnev signed in 1975, parents could assert the right to be reunited with their children. But the
agreement didn't seem to apply to these citizens. The Leviches
poured tea and talked wistfully of attending a scientific conference
in his name that British scientists were sponsoring in England that
summer. The state had not responded to his requests for a temporary visa. Since Levich had already been dismissed from his most
important scientific posts and had no intention of doing meaningful
work for the state, his treatment seemed cruel and pointless to me.
But I was very new to Russia then.

In mid-August, Eliza returned with our three children: Cornelia
(Nina), a determined almost-10-year-old; Brennan, a blue-eyed 8;
and Chandler, just 4½ and happy to sit in any lap he could find.
What would these three encounter in the years here?

Soon after Eliza's arrival, we went to the Leviches for dinner;
they entertained us with tales of Soviet life. One of Levich's first
points was that not everyone in the Soviet Union practiced communism with the same zeal as the Russians. The "Southerners"—the
rebellious Georgians, Armenians, and Azerbaijanis—did things differently, he said, and began describing life in Baku, the Caspian Sea
port that is the capital of Azerbaijan. "Did you know that it costs
four hundred rubles to have your appendix removed in Baku?"

"Really?" I said, as shocked as any Westerner who has heard of
the Soviet Union's free medical care.

"Oh, it's much better that way," Levich explained. "There is a fee
schedule—perfectly illegal, of course!—for each kind of operation,
so you know what you're paying for, and the service is much better
down there than anywhere in European Russia. Everyone else is
smarter about these things than the poor Russians! Up here, they
really try to make it impossible to get decent medical service!"

Later that evening, the Leviches asked if we had any photographs of the children. I had none; Eliza searched her handbag and found Chandler's passport. She showed it and the Leviches handed it back and forth. Then, Ben's eyes filled with tears. "What I would give to have such a passport!"

After the intervention of Senator Edward M. Kennedy and other Americans a few months later, the Soviets permitted the Leviches to leave. The decision came at a time when Washington and Moscow were searching for ways to improve their relations after several disagreements between the Kremlin and the new Carter administration. Freeing the Leviches suggested that the Kremlin wouldn't hesitate to trade bodies for better relations. But so what, I thought. The important fact is that they were allowed to leave.

One day in late summer, a Russian I didn't know telephoned me at the office and asked to meet. I went to a nearby vest-pocket park and a stocky man in his late 30s with a harried expression on his face wandered over and introduced himself as a lawyer from Leningrad. He showed me several identification cards and a small party membership card in a red plastic holder. Other than my own visa, driver's license, and press credentials from the Foreign Ministry, I hadn't seen many Soviet IDs; these looked genuine enough. "I want to tell you about political abuses in the Leningrad legal system," he said. My Russian was not good, so I arranged to bring a friend, whom I shall call Richard, to another meeting the next day to act as interpreter.

The lawyer was very tense and, to calm him, I drove well out of the downtown area. After a twenty-minute drive, during which the Russian swiveled nervously in every direction, I pulled to a curb near a shoe store and, with my American colleague translating, the man began.

"I'm sick of Soviet power and its distortions of reality," he began. "I have seen political interference in Soviet justice and I am ready to give you accounts of these and supply documents as well."

"Fine," we said. "Go on."

"But first, I want to ask you something."

"Go ahead."

"I want you to tell your embassy that I am ready to work for the CIA."

I turned to Richard. "This is incredible. Tell this man to get out of the car. Tell him we do not have any connections with the

U. S. embassy, that we have no connections with any branch of the American government, and that if he does not believe what I have said he is the biggest fool I've ever met."

Richard rattled out the message. For a moment, the man looked perplexed; then, sweating profusely, he got out of the car. He walked a few steps away, then returned and leaned in the window. "I understand why you had to say that," he said. "And I await your call."

I drove away, raving at my own stupidity. Then I stopped. "Do you think he was a provocateur?"

"He certainly seemed like it," Richard said with a laugh that told me what a fool I'd been. "But who knows? He might have been for real. They're all told we're spies so maybe he thought he was doing the right thing."

"That doesn't make me feel any better. What's going to happen to him? More to the point, what's going to happen to us—ah . . . me?"

"If he's a provocateur, he will report to the KGB that he was successful in getting us to solicit him for the 'special services.' If he's genuine, he'll keep coming back, somehow finding contacts with foreign reporters or diplomats until the KGB sifts him out and interrogates him. And they can make him say the same thing."

"You're not very helpful."

"I'm not trying to be. The point of it is, Kevin—either way it goes in the dossier they've opened on you."

In late August, we enrolled Nina and Brennan at Moscow Special School No. 5, one of about a hundred special schools among the eleven hundred public schools in Moscow. The specials function as a kind of private school system for the offspring of the elite and for the sons and daughters of other Soviet citizens who can qualify for enriched learning opportunities. The school specialized in teaching English, which began in the second grade. Most of the pupils were the children of well-placed party people and technocrats who knew that mastery of English, the world language, could be a ticket to astonishing foreign travel—such as to America, or England. We felt that if our children could get through the first difficult months, they would learn Russian well and gain special insights into a society that could only seem strange to them.

Special School No. 5 was located directly across the street from the KGB-guarded compound on Kutuzovsky Prospekt where we took up residence in the same low-ceilinged, four-room apartment in which every *Washington Post* Moscow correspondent had lived since 1967. On September 1, accompanied by their somewhat apprehensive parents, Brennan and Nina set forth for their opening day of first and second grades, respectively, in the Soviet school system. Because they knew no Russian, each had been put back two years. Since Soviet children begin school at age 7 and attend for ten years, this meant that our children were starting at and near the bottom. They would be tutored daily after class to help them with the language, and it was promised that, if things worked out, they might skip a grade or two later and join their own age groups. Chandler, not yet 5, could not read and write in his mother tongue, and we had decided that he needed more practice in English. He would attend the Anglo-American diplomatic school. But he came with us this morning, eager to watch his siblings go off to their first day of school.

Nina and Brennan were dressed in the customary Soviet uniforms—for the girls, chocolate brown dresses with white, lace-trimmed aprons, cuffs and collars; for the boys, blue twill trousers and Eisenhower jackets. They carried bouquets for their teachers, a national tradition for opening day. We joined a stream of children, parents, grandparents, uncles, aunts, cousins, and perhaps even out-of-town relatives who were filing into the schoolyard for opening day ceremonies.

Here was pandemonium. Children scrambled, parents milled, and teachers moved about nervously, dividing their charges into grades and classes. With all assembled beneath class placards, the directress appeared and exhorted the students to excel at their studies. When she finished and dismissed them, the children broke for the school building, where the seven hundred scholars faced nine months of six-day schoolweeks.

With our imperfect command of Russian, we struggled to understand the directions for newcomers. But some older students quickly took charge and escorted Nina and Brennan into the schoolhouse. Nina cast us a stricken look as she disappeared with a teenager whose English carried a distinct Oxbridge accent, the preferred language of the school.

Chandler watched all this with a mild detachment befitting one who was headed for the familiarity of the diplomatic school, where there were scores of Americans. And then, the vice-directress of the school suddenly materialized. Casting an intensely Russian look at Chandler powerful enough to melt an iceberg, she turned to us. "There's room for him as well!" she announced, clamping her hands on his wrist and giving a strong tug. Chandler froze.

"Oh, no, no," Eliza said, grabbing his other wrist. "He's going to the Anglo-American school."

"*Nyet, nyet,*" said Ludmilla Ivanovna gaily, "he's one of *ours.* We have a place for him." Another tug forward.

"No, no, really, that's very kind, but he's got to learn *English* before anything else." A tug backward.

"We have excellent English here. He is most welcome." Another pull.

"He really isn't ready for Russian schools . . . no uniform, no books. . . ."

The hostage now was completely terrorized, in abject fear of sharing his brother's and sister's fate beyond the schoolhouse door. Chandler uttered nary a word as the tug-of-war went on, but his silence was eloquent. In the end, Eliza prevailed; it was a near thing.

Eliza had been active in the Washington public schools during our years there and was interested in volunteering at No. 5 to help with English pronunciation or usage or to organize activities outside the classroom. She talked to various officials and just about the only response was a request for as many paperbacks of *Alice in Wonderland* as she might care to provide for the school.

After Nina was corrected one day in class by her English teacher for not knowing that the plural of "sheep" was "sheeps," Eliza renewed her efforts. The answer finally came back: could Eliza deliver a talk on trends in American public school education? Eagerly, she prepared. Here would be a chance to crack the ice and develop better rapport with the teachers.

On the appointed day, she was ushered into a fifth-floor classroom and treated to a polite round of applause from the thirteen teachers of English and the directress, a formidable woman who seemed less than happy about the presence of American children in her school. One of the teachers delivered a formal speech on ways to teach English grammar. Then it was Eliza's turn. Drawing on her experiences at the Columbia Road Children's Center and Horace Mann public school in northwest Washington, she described the general classroom scene, the role of teacher and teaching aide, and some of the subjects. She mentioned that Washington had somewhat smaller classes than did No. 5, where classes usually totaled around forty pupils. She pointed out the lack of emphasis on grades in the early elementary years in many American schools, and the fact that some schools had "open classrooms," with unstructured curriculum. For the benefit of the English teachers, she delivered her remarks in English; the head of the English department translated them for the directress, who neither spoke nor understood English. When she was finished, there was a slight pause. Then the directress took the floor.

"Very interesting. Now, I should like to mention that we also have teaching assistants in Soviet schools, who aid the teacher in preparing the class each day. We also have smaller classes in many schools in the Soviet Union. This is a well-known fact. First-grade children are not graded in their first term. In some rural schools, we also have open classrooms." On every point of information about American schools, the directress had comparable assertions about Soviet schools. If smaller was better, then Soviet school classes were smaller than American classes. If open classrooms were in vogue, then the Soviets had pioneered open classrooms. And so it went. Eliza found other outlets for her energy.

It was a December day, perfectly clear and quiet, as though a bell jar had been clamped over the landscape. The sharp air and temperature of about fifteen degrees below zero Fahrenheit pierced our nostrils. The sun, a watery yellow disk that would climb no more than a few dozen degrees above the horizon, yielded no detectable warmth. But its low-angled rays across the crystalline dust of new-fallen snow transformed the vast drifted field where we stood into a shimmering carpet. We were about sixty miles west of Moscow, surrounded by the solitude of the East European plain. We had come here in search of a Christmas tree.

The quest had begun a few days before, with a volley of telephone calls to various departments in the Diplomatic Service Corps Bureau, the apparatus that looks after resident foreigners in Moscow. Through Regina, our secretary, we sought permission to enter the "green zone," an area of the Moscow region closed to foreigners and well beyond the twenty-five-mile radius within which we could travel without permission.

After two days of conversations and some letters to officials, the bureaucracy produced slips allowing a car bearing an American family plus nanny into the countryside where we could chop down our own Christmas tree. The spirit of the season had prevailed. The Russians understood our hopes: they themselves celebrate the New Year with all the intensity and cheer with which Americans greet Christmas.

Although there is no official religious content to most of their activities, there is little apparent distinction between Western and Soviet winter celebrations. The Soviets have New Year's trees, which are cut down weeks before the holiday and trucked into towns and cities to be sold on street corners and in vacant lots. Because the average Soviet home is small, the trees are small. But when they are decorated with lights and glass globes, they are dazzling. Presents lie beneath the boughs, delivered by *Dyet Moroz*, Grandfather Frost, who looks, dresses, and acts like Saint Nick with his sack full of toys. There are, however, differences to the ritual: Grandfather Frost's sleigh is drawn by a troika of stunning horses with flowing manes and tails, and he carries his bundle of presents in through the front door. "The chimney is the devil's entrance," our samovar-shaped maid told us when she heard how Santa made his appearance in America. Grandfather Frost also has a beguiling companion who seems much more European than American—*Snyegoruchka*, the Snow Maiden, who accompanies him on his rounds from house to house. Chandler didn't find this especially appealing, but the rest of us did.

Nina's teacher smiled indulgently when I explained to her in my still-limited Russian that Americans celebrated Christmas and we had obtained permission from the authorities to cut our own tree out in the restricted green zone. "Have a good trip," she said with a holiday-like wave of her hand.

Once in the countryside, we stopped at a small government office to present our permissions and pay for the tree. There seemed to be one other customer, probably a privileged Russian or East European, who regarded us in a friendly way. It took us fifteen minutes and visits to three different ramshackle offices in the same building to have the permissions duly noted in purple ink in various ledgers. Four plump women sat in the steamy heat of the last office; protocol required visits and explanations to three of the women in turn. Each gravely proffered approval in the form of the right initials on the right forms. As I left, I called, *"S'Novim Godom"*—"Happy New

Year." The women returned the greetings in a pleased chorus and observed that the forest was not far.

We drove another twenty miles through numerous small villages, past old wooden houses set close to the road. Here and there women drew wooden sleds with large buckets of water for cargo; some children, so heavily wrapped in the Russian manner against the chill that they could barely move their arms, were being towed on their own small sleds along bumpy, hard-packed side roads. These were places that no plow would ever touch.

At our destination, we walked through a copse of birch. Some of the graceful trees had been bent double by the weight of a month of snow, and were arched over the narrow trail in a cathedral effect. Beyond lay a large, open field where snow was mounded in frozen waves over hummocks of dead pasture grass. The children threw snowballs and rolled in the drifts.

Then we moved into a dense forest of mature trees interspersed with stands of young pines. After much tromping around and inspecting of the trees, we chose three smallish ones—one for us and two for friends, all carefully arranged for and paid in advance. The young forester who had accompanied us seemed scandalized with our choices. "They're all right," he said of our prize trees, "but you should have something *bigger.*" He marched off and, then, to the delight of the children, returned with a magnificent spruce much too tall for our low-ceilinged apartment. Ignoring our protests, he tied the tree atop the car with its puny cousins and bade us goodbye. With the challenge ahead of sizing the tree and the thought of a turkey from Hungary waiting to be roasted, we were ready for Christmas.

Chandler was confident that Santa, or perhaps Grandfather Frost on a get-acquainted visit a few days early, would find the way to the right apartment. We agreed and he turned out to be right: there were presents beneath the tree on Christmas Day. We felt very much at home.

In early April of 1978, the story of an extraordinary escape attempt broke in Moscow. It was an adventure that a few weeks later would encourage the Soviet Union to shoot down a South Korean airliner that had blundered off course and gone far astray over northern Russia. That episode, in which two people were killed and 108 others aboard the plane narrowly escaped death, was to be repeated five and a half years later, when the USSR brought down another South Korean airliner, this time killing all 269 aboard, in one of the worst incidents in the post-détente era.

The 1978 escape attempt was organized by Ludmilla Agapova* and her husband, Valentin Agapov, a Soviet sailor who had defected from his ship when it was docked in Sweden in 1974. Ever since then, Agapova had petitioned the government to allow her, her 69-year-old mother-in-law, Antonina Agapova, and her teenaged daughter, Lilya, to emigrate and be reunited with her husband. The Kremlin ignored her pleas. A defector's family was almost never allowed to leave the country. The Swedes, who had granted political asylum to the Soviet sailor and took up his cause, also got nowhere. Husband and wife at last decided to take matters into their own hands.

Following months of cryptic telephone calls, conversations with intermediaries, and guarded correspondence, the couple forged a plan to fly the three women out of the country by light plane. The plane would make a treetop flight from a nearby Finnish airfield and land not far from the Soviet border north of Leningrad. The landing strip would be a frozen lake because it offered a flat, clear surface and plenty of room for taking off. Agapova and the other two women would have to penetrate the tightly guarded border zone and make their way to the lake in time to meet the plane.

Valentin Agapov found a Swedish pilot willing to risk the forbidden flight into Soviet territory. Meanwhile, beginning in January 1978, his wife began traveling from her home in Kaliningrad, near Moscow, to Leningrad and then about seventy miles farther north to the provincial town of Priozersk on the northwestern shore of Lake Ladoga. From there, she went by bus to a smaller lake, reconnoitering the rendezvous area numerous times and becoming familiar with ways to avoid detection. The Soviet border zone is a heavily patrolled fenced-off swath about thirty miles wide along the Norwegian–Finnish border. It is dotted with observation towers and similar security measures and only Soviets with special extra documents are allowed to live there. The region is heavily forested and most of the border zone population is employed in logging and similar work. Any Soviet traveling into the zone must pass through two and

*Women's names in Russian usually have a feminine ending of -a or -aya unless they are of foreign extraction.

sometimes three separate passport inspections. Agapova found that the people of the area reflected this security mania: they were vigilant and suspicious of new faces and felt comfortable with police and agents. But she mastered the complex permissions and official approvals required even to buy bus tickets to the small border hamlets and logging settlements.

She made her way to the lake that had been chosen and checked the depth of the ice to ensure that it could support the weight of a light plane. After several more trips to the general area, and when she was satisfied that they would not be detected, Agapova returned to Kaliningrad and communicated with her husband. Soon the first attempt was ready.

On March 10, the women headed north by train and bus to Priozersk. They faked their way past various officials and guard points and took a bus that would deposit them near the lake. The conductor worked his way down the aisle toward them. "Tickets and *propuski*, permissions," he intoned. Agapova looked up at him.

"We have them," she lied.

The conductor moved on.

"He didn't check to see," she told a group of correspondents later. "Not everyone works for the KGB."

The bus left them at an open-sided shelter in the deserted countryside. They shivered through the night and at dawn slogged on foot through heavy snow to wait beside the lake. The airplane never came. The three women spent the night in the area and another day beside the lake. Still no plane. They returned to Kaliningrad and word came from Agapov: bad weather had stopped the flight. They would try again on March 19.

At dawn that day, Agapova, Lilya, and Antonina were at the lake. But by the time the light began fading, at around 4 P.M., it was clear the plane would not come. Returning home, they learned that bad weather once again had prevented the lightly instrumented plane from making the flight. With spring moving into the Leningrad region, there would not be much time before the lake ice melted, putting off any possible landing until the following winter. A final attempt was scheduled for April 1.

The women set out again from Kaliningrad, confident only that they had mastered the timetable for getting to the lake at the appointed hour. After boarding the train for Leningrad they sat back, waiting for the departure that would ensure arrival in time to catch the first of the local buses. But the train sat on the platform. Ludmilla, by now frantic, suddenly realized that they were in the middle of the spring school holiday and families were thronging the platform, still trying to get aboard. After what seemed like an eternity, the train departed. The ride turned into a nightmare of long stops and delayed departures. They arrived in Priozersk so late that all the seats on the local bus to the way station had been taken. In despair, they took the next available bus, knowing they could never reach the lake by the 7:30 A.M. rendezvous time.

It was about 9 A.M. when they finally reached the lake. In dismay, they saw that the spring thaw had melted the rim of ice at the shore of the lake. Thirty feet of deep slush and water separated them from a patch of solid ice that looked big enough to land on. "We couldn't make it . . . we couldn't walk on water." The women turned back for the last time.

Meanwhile, not far away, at the small Finnish airport of Immolo several miles west of the Soviet border, startled Finnish authorities had taken into custody two Swedes who had landed their light plane there—*after flying in from the east.* The pilots told a fantastic story of how, flying just above the tops of the pines, they had dodged over the Soviet border, touched down briefly on a small lake inside Russia, and finding no one there, returned empty-handed.

Unknown to the Swedes or Agapova, at the very moment the rescue plane penetrated Soviet airspace, the Soviet Air Force was conducting a major exercise to check the air defense force's ability to intercept and repel imagined aerial intruders. The Russians never detected the small plane.

Just twenty days later, a Korean Air Lines 707 with one hundred ten passengers and crew aboard, on a trans-Polar flight from Paris to Seoul, via Anchorage, Alaska, lost its navigational bearings somewhere near the North Pole. Instead of continuing east toward Alaska and safety, the plane turned south to Soviet territory—and danger. Smarting from the discovery that a light plane had flown into the USSR and landed undetected during their recent defense exercise, the Soviets were determined to stop this intruder.

As the Korean plane passed over Franz Josef Land off the Soviet Arctic coast, two surface-to-air missiles were launched, NATO sources reported later. The Boeing was flying straight and level at thirty-five thousand feet, its airspeed about five hundred miles per hour. The rockets missed the target and the Koreans never saw them. The plane continued south, flying over Murmansk, home port of the USSR's northern ballistic missile submarine fleet. Soviet interceptors were scrambled and, after a few minutes in which they identified the target, a Sukhoi-15 fighter on command from ground controllers fired a missile at the airliner. The blast shredded fifteen feet from the port wing of the Boeing and shrapnel ripped into the cabin. Two passengers died, and ten others were injured. Pilot Kim Chang Kyu narrowly averted a greater disaster by diving down to a few thousand feet and landing on a frozen lake on the Kola peninsula south of Murmansk.

The Soviets interned the survivors for two days, accused the Koreans of plotting an espionage flight with American connivance, and then allowed the U.S. to fly the foreigners out. Six months later, Moscow billed the Koreans for about one hundred thousand dollars —for humanitarian aid, such as food, clothing, and transportation —provided to the survivors of the aerial attack and crash landing.

A month later, in May 1978, the regime put Dr. Yuri Orlov, a longtime human rights activist, on trial. He had been in prison under pre-trial arrest since February 1977 and held all but incommunicado in accordance with Soviet legal practice. For helping found an unofficial citizens' group to monitor Soviet compliance with the human rights provisions of the Helsinki Agreement on European Cooperation and Security, he was charged with anti-Soviet slander, which carried a maximum penalty of seven years in prison and five in internal exile. Orlov, a diminutive man with curly reddish hair flecked with gray, was then 53, and suffered from kidney problems which had gone untreated during his incarceration. His trial was the first of the major anti-dissident political shows of the late 1970s and much of Moscow's foreign press corps was on hand to record the event.

The trial was held in a district court in the eastern part of the city, about a twenty-five-minute drive from the downtown compounds where the correspondents lived. The courthouse was situated across from a railroad switching yard and behind an army barracks where pimply faced recruits with crudely shaved heads slopped green paint on picket fences and eyed us foreigners with something between guarded interest and blind fear.

The proceedings took four days in May. The weather had turned warm and lilacs in front of the courthouse came into bloom. Most of us kept vigil outside the court, where we interviewed Irina Orlova, the physicist's wife, whenever she emerged from the building. She was more than twenty years Orlov's junior, his second wife, and devoted to him. She, as spouse, and Orlov's two sons by his first marriage had access to the courtroom, which was otherwise packed with KGB agents and trainees who shouted and booed whenever the defendant tried to speak. The sons were harassed and one was barred after an altercation with the guards. Irina was stripped to her bra and panties and searched in full view of three male guards, but still managed to provide the most coherent account of what was happening inside. Each time she appeared, sympathizers and correspondents crushed in around her.

On the first day, the uniformed police and KGB permitted us to interview Irina on the courthouse steps. The second day, they barred this and herded the crowd away from the courthouse, up the street to the main thoroughfare and into the potholed parking lot of a decrepit supermarket. There the police staged a mini-riot, grabbing reporters, smashing tape recorders, and encouraging young toughs to spit on or slap the foreigners and pummel the tops of their cars when they drove off. There was nothing especially serious in any of this, but it was a nasty harbinger of what could happen if the police decided to get serious. That night, David Satter and I talked over what could be done to protect Irina, our sole source of information about the trial. The police could pounce on her anytime she appeared, drive her to the edge of the city, and dump her. There was the risk of injury. She was in jeopardy largely because the foreign press needed to interview her. The next day, we proposed to our colleagues that she be driven to any Western compound where she could be interviewed in peace. Fine idea, they agreed—but who would do it? Eventually, Satter and I did.

During the third day, David and I spread the word of our intention to correspondents and dissidents. When Irina emerged from the court, drawn and near collapse, the throng ushered—almost carried—her up the street and put her into the back seat of David's car. Two friends sandwiched her in, I jumped into the front passenger seat, and he pulled out of the parking lot. Suddenly, four KGB cars roared out behind us. As we pulled into heavy afternoon traffic, the police cars began weaving back and forth around us, a crude bumper tag. David drove coolly as we headed toward Kutuzovsky compound and the *Post* apartment. As we reached the compound territory, the agents' cars suddenly roared in front of us and then pulled to the curb, and the agents piled out on foot, chasing after us with videotape cameras. As daylight waned, they spent about an hour in the courtyard, staring up at our apartment windows, while inside Irina related what had happened in court that day. When she finished and had rested, some correspondents took her out past the agents without incident and, at her insistence, drove her and a number of her Russian friends to a nearby subway station. She'd had enough of autos for one day.

Orlov was convicted the next day and given the maximum sentence—seven years' imprisonment in a strict regime labor camp and five years internal exile. Irina's account of this was crucial. We would take her to David's apartment where the correspondents could interview her. Since the trial was over, it seemed possible the police wouldn't bother us, a happy prospect since it was my turn to drive. Irina sat in the back seat of my Volvo station wagon, between satirist Vladimir Voinovich and another man. David Shipler of *The New York Times*, who was standing on the sidewalk as we drove out of the supermarket parking lot, gave me a smile. "Have a nice trip."

"I'd rather be in Philadelphia," I said.

Satter's apartment, our destination, was in an old building with a narrow, arched entrance just wide enough to allow one car through. As we rolled along the Moscow Ring Road toward it, KGB cars completely surrounded us; there was even one in front. Four or five beefy agents were jammed inside each car and one man in each had a small videotape camera trained on us.

Then I noticed that, as if on signal, the taping had ceased in every car. *They've run out*, I thought. Immediately, another thought crowded past that idea: *they're saving tape for something still to come*. This bothered me plenty. But what? As the exit that would take us to David's building came into view far down the Ring, I suddenly recognized the scenario: the car in front of me would plug the building's narrow entrance like a cork in a bottle and then the other agents would attack as we moved on foot into the building. They were saving film for that.

Even as this realization was forming in my head, I began accelerating the Volvo. The KGB driver ahead had to stay in front of me by reading my movements in his rearview mirror. This man would have to be very good to stay with us. I began weaving from lane to lane. Now the car ahead was swerving awkwardly to keep his position. The exit was fast approaching on the right. But the goons ahead weren't sure I would take it. I whipped the wheel to the left, the lead car snapped out into the middle lane to cover, and, at the last second, I swerved to the right down the exit ramp. As we descended, I could see the KGB car stopped dead at the curb with rush-hour traffic bearing down on it from behind.

"Kouv-boy!" Voinovich yelled in delight. With the other police cars now trying to get in front of me, I floored it. As David shouted turns, we led them on a high-speed chase through winding back streets. With each turn, the KGB fell farther behind. This was David's turf; he had driven these streets daily for almost two years. As we crested the last rise a block from the compound, a stumpy babushka with string sacks groaning with groceries was square in the middle of the street. I hit the horn. She hunkered, hesitated, then leapt aside as we flashed past.

Moments later, I yanked the wheel to the right and we slid through the archway to the safety of the postage-stamp-size foreign compound. Two uniformed guards in the KGB booth beside the arch goggled at us through the glass as Satter and Voinovich hustled Irina inside. Then I heard the chase cars coming—horns blaring. The babushka was in the middle of the street again!

At that exact moment, I figured I was one for one and batting a thousand against the secret police.

Over the next three years, that average plummeted. You can't beat the KGB on its own turf. If they can't get you, they can get the people you love and respect, or those who have the courage to help you. In the end, I realized that the only way I could understand the true meaning and implications of the Soviet Union was through the stories of the people we met inside the closed society.

Russia
and the
Russians

1

The Workers' Paradise

*Capitalist production develops . . . only by
exhausting . . . the two sources from which all
wealth springs: the earth and the worker.*

—KARL MARX

I

Hᴀᴜʟᴇᴅ by a Czech-built locomotive, the red-trimmed, dark-green passenger express from Moscow boomed southward across darkened, rolling Russian countryside. It was December 1980 and passenger Alexei Nikitin was heading home to Donetsk, the Ukrainian coal-mining city, where the KGB secret police planned to arrest and imprison him.

He was a balding, 42-year-old Russian with a fleshy nose, cornflower-blue eyes set wide in his round face, and a mouth that held numerous stainless-steel teeth. His broad hands were callused from years of manual labor and he had the rough-and-ready humor of his peasant forebears. A sturdily built Soviet Everyman without privilege or *blat,* pull, he was thoroughly at home in the pungent, hard-class world of minimal comfort known to the Soviet proletariat. He fit right into the scene aboard Wagon No. 7 of the Moscow–Donetsk express.

Wagon No. 7 contained fifty-four blue plastic pallets arranged in nine open alcoves of six bunks each, with tiers of three facing each other across a small table that folded against the wall. The corridor ran down one side of the car, past cramped stool-and-table combinations of stainless steel and plastic bolted against the car beneath the windows. These could be adjusted into a narrow shelf that made up into an extra berth, and another berth dropped down from above the windows. In all, seventy-two humans could sleep in Wagon No. 7. Mother Russia on four steel wheels.

Here were ancient grandmothers like gnarled tree trunks; peasants with bleary eyes and alcoholic cheeks ablaze in suety faces; gaunt miners, with dark smudges of emphysema in the hollows beneath their eyes and the hawking rasp of black lung in their voices; children playing, crying, romping, or staring mildly at the world from behind the white plastic rings of pacifiers. Parcels, bags, cardboard suitcases, cloth-wrapped boxes, canvas duffel bags, plastic valises, boots, and shoes cluttered the aisle. Bottles of Borzhomi mineral water, beer, yogurt, sour cream, buttermilk, vodka, and cheap brandy rattled cheerfully on the tables as the train sped south. Sausages, bread, cheese, tinned fish, and meats swayed in string bags. Men wandered about in blue sweatsuits and slippers; a drunken couple snarled from the depths of an alcove; families gabbed or stared out the window, or conducted "Russian conversations" with themselves—silently eating sunflower seeds from cones made of the pages of *Pravda*, spitting the husks on the floor.

Already, some men and women had stripped to their underclothes and laid their shapeless, careworn bodies on the pallets, like gunny sacks of turnips, pulling the thin blankets up over their faces to cut out the harsh lights overhead. The air was a thick tang of peasant body odor, pickled vegetables, smoked meats, musty, unwashed clothing, cabbage flatulence, harsh Russian tobacco smoke, drying boots, beery perspiration, damp socks, babies' bottoms. An hour south of Moscow, the toilets at both ends of the car were wet underfoot. This Hogarthian world was the habitat of the *narod*, the masses, and the only detail distinguishing Nikitin from the scene was the presence of a thin-faced man sitting on a window stool a little farther down the car, and taking very seriously his responsibility of watching his quarry.

Alexei was a proud man and a warm one, who had made many friends in many different places, including some of the most sinister of the Soviet Union's numerous institutions of control and punishment. He had spent most of the previous decade confined to Soviet psycho-prisons as punishment for defending fellow miners cheated of long-promised bonuses. And because he had never given up his quest for justice, he knew that his present moment of freedom would be brief. But when the arrest came, his one consolation would be this: he had invited two American correspondents to accompany him to Donetsk to see for themselves the grim reality of living and working conditions in the workers' paradise. I was one of those two foreigners, and my close friend David Satter, of the London *Financial Times*, was the other. As Alexei said, with a rueful smile, our tour of this world would be worth the regime's anger.

We had met Nikitin earlier that year in Moscow, shortly after Poland's Edward Gierek was toppled from power in Warsaw and the Solidarity free trade union movement was surging to life. The Polish crisis promised to go on for months, and David and I were seeking information about possible reverberations within the Soviet Union's own labor force. This was no easy task, for there are few reliable channels of communication between the foreigners living in Moscow and average Soviet workers. The state has no interest in allowing accurate information about its exploited labor force to reach the West from inside the country and goes to great lengths to insulate foreign diplomats, correspondents, businessmen, and exchange scholars from simple laborers. For example, most factories and manufacturing enterprises are considered military objectives and are thus off limits to foreigners without special permission. To discourage all but the most sophisticated or courageous citizens from unauthorized Western contacts, Soviet propaganda routinely portrays foreign correspondents as spies. But Satter, resourceful and deeply knowledgeable after five years in Moscow, had found a way to neutralize all this.

One day he suggested we visit a former welder and metal worker named Feliks Serebrov in his southwest Moscow apartment, near the gleaming former Olympic Village (the games having ended, the apartments now were being sold as luxury cooperative flats to well-heeled party members and technocrats despite official press reports that the complex had been turned over to "ordinary workers"). Serebrov maintained contact with a broad range of activists from outside Moscow. A former political prisoner himself, he now was a member of a group gathering information about the regime's increasing misuse of psychiatry to punish and silence political dissidents. A number of worker activists had been dealt with this way and we hoped Feliks, a thin, wearied man of great intensity, might be able to put us in touch with some working men willing to talk with two American journalists despite the risks involved.

While we were sipping tea with Serebrov, the doorbell rang and Alexei Nikitin walked in. He had come to Moscow looking for help in his own fight with the state and other activists had sent him to Serebrov. Nikitin joined us over tea and, in the softened accents of his rural Russia, quickly offered to guide us around his hometown of Donetsk so we could see for ourselves how Soviet working classes lived and labored, and why the Polish upheaval would never penetrate the Soviet border.

We took him up instantly on his offer, but it was not until December that we were able to clear the time and go. By then, the secret police had found out that Nikitin was making forbidden trips to Moscow and he feared they would arrest him before we could get to Donetsk. On the theory that the police would be reluctant to create a messy incident by arresting Alexei in the presence of American newsmen, we decided to travel on the same train. It was the right decision, for there was no trouble en route. But when we reached Donetsk the next morning without incident, we made a grave error: we decided to separate, with Alexei going to the apartment of his widowed sister, where he lived, while we checked into the Hotel Donetsk and went through the formalities of turning in our passports for inspection by the local security men. We would meet later at Alexei's and spend the next three days with him.

Moments after we separated on the arrival platform, Nikitin sensed danger. While we, unaware, waited for a cab outside the station, he suddenly ducked off the arrival platform, shuffled inside, and slipped through a side door just as a squad of plainclothesmen appeared and began scouring the train and the crowds of passengers for him. But with his dark, fake leather topcoat and battered, fake leather valise, he looked like just one more beefy miner in a city filled with them. Nikitin vanished.

There were many places he could have hidden himself. He had six siblings, most of whom lived in Donetsk or the surrounding *oblast*, district, and they had helped him in the past. He could have retreated deep into the Ukrainian countryside, finding work as a carpenter, collective farm laborer, or woodcutter. He had done this once before when the police were pursuing him and thus had prolonged his freedom for weeks. Or, like thousands of other men in trouble, he might have tried escaping to Siberia, where he could have sought a job, few questions asked, from foremen at the remote oil and gas exploration camps scattered across the frozen wilderness where most of the USSR's vast mineral wealth is locked away. These bitter places were always desperately short of workers despite extravagant hardship pay bonuses. He even could have returned to Moscow. Although the capital teemed with police and informants as did nowhere else, it also promised anonymity that could be achieved nowhere else. Almost every day, an extra million or more citizens from the provinces rolled into the city in suburban *elektrichki*, commuter trains, creaking feeder buses, trucks and cars from outlying collective farms and gritty industrial complexes. They were looking for better food and clothing than they could get at home. If they came by public transport, they would live in the train stations and passenger depots while they spent the days shopping. If they came by private car or farm truck, they would park on a back street in the sprawling city and use the vehicle as a base, living in it and stocking up on food and supplies while taking care to guard their caches from thieves. They would stay until there was no more room left aboard, or the money ran out.

Nikitin could swim for months without detection in this threadbare tide. Far more important, in Moscow he once again could have sought help from the tiny handful of political activists who were still willing to assist other dissidents despite the gathering momentum of repression against them. Moscovites like Serebrov had precious contacts with the West that were more valuable than diamonds to an unsophisticated working man like Alexei from the benighted isolation of the Soviet hinterland. For it was the remote West, portrayed by party propagandists as the sworn ideological enemy of the Soviet state and each of its 270 million people, that was interested in the things Nikitin had suffered for and revered—justice and truth.

Chilling rain drenched a grim vista of industrial flats, factories, equipment yards, and clusters of timber and stucco cottages set in rubbish-strewn fields as Satter and I, blissfully ignorant of any trouble, drove up to No. 1 Denisenko Ulitsa. Nikitin's sister, Lyubov Poludniak, lived here in the last of a collection of small, run-down three-story cement and stucco apartment buildings on a narrow, bedraggled courtyard in the Panfilovski mining quarter about a mile from the center of Donetsk. A white, Soviet-made Fiat stuffed with beefy secret police had followed us from the hotel. Other cars, also crammed with agents, sat in the slop around the buildings, motors running. The men inside smoked and gave us dirty looks as we brushed past a sentinel sheltering himself under the battered tin roof of the apartment house stoop and climbed a filthy cement stairway to the top-floor apartment where Alexei was to meet us.

The door cracked open at our knock and we slipped inside. A heavy woman shaped like a *matrioshka* doll, wearing a dark, rough coat and brown wool kerchief, ushered us into the flat. Her round face was immensely sad and her brown eyes were red-rimmed from tension and tears. "They're hunting him!" she whispered.

Depressed and appalled by our naiveté, David and I sat at the dining table in the two-room flat's front room. The place was spotless. It gleamed with freshly painted floors, white trim, and a carefully dusted collection of chairs and the table. An iron bed stood in one corner and a traditional East European glass-fronted cabinet rose against a wall, filled with books, photographs, dishes, glasses, and other mementos in the eclectic, unpretentious Russian manner. Somehow, Alexei and his sister had managed to barricade the flat against the grimy world outside, where fly ash and sulfurous gases of spontaneous combustion from deep within a nearby mountain of mine wastes turned the air a grayish brown. We waited here; the room was tense and utterly quiet.

From time to time, Mrs. Poludniak reconnoitered around the neighborhood, returning with reports that various neighbors had said they had seen Alexei in the woods near the community. They figured it was only a matter of time before he eluded the "organs," the secret police. Nikitin's sister wasn't so sanguine, and she was genuinely frightened by the sight of a Red Cross van parked several blocks away. Foreigners would think it an ambulance and feel reassured. But Soviet citizens, remembering how the previous generation had been shipped to slave labor camps in boxcars labeled "Grain," would be apprehensive seeing this van. Once he was inside, a citizen could never be sure of its destination. And this Red Cross van was accompanied by cars full of agents. It could only be a *spets machina*, a KGB special vehicle. The organs possessed many disguises.

Mrs. Poludniak sat in the tiny kitchen, resting her head in her hands, warming herself in the heat of the coal cook stove. Light faded. The bare branches straggling toward the patch of sky visible through the apartment's double front windows began to recede.

Men keeping vigil in the courtyard below huddled behind the cellar door of the building opposite, their hands thrust into coat pockets as they tried to keep warm. The woman stirred, pulled on her coat, and slipped quietly downstairs. She was back almost immediately, breathless from the rapid climb. "He's coming!"

We ran down the three flights and into the muddy courtyard. The scene burned into my mind: rain slatted against the building from the northwest, borne on a biting winter wind, while down to the left, two unmarked Volgas were parked door to door, engines idling, agents dark inside. Across the narrow courtyard, five or six men peeped out from behind the cellar door. The sentinel huddled on the stoop, a stringy young man in a drenched and forlorn cheap fur hat, long nose dripping over a weak chin—defiant, humiliated, hating. Up to the right stretched an abandoned field of tall weeds and grasses intersected by some uneven muddy paths. Rusting hulks of machinery and concrete structural parts protruded from the destitute earth. On the periphery of vision, something moved in this field.

A man in a large floppy cap and a long green raincoat suddenly materialized out of the weeds and headed toward us. We edged away from the stoop, fearful of alarming the police and unsure of what we were seeing. Then—Nikitin!

He rushed out of the field and we embraced right there in the middle of the courtyard. As he stared around at the agents and watchers, his face twisted with loathing. "*Svolichi! Chekisti!*" Bastards! Chekists! Then we scrambled inside, Alexei safe between us, rushed upstairs, double-locked the door, and drew the curtains on the two windows over the courtyard. None of these precautions meant much. There is no protection from police in a police state. But we felt better. Alexei stood peering out through narrowly parted curtains, shaking his head with disgust and tension.

"What scum! You'd have to fire 70 percent of them to make it a decent organization! They're just in it for the money! You've got to pull them along to get them to do anything!" He flushed with the effort to master his fear of them. "Wolves in human skin," he said at last.

We settled down over a supper of bread, butter, fried sausage and potatoes, and tea laced with homemade raspberry preserves. His eyes troubled but aglow with the telling, Nikitin described how he had escaped the agents at the railroad station and gone to a friend's house where he borrowed some outsized clothing to alter his appearance.

Then he had easily penetrated the cordon of cars and agents around the Denisenko apartments. He walked along a railroad spur line that ran across the north end of the vacant field, taking a path that many Denisenko residents used, crossing the tracks on an unmarked footpath. This had been Nikitin's route home; he passed unnoticed in the stream of shoppers going to and fro on their daily errands.

Although we were checked into the official hostelry for foreigners, the Hotel Donetsk, David and I in fact lived with Alexei and his sister during our time in the city. We spent all but one of the nights sleeping on two comfortable steel-framed beds Nikitin had assembled in anticipation of our visit. We spent the last night at the hotel, because Soviet law states that foreigners and Soviet citizens cannot spend more than three consecutive nights together without police permission.

After our first night in the apartment, we awakened at five in the morning, brewed tea in the darkened kitchen to avoid alerting possible sentinels below, then bundled up and crept downstairs. The courtyard was impenetrable; it seemed empty. The temperature was 25 degrees Fahrenheit below zero. At 48 degrees north latitude, Donetsk is north of almost every major city in America. At that time of day during that part of the year, it is a place of biting wind and inky darkness.

We turned east, walking quietly away from Denisenko Street. Our destination was a bus stop on the other side of a small collection of one-story houses. We ghosted along over frozen mud and puddles, saying nothing. Here and there, lights were winking on and thick coal smoke from cook stoves rose from many chimneys. The working day approached and the miners soon would rush for buses to get to work on time to avoid an accusation of a "violation of socialist labor discipline" for being late, which could mean loss of vacation or of other hard-won benefits. But for now, the activity was inside the snug, low houses. We were alone outside.

Then we heard a car and turned to see parking lights creeping toward us from about a half-block away. Now we could hear the soft *crunch! crunch!* of other feet striding in time on the parallel streets to either side of us. The police were still out in strength. They were to shadow us throughout our time in Donetsk, on foot and by car, in pitch darkness and every kind of weather. In all, perhaps two dozen or more plainclothesmen concentrated on our comings and goings, even escorting our taxi to the airport when we left, and loitering in the ticket lines around us until we had been put aboard for the flight to Moscow. But with Alexei as our guide in Donetsk, we were able to learn much about the "workers' paradise."

II

DONETSK coal fires the hearths of hundreds of steel foundries and plants throughout the Don and Dnieper River basins, in the eastern Ukraine. The Donbas, as it is known, is the industrial backbone of the mightiest Communist power on earth, whose leaders have dedicated themselves and their people to expanding the ideology and influence of their vast empire to remote corners of the world, ostensibly for the benefit of the downtrodden and disenfranchised.

The city of Donetsk resembles many other regional centers in European Russia: a number of boulevards and marble and granite edifices grouped around a huge central square give the downtown area an imposing gravity and sense of official presence. A T-34 medium tank on a pedestal in the main downtown park serves as one of many memorials reminding the populace of the struggles and sacrifice of World War II. A few blocks from party headquarters and the sprawling main offices of the Ministry of the Coal Industry, the boulevards give way to a jumbled network of potholed streets, narrow side roads, and lumpy country lanes. Unfinished apartment blocks rise here and there behind sagging wooden fences. Industrial enterprises, factories, and institutes sprawl across the metropolis in no particular order. Tucked behind the taller, newer complexes are neighborhoods of small, dilapidated timber and cement houses backed up to each other against fences thrown together from scrap lumber and discarded building materials. In the summer, vines and flowers soften the lines of ramshackle neglect, hiding the henhouses, doghouses, privies, and communal wells that serve as magnets for the aged Slavic babushki who gather and gossip wherever there is potable water. But on the winter day we set off with Nikitin, everything was raw and weatherbeaten.

As morning began to lighten the pall of heavy gases drifting from smouldering mountains of mine wastes that dominate the city's squat skyline, aging buses creaked and groaned over slushy, pot-holed streets, beginning the day's first pickups of the workforce. Stray pedestrians scuttled about—pensioners and women with a day away from the mines already queueing at the chained and padlocked doors of milk and meat shops around the city, hopeful of getting something before the limited supplies gave out for another twenty-four hours.

A few blocks from the central railroad station near the center of Donetsk, the Panfilovski mining quarter awakened and faced an-other Monday of work. Hacking and coughing from years spent in ill-ventilated tunnels, the men gathered beneath a bus shelter at the edge of the community. They smoked as they waited and said little. Arching over them into the sky, a string of naked lights bobbed in the wind, casting a dismal glare over a narrow-gauge railroad track that climbed the side of the gigantic heap of smouldering mine debris. With a muffled rumble, a mine car suddenly emerged from behind the bulk of buildings at the Panfilovski pithead and slowly moved up the 150-foot-high discard mountain. Reaching the top, it paused and then dumped a new load of wastes onto the flanks of the pile. A dull clattering roar echoed through the district. The tunnel car retreated into the bowels of the mine. The Sunday night shift was still at work deep below the earth.

Extra work was normal at the Panfilovski mine and most of the forty-eight other shaft mines within the city limits. Indeed, extra shifts had been the custom for years in the land of the hammer and sickle. Ever since the end of World War II nearly four decades earlier, much of the Soviet Union's industrial workforce had labored through six- and seven-day workweeks, first to rebuild the country's shattered industrial capacity, and then to attempt to dominate the world and spread socialism—or, at least, defend its gains, as the state propagandists styled it. Nikita Khrushchev's 1960 boast that the Soviet Union would overtake the United States and establish a new world standard of life and leisure by 1980 was a thing of the past. Like Khrushchev himself, his promise was now an embarrassment better forgotten. The regime had its hands full simply trying to reach the unrealistic production norms set each year by central planners in Moscow. In the previous month, November 1980, the Panfilovski district miners had been called out every Sunday to work compulsory overtime shifts.

Many of them would never be paid the overtime they had earned. The double-overtime wages guaranteed by Soviet labor law were a myth. But there were no enraged outcries and no protest petitions from the miners. Like virtually all other laboring men and women in their country, Soviet miners simply endured what a capitalist workforce would have long since vigorously protested. Soviet workers had no power. The conditions for establishing meaningful worker solidarity to force better wages and living standards had been effectively eliminated by the massed power of the Soviet state. Beneath the carefully formulated surface of Soviet reality, exemplified by huge murals of brawny miners outside mine entrances across the city, was a harsh reality of another kind.

In this truer world, political control was exercised right down to the level of each individual worker—deliberately fostering divisions, resentment, and dissension bordering on hatred within the working class, sapping its unity and potential cohesion in the face of exploitation. Fealty to the party, however cynical, was rewarded by special privileges that guaranteed better tools, higher production, much higher wages, and the eventual promise of improved living conditions. This was one reason that party membership was kept to a tiny minority of the entire population. Those who complained too much about injustices, or acted out their frustrations against their privileged peers, faced draconian reprisals that could cost them their livelihood, ensuring bleak times for spouses and children for years to come. There were about one hundred twenty-seven million industrial workers in the Soviet Union in the early 1980s and, with Nikitin's help, we met some of them in Donetsk. The number was small, but it was a close enough look to tell us that this was how most Soviet workers lived and labored.

One night, Alexei took us to the home of a mining family he had known for many years. We went by taxi to a neighborhood of individual houses and slipped down a narrow alley between two cross streets. The alley dipped and turned, barely wide enough for a single person where it led between back fences. Even in the pitch darkness, Nikitin knew exactly where to turn. He abruptly ducked through a narrow gate, ushering us into a backyard the size of a modest kitchen. The gate was eased shut and we tiptoed up to a small house with eaves so low they almost touched my head. Alexei knocked and after a brief, whispered explanation, we were admitted. The family of Pyotr Borisovich* spent about four hours with us that

*The names of the coal-mining families who spoke with Nikitin, Satter, and me have been changed.

December night. It was an act of courage to welcome American newsmen into their house. But they had much on their minds and as they brewed up fresh hot chocolate for their guests and poured it out, they poured out their hearts as well.

Pyotr Borisovich had worked for almost fifteen years as a carpenter at the Butovka–Donetsk shaft coal mine, located within the city several miles from downtown party headquarters. His wife, Tatiana Ivanovna, had spent nearly twenty years at the same mine works, sorting coal by hand. Their daughter, Irina Petrovna, an activist in the League of Young Communists, the *Komsomol,* studied part-time while working as a clerk in the mine administration. The parents were indifferent to the party and in fact despised many party people they had to work with; they were not members. Their daughter felt the same, but she would join in a few years because it was one way for a pretty girl to improve her life.

The mine had been started up before World War II and now employed about three thousand of Donetsk's one million residents. It looked like any other shaft coal mine: a pithead with elevator works stark against the sky; ramshackle buildings of brick and concrete for administration, repair, and storage. There were receiving docks for supplies, conveyors running in various directions, huge stockpiles of different grades of coal, and an immense mountain of waste rock excavated from the shafts and tunnels. This pile of useless stone smoked and steamed; its interior had been afire for decades. The main Butovka shaft descended some fifteen hundred feet, with horizontal tunnels spreading at various depths to follow rich coal seams that honeycomb beneath Donetsk. So much subsurface material has been taken from the city since mining operations were begun late in the nineteenth century—by the British at the czar's invitation—that portions of the surface have collapsed and a number of areas in Donetsk are too undermined to allow construction. Butovka was dangerous, a place of heavy, fast-moving machinery, explosives, gas leaks, high-voltage electricity and high-pressure air, rockfalls, coal dust, damp, and noise.

There were three eight-hour shifts daily, beginning at 6 A.M. There was no meal break for most categories of workers—the miners either skipped food or ate on the run. They worked six days a week most of the year, and sometimes seven days. The official reason for this was that the mine was lagging behind production norms and had to make it up on weekends. Yet, many Butovka workers, such as Pyotr Borisovich, were convinced that the mine consistently exceeded production goals by many hundreds of tons. The mine directorate, party chief, and police were suspected of illegally speculating with the extra coal they had cheated from the state and workers. The miners believed that their bosses earned enormous fortunes selling hidden coal at exorbitant rates to factory and foundry directors who had been deliberately shorted of contracted coal by the Donetsk mines. In turn, it was thought that factory chiefs held back on their own production, speculating with their own unused materials to earn back the money they had had to spend on the coal. Weed-covered mountains of coal in remote parts of the city were said to be moved around on paper like the pea in the shell game. But all of this was beyond the sphere of any worker and, since the police were part of the hierarchy, there was no way to get an investigation started.

Miners' pay averaged two hundred rubles a month, about 10 percent higher than the Soviet industrial norm. This sum was worth about three hundred dollars at the official exchange rate, and considerably less at black market rates—perhaps forty dollars. In fact, the ruble had no hard currency value in Donetsk, since few foreigners from capitalist nations ever found their way there. There were bonuses for night work and work below ground, time and a half for working a sixth day, and double time for the seventh workday. There also were bonuses for exceeding production targets. But only a few bonuses were paid to nonparty workers, and there were kickbacks to team leaders and foremen whose teams did get bonuses. The bosses routinely offered time off in lieu of extra pay, and the workers usually accepted. But schedulers frequently moved the shift around so that, in a single month, a worker who failed to make payoffs to his superiors could receive numerous back-to-back shifts.

Tatiana Ivanovna told us how she had recently asked her shift supervisor in the coal-sorting department at Butovka to give her an owed day off on her husband's birthday. "If you try to take it," the supervisor replied, "we'll fire you. So go ahead and try it." She said she later felt like a fool for even asking, since her request had given the supervisor an opportunity to humiliate her. She figured she had only herself to blame.

About three hundred Butovka workers were party members, which guaranteed them higher pay and privileges than the rest.

Party members routinely were assigned to the best-equipped work teams and given the most productive coal faces to mine. These were the brigades of *udarniki,* the shock workers, and they were used to set higher norms that made it more difficult for regular shift teams to achieve bonuses. Frequently, they were equipped with foreign-made tools and machines, which were more efficient than Soviet-made gear. If the equipment was Soviet, as most was, it was abused and neglected according to the operative morality that, since it belonged to the state, it was to be either stolen or broken.

Udarniki customarily received about four hundred rubles a month. They were hated by normal workers. An air of strained anger and frustration hung over the pay line. Men took their pay and made a beeline for a vodka store near the Butovka territory to drown their bitterness. Dry throats clicking in anticipation, they queued, paid, and drank. Within moments, "three on a bottle" could drain it dry and be ready for more. But it never settled anything. Quite the opposite, for soon there was trouble: fistfights, brawls, men stupified with alcohol and rage flailing at each other or carrying their fury home to spill it on wives and children in the bleak flats and crowded communal apartments where all but the chiefs and their assistants lived. Where hatred of udarniki was great, the shock workers enjoyed extra protection. Not only were they party members and thus dangerous to tangle with, but the Butovka bosses, following Soviet industrial tradition, kept some professional brawlers as enforcers. A man who successfully beat up an udarnik could expect retaliation from an enforcer.

The shock-worker phenomenon arose in the Donbas in 1935, when an obscure miner named Alexei Stakhanov claimed that he had produced one hundred two tons of coal in a single six-hour shift, more than fifteen times the average seven tons per worker per shift. Within weeks, Stakhanovite madness swept the coalfields as mine after mine arranged competitions to catch their tyrant Stalin's favor. Record setters were hailed as heroes, but underachievers faced reprisals, which could take many forms. At the least, they could be docked pay or denied bonuses they had easily qualified for in earlier times. At the worst, thousands were sent into the rapidly expanding concentration camps of northeastern Siberia on phony charges of "sabotage" and "wrecking." Miners fled the coalfields. Stakhanovites were murdered. The insanity finally burned out toward the end of the decade. Many years later, after Stalin was denounced,

Stakhanov's original production claims were proved to be fraudulent. But the idea of herculean work to glorify the workers' state was a powerful tool for the regime. Campaigns of "socialist emulation" and "socialist competition," less bizarre than Stakhanovism, persisted. These campaigns were easily manipulated to favor party members and thus remained valuable in keeping the workforce divided against itself.

Pyotr Borisovich, a sallow-faced man in his mid-40s, kept clear of the brawlers and the drunks. A miner who was arrested could be shipped off to a "corrective labor camp" to learn "work discipline." A two-year sentence to such a place amounted to two years' free labor for the state on ambitious projects like the new trans-Siberian rail line being carved through the wilderness north of Lake Baikal to the Pacific coast. Police vigilance varied in response to demands from remote work sites for more hands. Public drunkenness that was tolerated one week might be an excuse for punishment in a labor battalion the next.

Mine bosses also conducted their own disciplinary hearings, which could easily become kangaroo courts to settle scores with unruly workers or to reward favored miners. These were called *Chisti Vtornik* or *Chisti Chetverk*, Clean Tuesday or Clean Thursday, sessions. Here the emphasis was on "comradely" criticism— crude denunciations of the offending worker to humiliate him before family and friends. Wives could easily be induced by the bosses to denounce their husbands; a petty infraction could become the excuse for neighbors to square long-festering accounts from overcrowded dormitories and communal apartment houses.

The bosses had absolute power to fire, reprimand, dock pay, deny vacation, or mete out any combination of punishment they chose. In theory, the workers enjoyed full rights to petition through their trade unions for redressing unfair treatment. In practice, workers usually agreed with their bosses. They were afraid to challenge them because they could only lose. A dismissed miner was in serious jeopardy, since the firing was marked permanently in the labor performance book, the *kharakteristika* every Soviet worker is required to show a prospective employer. The Soviet Constitution guaranteed a job for every able-bodied citizen. But a person without a job had four months to find one or risk being prosecuted as a criminal parasite.

The home of Pyotr Borisovich and Tatiana Ivanovna consisted

of two rooms in a small dwelling and a third room in a summer kitchen ten feet away across a tiny dirt yard, where their daughter, Irina Petrovna, lived. This room contained a bed, a coal stove for heating and cooking, and a sink with a cold-water tap. There was one naked lightbulb hanging from the low ceiling, and the room was decorated with a small, cheap, souvenir balalaika and pictures of Western actresses and Eastern European singers cut from magazines. In mid-winter, when the cold intensified, the daughter moved in with her parents to sleep on a bed in an alcove. Her parents slept in the main room, which also contained a dining table, chairs, a cumbersome television set, and a record player. The apartment had no running water and no bathroom. There was an outhouse in the yard.

There were not enough decent apartments available to house all Butovka workers and their families, so there was a long waiting line for private, modern living quarters. The shortage existed even though the workforce had been stable for years and the mine financed the construction of about a dozen new apartments yearly. The reason for the shortage was that the hierarchy took most of the new apartments for itself or its friends. So far, Pyotr and Tatiana had been waiting nine years for a modern apartment and believed they had another eight years to go. They stood in the ninety-first position on their particular list and lived in constant apprehension that some unexpected catastrophe would knock them off. Since the bosses took most of the housing for themselves, this item of life became a powerful weapon for cowing the workers. The chiefs sometimes demoted or dismissed workers, so they would lose all privileges, and then rehired them, forcing them to start again at the bottom of the list. The same danger surrounded vacation privileges, as Tatiana Ivanovna described for us.

She was a compact woman who exuded an air of energy and fortitude. On that night in December, she was wearing a dark, sacklike dress and her brown hair, cut short around her ears, was dyed henna red, one of the two hair dyes available in the provinces, the other being bleach. Her small hands were thickened from her work and her two upper incisors had been replaced with gold-capped teeth. As a coal sorter, she worked in a shedlike gallery near the pithead where a conveyor brought coal and waste rock to the surface in an endless stream. She and nine other women on her shift sorted the rock from the coal, sending the waste into mine cars that eventually were hauled up the rock mountain and unloaded automatically. Noise and dust filled the sorting gallery. Aside from cheap canvas mittens on their hands, the women wore no special protective clothing.

Uppermost in Tatiana's mind that night was the scheduling of her vacation in the coming year. She had borrowed money through the mine to pay for winter clothing for her family, and the credit would not be paid back until February 1981, two months hence. Meanwhile, she could not borrow any more money. She had asked to have her vacation of twenty-four days scheduled sometime after February, because by then she could borrow enough to get a bed at a rest house on the Black Sea. Even though it would be cold at the shore, the sea air would be good for her lungs. But her boss told her: "You've been given vacation for January and that's what you'll take." She would spend her vacation at home. Tatiana Ivanovna was 44. She looked to be in her mid-50s.

With few belongings and all three adults working, the family income was four hundred twenty rubles a month, which kept them generally in debt to the mine. Although they paid seven rubles for what was nominally a one-room apartment, the minimum monthly food bill was three hundred rubles, for which they ate poorly. Tatiana Ivanovna showed us a plastic sack that contained soup bones that had cost 1.90 rubles a kilogram, or about $1.30 a pound. "We bought it to make borscht," she said. Bones with meat on them cost twice as much at the state store—if they could be found—and four times as much at the farmers' market. Potatoes cost a dollar a pound, equivalent. Milk was sold out daily by 10 A.M. "Sour cream and curds are only available some of the time; cheese and eggs are deficit items." She laid the blame on President Carter for placing an embargo on grain in retaliation for the Afghanistan invasion. Shoes cost up to eighty rubles, or two weeks' pay for Tatiana Ivanovna; a man's suit was one hundred eighty rubles; a cheap fur hat, one hundred fifty rubles; a television set, between four hundred and seven hundred rubles.

Pyotr Borisovich spoke about Poland. "We all know about it. But what can we do about it? Our people are for the Polish workers and for peace. . . . They sympathize because our working classes are directed toward peace and friendship. But everyone reads the newspapers. . . . Everyone worries: if our leaders attack Poland today, it would be us tomorrow."

At the Butovka mine, as at virtually every other Soviet factory, enterprise, institute, and school, the bosses relied on a network of paid informants, *stukachi,* to keep track of worker attitudes, such as Pyotr Borisovich's. Through the so-called First Department, which appraised employees, the KGB paid close attention. There could be secretaries keeping track of bosses, department heads watching the political views of other administrators, udarniki monitoring members of their own privileged brigades, and pick-and-shovel men reporting on the complaints of other pick-and-shovel men. The web of listening and reporting was as much a fact of life as the network of underground tracks that carried coal cars from tunnel to tunnel.

In this world, caution and suspicion made sense. A crew could be lounging in a tunnel, grousing about skimpy food supplies in the state stores, or stupid supervisors, when a man from another crew might appear. Instantly, he was considered *chuzhoi,* alien. Without a pause, the talk would shift flawlessly to praise of bosses, condemnation of the United States, or acclaim for recent Central Committee decisions. The miners might despise their bosses and know next to nothing about the other topics, but the conversation would continue this way until the outsider moved on. Then the talk focused anew on shortcomings. The terms of life in the mine eliminated adherence to the truth.

This was driven home to us—and to the family—very soon after we left them. The morning after our visit, Alexei wanted to know if the family would see us for a second interview. It was a Saturday, and he expected to find one of them at home. But the house was empty and stayed that way throughout the day. He was sure something unpleasant had happened to them.

The following day, we went by their home again and knocked on the summer kitchen door. The sound of footsteps padded toward us, there was the sound of a lock, and the door cracked open. Tatiana Ivanovna stared out, her face a mask of fear. "Go away!"

"Can we talk again?" Alexei asked.

"Go away!" She whispered something to Alexei, then shut the door in our faces.

We retreated, feeling the weight of the state. Nikitin said that the family had spent the previous day under KGB interrogation—the price they paid for pouring out their hot chocolate and their hearts.

III

Down a potholed street, hard against a smoking hill of mine wastes so high it blotted out the rising sun until midday, stood the New Colony, a community of three- and four-story walk-ups where many retirees and pensioners from Butovka and other mines lived out the remainder of their lives. We went there one day with Nikitin.

After passing through the peeling entranceway of a long, pale cement and stone building, we climbed to the first landing and rapped at one of the two apartment doors. A woman with a strong jaw, high cheekbones, and piercing blue eyes let us in. She was Matriona Ilyichna Leonovna, 67, and she had lived in this apartment for nearly thirty years with her husband, Tikhon Feodorovich Leonov, who was 80.

Their home was one room about fourteen by fourteen feet, with a tiny kitchen off the back and one large window. A laundry clothesline crisscrossed overhead; greenish wallpaper hung in the corners in ribbons, and the woodwork was gray. Two daybeds stood along the walls, a large table took up the center of the room, and assorted chairs clustered toward the kitchen. The floor was grimy, with a threadbare carpet remnant spread across an uneven hardwood floor.

In 1938, Tikhon Fyodorovich had been guiding a mine car filled with rock waste up the Butovka "tip" when he slipped from his perch on the five-ton cart and fell beneath its iron wheels. In an instant, his right leg was severed at the hip and his left foot and ankle were gone. His working days were over. But he was lucky to be alive and he knew it. He was classified a state invalid of the second class and began receiving a pension that increased gradually over the years. In December 1980, his pension was forty-five rubles a month. This was five rubles below the officially acknowledged Soviet poverty line of fifty rubles per person a month, but Matriona Ilyichna counted the luck of it, no matter what kind of pension he received: he had kept his health, had lived long enough to see her successfully retired, and had seen their son and only child, Sergei Tikhonovich, employed at the same mine. Tikhon Fyodorovich lived in the kitchen on a small bed jammed into the corner near the stove, where he would be warm during bitter winter nights. He now was a frail-looking bundle of a man, swathed in blankets, with a thatch of white hair and a face and voice grown permanently quarrelsome from decades of frustration as a bedridden victim.

Matriona Ilyichna had worked at Butovka first as a machinist and then as an attendant in the workers' bathhouse, where she handed out towels and soap. Their son, a bachelor, lived at home with his parents and earned one hundred forty rubles a month. In 1978, he had received an award naming him a Victor of Soviet Labor for overfulfilling his norms. Matriona Ilyichna was contemptuous of this, for the award brought nothing more—no extra cash, no promise of a better apartment or even a can of paint for this one. Since her own pension was forty-nine rubles a month, money was a serious problem. The family helped make ends meet by renting out space in their one room to a boarder. For many years, a pensioned widow had occupied a spare bed in the room, the best arrangement she could find since her own pension was thirty-seven rubles a month. The widow recently had remarried, however, and now lived nearby with her new, but aged husband. The Leonovs were looking for someone else to rent the bed.

As we sat talking and taking notes, an ancient, birdlike woman dressed in a black padded jacket, woolen stockings and slippers, and with a dark shawl pulled around her face crept to the open door of the apartment and leaned against the jamb. When we peeked at her, she pulled her head back just enough so there was no eye contact. But it was easy to see that she was wearing rags.

"When we worked, there were no private apartments, only communal flats," Matriona Ilyichna said. "Now, as pensioners, we don't get what new apartments there are—the workers get them."

The ancient at the door nodded silently. Unexpectedly, another crone in near rags appeared at the door. She was bolder, and inched into the room and watched us steadily. She took in the two men with their suits, notepads, pens, and briefcases and understood immediately. "A commission has come," she said to no one in particular. She disappeared, but within moments returned—and now there were four elderly women hovering at the door, listening and murmuring about the "commission" that somehow had materialized to hear their stories and perhaps do something about the poverty and neglect ruining their final years.

Matriona Ilyichna invited the women in, and as they creaked inside and sat dispiritedly on one of the beds, we learned that the Leonovs had lived in New Colony since 1945. At that time, the apartments were built by German prisoners of war who were used as labor in the country they had tried to conquer and were then repatriated about a decade later. This seemed more than simple justice, for the Wermacht had swept through Donetsk itself, many Soviets had died, and later the Germans had destroyed much of the mining machinery before retreating. But life had moved on, and what was new in 1945 was a slum in 1980. "We've been waiting more than twenty years for a better home, but the relatives of the directors and the bosses get any new flats," Matriona Ilyichna said as the aged listeners nodded in agreement and one of them began weeping.

This was life in the fourth-largest city of the Ukraine, a Soviet Socialist Republic with its own voting seat in the United Nations as if it were a nation separate from the USSR. The citizens of New Colony got their water from a community well in a weed-choked field a hundred yards from the Leonovs' doorway. A journey of about forty feet in another direction took the residents to their sanitary facilities—six foul-smelling, rough-hewn outhouses.

While there is lively and sometimes harsh criticism of housing shortcomings by the official Soviet press as well as warnings of the impact of backward living conditions on worker morale, those pro forma protestations had little meaning for New Colony's pensioners. In seeking better living conditions, the old people found themselves treated the same way as the rock that must be broken up deep underground to get at the rich seams of coal: they were discarded.

With the neighbors paying close attention, Matriona Ilyichna continued her account. "They consistently violate the queues. For people who wait for years, it can be agonizing to see themselves passed over year after year when they are at the head of the queue. But if you complain to some higher authority, they refer it to the lower authorities, and they ignore the complaints or make up any kind of nonsense to explain it. The official union is worthless.

"Pensioners are always pushed to the back of the queue and ignored. They are on the list from the time when they worked and they grew up in an era when no apartments at all were available, so they are denied separate apartments in their own old age."

Hesitantly, the neighbors began telling their stories.

Lidia Yermolaevna Belozorova had spent many years before and after the war collecting rock at the mine and putting it in piles. In 1953, she found a better job at the Butovka mine—she performed the job of a horse. She was stationed at the bottom of inclined tracks while cars loaded with coal came down the incline, dumped the fuel, and then had to be turned around and sent back up the incline. This was Lidia Yermolaevna's work, which she did almost without a break during the frantic post-war reconstruction. In all, she said, she had worked eighteen years for the Butovka mine and had received an Order of the Red Banner for outstanding performance—but no housing, except for the squalor of New Colony.

In 1979, she decided that she deserved something better. She took her award and went to see Anatoli Dmitrievich Babich, chief of the mine union, to ask for a one-room apartment of her own. She described how Babich took her award, weighed it in his hands, and then put it back on the desk. "You've received the Order of the Red Banner from the state for your work," he intoned. "You aren't going to receive anything more."

Another of the women was Olga Grigorevna Famina, 80, a hunchbacked wisp with a toothless, crab-apple face. She said she had worked for sixteen years as a coal sorter and retired when she was 57. Her monthly pension was twenty-four rubles, less than half of what was considered the poverty level. "There is no money even for milk . . . I haven't seen meat in years," she whispered, peering intently into my face to be sure I comprehended what that meant for her.

Earlier that year, she related, she had gone to see one of the senior mine chiefs, a man named Anatoli Fyodorovich Bynba, to ask him for free coal for her cooking and heating. Like most Donetsk residents, Olga Grigorevna could obtain coal from the mines as a former mine worker. But there was a charge of thirteen rubles a month, leaving her only eleven rubles on which to live. In the late 1970s, a series of harvest disasters had sent the price of food spiraling upward and she was desperate.

When she walked into the office of the sleek *nachalnik*, chief, she was immediately buoyed up because she recognized him. In his childhood, he had been a sunny little boy of the neighborhood, doted upon by everyone. She showed him her documents that proved how much she had done for the mine and the motherland.

Bynba stared at her as she asked for financial help from the director's discretionary fund, and then he grabbed up the collection of worn papers and threw them on the table. "We don't have money for this! There's nothing in the fund for you!"

She gathered the pieces of paper. "Dear little son," she remembered telling him, addressing him in the same fond way she had when he was a boy, "my husband was a party member and when a party man dies, they say at the funeral, 'We are your family and will never desert you.' And now, dear little son, you're ignoring my appeal for help." Then she got up and walked out of his office.

Later that year, friends began giving Olga Grigorevna coal because she was destitute. In August, she had gone to the regional party committee and asked them for help, explaining that she lived in someone else's apartment in the New Colony community and thought she deserved something better.

"Do you have a table?" the official asked her.

"I have."

"Do you have a bed?"

"I have."

"That's enough for you! Get out of here!"

She fainted on the street outside and spent a month recuperating from nervous strain in a city hospital. She never received any help from the mine, she said, and as she related this in a subdued voice, tears welled and rolled down her wrinkled cheeks.

As the other women sought to comfort Olga Grigorevna, there was a commotion at the door and a tough-looking young man with a sodden *shapka*, fur hat, jammed down on his head pushed into the apartment. "What's going on here?" he said, his voice furious and tense.

"These are foreign correspondents talking to people and they are within their rights," Nikitin shouted back.

"I know who they are and they have the right," the intruder said. "But who are you and what documents do you have?"

"Nikitin, Alexei Vasilyevich," Nikitin said in the formal, official style, "and here are my documents." He held them up. "But who are you and where are *your* papers?"

"I'll get them and I'll be right back!" the stranger blustered and walked out. There was a stunned silence. With a sardonic smile, Matriona Ilyichna pointed to the window. We could see a bedraggled group of plainclothesmen outside in the windy rain and sleet, stomping their feet and looking angrily around the desolate New Colony. Matriona Ilyichna tried to get the other pensioners to stay, but the fox had made his appearance. The women filed slowly from the room. They knew the truth: no one was going to help them.

The day before we left Donetsk, one of the KGB agents in the car tailing us stuck his fist out the passenger's side window and waved it at us. It looked odd to us, because the man's thumb protruded between the fingers instead of being wrapped around them in the usual way. Nikitin got agitated. "See that? See where the thumb is?"

"Yes . . . what does it mean?"

"That's a Ukrainian curse sign; it's . . . something people fight over. A serious threat. It's like Khrushchev pounding his shoe on the table at the United Nations. In the Ukraine, that sign between Ukrainian and Ukrainian means a fight immediately. It's called a '*dulya.*' Any Ukrainian-American who reads that a KGB agent gave you a dulya will know what it means. It means: '*You're a fool—a loser.*' "

When we said goodbye the next day on the landing outside Lyubov Poludniak's third-floor apartment, there were bear hugs and intense looks. Alexei was busy installing an extra lock and a buzzer on the door. Somehow, it made him feel better, though we all knew there were no real precautions he could take short of fleeing. And the only place he would be truly safe was beyond the territory of the Soviet Union entirely—an impossibility.

"Be well. Safe trip! Until the next meeting!" We embraced, as we had when he'd escaped the dragnet.

"Safe trip!" he called as we dropped down the stairway. He smiled a sad smile. "Don't worry!"

We climbed into a taxi and headed for Donetsk airport. There was silence between Satter and me for many minutes. At last I said, "If they can do it, they'll put his head on a pike."

Five days after we returned to Moscow, the secret police smashed open the door to Mrs. Poludniak's apartment, seized Alexei as he struggled from bed, and jammed a needle full of drugs into him. When he had passed out a few minutes later, they bundled him in a heavy cloth, lugged him downstairs "like a man wrapped in a carpet" his sister reported by phone to David, and threw him in the back of the spets machina with the Red Cross painted on the side. He was taken to a prison for the criminally insane and the police resumed their torture.

2

Alexei Nikitin's Crime

Only a fool believes in his own ideas.
—PEASANT PROVERB

I

ALEXEI Vasilyevich Nikitin never thought of himself as a man looking for trouble or as a man with a mission. At first, he only wanted to right a wrong.

With his humble beginnings and modest early aspirations to conform and prosper within the system of his homeland as he had been taught, he hardly seemed a protagonist in a Kafkaesque odyssey through the interior of the Soviet police state. But when he took up the cause of fellow workers cheated of wages at the Butovka mine, and when he warned of safety hazards in the pit caused by profit-hungry bosses, he was branded a renegade, fired from his job, and expelled from the Communist party. When the mine exploded as he had foretold, killing seven men, other miners hailed him as an honest voice in a corrupt world: he was then arrested, thrown into jail, and judged insane by Soviet psychiatrists who never examined him. They imprisoned him in a police-run mental hospital where he was injected with hallucinatory drugs meant to bring on robotlike submissiveness.

No precise figures will ever be known, but there are hundreds of political prisoners like Alexei Nikitin locked away in insane asylums throughout the Soviet Union today, undergoing similar drug "treatments." Some are religious men and women who sought to have their children baptized, or to spread their faith to others. Some are citizens who were caught trying to escape from the motherland by sneaking across her closely guarded borders. Some are people who objected to political control of science. Some spoke out against the denial of rights to free speech and assembly. Some have been hospitalized for writing to people in foreign countries. Some have tried to reclaim land and houses they were forced to flee during the war on false charges that they were unpatriotic. Some are Jews who have agitated for the right to emigrate to Israel. Some are worker activists who objected to unsafe factories or demanded the ouster of corrupt bosses. Like Nikitin, many of those hidden away in the recesses of the hospitals had launched an exhausting effort to find justice—and with the same results.

Nikitin's story begins in the heart of European Russia, in the village of Fedorovsky, Rognedino *raion*, or region, Bryansk oblast. This is deep in the backwaters of the country, some two hundred fifty miles west of Moscow near the boundary between the White Russian Soviet Socialist Republic and the huge Russian Federation. Alexei was born here on February 20, 1937, the tenth and last child of Vasili Nikitin, a peasant farmer of the V. I. Lenin Collective Farm, a vast holding that took in miles of rolling fields and pasture, marsh, meandering streams and forests, and tumbledown impoverished hamlets. Beneath the flat, timeless vault of landlocked sky, life appeared peaceful, homey, and quaint, as much a part of every earlier century as of the twentieth.

The motor age was just taking hold here in the remote countryside. Trucks were irreplaceable, tractors a precious novelty, automobiles now in the hands of party chiefs and police as carriage horses and high-spirited thoroughbreds had earlier been in the hands of the landlord. Heavy iron-wheeled tractors lumbered across the fields, but horses also still drew the plough and the cart, cattle grazed in meadows of rank, green grasses, fowl scratched and clucked in dooryards, and drinking water was drawn from the communal well by families bearing wooden pails on heavy yokes. In summer, the sky glowed pale around the clock; night hardly seemed to touch the land. Children and women alike could go barefoot; there were small garden plots, places to fish, berries to be collected and preserved, bread to be baked—all manner of chores of home and hearth.

Contact barely existed beyond the horizon of the hamlet. In

spring and fall, the land became a quagmire of flooded streams, rutted rural paths, and fields sunk in water. Thatch roofs leaked; backyards disintegrated into muddy wallows. Mud was everywhere. Travel was impossible. In winter, storms raged and howled across the broad countryside, obliterating such signposts as there were; families stayed indoors for days on end, stirring only to dig for potatoes or turnips from root cellars, gather firewood, and feed their emaciated cattle. Horse-drawn sledges moved along ancient tracks, their passengers bundled against the frost. Like buns in a warming oven, children slept through the long, cold nights in nooks and crannies of the massive *pechka*, the clay and ceramic stove that heated the hut. One could leave such places behind, but they were the soul of the motherland.

There was another reality of pastoral life that was the opposite of this romantic scene. Nikitin's home ground was located in one of the poorest areas of an exceptionally impoverished region. Cursed with thin, sour soils and backward farming methods that promised only shortages of food and fodder, the land was peopled by peasants who had been cowed into sullen submission by the horrors of Stalin's forced collectivization. It was a place of alcoholism, family violence, illiteracy, and illness. Crude farm bosses and sinister party men ran roughshod over the peasants, confiscating what they pleased and groveling before the stern taskmasters from Moscow who applied knout and boot to the farmers to raise their production. Some peasants learned to read and write and went off to the raw new cities and industrial complexes that were being flung up as Stalin tried to vault the new nation into the big leagues of the powerful industrial nations. To leave without permission was to risk execution, and for those left behind, rural life was desolation. One of Alexei's older sisters had died in the great hunger that accompanied collectivization; all his family suffered and endured, deep in their "deaf place," as these provincial settlements were known.

On the morning of June 22, 1941, four and a half years after Alexei was born, Hitler's Army Group Center under the command of Field Marshal Fedor von Bock smashed across the Soviet frontier west of Rognedino raion and, within weeks, had swept through Bryansk oblast on the drive for Moscow. Even though the Nazis assumed victory was to be theirs, the empty, trackless miles of Nikitin's homeland overwhelmed them, haunting them with its barren reality. Letters and dispatches from the front spoke of endless spaces,

a vast horizon, and clusters of desolate hamlets huddled in melancholy gloom as the Germans marched to seize the distant Bolshevik
capital. Under Hitler's Plan Oldenburg, Nikitin's peasant family
and millions of other Russians were to be enslaved to the Reich; the
planners in Berlin foresaw starvation and death for millions if the
interests of the Reich were to be served.

Two of Nikitin's older brothers died during the Great Patriotic
War, as the Soviets call World War II. But the rest of the family
survived, only to face a great new famine in 1946–47, which nearly
swept them away. Years later, Alexei remembered that "they gave
grams of grain daily" to families the size of his. Although it was
illegal, as soon as the snow melted in the spring of 1947 people went
into the fields to gather "potato remains to mix with the flour and
make it into bread to keep from starving."

The youngest Nikitin child went off to the local elementary
school and proved to be a model pupil: energetic, concerned, and
bright. His grades were excellent and he seemed capable of much
more important future work than the life of a *kolkhoznik*, a collective
farmer. He became a Young Octobrist, the Soviet equivalent of a
Cub Scout, and then, like virtually all of his classmates across the
country, a Young Pioneer. This organization, the Soviet equivalent
of the Boy Scouts, was founded in tribute to little Pavel Morozov,
who was killed by enraged relatives after he denounced his father
to party officials for assisting some neighboring kulaks, landed farmers, during the collectivization in 1932.

Inspired by his school director, a decorated hero of the Battle of
Stalingrad named Filatov ("I loved him," Nikitin said), he joined the
League of Young Communists, the Komsomol, when he reached
the Soviet equivalent of the tenth grade. He quickly became the
secretary, or leader, of the organization. With his enthusiasm, resil-
ience, and goodheartedness, the role fit him perfectly. He was a
natural leader and eager for the responsibility of looking after others.
But in his final year of high school, an unpleasant episode occurred,
a harbinger of the serious troubles that awaited him as an adult.

One Sunday, as secretary of the school Komsomol, he was chosen
to lead a group of the senior class to a neighboring hamlet, Potsini,
to help dig potatoes at the local collective farm. It was an attempt
to save the harvest. There was nothing unusual in this; even in the
1980s, students, bureaucrats, and factory workers are pressed into
service to save various harvests. Even so, some 30 percent of vegeta-

bles and grains grown on the collective and state farms are lost because they never get harvested or are improperly cured afterward. The high-schoolers were told that they didn't have to carry their lunches because the *kolkhoz*, collective farm, would feed them. It didn't turn out that way. No meal was provided and, after trying unsuccessfully thoughout the afternoon to get something to eat, the high-spirited young workers from Fedorovsky angrily walked off the job. Nikitin was the last to leave and, the next day, the school Komsomol convened an emergency session to denounce him for failing to protect the interests of the students and then inciting them to a job action.

"This was the first time I saw that even though the blame was on the kolkhoz, I was blamed. They wanted someone who would accept anything," Alexei recalled during one of the lengthy interviews David and I had with him in Donetsk.

When he graduated from high school in the mid-1950s, winds of change were sweeping through the Soviet Union. Stalin's death in March 1953 had at last brought an end to twenty-five years of terror. By 1956, Khrushchev had moved much farther, denouncing the Great Leader as a bloodthirsty criminal. Khrushchev revealed that even the sanctified Lenin in his last days had concluded—too late —that Stalin should be eased from power. A new spirit was flooding the nation. The USSR led the world into space with the triumphant launch of the first sputnik in October 1957. Meanwhile, Khrushchev was successfully outmaneuvering Stalin's chosen heir, Georgyi Malenkov, and retiring him to run a power plant in the hinterland. These affairs of state had no meaning to Nikitin: like millions of other peasants' sons, he joined the torrent of migration from country to city that fed Soviet industry with willing new manpower.

With a gift for tools and machinery, Nikitin found himself drawn irresistibly to Donetsk and the mines. Founded in the nineteenth century, the city was called Yuzovka after Welshman John Hughes, who started an ironworks near the coal mines to make rails for the czar's expanding railroad system. The city was still called Yuzovka when the young Nikita S. Khrushchev began his professional life there and in pre-revolutionary years witnessed his first Jewish pogrom. Later, when Stalin's name and granite profile multiplied across the land, Yuzovka became Stalino. That lasted until 1961, when Khrushchev had the name changed again, now calling the city after the Don River tributary that flows nearby. But John Hughes and the original name had never been forgotten, in part because as many as five families now lived in each of the one-story stucco houses originally built by the British for two families.

Nikitin lived in rough workers' dormitories, joining the Butovka–Donetsk coal mine as an apprentice electrofitter, repairing motors in the electric repair shop. Even then, he was appalled by the carelessness and waste: used motors lay out in the rain, spare parts were scattered everywhere, tools were lost or stolen, and equipment was abused or intentionally destroyed. He began to attend classes at the well-respected Donetsk Polytechnic Institute, studying electrical engineering. But he was in Donetsk only a few months before he was drafted into the armed forces and sent to duty with the Soviet northern fleet, which was based in Murmansk, the ice-free port well north of the Arctic Circle.

Mustered out in 1961 after receiving various commendations for meritorious service, Nikitin returned to Donetsk and resumed his Butovka mine job and his studies. He was reaching out to the world around him, meeting women, becoming active in the Butovka mine trade union and in the community council of the dormitory where he lived with dozens of other young, unmarried miners. "I left the army without any sense that the party was against the people," he said of this golden and easy era of his early adulthood. "I was raised in the idea that the party senses people in the best spirit. I never listened to foreign radio stations, I read Soviet papers and assumed they were truthful." He knew of people who fought against "socialist shortcomings," but that was simply part of life, the work of improving the country. There was no reason to think something was fundamentally corrupt or beyond correcting.

On January 1, 1965, Alexei was married; his bride, Natalya, was a staunch party member, and her entire family belonged to the party. They lived in a dormitory for married workers, where Nikitin quickly became deputy chairman of the hostel's worker council and established a friendship with a man named Kirill Sarachev, party member and instrument maker at the Butovka mine. Soon Sarachev was urging Nikitin to join the party. So Alexei went to a few party meetings to see what it was all about. He found them boring. But Sarachev persisted, and any level-headed person could see the sense in it anyway. Party members stood at the top of most lists for new housing, their pay was better, and the party offered a genuine opportunity to work for the common welfare of everyone.

Nikitin was accepted as a candidate member—on probation and without the right to vote in the closed meetings.

As an activist agitator in the Butovka trade union, he began hearing complaints about miners cheated of bonuses or transferred to menial jobs because they spoke out. Several men were dismissed for the same violations of labor discipline that others had been forgiven. Alexei began working to get these men reinstated. When he succeeded, he began to hear of even more abuses.

As he gained experience, his views matured and he began to realize that the closed party meetings where these matters were discussed were farcical at best and malign at worst. He felt that his mentor, Sarachev, was a principled man, but whenever some serious problem of wage-cheating or repressive actions by the mine chiefs was brought up, Sarachev deflected the matter with a joke or an anecdote that throttled serious talk. He seemed to play the role of a deliberate court jester. Most of the time, the party sessions dealt with mind-numbing—and utterly irrelevant—twists and turns of the party's international policies, or the decisions of whatever recent party congress was still thought to be important. Nikitin concluded that every major question had been decided in advance by the Butovka chiefs. They had no interest in seeing their judgments challenged by rank-and-file party men or self-righteous activists like Alexei.

The Butovka mine director was Viktor Filipovich Savich, who had married into the family of the Donetsk oblast party chief, Vladimir Degtyarev. Savich was openly known as the "prince" of Butovka; Degtyarev was called the "czar" of the region. In coordination with his regional peers, this man ruled several million subjects with absolute authority, and he inspired fear and awe in his fiefdom. Nikitin himself had once chanced to hear Degtyarev make a speech at another mine; Alexei came away from the experience with the strong feeling that the party chieftain was a cultured, ruthless, and capable leader. Within a few years, Nikitin would find himself in direct confrontation with this man.

Degtyarev had spent most of his life in the shafts and tunnels of the party in the Ukraine. He was an engineer, a mover, a shaker—and a survivor. He had lived through the Terror, and any man who achieved that lived ever afterward with the knowledge that Moscow could strike without warning or provocation. The 1930s had decimated the Ukrainian party, as one survivor of that time recalled for us in an interview in Moscow. At the Donetsk steel works alone, this source once told us, the purge cut down all but a handful of the more than two hundred engineers needed to run the factory. "They just disappeared, and it was never clear whether they were shot. . . . None of us could sleep at night. No one criticized anything. We didn't trust anyone."

In the aftermath of the purges and the war, Degtyarev moved up in the party and began living more like provincial nobility. His home was on Velikaya Otechestvenaya, Great Patriotic Street, and the city militia watered his flowerbeds. He made housing a major priority, and whatever else he may have been, city residents thought he had succeeded on that score. "Whatever he wanted, he did, and he built a European city," said one elderly woman who had never been to Europe and who despised the Soviet regime. "People trembled when they spoke of him . . . he was a great chief," she acknowledged with grudging respect.

As Nikitin was to find out, this mighty leader was not interested in miners' complaints. As a one-time Donetsk resident said, Degtyarev was like a character in Alexander Solzhenitsyn's *Cancer Ward* —a man who loved the Russian people and hated the Russian population. In September 1969, Degtyarev's views on labor problems were published in the newspaper *Pravda*, the powerful voice of the party. He complained that "often, an artificially exaggerated 'affair' gets outside the framework of an enterprise, and makes the rounds of the city, oblast, and even central organizations. . . . In principle, any labor conflict at a plant can be solved internally, without the intervention of higher authorities." Even as the party chief was delivering himself of these blunt and threatening views, Nikitin was heading toward a crisis in his relations with the men who ran Butovka, including Degtyarev's relative, Savich.

Throughout the second half of the 1960s, Nikitin had struggled to give substance to the title of Communist party member. He reckoned later in conversations with us that he had helped restore nineteen miners to jobs from which they had been illegally or unfairly fired. He had a reputation as a person who cared, and years later when we walked with him on the streets of Donetsk, I was astonished to see other miners, braving the secret police lurking behind us, walk up to Alexei, shake his hand warmly or clap him on the back, and offer a few words of encouragement.

With the birth of his daughter, Irina, in 1966, Nikitin achieved a family life that succored him and gave him reason to trust in the future. Yet the abuses did not cease. In fact, it seemed to him that, under the corrosive leadership of Savich, safety conditions at Butovka were deteriorating. His job repairing and installing electrical equipment took him all over the mine and its tunnels. He was appalled to see the sloppy way explosives were stored below, the dangers of improperly maintained equipment, and the general disregard for safety precautions. The chiefs made clear that they cared about only one thing—beating the quota. Nothing else counted.

Alexei began raising the question of safety at the closed party meetings. Each time, his questions were deflected in the usual way. When he couldn't stand the bosses' smugness any longer, he took a fateful step further: he complained to the oblast party committee. Within days, he was called in and told he was not qualified to judge safety matters and he'd be very smart to keep his ignorant mouth shut.

Nikitin's conception of what his country wanted from its people changed. He began reflecting on the string of solemn promises from the succession of Soviet leaders, including the Great Lenin himself, of a better life to come. His party history books could tell him that on March 22, 1919, the party had adopted a program of Lenin's promising an eight-hour day, a month's vacation, and free medicine and medical help for pregnant women and other classes of workers. There would be safety inspections of the workplace and the state truly would defend the worker. But, so far as he knew, even the promise of an eight-hour day was something of a myth since there was so much extra work to be done to reach plan norms. The rest of the promises of 1919 had never been met. Lenin had decreed that trade unions should function as "transmission belts from the party to the people," guaranteeing that real power would remain with the party. The concept embodied in this assured that the party defended its power and not the people. Trade unions had no power in such a system and were utterly subservient to the party in any clash of interests. Khrushchev's program at the beginning of the decade had promised a thirty-five-hour workweek, free food at the workplace, free medicine, free housing, and free transportation to most places. Not one promise had been fulfilled and it was considered offensive to raise the former leader's name in party meetings. Nikitin was losing his faith.

And then, twenty Butovka miners came to him complaining that they had been cheated out of a bonus promised if they fulfilled the plan that month. Nikitin listened and knew that what the men demanded should be given to them. He suggested they organize a delegation to raise the complaint with the directorate. Anything less than a delegation would be ignored; at the same time, it seemed unlikely that there could be a reprisal since the group was so large.

They went as a group to see the Butovka party chief, Yuri Demisov. He listened to them impassively and then shrugged his shoulders. "There's nothing I can do," he said. "Go to Comrade Savich." Only the chief of the mine could decide the complaint.

The protest grew and by the time Nikitin and some two dozen other miners got an appointment to see Savich, they were carrying a petition with one hundred thirty signatures on it. That was a challenge the directorate must not ignore. It was December 1969, the invasion of Czechoslovakia had occurred the previous year, and the economic reforms that Premier Alexei Kosygin had once backed had been stifled by the power of the fiscal and ideological conservatives behind Brezhnev. The Butovka complaint was to be handled in only one way.

Nikitin spoke for the delegation, explaining carefully to Savich that, thanks to advances the country had made under Soviet power, the miners were literate and therefore they could read the production charts as well as anyone. They knew almost to the kilogram how much coal was produced daily and, therefore, what was owed them. Down to the last kopeck.

With the portrait of the Great Lenin surveying the scene from the wall, Savich regarded the miners before him. This was the kind of confrontation he knew how to handle. Savich was only a baron and mine director and therefore had to be careful he did not run afoul of a higher princeling. But he also was a relative of the region's czar, Degtyarev. Savich knew his own position in this situation: he held every card in the deck.

So he said: "I'm the boss! If I want to pay a bonus, I'll pay it! If I don't, I won't!"

"In that case, we'll find a boss who is higher than you," Nikitin shot back.

"Get out! Get out!" Savich shouted, pounding the desk. "Go complain to anyone you want!"

They did. The declaration now became a letter from thirty party members and another hundred nonparty miners. Ignoring the local party men since they were controlled by a relative of Savich's, Nikitin sent the letter off to Nogina Square in Moscow where the Communist party's Central Committee is located, just down the street from KGB headquarters at Lyubyanka Prison. The Lyubyanka was itself across the street from Detski Mir, the Children's World, the best-known toy and department store in the USSR. The juxtaposition was important in Soviet mythology: Feliks Dzerzhinsky, the first chief of the Soviet secret police, was said to have loved children. His statue graced the wide traffic circle that the prison and the children's store both faced. Intourist guides liked to point out Children's World to foreigners; they seldom mentioned the bizarre positioning of the statue of the savage Dzerzhinsky with the toy store. Foreigners could not be expected to understand these things—or to understand them too well.

The miners waited for a retort from the Central Committee. From Moscow came only silence. And then one day early in 1970, Nikitin was called in to the local party committee, where he was denounced and expelled for unsatisfactory performance. Some days later, the scene was repeated: he was fired from his job at Butovka. A door slammed shut on his life. He never was able to open it again.

II

During his years as activist and party man, Alexei had carefully amassed enough blat to improve his family's position greatly. For example, he had been able to move them out of dormitory quarters for married workers and into a small apartment near the Butovka mine itself. This represented a gain of years on the housing queue. But in two swift strokes, the party had severed the trouble-maker from the intricate system of reward and privilege that kept most of its members obedient. Now, he was no better off than most of the other 94 percent of Soviets who are not party members. And because he had been disciplined and yet remained defiant, there was real danger of further reprisal from the authorities. No one knew this better than Natalya Nikitina, daughter of party people. "You're a fool to defend the workers," she told her husband. "Why don't you steal the way the others do?" This hard-bitten cynicism was in accordance with an iron-clad provincial proverb: only a fool believes in his own ideas.

As a longtime Donetsk resident told us, "They may applaud Nikitin and in fact admire him, but they also think he is stupid, for what he did earns nothing. It simply isn't profitable. It goes against their mercantile instincts."

Meanwhile, the state lost no time in rooting out the dangerous dissatisfaction that Nikitin's petition represented. Each miner who had signed the offending document was called in to the mine directorate, denounced, and threatened with punishment if he did not repudiate it. While a city committee *apparatchik*, bureaucrat, looked on, a number of the miners grudgingly wrote out renunciations and signed them. But many others refused—and were summarily transferred to other mines. The authorities feared so large a group of disgruntled workers in one place.

If he was shocked or chastened by his harsh treatment, Nikitin gave no sign. His hardy constitution took the blows. "I am a Russian and I was raised in a patriotic family," he mused later. "Like all Russians, I deeply love my people, our land, our folk songs. But I began to believe that to live in this country is impossible—unlimited terror by the authorities without any law. This happened because I started to defend workers without the bosses' permission."

Alexei took up his own cause with the same energy he had devoted to his colleagues. He began petitioning every level of the Donetsk hierarchy with letters, visits, and telephone calls. He burrowed into the maze of bureaucrats, ferreted out secretaries and their nachalniki, and spent hours waiting for a few moments' confrontation with the party men. In every case, his complaint was bucked somewhere else. But he persisted. At last, he was permitted to present his case to the local Party Control Commission, which was charged with adjudicating disciplinary matters. The commission was headed by the city party chief himself, A. A. Kubyshkin. Aside from having little inclination to find fault with his own underlings, Kubyshkin was a crony of Degtyarev's, and his review board exhibited the same seamless face of power as the Butovka mine directorate itself. Commission members included senior factory and mine directors, senior party officials, and senior representatives of the police and KGB. Nevertheless, Nikitin pressed for a hearing.

Some seventy officials were on hand when the case was heard. While Nikitin sat before this segment of the local leadership, a pensioner droned through the tale of Alexei's expulsion. The attention of the listeners focused with ferocious intensity on the petitioner. The old man had barely finished when Kubyshkin raged to the attack. "So you defend the people, do you?" he screamed at Alexei. "Well, you're a literate fellow, you've read your history and in the history books it's written that those who tried to lead the masses—they lost their heads!" A heavy silence fell. Everyone there knew that Kubyshkin was talking about Cossack rebel Stenka Razin, who was beheaded in 1672 at the Place of Execution in Red Square across from the Kremlin, and Yemelian Pugachev, the other famous Cossack rebel, who was executed by quartering at the command of Catherine the Great in 1775. But Nikitin was not intimidated.

"I grew up amid the people and if defending them means losing my head, I'm ready!"

At this, Kubyshkin began screaming for the police chief, Voronov: "Open a case against him!"

Nikitin stalked out. Within days, agents began shadowing him. Ostentatiously, they took his photograph on the street and from time to time showed up at the apartment to question him about various city crimes. Oblast party chief Degtyarev reviewed the case and the regional czar told Alexei: "If you stick your nose into our business, I'll mix coal with your blood and take your body and grind it into fertilizer!"

With the pressure all around him, Alexei found his personal life crumbling. When former mine colleagues came by to chew the fat, bringing vodka or homemade hooch like old times, he was suspicious, fearing that these friends had been brought under KGB control and that he risked arrest on a drunk charge. He sipped his liquor slowly and kept his counsel. He earned small amounts of money from odd jobs in the city and countryside. Part of the time, he returned to Bryansk oblast where he had been born. It was just as impoverished as he had remembered as a child, but he found work on state and collective farms, where the sloth and drunkenness appalled him. The oblast was exploited by the production system. He was outraged to find, for example, that, while the farms in the area raised wheat that was shipped off and ground into flour for refined white bread for the rest of the country, the farmers themselves had only brown bread to gnaw on. "They never got the white flour back," he remembered.

The Lenin Collective Farm now was run by a Nikolai Gaponov, "a pirate." In the late 1970s, Alexei said, shortages were imbedded

in Bryansk life. Local state stores lacked cereal, meat, noodles, maca-
roni, paper supplies, and milk. "Bread supplies were poor and if it
rained, there might be no bread for several days because of delivery
problems. There were never sweet buns, and no white bread—only
brown bread."

His wife grew frantic with him for refusing to bend, apologize,
and put his once-promising career back on track. Meanwhile, the
party called her in and suggested a way she could help to "re-
educate" him—and put some daylight between herself and her husband. The apparatchiks counseled her to denounce him for anti-
Soviet activities. She resisted, but in the end concocted an appeal to
the party for help, accusing Alexei of staying up at night writing
anti-government tracts. Nikitin got wind of the denunciation and
somehow obtained it. When he had satisfied himself that it really
was in her handwriting, he knew they would never again live together as husband and wife. They struggled on together for almost
two more years until one day Natalya disappeared, taking Irina with
her. Fearful that he meant only trouble for his beloved daughter,
Nikitin vowed he would not try to find her. He never saw Irina
again.

With every avenue of appeal denied in Donetsk, Nikitin took the
same route he had with the miners' complaints. He turned to the
Center—Moscow. Even though Moscow had dealt harshly with the
miners by throwing their petition to the same local wolves from
whom the workers had sought relief, he reasoned that this had
occurred because the central authorities didn't fully comprehend the
degree of abuse in Donetsk. The fault was with local bureaucrats
and some party men who exceeded their own authority; there was
still a likelihood that the misunderstanding could be rectified once
Moscow was in possession of all the facts. They would see that he
had been unfairly punished. This notion of the rectitude of the
Center was traditional and important in Russia. It had helped citizens live with themselves during the Great Terror, when they could
blame brutish local police and party authorities while revering the
tyrant who was busy ordering the sacrifice of their lives. After his
Donetsk experience, Alexei knew the effort would take a great deal
of time. But there was no worry there—he had plenty of time on
his hands. He headed for Moscow.

Over the next two years, he would spend months in Moscow,
living the strange life of a "truth seeker," a historic calling in Russia.

Truth seekers were as much a part of the country's ritual and tradition as the icon. The existence of an unkempt and stubborn petitioner in the faceless, intimidating reception halls and corridors of government buildings implied that wrongs could be corrected and that the individual had personal rights the government was interested in protecting. Thousands of truth seekers had thronged czarist St. Petersburg and thousands congregated in Moscow during the Brezhnev era.

With his documents in his valise, Nikitin trudged the streets of the capital, looking for justice. He found himself shunted from the Central Committee to the headquarters of the All-Union trade organizations; to the state procurator, then on to the national parliament, the Supreme Soviet; and then to the Supreme Court—and back again. Everywhere, there were lines of shuffling, unhappy citizens, ready to mumble their tales of woe to anyone willing to listen. These regional folk peopled the gloomy, echoing granite halls of certain government and party buildings. The petitioners were never allowed to be comfortable. Grim-faced policemen in gray uniforms, plainclothesmen, and civilian guards, the *druzhinniki*, kept vigil over the petitioners. Nikitin learned from veteran truth seekers, men and women who had spent years searching for vindication, that microphones overheard conversations in some reception halls and that a petitioner careless with his anger could find himself hauled out of line and sent off to a mental hospital for involuntary observation. A stay in a psychiatric hospital could mean plenty of trouble from local authorities when the petitioner got home.

Regardless of which line or what institution, the routine was the same. The petitioner was made to fill out fresh forms for each visit, a painstaking process that took on nightmarish qualities as he or she worked through a meaningless series of questions and answers. The forms were good for a short time and then had to be filled out anew. Only certain officials were empowered to handle certain kinds of complaints, and if the examiner happened to be away from his desk or office—often the case—no one else could handle the petition. Sometimes, a supplicant could wait for days or even weeks for the right bureaucrat to appear. Finally, the official would review the documents, listen with an utterly indifferent expression as the petitioner elaborated, and then hand out a decision: "Settle this in the local organization."

"I already tried there—without result. Which is why I am here!" the petitioner would say.

"Go back anyway. Next petitioner!"

Pretty soon, the faces of the truth seekers became familiar and Alexei discovered many of them returning with new petitions from their homes, new arguments, and new hopes for vindication. But during the months he spent with them, he was sure that not one of them had obtained satisfaction.

Like many of the truth seekers, Alexei had family to stay with in Moscow. But other petitioners were forced to live like vagrants, one step ahead of the police. In the summers, the drifters could find almost idyllic shelter from harassment along the peaceful green banks of the Moscow River where it meandered outside the grimy industrial sections. Keeping to themselves when they weren't standing in lines, they could rest beneath the soft, northern summer sun, catch fish, and refresh themselves. In winter, they could shelter with thousands of others in the rancid, sodden waiting rooms of the capital's numerous rail stations. There was greater danger in these places because the police customarily searched there for fugitives. There also was a measure of safety to be found in such unexpected places as the Lenin Stadium, the huge coliseum lying within the south bend of the Moscow River, where the roof provided shelter and some warmth in fall and spring.

Toward the end of his second year of travels to Moscow, Alexei got permission to present his complaint to the highest party review board in the USSR, the Party Control Commission. Headed by Arvid Pel'she, a dour 71-year-old Latvian who was a member of the Politburo, the secretive inner ruling council, the commission was the court of last resort for faithful Communists in trouble with their party. Brezhnev himself liked to talk about the work of the commission as a force for bringing justice and new blood into the party. If there was one place Alexei could hope for vindication, this was it. Several weeks before his appointed day, he reviewed his case with an elderly functionary of the commission who would make the initial presentation, followed by Nikitin himself.

The day came when Alexei, freshly shaved and in carefully cleaned jacket, trousers, shirt, and tie, was solemnly ushered before the highest party tribunal of all. Some two dozen party men in conservative suits stared reproachfully at him as he stood to request a review of his expulsion. The focal point of the ornate room at

Central Committee headquarters was Pel'she himself. A longtime confidante of Brezhnev's, Pel'she had helped establish Soviet power in his previously independent country when the Red Army invaded in 1940. The Soviets had been pushed out by the Germans in 1941, but Russians returned four years later, driving the Germans out, and Pel'she emerged again. Many of his Latvian countrymen regarded him as a quisling, but he was important to the conservative Brezhnev coalition in the Politburo. His status as a voting member of the inner sanctum was enhanced by the fact that he was a member of a tiny European-oriented minority among a ruling body utterly dominated by the Great Russians. In addition, having Pel'she within the Politburo served as an unmistakable rebuff to the United States, which had steadfastly refused to recognize Soviet hegemony over Latvia or the two other Baltic states, Estonia and Lithuania.

Pel'she could have had no interest whatsoever in this complainer from Donetsk now standing before him. The powerful party sachem watched Nikitin without a flicker of emotion. The only movement to be seen in his gaunt, cadaverous face was the blink of his large, dark, impassive eyes.

Alexei's voice rose and his hands sketched in the air as he described the injustice. His performance was lively and compelling, the only way he knew how to approach life. No one asked him a question. The commission members regarded him with steely, numbing contempt. He spoke for a time and then sat down. He had barely stopped speaking when a commission bureaucrat rapped out the decision: "Appeal denied." As he walked from the reception room, Nikitin carried with him one indelible impression: Pel'she's severe expression betrayed a desire to punish.

III

ALEXEI never gave up his efforts to be reinstated in the party or the Butovka job, but when he left the Control Commission and found himself once again drifting through the streets of Moscow, an outcast, he knew he had reached a point from which he would never return: "I saw that my fate was decided. These Communists weren't building communism, but some kind of society of hangmen."

Was there no place within his country where he could find satisfaction?

On April 15, 1971, Nikitin walked into the Embassy of Norway at No. 7 Vorovskogo Ulitsa in the heart of Moscow and asked to see a diplomat.

It was an extraordinary stroke of luck—and an example of his cunning—that he had not been intercepted on the street by the uniformed KGB police who patrol every foreign chancery, compound, and residence to prevent Soviets from free access to outsiders, regardless of their acceptability. The KGB guards at the East German embassy perform the same function as their colleagues outside the American embassy. That paranoia, reinforced by xenophobic state propaganda, made Nikitin's appearance at the Norwegian embassy even more remarkable. For, of all the potential foreign enemies surrounding the motherland, the NATO countries are portrayed as the most threatening. Indeed, as Alexei told us, he had specifically chosen the Norwegians because of all the warnings of their perfidy he had received during his military service. If any foreigners would be interested in helping him against Soviet power, he reasoned, it would be these people.

A young diplomat appeared and listened while Alexei explained his predicament and asked for assistance in sending some documents to the United States, the United Nations, and several international labor organizations. The Soviet postal system would never let them out of the country. Quite to the contrary, Nikitin knew, the mailmen would make sure that he was arrested. The Norwegian refused.

Then he suddenly shut the door to the interview room, cutting off the prying eyes of Soviet clerks who were employed by every foreign chancery and who reported whatever they could glean of interest to the KGB. The Norwegian accepted the petitions and gave his visitor the telephone number of the American embassy. A few moments later, Nikitin was back on the sidewalk and away before the guards realized what had happened. He would never be so lucky again.

Alexei phoned the Americans and spoke with a man there about visiting the chancery, located on the Tchaikovskogo section of the central Ring Road, a few blocks from the Foreign Ministry. Next to the hated Red Chinese in their massive compound near Moscow State University, the U.S. embassy was the most heavily guarded legation in the city. There were uniformed KGB police at each of the three entrances to the aging yellow-stucco building and an unmarked Volga sedan was parked nearby, ready to add agents should any Russian be foolhardy enough to attempt to get into the building without an official invitation supplied ahead of time by the Americans or a consular officer as escort and witness if the police attempted to stop the Russian guest. A small wooden guardhouse stood around the corner on a side street. The Americans accurately called it the "beat-up shack."

The American diplomat agreed to send Alexei an official entrance permit, which would help get him in past the guards. At Nikitin's request, the form was sent to the central city post office on Gorky Street to protect the Moscow relatives Alexei was staying with from a police visit. On April 17, Alexei went to the post office and was told that a package, but no letter, awaited him. Apprehensive, he replied that the parcel couldn't be for him, and walked out. Two days later, he returned and this time the clerk said that there was neither letter nor package. When Alexei left, two men darted out of the daytime crowds on Moscow's busiest shopping street and forced him into a waiting car. He spent two weeks at a community psychiatric hospital in Moscow. The experience left little impression on him. "There was no treatment; they did it to frighten me," he told us. He wasn't frightened and those two weeks were so innocuous that they offered no foretaste of what lay ahead.

When he was released, the police put Alexei on a train to Donetsk with instructions to stay there. He ignored them and toward the end of 1971 returned to Moscow with new petitions to be sent abroad. Again, he made contact with the Americans and successfully passed the material on to them. Among the items was a written renunciation of his Soviet citizenship. Then he returned to Donetsk, comforted by the knowledge that somewhere in the world beyond Soviet boundaries it could be learned how he had been dismissed from work in violation of his own nation's laws.

On December 22, 1971, Nikitin's life was changed forever. Early that morning, the safety violations he had first warned about more than two years earlier caught up with the bosses of the Butovka mine. Around 6 A.M., with the night shift of miners just emerged from the tunnels at Butovka and the day shift preparing to descend into the pit, the Butovka–Donetsk coal mine blew up.

The explosion ripped through underground galleries and thundered aloft over the pithead. Emergency vehicles and hysterical families raced to the shaft. Amid the pandemonium, rescue teams descended and slowly penetrated the web of tunnels, bringing up survivors and counting the victims. Seven miners were killed and more than a hundred injured. Everyone knew the toll would have been much higher if the shifts had not been changing. With the families had come the KGB—carloads of agents to control the milling throng of frightened and angry miners and their families. As the death toll rose, so did the workers' fury. They began shouting: "Nikitin warned you!" The KGB ringed the territory and commanded the workers to disperse.

An earlier uprising in Novocherkassk was well known to many Soviet workers. During that episode in 1962, textile workers in a southern Russian city of that name rose up over poor food and poor pay, seized party headquarters in the town, and demanded talks. Khrushchev ordered in the troops, and in the ensuing face-off, the soldiers fired on their countrymen. There had been many deaths and many wounded. Now, the angry Butovka miners slowly went home.

A day or two later, miners going by bus to the cemetery for the burial of one of the victims found themselves under surveillance by KGB men. Resentment flared. One of the miners burst out: "You fired Nikitin for warning about an explosion!" The Chekisti leaped on the man and tossed him off the bus.

When Alexei heard this tale, he figured his own days might be numbered. His problem worsened when some of his old friends began coming to see him at home to complain about the negligence at Butovka and the indifference of the nachalniki. He was sure the authorities would not allow him to remain free as a living reproof of the Butovka directorate. He began moving from house to house, living in Donetsk on the run from the organs. It didn't last long.

The KGB seized Alexei on January 13, 1972, and jailed him. He was charged with violating Article 187 of the Ukrainian Criminal Code: dissemination of knowingly false fabrications discrediting the Soviet political and social system. Penalty: three years at hard labor.

Alexei was held incommunicado for five months. He had almost no contact with his brothers and sisters and never had access to a lawyer or any other person who might have been able to help him defend himself. This was in accordance with Soviet criminal law, which presumes a person guilty. He had almost no contact with the police either; he seemed to have been forgotten. But on June 19, the man who once had only wanted to right a wrong was hustled out of the city jail and herded aboard a prisoners' train with other inmates. They were locked into a passenger car that had frosted windows, and the train rolled out of the terminal. Toward the end of the day, the train stopped at a siding in the Ukrainian country-side. A flock of police vans, stood nearby: the prisoners were loaded into the trucks and the journey resumed. When they finally climbed out, they found themselves at the main jail in the city of Dneprope-trovsk.

Along with Donetsk and a few other grimy cities nearby, Dne-propetrovsk dominated life and commerce in the southeastern Ukraine. The Dnieper River, third longest in Europe after the Danube and the Volga, flowed through the city and its bargemen, dockers, and inland sailors lent a swaggering edge to the scene. Like Donetsk, it was a place of muscle and raw manpower and most of its eight hundred thousand souls labored in the heavy machinery factories and foundries that consumed Donetsk coking coal.

For all its grime, the city has a genuine royal past: it had been founded in 1783 by Catherine the Great as Ekaterinoslav (Glory to Catherine), before the disbelieving eyes of Joseph II of Prussia, whose diary entry for the event is worth recalling: "Here, human life and effort count for nothing," wrote the Prussian potentate, perhaps enviously, of Catherine's Russia. "Here, one can build roads, ports, fortresses, palaces on marshland; one can plant forests in the desert; all without paying the workers, who never complain even though they lack for everything, sleep on the ground and often suffer from hunger. . . . The master orders, the slave obeys."*

Ekaterinoslav–Dnepropetrovsk has two, more modern distinc-tions. In 1938, Khrushchev, who then was a power in the Ukraine, sent a bushy-browed young comer named Leonid Ilyich Brezhnev to the city to assume command of the local party in the aftermath of the savage purge of the Ukrainian party. Brezhnev did well, taking one more upward step in the long climb to power that culminated with his ouster of Khrushchev from supreme leadership twenty-six years later.

The final distinction is this: on maps of the Soviet Union that the Foreign Ministry sometimes hands out to foreign travelers, the city appears circled in red. This signifies it to be closed to foreigners. Its closed status made Dnepropetrovsk ideal for certain state functions

---

*Henri Troyat, *Catherine the Great*, p. 320. (See the bibliography on p. 335 for full details of the works cited.)

that demanded a special measure of secrecy. In 1968, the Ministry of Internal Affairs, the MVD, opened a facility there which Nikitin and most other Soviets had no idea existed. Now, Alexei was taken from the city's main jail to this clandestine place. He found himself inside a double-walled fortress surmounted by watchtowers manned by uniformed guards carrying automatic weapons. This strange and forbidding prison was called the Dnepropetrovsk Special Psychiatric Hospital for the Criminally Insane.

It was June 20, 1972. Barely a month earlier, responding to the yearnings of millions for a more peaceful, just world, President Richard M. Nixon had arrived in Moscow for his first and most successful summit with the apparatchik from Dnepropetrovsk, Leonid Brezhnev. The age of détente was about to begin.

3

. . . and Punishment

For the kind of social experiment you are making, I would not sacrifice a frog's hind legs.

—IVAN PAVLOV, LETTER TO STALIN

I

THE white-garbed criminals who functioned as orderlies at the psycho-prison stripped Nikitin naked. Methodically, they listed each article of his clothing and put it aside for storage. Perhaps this meant he would be released soon, since they must be saving the clothing for a reason.

But they said, "Now, dear comrade, you're going to be here for life."

"How do you know . . . for life?"

"Little friend, they've decided you're a fool and you've got a political offense. . . . So don't worry about your clothing . . . you're here for life."

He was sent to disinfecting baths in the basement, then brought back and dressed in black prison trousers and a felon's loose-fitting striped shirt. Then he was escorted through grim corridors by an orderly who confided that Nikitin was about to be given a pill and he would be smart to take it without complaint or resistance. Otherwise, they would force it down his throat.

They arrived at a dispensary room where other orderlies attended to a line of inmates. A middle-aged medical sister thrust a cup of water and a pill at him.

"I'm a healthy man and I won't take any medicine that I don't need."

They explained his situation to him this way: "You were brought here forcibly and you will be treated forcibly if you refuse to cooperate. If you don't want to take this pill, you will be bound and then injected with it."

He saw that they were dead serious. Even though they wore white hospital smocks that gave them the look of hospital personnel, they themselves were prisoners—criminals who would have no compunction about beating him if they wanted to. They are Fascists and I am in the hands of the Gestapo, Nikitin thought. He would take the medicine in the hope that nothing worse would befall him. He washed the pill down. It was majeptil, a powerful tranquilizer that had triggered suicides in other psycho-prisons when inmates were overdosed with it.

"The shock was enormous—so much that when I stood up, I was off balance and the world was spinning around me. It was hard to move. I felt hot, burning." Subdued, Nikitin was marched through the prison and deposited in front of a heavy wooden door. An orderly unlocked it and swung it open.

"It was a nightmare that no one should ever see." Dim light from windows high up on the walls filtered weakly into a room about twenty by thirty feet in area. So many dormitory-style, iron-frame beds jammed the floor that there was hardly room to move. Yet, strange creatures were in motion beneath a high ceiling where caged lights burned feebly day and night. The faces that turned toward Nikitin were a faded yellow from endless days out of reach of the sun. They had a wan, pasty look from lack of exercise and a starchy diet. Some of the faces were contorted into frightening masks, with the features bunched to one side or the other, brows pulled close, eyes staring or flitting at high speed from point to point. Some of the inmates had fragile frames made even weaker from years of inactivity. Some chewed their tongues, drooled through slack jaws, or made licking and swallowing motions. Some stood hunched and swaying, hands moving spasmodically, fingers curling or rolling imaginary ball bearings or other objects across their palms. There were murmurs, sobs, groans, sighs, and, here and there, snatches of furtively spoken words. Some men lay on their stomachs on their beds and could not turn over. Others seemed possessed by devilish spirits that caused them to roll and turn incessantly or pace back and forth like crazed animals, while some lay in dazed stupors, inert and uncaring.

A heavy, musky odor laced with the sharp smell of urine and the stench of vomit and excrement permeated the air. From time to time, someone crept forward to implore the orderly at the door to let the prisoners out to relieve themselves in foul-smelling toilets elsewhere in the prison. If they were denied, the men soiled themselves in the ward. Men coughed and hacked up phlegm and spat it on the floor, and men in the grips of drug treatment vomited. Others ignored these commonplace calamities.

Many pairs of eyes pried at Nikitin. Was this stocky man with the roughened hands of a workman and the dazed look of a newcomer a murderer? Rapist? Homosexual? Religious believer? He could be any of these things, for the ward contained every kind of transgressor of socialist order and there were many wards in the Dnepropetrovsk citadel.

The door closed behind him.

Soon, Alexei was put in the hands of two physicians who led the examination of what they called his "case." Captain Nikolai Karpovich Alexeev ran the sessions, assisted by Viktoria V. Blokhina, a psychiatric professor whose husband was a KGB colonel. Alexeev was a senior captain in the uniformed national police run by the Ministry of Internal Affairs, the MVD. It was a peculiarity of Soviet public health policies that its hospitals for the criminally insane were run by the MVD, which together with the KGB functioned as a successor to the dread NKVD which had run Stalin's Terror and his concentration camps.

It is not possible to know what was asked or how the physicians went about determining Alexei's health. But the universe within the closely guarded walls of Dnepropetrovsk was an unusual one when measured against most Western psychiatric traditions. It had been shaped largely by the theories of Ivan Pavlov, the world-famed behaviorist who early in the century had gained insights into human behavior by closely studying dogs. His best-known theory was that of the conditioned response, in which he demonstrated that, with the proper combination of punishment and reward, dogs could be trained to salivate when they heard a bell, a signal previously associated with the sight of food. They would water at the mouth whether or not food came. The notion of the conditioned reflex had unique appeal for a totalitarian state that permitted only one ideology.

In 1950, at a series of unprecedented Moscow conferences, a psychiatrist–politician named Andrei Snezhnevsky, maneuvering in the twilight of the Stalin era, successfully shifted Soviet psychiatric practice away from the precepts of the foreigner Freud, with his emphasis on the importance of individual self-reliance and independence within a society. Snezhnevsky brought the country's concepts of psychiatric practice home to the teachings of the native son, Pavlov. Freudians were suppressed and Pavlovians gained power.

Operating from the Serbsky Institute of Forensic Psychiatry, an unassuming, walled structure in central Moscow a few blocks from the ornate official residence of the United States ambassador, Snezhnevsky moved Soviet standards of diagnosis and treatment of mental illness in an unmistakably authoritarian—and punitive—direction. During the next three decades, the concepts of who was mentally ill and what kind of behavior constituted derangement came more and more to reflect Communist ideology, which emphasizes the needs and goals of the collective ahead of the individual. Since the party was inseparable from nationhood and a well-adjusted Soviet citizen was loyal to the motherland, it followed that it was disloyal to question the party. In practical terms, a person who could not submit to the dictates of the local party committee, trade union, farm management, factory, or mine directorate could be more than a troublesome nonconformist, or disloyal. Within the framework of Soviet insistence upon conformity it was apparent that those who rejected conformity—the norm of the community—in some cases might be deranged. Conformity had a special role in the Russian psyche, anyway. "The tallest sunflower gets harvested first," peasants said in czarist times, and the adage still held true in Soviet times.

One other major factor reinforced this uniquely Russian perspective on the nature of conformity: party ideology. Soviet medical students devoted about a quarter of their courses to the study of ideological matters: Marxism–Leninism, Marxist economics, dialectic materialism, scientific atheism. A psychiatrist encountering a religious believer would be dealing with a citizen who adamantly rejected the theory of scientific atheism. The state psychiatrist could feel right at home concluding that the Baptist was mentally ill. Snezhnevsky's pet theory held that virtually all mental illness stemmed from one of three forms of schizophrenia, including a variation in which a victim of the disease could retain every outward sign of normality while inwardly harboring deranged visions of "reforming" Soviet society. From the 1960s onward, the Ministry of Public Health and the MVD issued a series of regulations broadening the state's power to incarcerate citizens suspected of dangerously "reformist" views.

As these powers expanded, the system of psycho-prisons also grew. In the post-Stalin years, there may have been no more than half a dozen special psychiatric hospitals, or SPHs. By the late 1970s, it was believed in the West that there were about two dozen of these hospitals in operation, all of them under the control of the MVD. Other countries might find it at least odd that the care and treatment of criminally insane citizens would be entrusted to the mercies of the national police. In the USSR, such thoughts were disloyal.

Thus it was that Nikitin found his doctors wearing police uniforms under their white surgical smocks, an oddity which made clear for him that the only reason anyone wore white at Dnepropetrovsk was to make it look like a hospital. During sessions with his doctors, Alexei never learned that under Soviet law he was entitled to the services of a medical commission to review his incarceration and that the law gave him the right to name a physician of his own choice to the group. No one told him the same law required a review of his case every six months. And no one told him that the charge of anti-Soviet slander had been dropped and that, while the original crime for which he had been thrown into jail carried a specific sentence, there was no limit on how long he might be held at Dnepropetrovsk.

Alexei learned that as a "patient" he would be allowed only minimal contact with his family, including the equivalent of two postcards a month; that he was forbidden to write to any Soviet official; and that he would have nominal library privileges. The place was organized like a prison, and not a hospital at all. The bars on the windows of the wards, corridors, treatment bays, and eating halls were no accident.

After two weeks of sessions with Alexeev and Blokhina, Alexei was diagnosed as deranged, suffering from "psychopathology—simple form." Treatment: unspecified. Length of incarceration: indefinite.

II

THE psycho-prison was a strange and lawless place. The most dangerous of all the denizens seemed to be the MVD doctors and nurses who ran the SPH and who believed that punishment with drugs was the most effective remedy for deranged behavior. The doctors' eyes and ears in the crowded wards were the orderlies, criminals who had the authorities' trust. From the time of Stalin's prisons, Soviet jails used common criminals to help run the penal system. The orderlies were thieves, muggers, and rapists and they hunted ceaselessly for excuses to beat patients. They bullied and insulted in hopes of finding a hint of resistance from an inmate. Any sudden move of a hand, an unguarded laugh, a sigh, or even a cry of despair or pain could bring the orderlies. Whatever precautions the inmates might take, the predators always found prey.

Then, two or three well-fed criminal orderlies would pounce on an enfeebled, drug-ridden patient and spread-eagle him in a "crucifix" as they dragged him into a punishment cell, pummeling his kidneys and stomach. They would truss the unconscious victim to a bedstead, where he might be left for days, defecating on himself and trying to feed himself with hands tied to the bed. Sometimes, the prisoner was thrown into solitary confinement—a tiny, unheated cell with a steel pipe bed frame, without mattress or blankets. This was called "the wall treatment," and could go on for years. Sometimes the offending patient would be disciplined with the "wet pack" or "roll-up"—wrapped like a mummy in wet canvas strips that shrank as they dried, grinding the body like some medieval torturer's machine, compressing the joints. The victims shrieked with pain. But mostly the doctors and nurses came running with their syringes and vials eager to inject a punishment dose of sulfazine, a form of sulfur suspended in peach oil.

Of all the many drugs administered at Dnepropetrovsk to impose discipline, sulfazine stood at the pinnacle of pain. Originally used more than fifty years earlier to treat malaria by inducing a high fever (giving sulfazine its oddly sinister classification as a "pyrogenic"), the concoction had been used intermittently in European and American mental hospitals in the 1920s and 1930s to treat some kinds of extreme and chronic schizophrenia. Despite its bizarre power to subdue even a violent person by inducing high fever, nausea, mental disorientation, and severe muscle spasms, most Western psychia-

trists found that sulfazine had no therapeutic value and discontinued
its use.

These were the qualities that made it so attractive to the MVD
doctors at Dnepropetrovsk. "People injected with sulfazine were
groaning, sighing with pain, cursing the psychiatrists and Soviet
power, cursing with everything in their hearts," Alexei told us.
"People go into horrible convulsions and get completely disoriented. Their body temperature rises to 40 degrees centigrade almost
instantly, and the pain is so intense they cannot move from their
beds for three days. Sulfazine is simply a way to destroy a man
completely. If they torture you and break your arms, there is a
certain specific pain and you can somehow stand it. But sulfazine
is like a drill boring into your body that gets worse and worse until
it's more than you can stand. It's impossible to endure. It is worse
than torture, because, sometimes, torture may end. But this kind of
torture may continue for years."

Sulfazine normally was "prescribed" in a "course" of injections
of increasing strength over a period that might last up to two
months. The mixture caused a violent, long-term reaction in the
muscles at the site of the injection, normally the buttocks. Within
hours after the first shot, the pain was so excruciating that a victim
could not sit down and was forced to lie on his stomach to sleep.
He could not lift his legs, which meant that some men were trapped
by the maze of bed frames in Nikitin's ward, unable to propel
themselves to toilet or dining hall. They languished in misery, dependent upon the whims of the orderlies or the compassion of other
inmates for food and companionship. The stench from their suffering hung in the air.

"There were baths once a week in the spring, summer and fall,
and in the winter, a bath every ten days," Alexei said. "The water
was frigid and no one wanted to go to bathe. But they were sweaty
from the effects of the medicine and the place stank with sickness."

Behaviorist Ivan Pavlov had staunchly maintained that mental
illness was a consequence of chemical imbalance in the brain and
nervous system, best treated by chemicals. So there was an inclination toward drugs within Soviet psychiatry that was reflected in
everyday life at Dnepropetrovsk. The doctors had many other drugs
with which to control and punish. Most of them eventually were
used on Alexei. Aminazin is a powerful tranquilizer, equivalent to
thorazine in the West, and used freely for "severe schizophrenia."

It causes depression, weight loss, low blood pressure, skin pigmentation changes, and sensory distortions that could last for months after use. Haloperidol, another tranquilizer, was used very widely at Dnepropetrovsk and seems to have been the principal cause of the "pill-rolling" motor distortions Alexei saw when he first entered the ward. Haloperidol when used alone causes severe disruptions in muscle control that will bring on head-rolling, swallowing, stammering, lip-licking, convulsions, and other Parkinsonian-like side effects. To avoid these unpleasant accompaniments, the Soviet doctors needed to use other drugs in consort with haloperidol. At Dnepropetrovsk, this was never done. Other drugs in the pharmacopoeia included sanapax, triftazine, and tizerpin; each had its specific pain.

But the drug of choice remained sulfazine. Shortly after he was "diagnosed," Nikitin was called into Dr. Viktoria Blokhina's office. She looked at him and announced, "We'll do this." She prescribed a "course" of one needle of sulfazine a week for the next two months.

"Every part of me was sick. They did this without any reason. Those were horrible days." At the end of the two months, Nikitin was taken off sulfazine but regular doses of haloperidol and other disorienting drugs continued the entire time he was imprisoned.

Because they took exceptional care not to cross the orderlies, Nikitin came to believe that most Dnepropetrovsk patients were not demented. Their behavior made clear that they recognized danger and how to avoid it. After months of watching and surreptitious conversations, he concluded that perhaps as few as 15 percent of all the inmates were insane. "Even the worst of the killers seemed perfectly healthy psychologically," he said. "The killers supported me. We were all in the same situation. They knew they were guinea pigs. There were killers in there, but most of them were inside because of the need for experiments, like rabbits. They said, 'We know our lives are simply going to be a slow death.' " They had given up any hope of ever leaving the psycho-prison. After they had been punished with sulfazine, the murderers writhed on their beds, moaning for "a Kalashnikov assault rifle, a balalaika, and I'll settle with them for good." But no one allowed them to settle anything. "The doctors controlled them by needles."

The inhabitants of the prison were extraordinarily diverse. There were nationalists, religious believers, anti-Soviet agitators, complainers, uncompromising truth seekers, and even some men who had tried to escape their motherland by walking across her tightly guarded borders.

There was Vasili I. Sery, in his mid-40s, a geography teacher from Odessa, who had hijacked a plane and been sent back to Soviet territory. He was lucky he hadn't been executed, he told Alexei. He had been through three court hearings and at last they had sent him to Dnepropetrovsk as punishment. His wife had moved to the city to be near him and, although he could never hope to be freed, she saw him once a week. It was something to live for. There was Yeroslav M. Stolar, a 26-year-old former Komsomol member, arrested as a spy for collecting information on military matters. He said he had copied the information from his own military unit. He had once been a regional journalist with a blemish-free record of service to the country. Alexei thought that perhaps he was being punished because he had relatives living in West Germany. Nikolai Valkov was a Ukrainian nationalist, arrested for publishing an underground journal that opposed Soviet power in the Ukraine. Valkov had company: Viktor Parfentyvich Rafalsky, a school director from the southern Ukraine, also was a staunch nationalist; and a man named Boris had designed a flag for an independent Ukraine and had been arrested as a "reactionary nationalist" after one display of it.

Viktor Pollezheyev was a former Soviet fleet marine who had been stationed in Egypt before the 1973 Yom Kippur War and had tried to defect. He had shot several soldiers in the attempt, but instead of execution, he, too, was in the psycho-prison. He worked as a prison cook and the doctors reduced his drug dose so he could work better.

Mark I. Stioba had a remarkable tale to tell: he had escaped from the Ukraine during the war and managed to make his way to Australia, where he married, settled down, and fathered two children. But a disease then left him impotent, he said, and he relayed this unfortunate fact to his sister, who had stayed behind in the Ukraine. Soon she wrote back that the Soviets had recently perfected a foolproof cure. He applied for a visa and quickly received one. When he set foot on the soil of the motherland, the KGB arrested him as a traitor. Eventually, he wound up in Dnepropetrovsk.

There was a man named Lukhanov who had collaborated with

the Nazis and then escaped and built a new life in the West. But years later, he yearned to show his children his homeland. When he entered Soviet territory with a valid Soviet visa, he was arrested and sent to Dnepropetrovsk.

There were many others as well, but perhaps the one who stood out most sharply in Alexei's memory was Pyotr Muravyov. Many years before, Muravyov had written angry letters to Nikita Khrushchev denouncing him as an illiterate peasant who was unfit to be chief of state. Muravyov was arrested in 1957, Alexei said. "He spent twenty years in prisons and hospitals for reaching the same conclusion about Khrushchev in 1957 that the Politburo itself reached in 1964!"

III

DESPITE the horrors and dangers around him, Alexei managed to steer a course among the orderlies. His easy manner, savvy smile, and air of knowing competence made him an unlikely target for the predators. They left him alone. He found it possible to do repair work and odd jobs around the hospital and that convinced the medical authorities to reduce the drug dosage which was forced on all prisoners to keep them docile. "I went to work drugged because I believed this was the only way to keep my health." Soon, he was made a doorkeeper for the ward. It hardly qualified as work: "A man sits in the corridor, the door opens or closes, and he simply has to look straight ahead." But it was a job, and it refreshed him, in part because the air was far cleaner and healthier than in the stuffy ward. "They gave me the work because they knew I wasn't sick," he said.

The months stretched into years. Alexei's situation remained unchanged. He made surreptitious contact with a variety of political prisoners and resolved to pursue his quest if he ever were released. He misstepped once, getting caught in a political conversation with Vasili Sery. Inmates were allowed to talk to each other about things like the weather and the food—but never politics. The transgression cost him one "course" of sulfazine. But the orderlies never caught him again.

Late in 1974, a psychiatric review board took up Nikitin's case and, after the usual delays, determined that he was sufficiently recovered from his "psychopathology—simple form" to be released from Dnepropetrovsk. On March 31, 1975, he was transferred back to Donetsk, where he was incarcerated in the city psychiatric hospital for further unspecified observation. Another year passed and, in the spring of 1976, he was adjudged "recovered" and released. After that, he moved in with his sister, Lyubov Poludniak. She was older than her brother by several years, and also had suffered immeasurable sorrow. Her husband had been killed in a mine accident years before and their only child had recently died in another accident. Now, she lived alone on the top floor of the Denisenko Street apartment building. It was a life that offered very little. The arrival of her younger brother, even with all his troubles, brought comfort and companionship.

Alexei resumed his rounds of the local reception halls, where he showed his documents and told his story—and was rebuffed at every turn. Sometimes when he came back to the flat at night, the police were waiting for him and tried to provoke him. "Did they help you?" they would jeer. "Have you found a job yet?"

"You won't get me to say something anti-Soviet," he told them. "Don't waste your time."

"We'll lock you up . . . not right away, but we'll find the way," they promised.

He went to city health authorities and got an interview with a senior official. Alexei wanted a certification that, since he had been treated in a mental hospital, he was an invalid under the rules of the state, entitled to a pension and a permanent excuse from working.

"But you're perfectly healthy!" the medical man said. "You can work." Besides, said the official, there is no such place as Dnepropetrovsk Special Psychiatric Hospital for the Criminally Insane.

Alexei found a variety of part-time jobs, keeping busy enough to bring in some rubles for the household and avoiding the criminal classification of "parasite" which the police would have liked to hang on him. Finally, he found a permanent summer job as a construction worker at the Avdaevski *sovkhoz*, state farm, eleven miles outside Donetsk in Yasinovatski raion, where wheat, sunflowers, and market vegetables were traditional crops.

"State farms generally don't have enough people to do all the work they want," Alexei explained; boredom and impoverishment have driven the population from the countryside throughout European Russia. "If they want to build something and get it done in time, they hire outside workers and pay them well." One of his neighbors, for example, worked in the summers on special farm projects making hundreds of rubles a month, and then spent most of the harsh winter snug at home in the relative comfort of Donetsk. Alexei became part of an eight-man building team that took on special projects for the sovkhoz which its own indifferent and demoralized workers could not build for themselves.

"The work situation in general in our country is bad, but at least at a coal mine there is the possibility to work round the clock to fulfill the plan," Alexei said during one of the humble but tasty suppers we shared in his sister's apartment. "On the farm, generally they can't work that easily at night, or when the equipment is bad, so they lose part of the harvest. But the workers don't blame the bad equipment—they don't blame anyone in particular. People at Avdaevski simply don't want to work because they are paid poorly—they receive 2.40 rubles per work shift, and that isn't enough to make them want to work. So, they work slowly, talk a lot, take a lot of rest. They try to do as little as possible, since they won't get paid any more if they work hard or not."

Like thousands of other state farms, the sovkhoz was an amalgamation of numerous separate holdings drawn together into a single entity totaling thousands of acres and numbering several hundred peasant families. Avdaevski sovkhoz was organized with a central administrative village and outlying hamlets controlled by the center. There were granaries, stock pens, food stores, a dispensary, machinery storage and repair buildings, headquarters buildings, schools, a cafeteria, cultural hall, apartment buildings, fuel bunkers, and many other structures concentrated in the center and scattered as well around the holding wherever geography and need dictated. Buses, tractors, and trucks carried workers from home to field. Reflecting the nationwide drive to industrialize agriculture, the Avdaevski farm, like thousands of others around the country, was steadily building high-rise apartments in central locations and moving the peasants out of the far-flung hamlets. This meant a constant stream of building projects. There were two construction teams at Avdaevski—a group of forty-five men drawn from the sovkhoz population and an eight-man team of outsiders from Donetsk.

"Our eight did twice as much work as their team of forty-five men," Alexei said, with a mixture of pride and contempt. "We built two stores, and two, two-story apartments, with room for four families apiece. We got about two hundred rubles a month, much more than the sovkhoz team. But the farm builders didn't argue with the temporary workers because they knew we would work as poorly as they themselves did if we were paid as little as they. It's just a matter of indifference. The *sovkhozniki*, state farm workers, show their indifference by arguing with their leaders and complaining about the low pay they get—and doing no work."

The focus of life on the sovkhoz was each peasant family's private plot—a piece of land of up to three acres where fruits and vegetables could be raised and sold privately. "Each raises his own food for his own family and for the market place, and here, they don't waste time or laze around," Alexei said. "On their private plots, they raised twice as much as the norm." He acknowledged that outsiders to Soviet life generally found it impossible to believe that nearly a third of all fruits and vegetables that reach the marketplace in the USSR come from only 3 percent of all the land in the nation under cultivation—the 3 percent in private plots.

Part of the explanation for high yields on the private plots was that the peasants stole fertilizer, seed, tools, and anything else they needed from the state to help their own productivity. "Thievery on the sovkhoz is fearsome," he said. "They take whatever they can get away with. There is this kind of saying in the countryside: 'It's all ours, so it's all mine.' "

At sowing and harvest time, the farmers were supposed to begin their workday at 8 A.M. Few did. Team leaders chugged around the vast fields on motorcycles, checking up on the laggards. The problem was so great that the chiefs tried to solve it by imposing fines on every harvest team member if one of them was late to the fields. The scheme backfired: resentments ran high and the embittered teams rested on their hoes even longer than usual. The days became skirmishes between chiefs and workers, divided by long breaks for hot meals that were brought to the harvest brigades in the fields by the sovkhoz women.

Between meals and looking out for the roving leaders, the sovkhozniki continued their looting. "They pick the absolutely top-quality stuff to steal," Alexei recalled with a kind of dazzled admiration. "Tomatoes, potatoes, cucumbers, beets, carrots, everything!" The peasants cached the booty, then collected it to feast on the produce themselves or sell it in the farmers' markets as their own. Meanwhile, they nurtured their own crops with great care until the best moment for the best profit. Theft was so great that it sharply reduced Avdaevski's production results. The police were called out during harvest time each year to sweep for thieves on the trucks and buses heading for the farmers' markets in Donetsk and other cities in the region. One day, Alexei was heading home with a large rucksack of cucumbers which were to be salted down for the winter by his sister when he was stopped in one of the police dragnets. The militia accused him of theft.

"Why can't I take these with me?" Alexei demanded in injured tones. "I worked for them—and besides, the party hacks can get theirs for free!"

This was no stab in the dark. For some weeks, he had been working in a repair shop near the main Avdaevski administration building, which gave him a bird's-eye view of the official comings and goings of the local chiefs. At the height of harvest time, the sovkhoz directors had plenty of visitors. While team leaders were exhorting fieldhands to get to work on time and hold back on their thieving, the private limousines of senior party, KGB, and MVD chiefs were rolling up to the headquarters building. As Alexei watched in sardonic fascination, the chauffeurs loaded bulging burlap sacks of tomatoes, cucumbers, potatoes, and other produce into the leadership's cars and then roared off to the private precincts of the privileged. In all, Alexei counted ninety-seven chiefs' cars in two weeks. "They used the produce themselves, or they sold it in the farm markets—or they did both. Just like the workers!"

Meanwhile, the police were sweeping the buses to arrest sovkhozniki who had a few tomatoes stuffed in their valises.

IV

YEARS earlier, Nikitin had taken what for an ordinary Soviet was the extraordinary step of sending documents about his case outside the country. Now, he wanted to follow them. In late February 1977, he made a cautious appearance in Moscow. For several days, he ghosted through the streets of the capital, sensing its life and rhythmns and carefully casing the security around various foreign embassies. The Third World nations were the least well guarded, but since most of them were currying favor with Moscow and vice versa, they did not attract him. As before, the U.S. embassy was strongly guarded by the KGB. In the end, his quest stopped at a familiar place—the Norwegian embassy on Vorovskogo Ulitsa.

February 22 was bitterly cold and snowy in Moscow. Alexei dressed warmly and moved cautiously toward his objective: he had no right to be in the city and had to act with the care of a man in hiding. He made his way through the byways toward the Norwegians. A scrim of icy mist hung over the city, and vehicles and pedestrians alike trailed plumes of frozen vapor. Steam rose from ten thousand vents in the streets, while the metro stations deep below ground seemed cheery and warmed from throngs of heavily clad, thickset passengers who rocketed across the platforms and surged up to the frigid streets above. Alexei joined the flow of bundled pedestrians, drew his head down under a thick, warm hat, and, clutching his briefcase, strode toward the foreign chancery. There were fewer pedestrians here—Vorovskogo Street was a handsome old street that had survived pre-revolutionary times, running to the northwest for a few blocks between the old Garden Ring Road and the traffic-choked Ring Road farther out from the Kremlin. Without glancing at the pair of hostile eyes that scrutinized the street from within the sidewalk guardbox next to the chancery, he darted into the foreign grounds, found a door, and pushed inside.

A man about his own age appeared, led him to a room, and in good Russian inquired who he was and what he wanted. Nikitin knew what had happened to men who tried to get out of the Soviet Union on their own—not one had succeeded and most wound up in torture chambers like Dnepropetrovsk. The Norwegians had helped him before and they would help him now. The peasant's son from Fedorovsky had given up on the motherland.

"I'm here to ask for political asylum," Nikitin declared.

The diplomat stared at him. "Why?"

Just the question. Alexei had plenty to show to answer it. He reached into his briefcase and began pulling out documents from the distant past. The Norwegian hauled out a pad and as Nikitin talked his way through the documents, the other man took careful notes. Alexei became so engrossed he hardly noticed that here he was, a political defector, and he had not even been asked to take off his overcoat. Oblivious to the heat in the little room, he unreeled the long, complicated truth of what had befallen him ever since he had tried to defend workers against the state's depredations. It was very peaceful and quiet in the embassy and he was pleased at how well the session was going. He even showed the diplomat his diplomas and citations from military service, high school, and the polytechnic institute—as well as his Soviet internal passport, which every citizen must carry with him at all times. This was the hated document Alexei wanted to give up for good.

After a while, the diplomat left him. As Nikitin sat there in the quiet room, a woman with a pleasant face suddenly appeared and in a gracious tone asked him if he would like some hot tea. Her manner was reassuring and friendly. He looked at her blankly, hiding his revulsion. No matter how many years this Soviet had worked at the embassy, enjoying privileges beyond the dreams of ordinary Russians that were granted her by the foreign diplomats, she really had only one boss and she and Alexei both knew it—the KGB. Any sympathy she might show him was overpowered by that single fact. As a loyal employee of the organs, she could not be trusted. He ignored her. She disappeared and returned with some tea and put it down for him with milk and sugar. He had spoken with the diplomat about two hours and his throat was dry and he was nervous from the strain. The tea would taste wonderful. He let it get cold.

The diplomat returned to say that they had carefully recorded everything and had found Nikitin's story compelling. "Now, if you leave the Soviet Union and apply for political asylum from another country, we'd be happy to give you asylum," the man said.

"What?" Alexei couldn't have heard correctly.

"We can't give you asylum here. We don't have the right," he said. Then he repeated the formula: "But if you want to apply from another country, we can do it." He mentioned something about a Helsinki Agreement. Alexei didn't know what the diplomat was talking about; he'd been in a psycho-prison for nearly five years and had never heard of this agreement. Nikitin's belief was very straight-forward: "I thought Norway was a NATO country and would support me."

"We don't have the right," the Norwegian repeated.

Alexei stood up, gathered his documents, put them in his battered briefcase, and pulled his coat tight around him.

"You'll have to go," the diplomat said. Escorting Nikitin to the outer door, he opened it and shut it firmly behind Alexei. Even though he was wearing very heavy, woolly mittens, his hands felt oddly congealed. His heart was in a vise. He took three steps on the sidewalk. A bulky officer in a gray overcoat with captain's shoulder pips clamped a hand on his arm: "Come with me."

He was shoved into the guardhouse, while the KGB officer, who stood a head taller than Alexei and had a tough face, took the passport Nikitin had never wanted to see again and telephoned somewhere. The captain was silent. An incident like this would mean endless explanations and possibly some reprimand. After a while, a Volga pulled up and Alexei was hustled into the car. As he was being driven away, Alexei caught a glimpse of the street and the embassy. Diplomats peeped out at him from every window.

Alexei was jailed in Moscow and then sent to Donetsk, where he languished in the city jail for weeks. Once again, they seemed unsure or uninterested in deciding what to do with him. In the end, he was returned to the Dnepropetrovsk psycho-prison. He arrived back in the crowded ward on September 22, 1977. Jimmy Carter was now president of the United States and relations between Moscow and Washington were sliding rapidly downhill. The era of détente was coming to a close.

It didn't mean much to Alexei Nikitin. There had been only one important change in his absence: Nikolai Karpovich Alexeev, the senior psychiatrist, must have been good at his work. He had been promoted to major in the MVD.

4

The Doctor

*The courts must not ban terror . . . but must
formulate the motives underlying it, legalize
it as a principle . . . as widely as possible.*

—LENIN

I

ALEXEI was released for the second time in May 1980. He had
spent nearly eight of the previous ten years in psycho-prison, but
he remained virtually unchanged. His defiance and refusal to accept
the state's crushing power in determining his fate burned as brightly
as ever. He had not been "cured." And like an iron filing to a
magnet, he once again made his way to Moscow.

But if Alexei had not changed, the same could no longer be said
of his country. During his long imprisonment, an unexpected series
of developments had broadened and intensified political activism in
Russia even as the Brezhnev Kremlin sought to tighten internal
control after the seemingly wide-open Khrushchev years. Not only
was *samizdat*, the underground press, flourishing, but disaffected
citizens with increasing boldness and success formed groups to
gather information about political and legal abuses in the country.
At first, these activities were an outgrowth of the Brezhnev repression of anti-Stalinist intellectual ferment. But in the 1970s, the activities of the dissenters and opponents of the regime took on a new
character—moving away from a focus on the crimes and suffering

of the Stalinist past and attempting to define moral and political principles other than police state totalitarianism upon which Soviet power should rest. What had been individual activism broadened into a small number of groups and self-styled committees whose members took upon themselves the risky task of calling the world's attention to their country's lack of individual rights.

There was no overall design or coordination to these efforts—that, emphatically, is not the Russian style. But the effort to search out truths about the Soviet Union was a phenomenon without direct parallel since the advent of Khrushchev in the mid-1950s. The ferment had a feverish and exciting character all its own and, eventually, it spread from the Center, Moscow, to other cities. Groups formed, were active for a time, then ran out of steam and faded from view, to be replaced by other groups representing slightly different interests, but frequently including many of the same people who had participated in the earlier efforts. It was a time of activism and experimentation with forms of political self-expression and basic fact-finding.

Throughout the years of détente, activists gained important practical knowledge about political and legal abuses in their country—and how to put this information into the hands of foreign journalists. The role of the journalists was indispensable, for their reports about Soviet internal repressions became a staple of Western media and were broadcast back into the USSR by the Voice of America, (VOA), the BBC World Service, Radio Free Europe, the West German Wave, and others. As the years passed, millions of Soviets were learning remarkable truths about their motherland through this informal system of information-gathering and dissemination that routinely encompassed a quick, ten-thousand-mile round trip from Moscow to Washington or New York, and back again.

Among the groups that had a distinctive if brief impact on the life of Moscow activists in the mid-1970s was one with an unusually long, but perfectly accurate name: the Working Commission for the Investigation of the Abuse of Psychiatry for Political Purposes. Founded in early 1977, it was largely the brainchild of a young Moscovite named Aleksandr Podrabinek, who burned with a reformer's intensity to expose the regime's growing use of mental hospitals to silence dissenters. The Working Commission was unusual in several ways, but like a number of groups of the period, one of its most important meanings was that it joined intellectuals and common working folk within a single organization. This was a rarity in Russia, where intelligentsia and narod traditionally had very little to do with each other.

Although Podrabinek was the son of an intellectual Jewish family, the commission was not solely concerned with the fates of intellectuals and/or Jews. It sought to understand and report every aspect of the phenomenon of political psycho-terror and gathered information about the most brilliant and the most ordinary of Soviet citizens —all of whom had received similar punishments. By 1980, the self-styled commission had publicized nearly two hundred of these cases, sparking Western protests and even wringing an official rebuke against Soviet mental health officials from the prestigious World Psychiatric Association (WPA). In time, the controversy would reach such proportions that the USSR, facing censure or worse at the 1983 congress of the WPA, resigned from the international organization. This step backward was one of the first foreign diplomatic moves of the new Kremlin leader, Yuri Andropov, the former KGB chief who succeeded Brezhnev at the close of 1982.

But that effect of the commission's efforts was still years away when the secret police began their swift and severe retaliation against the group at the end of the 1970s. Podrabinek and other members were rounded up and sent to labor camps or banished to internal exile. By the time Nikitin arrived in Moscow in May 1980, only Feliks Serebrov, the former metal worker, and a few others were still free. Alexei met with him and related his story. And on September 6, Alexei reappeared at the apartment and presented himself to yet another Soviet psychiatrist for an examination and diagnosis. But this time, his actions were voluntary and the man who examined him was not a physician in the pay of the Ministry of Internal Affairs, but a doctor seeking to practice medicine free of state interference.

This man was Anatoli Ivanovich Koryagin, then 41, a staff psychiatrist in a mental health clinic in the eastern Ukrainian city of Kharkov. For more than a year, Koryagin had served as an unpaid consultant to the citizens' group, examining former psycho-prison inmates to see if their political indiscretions meant they were mentally deranged.

Koryagin and Nikitin sat together for many hours that autumn day, with Alexei describing the course of his life under the doctor's barrage of questions. Koryagin recalled later that Nikitin showed the same personality traits as other dissidents he had examined—strong-minded independence, an acute social conscience, genuine sensitivity to the needs of others, and a dedication to improving life for the citizens of the motherland. He found Alexei's hardy optimism infectious and engaging.

"On the basis of personal history and examination, it should be concluded that Alexei V. Nikitin suffers no psychiatric illness or character disorders, and there is no evidence that he has ever had either of these conditions," Koryagin wrote in his medical conclusion. "His admissions to the special psychiatric hospital in 1972 and 1977 should be considered as totally unjustified." Koryagin's diagnosis of the man who had been subjected to years of drug treatments to cure what the state said was a psychosis: "No psychiatric disorder."

Who was this Soviet doctor from Kharkov who took the time, trouble, and risk to befriend Nikitin, a man he had never met, and declare him sane? He was a remarkable person—as tough, resilient, and determined as Alexei himself.

I happened to meet Koryagin several days after he had diagnosed Nikitin in Moscow. This occurred even before I had met Nikitin or knew of the connection between the two. The psychiatrist made an indelible impression on me.

As so many episodes in Moscow do, this one began with a cryptic message from a friend to meet him later that day for a "visit" somewhere. The friend, again, was David Satter. He didn't say, and I didn't ask, what the substance of the visit was to be, or where we were to go. But he meant activists and no questions were needed. A number of American correspondents in separate, guarded telephone calls agreed to make the "visit" together. So, with autumn darkness gathering early and fast over the city, several newsmen headed out into Moscow traffic for a meeting with some unknown activists. Even in heavy, rush-hour traffic, the city police had little trouble picking out the foreign journalists' cars. The license plates were black letters and numbers on a white background, distinctively the opposite of standard Soviet plates. In addition, the foreigners' plates had simple codes that made everything clear at a glance: "K" stood for "correspondent"; "04" meant the United States; and the three-digit number "725" was assigned to *The Washington Post*.

When I wheeled out Kutuzovsky Prospect 7/4 compound about 5 P.M. and turned east toward Red Square and the city Center, the

KGB men manning the *butka,* the booth, at the compound entrance telephoned news of my departure as they did of every foreigner or Russian who entered or left the compound. Presumably, the calls went to the Bureau of Comings and Goings. Soon, the traffic cops in their blue-gray uniforms who are stationed at every major intersection in downtown Moscow were reporting the progress of my newspaper's dark-blue 1977 Volvo station wagon through the city, radioing the information via walkie-talkie, which each carried. Regardless of the destination, it would not take long for the central dispatchers to figure out generally where we were headed. While we wanted as much as possible to protect anyone we saw from police reprisal, we also were determined to conduct ourselves openly: we were pursuing our professions; it was theoretically legal in the USSR for foreigners to speak with Russians; and the Kremlin had signed various international accords guaranteeing our legitimate rights. So we weren't skulking or seeking cloak-and-dagger drama.

The address was Novoalekseyevskaya No. 5, about two miles north of the Kremlin. This turned out to be one of a cluster of slab-sided cement high-rises in an overgrown field along a busy side street. The buildings had all the exterior charm of a flotilla of aircraft carriers stood on end. Outside the building, the usual group of busybody grannies congregated on sagging benches, keeping to the ancient Russian custom of sharply challenging any stranger who happened onto their turf. An aggressive question from one of these babushki about whom we were visiting, a vague answer that fooled no one, and then we went into the small, battered elevator for a creaking, hesitating ride up. Apartment 66 was somewhere toward the top of the building. At the ring of the buzzer, the door was swung open and a young man silently waved us inside with a resigned expression. We were people he had never met before and likely would never see again.

This man was Vladimir Neplekhovich and this was his apartment. He was not a dissident, but a fiercely loyal spouse in a country where that can be dangerous. His wife, Irina Grivnina, was a member of Podrabinek's commission to investigate psychiatric abuse. She had been a familiar participant at activists' press conferences in the previous two years, a slightly built 29-year-old with light brown hair and a wan but determined manner. But the KGB had been at the apartment two days earlier and had arrested her. Grivnina now was being held at Lefortovo Prison, a KGB detention and interrogation complex in eastern Moscow; the flat was still heavy with the sense of her arrest. It was dimly lit, as though in mourning, and quiet. One lamp seemed to be working in the living room–bedroom; the rest of the place stood in shadow. We filed in, and a man in a brown suit stood up from the daybed–couch in the main room and, with a dignified nod, very quietly introduced himself: Anatoli Koryagin.

He was nearly my height, which put him over six feet, and thus unusually tall for a Russian. He spoke calmly and with precision, belying none of the passion that in fact burned in him. He seemed nervous and on his guard, hardly an unreasonable reaction for a man who was meeting the bourgeois American press for the first time. This was a private man's debut before a group of people who must have seemed very strange and different from anyone he had ever met before.

Koryagin had come to Moscow on business for the commission, he said, and he wanted to take the opportunity to meet with us and make clear that the commission's work would go ahead despite Grivnina's arrest and the likelihood of further reprisals. At the same time, he did not want to be quoted or referred to in any way, for that would not be helpful just now. We moved on to other topics: his own background and intentions. With a smile of pleasure, he pulled out a photograph of his family. It was a professionally done studio portrait of Koryagin with his wife and their three small sons. Happiness and contentment radiated with such warmth that I almost could feel it in my hand. The picture surely had been made at a better moment in their lives; there wasn't a hint of worry in their faces.

As we talked about the commission's efforts, I became increasingly depressed. Why didn't Koryagin take the course most of us would have chosen and turn away from what he must realize was a sure collision with the state? At that moment, I hadn't met Nikitin and had little idea of the world of psycho-prisons. I held an understanding of the commission's work, but nothing stronger than that. And yet, there was nothing abstract about the situation in which Koryagin was enmeshed. Podrabinek had been arrested; Grivnina had been seized—Koryagin's would come as well.

The smiles of his three children persisted in my mind's eye. I wanted to know why he was doing this, and yet reluctantly comprehended it at the same time: sacrifice inspires and disturbs at the same moment. I didn't want to know what it was that could out-weigh his responsibility to his family—particularly since his sacrifice wouldn't make an iota of difference one way or the other in the eventual grinding out of the fate of his immense nation.

So I asked: "Why are you doing this?"

He answered me with a question, as I knew he would. My notebook records it, scribbled in haste and semi-darkness: "What choice do I have except to do my duty?"

II

ANATOLI Ivanovich Koryagin was born on September 9, 1938, in Kansk, a remote city located more than two thousand miles east of Moscow deep in Siberia. Founded as a czarist fort and trading post in 1640, Kansk was worlds removed from the terrors and hardship of World War II that engulfed Alexei Nikitin's birthplace. Yet the distant conflict drew blood from the Koryagin family: his father was killed at the front and a beloved sister died from starvation brought on by the war. Anatoli Ivanovich grew up "accustomed to hunger and unheated huts, the tears of widowed mothers," he wrote many years later in trying to explain why his life took the course it did. "We didn't grumble, complain, or seek explanations of our circumstances. Daily and everywhere, people survived those times of difficulty, shortages, restrictions." Misfortune was "the inherent characteristic of life." Yet, people consoled themselves in the most difficult moments with the belief that whatever sacrifices had to be made, "the party and government existed to overcome such problems."

Koryagin graduated·from high school in 1956, the year Khrushchev denounced Stalin at the 20th Party Congress, and he enrolled in a provincial medical college in nearby Krasnoyarsk, a rapidly growing Siberian center on the Yenisei River. For three hundred years, the town had been a Russian outpost amid the nomadic peoples of the vast, empty quarter of the river. Despite the rising tide of Soviet technicians and bureaucrats, the city's raw streets were alive with the faces of the ancient Siberian races: Tuvinians, Yakuts, Evenki, Khakass, Ougirs. There was an air of pioneering independence about the town. Even Lenin, who had spent three years in exile from 1897 to 1900 in a hamlet one hundred fifty miles south of Krasnoyarsk, was struck by the self-reliance of the region's peoples.

While in exile, he wandered the limitless forests and fields in his favorite pastime of bird hunting and composed what was to become one of the influential pamphlets of pre-revolutionary times, "The Tasks of the Russian Social Democrats." The tract envisioned struggle, sacrifice, and high moral commitment to the principles of political freedom in Russia.

Half a century later, medical student Koryagin, like Lenin a passionate bird hunter, was struggling to find evidence of high moral commitment in the society Lenin had founded. "The drive for material security" that his colleagues were pursuing so hard "now seemed to me the wretched and worthless delusions of a primitive mind." Devoid of religious belief, "I inherently felt that spirit, intellect, ideas, and knowledge were more significant for man than any material possessions." He settled on psychiatry as a way to probe "the spiritual side of man."

The state's interests didn't exactly match his. The Ministry for the Preservation of Public Order, which helps run Soviet prisons and labor camps, sought to recruit him during his final year of study. He ignored their invitation to an interview. It turned out to be the sort of gesture of independence that could not be overlooked. His academic supervisor demanded an explanation of Koryagin's high-handed snub.

"I don't want to work in the camp system," Koryagin replied simply.

"Conditions are better there than anywhere else, the pay is higher, and you can specialize at once!"

"Then perhaps it's because I was raised among people who didn't like police and wardens very much."

"But there are sick people who shouldn't have to suffer. And someone is obliged to work there."

"Obliged is the wrong word in my opinion," Koryagin said. "Let those work there who can and want to. I'm not one of them."

"But what if all acted the way you do?"

"Do you think such a thing would happen? What about the specialization? The wages?" Koryagin's words mocked.

"Your unhealthy opinions can end up hurting you," the now furious supervisor threatened.

"It isn't opinions that hurt a person," Koryagin shot back. "One is hurt because of them."

Upon graduation in 1964 he was sent one hundred fifty miles

southwest to Abakan, a regional town of about eighty thousand which served as the capital of the Khakass Autonomous Region. The region, on a high plateau along a tributary of the Yenisei ringed by nearly impenetrable mountains to the west, south, and east, was misleadingly named for the once-dominant Khakass, Turkic nomads of Siberia who now were a distinct minority in their own homeland. Noted for its rich gold, copper, and iron deposits, which had attracted hordes of Russians and Ukrainians who ran things, the region possessed another distinction: there was not a single psychiatrist among its half-million inhabitants.

The young doctor's work was cut out for him. The mental "ward" at the municipal hospital was a small *izba*, wood cabin, heated by a stove. It had electricity but no running water. There were ten cots for fifteen chronic patients; violent or psychotic patients were locked into tiny isolator cubicles. Meals were passed through hinged steel gratings. The staff was made up of semi-literate peasant women who needed the money to supplement meager pensions. Every bit as tough and drunken as their kolkhoznik husbands, the women routinely beat the patients to control them.

Koryagin turned for help to B. P. Gordovsky, the elderly surgeon–director. Imprisoned during the Terror, rehabilitated by Khrushchev, and assigned to this backwater, Gordovsky was tenacious and wily, a combination that had wangled genuine public health improvements to his area. Koryagin described what he had been taught were the "pillars of Soviet psychiatry: nonconstraint and an open-door regime." The cages must go.

Gordovsky bluntly disagreed. "Without the gratings, your fools will run off. Before you came, one escaped and jumped off the railroad bridge. A lot had to be written—and only for form! But this way, you and I can take it easy!"

"The mentally ill aren't wild beasts," Koryagin retorted. "How can they be kept in such conditions? The district psychiatrist will reprove me for the inhuman way of dealing with patients—and she will be right."

"She won't reprove you," Gordovsky said confidently. "You'll send her to us. Perhaps a fuss will come of it, but finally, it'll be hushed up."

Koryagin turned his attention to the rough-hewn farm women who looked after the patients, appealing to their "better instincts," as he put it—mixed with threats to fire them.

"But when I'd gone home," he wrote later, "the attendants did as they pleased, put the 'dangerous ones' behind bars, turned off the lights, and went to sleep. Just like home." When the rest of the hospital medical staff realized they had a zealous reformer in their midst, they closed ranks against him. "All my efforts met with total lack of support of any kind."

In the end, Koryagin, without permission, took it on himself to throw out the window grates and prison doors. Gordovsky, a former *zek*, political prisoner, was shocked—and scared. "Now you're responsible for everything . . . pray God it won't boomerang!"

But nothing happened. No one in the medical hierarchy noticed, or if they did, they didn't care.

After four years, Koryagin left Abakan for postgraduate studies at the Research Institute for Neurology and Psychiatry in Kharkov. He wanted to steep himself in pure research. But, fresh from the crude routine of provincial psychiatry, he ran headlong into something equally unrewarding: dry academics interested only in insulating themselves, "driving off able graduates and surrounding themselves with toadies so they would appear the most imposing figures." Actual research conditions, Koryagin found, "were disgusting: a low stipend, extremely poor housing, routine methods, no conditions for conducting scientific work." Rampant mediocrity was the rule: "People of science rummaged in the dung of insignificant facts, settling their scores of prestige."

The more he thought about all this, the more he blamed the Soviet state. "The state needs healthy, hard-working members of society, but mental illness most often limits or eliminates a person's ability to work hard. . . . The psychiatric service cannot effectively restore a patient's [full] health, so what use is it to the state? Surgery, for example, is an entirely different matter: the result of an operation is apparent—either into a box or back to the workbench. But when a person gets mentally ill, he is sitting on the state's neck, from sick pay to pension."

Koryagin had been taught that "the humanism of a society could be determined by how it deals with its mentally ill." But the facts didn't stand up to his idealistic scrutiny. Disillusionment deepened. "That's how my conviction arose regarding the anti-humanism of our state," he wrote. "I understood that the rulers of our country spit on this humanism since they require ever greater labor—devoted not to the citizens, however, but only to the military–economic might of the State, where their power resides."

A man so estranged was a loose cannon on the deck of Soviet conformity—and Koryagin knew it. So when he completed his graduate work, the psychiatrist returned to the remote countryside "as part of an attempt to escape the many pressures that bear on each person in a society with a totalitarian regime."

The place he found was the isolated eastern Siberian town of Kyzyl, the capital of a small ethnographic region called the Tuvinian Autonomous Soviet Socialist Republic. It was a lamb-chop-shaped territory near the geographic center of the Asian land-mass, at the headwaters of the Yenisei River, hemmed in on two sides by the saw-toothed Sayan Mountains and bordered to the south by Mongolia. From Kyzyl, it was about two thousand air miles to Moscow, seventeen hundred to the Pacific, and seventeen hundred north to the Kara Sea. The ASSR abounded in exotic names—Chaa Kol', Kungurtug, Systyg Khem, Ak Dovurak—that reflected its Mongolian heritage. And with their lank black hair, high cheekbones, and exotically tipped eyes, there was reason to think of the Tuvinians as latter-day descendants of the Golden Horde who had controlled southern Russia for more than two centuries and terrorized much of Europe in medieval times. But now, it was the Europeans who ran the show: like the Khakass, the Tuvinians were a minority in their homeland.

Tuvinia was an obscure corner of the world but it owned a curiously modern history: once part of Imperial China, the region was annexed by Czar Nicholas II in 1914 and enjoyed a semi-independent status until Stalin swallowed it in 1944. This put Tu-vinia on the same footing as the Baltics. When Westerners asked if the Kremlin could be trusted to withdraw from Afghanistan in the face of international denunciations after Soviet troops took control of Kabul in December 1979, Soviets with good memories liked to recount the history of Tuvinia.

Although a continental climate gave the region harsh temperature extremes, it was a remarkably beautiful place, with chains of high mountains, upland farming areas, and dramatic seasons when the landscape seemed to change almost overnight. So far from the Cen-ter, a person could lose himself here and never return to civilization. This was Koryagin's intention. But like Nikitin, Anatoli Koryagin's situation had little to do with physical locale. His travels were outward hints of a complex and inevitably dangerous internal migration that had taken him from hopeful student of psychiatry looking for clues to man's spiritual nature to uncompromising realist about the character of his homeland. He had traveled much, but, in fact, he had reached a place inside himself from which he could neither return nor go farther.

"My duties brought me into contact with representatives of various levels of our society, significantly broadening my outlook," he recalled in a newly sarcastic tone. "I began to fathom more deeply the meaning and role of the bureaucratic party elite, the *nomenklatura*, as a parasitic class, [and] the estrangements of these representatives from the interests of the people. Slogans, posters, radio chatter, and televised puke—all these were means of stupefying the masses. I fought as much as I could against stupid orders and senseless laws. . . . I didn't offer bribes, I didn't hand out presents, I didn't stand them to drinks, I wasn't obsequious, and I didn't join their party. . . . This was a protest."

There were some other doctors who apparently felt just as estranged as Koryagin did and the local apparatus finally moved against them all: "They separated and scattered us to the ends of the country," Koryagin wrote.

III

KORYAGIN was sent back to Kharkov where he found an apartment at No. 10 Poznanskaya Ulitsa and settled in with his wife, the three boys, and his mother. He had not sought this transfer, but now that he was in the city, he determined to follow the increasingly strong dictates of his conscience. Ministering to the sick who thronged the psychiatric clinic where he worked was simply no longer enough. "I got the firm conviction that a person had to fight against dirty tricks, complain loudly against all illegalities [that were] painted as blessings of 'developed socialism.' A person had to shout about all of the parasitic dirty tricks, such as Soviet bureaucratism, which is based on naked violence."

Aside from being just five hundred miles from the Center, Kharkov had its own strong intellectual traditions. It had originally been the Soviet capital of the Ukraine and was a major rail and road hub for European Russia. There was an active intelligentsia and, perhaps as important, a large Jewish population. Thousands of Kharkov

Jews had emigrated abroad through the 1970s, and the constant stream of families up to Moscow for exit visas and then out to Israel and the West had kindled a spirit of challenge in some parts of the city's life. Anatoli Koryagin found it a congenial place to resume his own quest for ethical peace of mind. It was only a matter of time before he made contact with the Podrabinek group and, in 1979, he became its psychiatric consultant: examining Soviet citizens who had been incarcerated in psycho-prisons to cure or to punish them for their deviant activities of challenging or criticizing the state. At last, he was doing useful work.

"All the people I examined had joined the ranks of the mentally ill because they did or said things which in our country are considered 'anti-Soviet,' " Koryagin wrote many months later.* "Some had tried to leave by crossing the frontier or asking for asylum in foreign embassies; some circulated leaflets with . . . poems. Others stated that they disagreed with the existing order in the country and described how their economic, religious, and other civil rights had been flouted by the administration at their place of work, and by party and government institutions. . . . The overwhelming majority of them were noted from early childhood for qualities typical of strong personalities—energy, enterprise, a marked ability to communicate, leadership, and good or excellent marks at school. They showed early signs of independent judgment and behavior and determination in overcoming difficulties and achieving their aims. . . . All these people were 'positive' Soviet citizens with real prospects of succeeding in society—but all of them, eventually, came into conflict with that very society.

"The moment these people came into conflict with the state system, they came under the observation of psychiatrists who judged their behavior to be abnormal. From this moment they assumed the clinical and social status of the mentally ill, with its consequences: compulsory confinement to hospital and compulsory treatment, a definitive diagnosis of psychiatric illness in some cases, invalid status due to mental illness was imposed and the right to function normally was taken away.

"Dr. A. Butko's psychiatric odyssey began when he attempted to swim to Turkey; that of engineer and former Communist L. Pribytkov when he renounced his Soviet citizenship; that of engineer A.

*The Lancet, April 11, 1981.

Paskauskiene when she circulated nationalist leaflets."

There was no end to the variety of offenses against accepted order that could land a citizen in a psycho-prison. Koryagin worked through 1979 and into 1980. He wrote: "Leaving to the doctors' own consciences their flagrant, almost criminal disregard of professional duty, it is legitimate to pose the following question: how does it happen and who is responsible for the fact that, in a country like the USSR, where every aspect of economic, political, and social life is strictly controlled by the state, perfectly healthy people are treated as though they are mentally ill? There can be only one answer: these things are done by those who have the power and for whom it is convenient to do so."

By early 1981, Koryagin had examined fifteen others besides Nikitin and found all of them victims of unjustified psycho-imprisonment. His reports went to Moscow and were smuggled out of the country, where Western organizations like Amnesty International and a British-based group of physicians and sovietologists called the Working Group on the Internment of Dissenters in Mental Hospitals publicized the cases. The authorities would not allow this to continue.

Agents swept into the Koryagin apartment and ransacked it, carting off boxes of books, papers, letters, and anything else that appeared to be samizdat. They made another raid a few months later. None of the material was returned. Meanwhile, the state began the process of legitimizing its moves against Koryagin. In early February 1981, his colleagues at the Kharkov psychiatric clinic were called together to deal with what they were told was a crisis. After a round of denunciations of his deviations from work norms and disruptive habits at the clinic, he was censured for actions "hostile to the state." It didn't matter that his colleagues were not informed what his "actions" had been—it was his skin or theirs.

On February 13, Koryagin set out by train for Moscow for more commission examinations. He never made it. He was arrested during a local stop and brought back to KGB headquarters, Kharkov. In a statement he had prepared in advance that was smuggled to the West later, Koryagin denied committing any crime.

"I regard my arrest and prosecution as a predictable act in a logical chain of reprisals by the authorities as their revenge for my participation . . . in the working commission. The diagnosis of mental illness is my professional duty and can be discussed only by competent professionals, not by officials of the KGB, the Procuracy, or a court. The outcome of the investigation and trial is predetermined. I refuse to take any part [in this] blatant illegality."

Colonel V. Sidelnik, senior investigator of the Ukrainian KGB in Kharkov, had other ideas. Koryagin was accused of violating Article 62-1 of the Ukrainian criminal code, "circulating anti-Soviet propaganda." In case that didn't stand up well enough, Koryagin also was charged with illegal possession of a firearm, his old, inoperative hunting rifle. Then he was subjected to the "conveyor belt," as Soviets call nonstop interrogation. After four days of questioning, Koryagin collapsed and was carted off to Kharkov jail where he was thrown into an unheated stone chamber, put on bread and water, and ordered to sleep on a bunk that had no mattress. He recollected signing some kind of deposition and reading what was said to be the legal indictment against him. Then he refused to participate any more, ignoring their threats against his family and shouted assurances that he would die in prison.

Koryagin's trial opened in Kharkov Regional Court on June 3, 1981, and ran for three days. Nominally open to foreigners, the city was closed to Western journalists "for reasons of a temporary nature" by the press department of the Foreign Ministry. As at other political trials, KGB trainees and druzhinniki packed the courtroom and only the psychiatrist's wife was allowed inside. Despite the secrecy, a comprehensive account of the proceeding surfaced in the West about a year later.

Procurator V. I. Popov, an assistant regional prosecutor, and presiding judge Navalny* opened with a reading of the indictment, which totaled twenty counts of criminal subversion against the state, plus the gun charge. The charge sheet preamble noted that there is "ideological warfare with Soviet power and the Communist party, conducted within the USSR as well as abroad. Radio Liberty, Radio Free Europe, the German Wave, the Voice of America, the BBC, and even the Voice of Israel regularly broadcast slanderous lies about our reality. Various ideologically unstable persons fall under the influence of enemies of Soviet power and the party.

"Koryagin is a clear example of this type. Regularly listening to broadcasts of anti-Soviet [radio] stations, reading anti-Soviet litera-

---

*No other identification available.

ture, and associating with persons who previously had been convicted of anti-Soviet activities, Koryagin himself was launched on the criminal road of activities harmful to Soviet power and the party."

Some of the criminal counts:

"In January 1980, A. I. Koryagin with his own hand prepared and distributed an article of slanderous content entitled 'Involuntary Patients,' in which he defames Soviet power and the Communist party. It was published abroad in 1981. . . .

"With his own hand, he prepared and distributed an individual account of the examination of A. A. Butko, in which anti-Soviet slander is purveyed in the guise of an interview with the patient. . . .

"With his own hand, he prepared a letter to Yu. Belov, of anti-Soviet content, defaming Soviet society, the peace-loving policy of the USSR, democratic principles, the party, etc. Seized during a search of his apartment. . . .

"He prepared writings defaming the historic past of the USSR and the Communist party in the Stalin era. . . .

"He prepared writings of malicious, slanderous fabrications on democracy and the management of the Soviet state, as well as excerpts from Solzhenitsyn's libels on how to conduct oneself when interrogated, arrested, or followed. . . ."

In addition, claimed the state, Koryagin had violated Soviet law by writing poetry whose opening line was: *"In the world of the abnormal. . . ."* He also had committed crimes by keeping "foreign magazines" at home and by corresponding with a relative who lived in the West and who was described in court by an investigator as "a fugitive White Guard officer, and this is at the bottom of his harmful activities." The psychiatrist had "conscious criminal intent," the indictment charged.

"His guilt and responsibility are aggravated [because] Koryagin understood he would commit a crime by acts hostile to Soviet power and the party, realized and foresaw the consequences of his actions, but nonetheless, with malicious intent, conducted agitation and propaganda aimed at subverting and weakening Soviet power. [His] criminal activities extended right up to the time of his arrest and detention on February 13, even after suppression of his activities. Koryagin did not at all repent his criminal activities. Koryagin refused to participate in the investigation and made no deposition of any kind."

Asked how he intended to plead, the psychiatrist declared: "I do not consider myself guilty, and I refuse to speak since this is not a court but a punishment for participating in the working commission." Later, however, he changed his mind and denounced the trial, asserting that he had been arrested because of "my activity as a medical consultant helping the working commission." This work, he added, "led to the determination of facts regarding groundless and illegal hospitalization in mental asylums of mentally healthy people who are forcibly detained and treated [for] a kind of mentality that does not correspond to the principles proclaimed by official Soviet propaganda. In this, I was guided by considerations of medical humanism, personal justice, and civic responsibility. I do not consider myself guilty before anyone, but responsible to my own conscience. . . . I refused . . . to engage in any defense because I consider [this] a planned persecution, concluding with punishment."

A Soviet judge has wide responsibility to intervene in any trial, aggressively questioning witnesses, plaintiff, and defendant alike to help shape the search for the facts and uphold the state's legal powers. Since a defendant is presumed guilty, the judge's activities generally favor the prosecutor in a way that helps him prove his case. The two function as a team. The two "citizen assessors," who together with the judge comprise the jury, seldom have much to add, since they usually lack any legal training and tend to defer to their more learned colleagues. In political cases, they function solely to strengthen the state's hand.

Although the charges rested on the assertion that Koryagin's writings slandered the state, the judge and the two assessors never sought to look at these materials or to hear arguments between the psychiatrist and the prosecutor on the question of what constitutes anti-Soviet propaganda. There was no attempt to determine how widely Koryagin disseminated his views. Koryagin and his wife, as well as the other figures in the trial and the trainees packed into the courtroom, all understood that the point of the procedure was the opposite of establishing facts and then determining guilt. Instead, the trial was designed as a forum to label Koryagin chuzhoi, foreign, an outsider.

Prosecutor Popov called nine witnesses against Koryagin. One refused out of sympathy with the psychiatrist to testify against him and, in turn, later was prosecuted. But the others whose testimony was important to the state drew a portrait of an aloof, independent man who insisted on going his own way, arrogantly refusing to conform to the norms of behavior expected by his medical clinic colleagues. He was indifferent to them and kept to himself, and this made him untrustworthy—subversive—in their eyes.

The questioning of the first witness, medical worker V.P. Rudometov, set the tone.

CHAIRMAN (JUDGE NAVALNY): Where and how were you acquainted with Koryagin?

RUDOMETOV: I knew Koryagin from January to November 1979. I worked with him at the medical commission of the military registration and enlistment office, where he served as a psychiatrist. From the start, he seemed to me educated, erudite, well read—all in all, an intelligent fellow. It was interesting to talk with him. I even grew fond of him, but only at first.

CHAIRMAN: What did you talk about . . . politics?

RUDOMETOV: Yes, we did. For example, about Stalin, the Stalin era. I consider Stalin to be a person who, though he erred, did much good. Koryagin had an ultra-critical approach to this subject. He called me a Stalinist and said I knew little, but that if I knew more, I would change my opinion of Stalin. He promised to bring me something to read on this period. He did bring it, but not home, so I read it at work during the break.

CHAIRMAN: Did you talk with Koryagin alone or in the presence of witnesses?

RUDOMETOV: I don't know. I visited him often and he would hide something under a newspaper—some sort of book. Since I noticed that he didn't offer it to me, I didn't ask him to, so as not to have him refuse me, though I do like books very much and have a big library. Well, these talks stretched out about a month to June, then I realized there was something wrong in his views. He sang the praises of Solzhenitsyn. It was clear that Koryagin was well acquainted with his work, having read his books.

CHAIRMAN: Have you read Solzhenitsyn?

RUDOMETOV: No, I haven't. I simply know he fought in the war, left his outfit in 1942, and was taken prisoner, but he was convicted after his liberation.

CHAIRMAN: From what source do you know all this?

RUDOMETOV: Well, I simply know it, I don't know from where. But I don't find him likable. His works don't promote Soviet patriotism. And in general, Solzhenitsyn does not arouse my sympathy.

DEFENSE COUNSEL: But why did Koryagin talk especially with you? It means you, not anyone else, were disposed to these conversations. And why didn't you put a stop to [them] if you felt they showed Koryagin's hostile attitude to Soviet reality?

RUDOMETOV: I don't know. At first it was interesting, then I couldn't say I won't listen to you—after all, I'm a courteous person. But the conversations became less and less frequent.

CHAIRMAN: Did he propagandize you? Thrust his opinions on you?

RUDOMETOV: No. He simply talked, conversed. When we had a confrontation he said he couldn't reach me at the level of a real human being.

CHAIRMAN: How did Koryagin fulfill his obligations as a doctor? How did he behave toward his associates?

RUDOMETOV: Koryagin is a reserved and arrogant person. He spoke scornfully and condescendingly of the medical commission workers, and called a military commander a crude soldier. He was conscientious at work, but somehow tried to complicate the work of the medical commission and to bring disorganization into the process. And my job was just to impose organization on these things.

CHAIRMAN: But what happened there—these four cases that were reversed of soldiers who had been examined?

RUDOMETOV: Yes, at our military commission we had four cases reversed, because of erroneous conclusions of the psychiatrist [Koryagin]. That was a lot, a high percentage of mistakes. So we had to send a letter requesting that Koryagin be replaced by another psychiatrist. Our request was granted—they sent us another doctor. Afterward, Koryagin and I never met.

The testimony of Serik, chairman of the local trade union, hammered out the same profile.

SERIK: I knew [Koryagin] from the day he joined us at the [Kharkov] clinic. Our relations were normal, concerned only with work.

CHAIRMAN: What can you tell us on the subject of this case?

SERIK: Koryagin behaved arrogantly, maintaining a reserve to those he associated with. . . . He didn't participate in the social life of the collective. Once, when we decided to employ him as a propagandist, he refused because he couldn't propagandize others in what he didn't believe himself. I reported this to [the] chief doctor. When we wanted Koryagin to appear for a discussion clarifying this matter, he refused to speak to us at all, let alone give us any explanation. He said this was his private affair, that he wouldn't even give his own mother such an accounting. Then we assigned him to work in political information. He agreed. He conducted political information sessions when it was his turn. He almost never appeared at sessions conducted by others or at meetings, staying in his office, where he said he belonged.

PROSECUTOR: Did Koryagin originate conversations of an anti-Soviet tendency?

SERIK: No, I never heard anything like that. He never talked with me about anything of that kind.

DEFENSE ATTORNEY: Did Koryagin introduce any unnecessary expressions into his political information sessions? Did he conduct them conscientiously?

SERIK: As I've already said, he conducted political information sessions when it was his turn, though he showed no initiative for it. He said everything correctly, as he was supposed to.

Chief of the clinic was a physician named Nikitin—no relation to Alexei. His authoritative testimony put the finishing touches on the portrait of Koryagin.

DOCTOR: [Koryagin] generally maintained a reserve and acted arrogantly to those who weren't his friends. We arranged excursions to famous battle sites and we went with our families to take a holiday. Not once did Koryagin travel on such an excursion. He didn't participate in social life.

CHAIRMAN: But why did he refuse to work as a propagandist? Did you talk to him?

DOCTOR: The chairman of the local committee told me he had asked Koryagin to work as a propagandist but he had refused. However, he did spend some time in political information sessions.

CHAIRMAN: What other cases can you recall?

DOCTOR: Once, Koryagin told me he had been proposed for a position as deputy chief doctor at Hospital No. 15. He asked whether I would release him. I said, of course, if this work suited him, but I remarked that this was a responsible job, a high position that should be filled by a worthy party member. He answered, "I could have obtained that meal ticket long ago if I'd wanted it, but I didn't want it."

CHAIRMAN: What sort of incident took place in January?

DOCTOR: Well, in February we received a letter at the clinic from the Kharkov procuracy that spoke of Koryagin's subversive activities. We decided to talk it all over at an open meeting in order to arrive at an objective assessment.

CHAIRMAN: Did Koryagin come to the meeting?

DOCTOR: He came, but when we began to read the letter, he made a show of rising and declaring, "I can't do anything at this meeting, so I'm going to my office." Therefore, the meeting continued without him, with twenty-two people. All condemned Koryagin's harmful activities, of which we had learned from the procuracy's letter. . . . Around this time, Koryagin received a letter from France, addressed to the clinic. This letter expressed a kind of gratitude to him for his noble activities. Something like that, since I didn't read the letter and don't know it exactly.

CHAIRMAN: What relations did Koryagin have with other co-workers, especially the nurses?

DOCTOR: He behaved arrogantly, was often rude, and in his conversations tried to wound the other person's weak spot. Nurses were often reduced to tears . . . yes, tears.

CHAIRMAN: Didn't you as chief doctor discuss this with him?

DOCTOR: Yes . . . but these talks didn't have any positive results. It was generally difficult to influence him. Conversations with him usually led nowhere. . . . He kept his own counsel.

CHAIRMAN: What is your opinion regarding Koryagin in general . . . well . . . whether he is mentally healthy?

DOCTOR: Koryagin is completely normal, in perfect mental health. But you have to realize that psychiatry has the concept of psychopathic features. This isn't an illness. Rather, as one might popularly say, it is simply a difficult disposition, inclined to abruptness and rudeness, easily excited. I already said that Koryagin behaved arrogantly, was often rude, but we attributed that to his being a candidate of sciences, who evidently considered that he deserved to be more than a district doctor.

The rest of the trial moved along the same track and, in keeping with most human rituals, it conveyed both overt and hidden messages to the spectators and, by extension, to all of Soviet society.

For an outsider, the distinctive feature of the trial was that the procurator and chief judge made no attempt to prove the state's charge that (a) Koryagin's writings were anti-Soviet slander or (b) that he had disseminated them. This was because the authorities never intended the Koryagin trial to be an example of justice. On the contrary, it was designed to be the exact opposite: an example of repression. Dressed in legalistic trappings to sharpen the message, the proceeding was an unmistakable warning to Soviet citizens that the state would take the law into its own hands to preserve its absolute powers. No citizen had the right to interfere with or question the state's methods of control—in this instance, the forced hospitalization and drugging of political dissenters as deranged mental cases. The one fact that emerged from the trial was that meddling in state psycho-terror by Koryagin or anyone else was prohibited. This was the overt message. The hidden message—that psycho-terror in fact was part of the state's arsenal of control—was conveyed by the prosecutor's refusal to deny the substance of Koryagin's accusations, in effect, letting them stand.

Since the state had no interest in getting to the bottom of things (everything Koryagin engaged in was lawful under the 1977 Soviet Constitution), there was a surreal, almost Mad Hatter flavor to the courtroom exchanges. Yet, the pose of airing genuine charges and making real findings of fact was intended to resemble reality. Like any work of fiction, the trial allowed room for suspension of disbelief. Fiction as fact, from the land of Gogol and Dostoyevsky. The Koryagin trial was a direct descendant of the great show trials of the 1930s, when Stalin perfected these rituals and embedded them in the conscience of the nation as a mystical confirmation of his unlimited power over all human life in the new Soviet state.

Koryagin, the student of human psychology and Soviet behavior, understood the make-believe framework of the process. "Not a single fact about dissemination of anti-Soviet materials has been proven either by the investigation or the trial," he declared in the summation. "I was accused of verbal anti-Soviet agitation and propaganda. Not a single witness confirmed the fact. . . .

"I know the sentence will be brutal. I don't ask anything of this court. Despite the sentence I will receive, I declare I will never abase myself in view of the situation prevailing in our country, when mentally healthy people are confined to mental hospitals for trying to think independently. I know I will be punished by long years of physical isolation, humiliation, and mockery. I accept all this in the hope that it will offer others the chance of living in freedom."

The chairman and his two lay assessors withdrew to chambers

and waited a plausible amount of time, then returned to announce the verdict:

"Koryagin is fully guilty of these crimes and subject to punishment. The court imposes altogether as punishment seven years of imprisonment in a strict regime labor camp followed by five years of exile." It was the maximum.

"The longer the sentence, the more shameful the court!" shouted Koryagin.

He was sent to a strict regime labor camp in the harsh Perm region in the foothills of the Ural Mountains east of Moscow. There are a number of prisons, camps, and forced-labor factories in the area; some of the factories turn out souvenirs and trinkets that the state hawks to Western tourists for hard currency. Strict regime meant minimum food, grim barracks conditions, and not more than one extended visit from relatives per year. In the spring, it was customary in such camps for the inmates to forage for fresh grasses and berries to supplement their diets.

Koryagin appealed his case without success. Then he became just one more of the estimated ten thousand political prisoners who inhabit the remnants of the Gulag.

In July 1982, Koryagin was transferred to Christopol Prison in Tartaria, and sentenced to three years' confinement there as punishment for attempting to give medical aid to fellow inmates in his Perm labor camp. Unexpectedly, an account by Koryagin of life in the Perm camps has surfaced in the West, published in 1983 by the London-based International Association on the Political Use of Psychiatry. Koryagin's report is chilling:

"The basic human right is the right to life," he wrote. "Soviet propaganda currently uses [this] as a major slogan in its worldwide campaign. As a Soviet political prisoner and doctor, I state that conditions in which prisoners are held in political camps are designed to break their physical and mental health—through starvation, cold, and deprivation of sleep.

"Camp food rations are specially reduced. A small bowl of soup or three or four spoonfuls or porridge cannot meet the basic needs of the human organism. You always feel starved and constantly think about your next intake of food. . . . This feeling is so prolonged and intense that it has the effect of genuine torture. In the 'cooler' (the isolation cell) one gets only bread and water every other day. The torture becomes almost unbearable."

Koryagin is known to have spent thirty-seven days in the isolation cell for attempting to help other prisoners. "In winter, the temperature in the prison cells was mostly between forty-eight and fifty-seven degrees Fahrenheit. Even when wearing a jacket, one felt frozen. When the temperatures rose to sixty-seven degrees, the guards promptly took the jacket away.... The cold made it impossible to sleep. The night becomes an endless torment. Sleep consists of brief moments of dozing, ended by fits of uncontrollable shivering and the cold. Feet froze solid, and so does one's head—shaved bare especially for the cooler! The night lasts forever.... Feelings of hopelessness and frustration, outbursts of desperation and anger —these are the common emotions of prisoners in the cooler....

"I have repeatedly been punished for my refusal to talk with the KGB. The last agent to visit me made this threat: 'The longer you stay silent, the longer you'll stay in prison.'"

If he survives, he will emerge from imprisonment and banishment sometime near the end of the decade. The court process may have been a piece of fakery, but there was nothing make-believe about the fate meted out to Anatoli Koryagin.

Meanwhile, the state had not forgotten Alexei Nikitin. After his last arrest in December 1980, he was held at the Dnepropetrovsk psycho-prison for some months and, toward the end of 1981, was shifted to another SPH—this one in Alma Ata, the capital of Kazakhstan, deep in the Asian heartland two thousand miles from Donetsk. Here, it was virtually impossible for his sister and other family members to visit him or for the world outside to pay him much attention. As of this writing, relatives have reported that Alexei was given a variety of drug treatments that left him disoriented and psychologically depressed. The drugs also have had an unexpected side effect: Nikitin is going blind.

In his long fight for justice, Alexei Nikitin lost his family, his freedom, and his future. There are many ways to crush the human spirit and, after sixty-six years in power, the Soviet regime knows all of them.

5

The Hidden Empire

*When Westerners think of the KGB, they
think of spies. When we think of the KGB, we
think of our neighbors.*

—IVAN T.

I

Ivan T.* knew his way around the hidden empire of the secret
police. He had been a Soviet lawman for more than thirty years
before going on pension. He had handled most kinds of violent
crimes as well as politically sensitive offenses such as black market
dealings by middle-level bureaucrats. He spoke knowingly of senior
officers in the MVD and the KGB. Ivan T. became a guide and
interpreter for me as I delved into their world.

We met at a raucous wedding reception of some Russian friends
who had shed their first spouses and, despite a tempestuous, brief
courtship, were hell-bent on matrimony. The new husband had the
widest circle of friends of anyone we ever met in Moscow—from
several American correspondents, to writers and dancers, to an auto
mechanic and a keeper at the Moscow Zoo. In the Soviet manner,
these friendships had been more or less compartmentalized. But the
compartments were shattered at the wedding and reception afterward, where more than a hundred people crushed into the couple's
two-room apartment in a high-rise in a new development of co-ops

*Not his real name.

in the northwest region of the city. We passed steamy hours in shouted conversation, while sampling from plates and platters heaped with fresh *zakuski*, snacks, and salads. There was Bulgarian red wine, coarse and robust; Georgian tsinindali, the most popular white wine; Armenian cognac; Russian vodka; and semisweet Soviet champagne.

The din seemed to shake the walls and, from time to time, a guest, brow glistening with sweat, would lean panting for fresh air against one of the heavily frosted windows. In this crowd was the lawman. When I learned what he was retired from, I asked to visit him. He indicated that that would not be possible—ever. Some weeks later, I went to see the newlyweds and asked about him. And the next time I went to see them, he was there. Perhaps he was bored with his retirement, or perhaps he was intrigued by the near-anonymity of our first meeting, jammed together with forty or fifty other people. Although the organs could identify him if they wanted to, his only ground rules were that his identity be obscured. At bottom, he had an urge to talk to an American correspondent. I visited him in his own apartment or at another person's place, and either we talked about broad questions, such as the role of the secret police and the national Soviet psychology, or he commented on specific incidents. There were perhaps ten extended conversations spread over two years, sometimes with my wife, Eliza, present. What follows is a compilation of our talks, arranged in a way that duplicates their development over the months.

"The first point to be remembered," he began in what was a slightly pedantic—and therefore utterly Soviet—style, "is that we are Asiatic in a way that you are not. In fact, while we think we look and act like Americans, we are completely different from you. As I understand our character, it is that we have the essential characteristic of Asians, which is the possibility of carrying two kinds of thoughts in one head. This makes it relatively simple for people to accept the idea that the rights set forth in our fundamental law [the Soviet Constitution] exist here as a lie. So we understand as well that the existence of freedom which the party claims to have achieved for us is a factual myth. Yet, we can quickly mouth the slogans that show freedom exists here, and in fact, in a certain way, we can believe this.

"Because of what happened under Stalin, when so many died and so many others 'sat' [as Russians call prison sentences], we learned how to live with internal contradictions like this. In the nineteenth century, the Russian proletariat was one of the most revolutionary in Europe. We are hardly a revolutionary vanguard now, but now we say we are in the vanguard of revolution and many in fact believe that—even when they make jokes about it. Part is ignorance, of course. But part is obedience.

"If there is a stereotype, it is that Germans are obedient and Russians chaotic. Partly, this is true, as I saw for myself during the war. But it is partly untrue as well. It is we, the Soviets, the Russians, who are obedient. We are obedient to the lessons of Stalin, which outlawed revolution, and obedience is easier to maintain now than before Stalin. Because so many were killed under Stalin, there won't be the same need to kill so many next time to achieve complete obedience. Like an alcoholic who only needs one drink to get drunk. So the next time there is need to impose fear, it probably could take just ten thousand deaths to achieve the same effect as it took Stalin to achieve only by killing millions. Obedience is now a genetic factor in us."

In his retirement, Ivan T. was reading Solzhenitsyn, Georgi Vladimov, Vladimir Voinovich, Pasternak, and other contemporary Soviet authors whose works have been repressed.*

He called this part of a phenomenon of "greater freedom within ourselves," which he saw as contradictory to the effects of Stalin. "The notion of greater freedom is purely an aspect of humanity, not because of anything special the regime has done. Mostly, it is because, in conditions of anything other than abject terror or deprivation, humans contradict their own passivity and reach out for things. In the coming twenty years there will be a further development of this kind of internal freedom, even if the organs and the party try to keep the status quo.

"This can be proven by the fact that there are millions of people who listen to the Voice of America and, as a result, they are slowly being torn away from their old beliefs. Whatever meaning the dissident movement has outside the country, it has great meaning inside the country—far more than even correspondents like you who are instrumental in the dissidents' activities can ever know. Dissent has a specific impact on our lives. Those who are activists have not come to the surface solely because of their own internal inspirations. They

*A Pasternak rehabilitation is under way. See Chapter 14.

are players on a stage and see themselves in that light. An international stage. The organs know this. To some extent, they are helpless before this general historical development. They do what they can by arresting dissenters and making examples of them. But it is somewhat like bailing out the sea, I think. Nevertheless, whenever a dissident is arrested and punished, part of the public defamation that follows is that the activist was led astray by foreign influences. This is sound psychology for the *Gebeshniki* (slang for the KGB) because it is clear that the Soviet people themselves are worried about foreign influences—even as they are attracted to them. The organs play on these things.

"Soviets in most classes of our society don't have a very clear notion of the ideology of either Marxism–Leninism or the brand of communism practiced here. They've never concerned themselves with it, merely had to live under it. So if papa listens to VOA, the son will do as well. The zeal that we relied on in earlier decades to split the generations is dead."

"Then Stalinist fear is a thing of the past, contradicting what you said earlier," I said.

"Certainly, even our cowed people have started to think their own thoughts, even though the average man doesn't have a clear idea of who these people—the dissidents—are. They think [Vladimir] Bukovsky was a criminal and [Anatoli] Scharansky a spy. It is natural for us not to be involved in political matters, and because of this trait, it is much easier to reach those kinds of conclusions. At the same time, they are questioning the regime in certain ways, because they see with our mediocrities running the country that Brezhnev and his colleagues are not all-powerful. But even though Stalin has been dead almost thirty years, the people know that the leadership succeeds here more because of the fear we have of our leaders rather than anything the leaders do themselves.

"The basic truth that binds the country is probably that, from bottom to top, no one wants change, no one wants to rock the boat. This is why the system keeps going in the same fashion. It is a kind of fear of the unknown which perhaps seems hard for you to comprehend but is very real with us. There are many different kinds of fears in this country and, to some extent, they are connected together. Perhaps it comes from this: if you ask any Russian where he was and what he was doing the day Stalin died, if he is of an age old enough to remember—he remembers! I remember and, like everybody I knew, it was as though the world had been torn apart. It was the most frightening day of my life."

My wife and I looked at each other and shook our heads in wonderment. We had heard this phenomenon described before, but it never ceased to amaze us.

"You *can't* understand it," Ivan said. "But we all thought—all of us—'How will we live? How will the country survive?' We were surrounded by enemies then and, without Stalin, who could protect us and lead the nation? And to many millions of Soviets to this day, those questions have never been satisfactorily answered. Even though any sane person would have reacted only with relief that Stalin died! The whole country should have done what only very few did—gotten down on its knees and thanked God. But we didn't. Today, he is venerated by millions. You can see his picture on the dashboards of taxis and trucks."

This is startlingly true. "Most people I've asked say that Stalin stood for law and order," I said.

Ivan nodded his head. "We want order in our country. Khrushchev denounced Stalin and frightened millions of us. Who wants to talk about the past? Let the dead lie where they are.

"This brings us back to the beginning. People always wonder: which is greater, the party or the KGB? The party has never fully discussed its crimes and it never will; there are two reasons for this. If it did, the effect might be to assuage the apprehension and fear which limit us and keep us subservient to the party. And the Chekists continue to function as the agents of the fear to this day. So even the question can't be asked because it's like two sides of the same coin—and the coin is fear. Stalin minted it that way."

II

"DURING Stalin's time, when the doorbell rang at night, terror seized the house," Ivan said one day. "Now, if someone knocks, I go peacefully to answer it. So you can't say it is as bad as when we were children. But I know exactly what I can say, and who I can say it to, and where I can say it. This is true for all of us. Anyone who forgets this is flirting with trouble.

"For example, the conditions of life in our country are the lowest in the developed world. We know that and so do the organs. It is more dangerous to the regime than the activists because it is tangible. But no one complains because, aside from being used to shortages, they are simply scared to express themselves in public. Millions of people 'sat' and they cannot forget that."

Among our friends was a woman I'll call Nadya, a gaunt, 37-year-old "engineer," a word so favored for its vague, yet heroically modern sound that it has become a catchall to describe everything from assembly-line work to actually running a diesel engine. We met over tea in her apartment from time to time to listen to tales of life for a divorcee in the USSR. She lived a strained existence, reinforced by worries over the delicate health of her son, who had had rheumatic fever. One day when we showed up for a visit, Nadya was beside herself with worry that bordered on grief over an incident she had sparked when she queued in a meat line the night before.

It was early in 1980 and, with the long-awaited Summer Olympic Games to open in Moscow the coming July, crash efforts were under way to polish the public image of the world's first socialist state for the foreign crowds who would throng the capital. While thousands of shock workers face-lifted the city's unique monuments and rushed to complete the sports arenas and other new facilities for the athletes, Soviet media were telling the populace that the virtues of the system would be extolled. Moscow's tough party chief, Politburo member Viktor Grishin, had recently called for renewed ideological vigilance to guard the country against dangerous foreign influences that the capitalist visitors would spread. Like most of her countrymen, Nadya had ignored the ideological preachings and hoped only that the effort to fell the visitors with the wonders of the system would in fact unleash onto store shelves a torrent of foodstuffs that the state was known to be hoarding for the big show.*

Meanwhile, here she was at the tail end of a line that stretched along filthy glass display cases against the meat shop's back wall, all the way through the store and out the broken doorway, then down the street where gusts of wind pried at the shoppers. On the street there was the usual rough camaraderie of people sharing adversity —they had no choice. But the feeling of the crowd inside was different. Warmed by the superheated temperature of the room, the inside line peered past the truculent stares of the shopgirls and

*It did. Moscow stores were heavily stocked for the Games.

cashiers with their abacuses to the slow weighing out of hunks of stringy steer meat. Through a door, they could hear the *chunk! chunk!* of the butcher flailing at some carcass draped over his chopping block. Everything seemed only to embitter the queue and, as they warmed up and watched the minutes tick by, they began giving voice to their thoughts. By the time Nadya squeezed inside, the state was suffering.

She was shocked at the frankness of what she heard. Bureaucrats were to blame. Thieving railroad workers. Kolkhozniki no better than cattle. "Because that's the way they're treated." "Life in communism is queues!" "For what? Stringy beef!" "The choice pieces go out the back door!" "The party will always get *its* packets!" Raucous laughter. Nadya felt something kindling in her in the warmth and greasy whiteness of that state meat shop, and suddenly it spilled from her tongue in a torrent. In anguish, she spoke about her son. What future could he have in a country where there were lines for food and bribes for medicine and lying about all of it? She heard her own voice and couldn't believe it was so loud . . . so reckless. She lost control. A ripple passed through the women near her and, somehow, a man had materialized next to her. He said something but now her head was ringing and she couldn't hear him and her insides were turning to water. He was telling her to accompany him somewhere. Her face felt scorched and she could hardly find strength to walk. The room was silent.

Now, she was out behind the store where trucks delivered. The courtyard was frigid and reeked with foul smells. "What are you doing?" she managed to ask the man. She was shoved into a car, driven a short distance, and shown into a brightly lit office. A uniformed police officer and a florid-faced man in a dark suit took her documents and carefully recorded everything in them. Then, they began to scream at her. She was harangued for nearly two hours and when she stumbled out into the winter night, shaking with fear and rage, she knew that only a miracle could save her from having her police permission to live in Moscow revoked. (A special permit, or *propusk*, is required to live in any Soviet city.) But in time, the charges against her apparently were forgotten and Nadya stayed on in the city.

"This shows that the system of surveillance, of vigilance and denunciation, can be activated at any time for whatever useless reason the state gives," commented the lawman as we munched some smoked sturgeon delicacies one sweltering June night that year. "Imagine the effort if the reason was more serious than the Olympics. Imagine the results! I think the Terror could be rekindled at any time and, if you were me, you would think of the preparations of the sort you have described as proof that I am right. You should also think of it as a training exercise."

Nadya had been sieved out of the grumbling crowd by an agent of the Political Security Services of the Second Chief Directorate of the KGB. Russians call this section simply *sluzhba*, service. It is the largest domestic political spying organization in the world. Its curiosity reaches from the mines of the Donbas where Alexei Nikitin first ran afoul of the state, to lines of shoppers at Moscow meat stores. Its ears are everywhere and the scene with Nadya keeps fear alive.

Political control of this sort existed in Russia long before Lenin set up the *Cheka*, the first Soviet secret police organization. Indeed, Ivan the Terrible, perhaps the greatest slaughterer of Russians up to Stalin, divided his kingdom in two in the sixteenth century solely to facilitate a reign of terror in half the realm to break resistance of the boyar nobility to his despotic rule.

Lenin's Cheka was itself a reincarnation of the czarist Okhrana, the Department for the Defense of Public Security and Order. The Okhrana had been set up in 1881, the year anarchists assassinated Alexander II. After the February 1917 revolution brought down Nicholas and Alexandra, the Provisional Government that gave Russia its brief taste of political freedom abolished the Okhrana.

Then the Bolsheviks came to power.

It took them two months to appreciate the Provisional Government's error. On December 20, 1917, the new regime established the All-Russian Extraordinary Commission for Combatting Counterrevolution and Sabotage. The Cheka (pronounced Che-KA) was born. Over the next four years, Chekists shot, stabbed, garrotted and bludgeoned three hundred thousand citizens. The seeds of Soviet domestic terror were planted deep.

In the decades since, the secret police were reorganized numerous times to face-lift them. But, whatever the names or organizational chart, the secret police have been the harsh enforcers. The OGPU, or Unified State Political Directorate, carried out forced collectivization; the NKVD conducted the purges of the 1930s.

The execution of Beria by Khrushchev in 1953, and the subsequent reorganization of the secret police into the KGB, or Committee for State Security (Komitet Gosudarstvennoy Bezopasnosti), did little to erase the bitter past. KGB men are still called Chekists by Soviets, a name that conveys fear, loathing, and contempt.

Moscow is the most heavily policed large city in the world, with fifty thousand uniformed police and tens of thousands of KGB operatives assigned there in normal times. For the 1980 Olympics, the police were quadrupled to two hundred thousand, with about half of them assigned to plainclothes duties. The party was intent on eliminating any chance that foreign athletes or tourists could protest the Soviet invasion of Afghanistan, which had triggered a walkout by the United States, Japan, West Germany, and a number of other nations; it also wanted to prevent any visitors from staging demonstrations in defense of human rights activists who had been jailed in the same wave of repression that rolled over Nikitin and Koryagin.

To help armor citizens' attitudes, staffs at restaurants, shops, movie theaters, and the city's public baths were lectured on the dangers of foreign enemies posing as tourists and depositing time bombs beneath restaurant tables or in bathrooms and changing rooms. Schoolchildren were warned against accepting chewing gum and candy from tourists because the sweets were likely to contain poison or be injected with contagious disease germs. As the games approached, the city took on the appearance of a garrisoned town, with roving patrols everywhere, intensified traffic control, and streets emptied of normal vehicle and pedestrian hustle.

"When the police are assembled in mass force this way, two goals are achieved," Ivan T. continued that June night. "When we stage this kind of show of force, it has an absolute effect of intimidating people from almost anything. This is a standard police custom anywhere in the world. But, with us, there is another aspect, more psychological. We are telling our own people that they cannot be trusted to behave themselves without 'help' from authority. This is a good relationship for police to have with their own population . . . very profitable. In the end, they thank us for that. It is a paternalistic relationship and this has advantages. Psychologically, the people are trained to believe they cannot function without us."

He beamed and mopped his sweaty forehead. "As it is, this conforms with reality here, for the 'organs' don't believe the people should function without them anyway.

"When salaries are nothing, and the requirements for initiative by the police also are not very high, it is cheap and easy to keep plenty of uniforms around. And the people can remain children. We relieve them of worrying about how they will behave. This makes it more difficult for the masses to restrain themselves when no one is looking. For example, at the factory. We are concerned about public signs of deviation and are quick to notice if someone violates community norms—that could threaten public order. But there is probably more theft in this country than in capitalist, corrupt America. Everyone does it here."

This series of observations brought something else to my mind: the first parade I ever attended in Red Square. It was the sixtieth anniversary of the Bolshevik Revolution, November 7, 1977. As I streamed with the rest of the crowd up the cobbled side street that leads into the square from Karl Marx Prospekt, I got a chance view through the tall, heavily timbered gate of the ancient Arsenal that occupies the northwest corner of the Kremlin. The door through the portal was ajar and, as I drew abreast, my eyes caught the gleam of daylight on gun barrels. I paused for a longer look. Just inside the door stood at least a squad of jackbooted troopers in full dress, carrying weapons. Since it was the anniversary of the revolution, the square didn't lack for men with guns of all sorts. But this group was a riot squad—in showy reserve.

"A deliberate glimpse of the truth is what I would call it," Ivan said. "Just in case anyone should be so foolish as to mistake the outward appearance of the event. The state has fashioned various realities for us to perceive, and the literal-minded among us sometimes require some help in fully comprehending the most important reality of all."

"Which is what?"

"Which is the fact that, while the people fear the organs, the leaders fear the people. As a person with a degree in English literature, you should recognize this."

"Meaning what?"

"Meaning *Macbeth.*" He gave me a delighted smile.

"Almost every man eventually has his price," Ivan commented another night, "and the organs have so much power they can discover what that price is. Since the individual has no power, they can go at him again and again and again. A person is powerless in this. From time to time, someone will be singled out for the purpose of demoralizing others. They will do anything they can to break him. This makes it very difficult to determine who is a friend and who is not . . . because every man has his price."

Among our friends was a Jewish mathematician and his family who perhaps three years before we met had applied for exit visas to emigrate to Israel. The husband, whom I will call Grigori, was fired from his research position and forced to take a job as a watchman. He was never given a specific reason for having been barred from leaving the country and, each six months, he and his wife re-filed the lengthy exit documents in hopes that permission would come and they could join the more than two hundred thousand Jews who left the USSR in the 1970s. But years went by, and the answer was always the same. One day not long before we left Moscow for good, Grigori was intercepted by a man as he stood at a bus stop. "Come with me."

"I have no wish to."

"There is something to be said to you."

"But I have nothing to say to you."

"You will come with me anyway." He took Grigori by the elbow and soon he was in a local KGB office. With the barest of preliminaries, the agent said, "You're a smart man, your record is very clear on that point." He spoke intelligently and had a calm manner. "Surely, you care for your children. That's probably why you have decided to emigrate." He smiled, eager to engage Grigori in some kind of conversation—anything would do, so long as there was a response.

"I have nothing to say to you."

"You can achieve what you want for yourself and your family," the man said, unperturbed. "All you have to do is give us what we want. And then I'm sure visas will come right through."

"I do not have to listen to this."

"Please take your seat. I have something else to say."

Grigori sat down.

"The information we are seeking is really quite minor and it won't hurt you or any of your friends. Besides that, they will never know, and you need have no worries on this point. It remains confidential. In fact, you are forbidden to mention this conversation to anyone . . . and of course, I never will either."

The agent then mentioned the case of a family who had been refused for a number of years and then suddenly were granted exit visas. The family's friends had been overjoyed, but also mystified about why permissions had come.

Grigori sat numb and shaken. The agent had just implied that the recently departed family had cooperated—and gotten permission. Was it true? Or was it a fabrication to defame people who had been friends? And even if the Chekisti weren't telling the truth, what difference did it make? If they chose to fabricate something similar about Grigori, they would do so—whether he cooperated or not. So in the end, it would make no difference at all. The organs could win. Only he would be naive and stubborn enough to be a loser. He could feel tightness in his chest; perhaps he was having a heart attack. His head swam and a wave of bone-weary exhaustion swamped him. He pulled himself to his feet and looked at the other man. He wanted to say more, but all he could manage was, "Goodbye."

He got himself home and his wife spent the next few days comforting him. This forced her to cancel the lucrative private illegal tutoring she conducted for university applicants and others trying to master French, which she spoke fluently. She had been forced to become a tutor when her husband had been fired from his research job and could only find watchman's work, at less than a hundred rubles a month. Most of her pupils normally qualified for admission into the prestigious Foreign Languages Institute or Moscow State University. Few were Jews, since Jews were all but barred from these places of learning. Most of her students went on to advanced academic training and many hoped eventually to get posted to the West as members of a diplomatic or trade mission. In order to qualify for those sensitive and coveted postings, many of these former students joined the KGB. Grigori's wife was one of the most sought-after illegal tutors in Moscow.

Even the cynical Ivan seemed subdued in the aftermath of this tale. Our visit ended early and, as we waited for the elevator to creak its way to the floor in the brand-new building where he lived, he gave me a curious look and then said, "Do you think your friend was telling the truth?"

"About getting pressured? Of course."

"No, I don't mean that." He was scowling. "I mean, do you think he really turned them down the way he said he did?"

6

Andrei Dmitrievich Sakharov

Today, as always, I believe in the power of reason and the human spirit.

—ANDREI D. SAKHAROV

I

TUESDAY, January 22, 1980, dawned cold and uncomfortable in Moscow: bundled crowds scurried and queued beneath a seamless, iron-gray sky. Smoke, steam, and urban grit shimmered on blasting wind. The harsh moment matched the mood and expectations of the Russians.

Less than a month earlier, Soviet paratroops and airborne had ridden the hulking freighters of Aeroflot's military arm into neighboring Afghanistan and, in a bloody coup, had killed the Marxist strongman then holding Kabul and replaced him with another Marxist more to the Kremlin's liking. Reinforcements were moving down from marshaling points in Soviet Uzbekistan and meeting fierce resistance. Russians were killing turbaned Moslem tribesmen in the name of Lenin, which was permissible. But the Afghanis were fighting back, spilling Russian blood in the name of Allah.

Very little about this remote adventure was familiar: it bore no comforting resemblance to Hungary in 1956 or Czechoslovakia in 1968. National television showed friendly Afghanis welcoming their Soviet comrades, but tales of maiming and butchery accompanied the coffins homeward from far mountain passes where the young men were dying. Soviet troops were at war for the first time in thirty-four years and Moscow stood condemned by most of the world. State propagandists portrayed the intervention as aid to a fraternal regime endangered by imperialist subversion, but most statesmen of the world regarded the surprise invasion as a historic new step by Moscow toward a prize that had beckoned Russians since czarist times: access to a warm-water port on the Indian Ocean. Even though the Western powers had all but abandoned assistance programs to Afghanistan in the 1970s, the overt Soviet move had turned a buffer zone into a battle zone. Few world leaders applauded.

American wrath went beyond words. Just seven months earlier, Jimmy Carter had embraced and kissed Leonid Brezhnev in a moment of saccharine sentimentality at the signing of a new strategic arms treaty in Vienna. The invasion ridiculed Carter, whose domestic popularity was plunging to new lows anyway because of the Iranian hostage crisis. The president reacted with startling fury to the Soviet incursion, suspending all bilateral exchanges and canceling a massive grain shipment to Russia that Moscow had counted on to help feed its vast, undernourished livestock herds through the winter. There even was a move to boycott the Summer Olympic Games, scheduled to open in Moscow in mid-July. The Soviets had sought the Games for years and spent hundreds of millions of rubles to build new sports facilities and face-lift ancient cathedrals and other neglected historic sites in Moscow and other major cities. The Games had long been planned by the Brezhnev Kremlin to show-case Soviet-style communism while reaping millions in hard currency from Western spectators. Now, it appeared, cynical Washington was acting as though there never had been a Vietnam war, as though Moscow had not negotiated some of the most important post-war agreements with the Americans, including the first strategic arms limitation treaty in 1972, even while U.S. bombers were blasting Moscow's staunch ally, North Vietnam. Carter alone wanted to kill détente.

Incredibly, there was a powerful voice from Moscow itself joining the American hardliners. Dr. Andrei Dmitrievich Sakharov, the much-decorated nuclear physicist who was the country's most influential political dissident, supported stern countermeasures by the West to punish Soviet Russia for invading Afghanistan. Though millions of Soviet citizens had never heard of him, and millions more thought him an anti-Soviet wrecker, there were other millions who silently agreed with Sakharov when they heard his calls for political, social, and economic reforms broadcast back into the country by Western radio stations. And in an interview a few days earlier with ABC correspondent Charles Bierbauer that now was being repeated by the foreign stations, Sakharov had supported most of the Western sanctions, including an Olympic walkout.

Winter had hardened into a bleak passage of time. It was about to get worse. Around 2 P.M., a black, official limousine could be seen moving through traffic on broad Leninsky Prospekt west of the Kremlin. It was a car from the prestigious Soviet Academy of Sciences, making a weekly trip from an apartment in central Moscow to the famed Lebedev Physics Institute. The sedan's lone passenger was a tall, stoop-shouldered man with deepset eyes, a straight nose, and a high, intellectual's forehead that arched upward to a bald dome ringed by a nimbus of wispy white hair. Although his income was enormous by Soviet standards—about seven hundred rubles a month—his clothing was nondescript, even shabby, in the genuinely offhand manner of most Russian intelligentsia. Fatigue and age lined the corners of his mouth and nose; his skin was so pale that in places, especially around the eyes, it seemed almost transparent, a chalky gray. Such a pallor is common in wintertime Moscow, when lack of sunlight, exercise, and fresh fruits and vegetables visibly drain the inhabitants of vigor. But chronic heart disease and immense, inconsolable human burdens had etched themselves into the man's demeanor as well: he seemed surrounded by stillness and silence, and his face in repose carried a solemn, somewhat guarded, mournful expression. At 58, Andrei Sakharov had spent most of his life in titanic struggle and he looked far older than his years.

In recent years, the state had grown tired of Sakharov's criticisms and had become increasingly concerned about the effect of his views on the citizens. The KGB had tried persuasion, vilification, threats, intimidation, and denunciation to deflect Sakharov from his dissent. All to no avail. He continued speaking out and the regime had to accept the bitter truth that its attacks not only had been ineffectual but, perversely, had strengthened Sakharov by making him a martyr. For example, when the organs in 1973 opened a press campaign against Sakharov which may have been designed to prepare the country and the West for his arrest, prominent Americans and West Europeans bluntly warned that scientific exchanges would be halted if Sakharov were not left alone. The Western threats were taken seriously by the more than three hundred other men and women who, like Sakharov, were full members of the Academy of Sciences, an institution venerated in the country as the flower of Soviet intellectual might. These scientists, who cherished their trips to the West as confirmation of their own status, were deeply worried by the foreign reaction to the attacks on their colleague. Such meddling in internal Soviet affairs was intolerable. But the party capitulated since the exchanges were proving vital to efforts by KGB agents and Soviet scientists to glean information from the technologically advanced Americans.

The situation of Sakharov vs. the State took on new dimensions in 1975, when the rogue scientist was awarded the Nobel Peace Prize. Kremlin outrage was boundless. No Soviet leader had ever won the prize, and 1975 seemed ripe for Leonid Brezhnev, whose statesmanship was viewed in Moscow as the key to the successful signing of the Helsinki Agreement on European Cooperation and Security. The accord had strengthened understanding between the USSR and Western Europe—and extended legal recognition to Soviet hegemony in the East European bloc. But Sakharov had gotten the prize instead—for what the regime could only consider as his seditious activities against the motherland.

Despite the affront to Moscow, the Politburo had allowed Sakharov's wife, Elena Georgevna Bonner, to travel to Western Europe and, while there, deliver an acceptance speech for the Peace Prize. The Kremlin could not punish her as it was inclined to do, since the Helsinki Agreement purportedly guaranteed rights to free expression among the citizens of the signatory nations. An effective program to counter this aspect of the agreement had not yet taken full form in the policies of the Kremlin's police organs.

This was the web of circumstance that had protected Sakharov down through the years. But now, the Afghan invasion and the West's bitter reaction had swiftly altered the equation. Washington itself had called a halt to the scientific exchanges, threatening to break all dialogue until the Soviet Army returned to Soviet territory. But Moscow already had secretly extended the military defense perimeter of the USSR to include all the territory of Afghanistan, making retreat unthinkable. The dimensions of the commitment were so great that, in fact, if foreign forces crossed the new perimeter, Soviet national interests would be at stake. Moscow at that moment had no intention of quitting Afghanistan, regardless of Western pressure. Furthermore, it no longer mattered that Jimmy Carter had once tweaked the Kremlin by sending a personal letter of support to Sakharov via the U.S. embassy, or that Sakharov had impudently used his revered position as an Academician to summon an Academy limousine to retrieve the letter. The way now was clear to deal with Academician Sakharov.

A traffic policeman on the busy boulevard suddenly pointed his white-tipped baton at the Academy car and flagged it to the curb. Nothing unusual here: corrupt police scour for bribes everywhere in Moscow, regardless of weather conditions. But now, the policeman departed from the usual script: instead of putting out his hand, he ordered the passenger from the car. Sakharov gathered his ever-present briefcase, pulled his overcoat more tightly around himself, and clambered out. In moments, he was ordered into another car and whisked away.

Sakharov's next stop was the Moscow procurator's office. There, he was taken before deputy state prosecutor Aleksandr M. Rekunkov, who informed him that, this time, Sakharov had gone too far. The state would no longer tolerate his anti-Soviet activities. He was to be stripped of his awards and banished from Moscow. His wife, Elena, would go with him for now, although the exile would not apply permanently to her. He was to call her and tell her to be ready to leave in two hours.

At that moment, Sakharov's wife was at home in their apartment on the Chkalov segment of the Moscow Ring Road. The eighth-floor flat, No. 68, consisted of two high-ceilinged rooms with a view to the southeast toward the modern antiseptic bulk of the Rossiya Hotel and the ancient spires of the Kremlin beyond. The apartment was crammed with books, papers, mementos, and photographs. There were several typewriters and tape recorders scattered about and multiple onionskin copies of *zayavlenie*, declarations, by dozens of disgruntled and disaffected Soviets. For years, the flat had been a mecca for an endless stream of Russians seeking solace or, at least, a sympathetic hearing of their complaints. Almost every day, new faces appeared at the large, heavily framed wooden door to beseech a brief moment with the physicist. Sakharov seldom turned people aside and, as a result, along with the rows of international scrolls, declarations, and medals struck, illuminated, or embossed in his honor and smuggled into the country by sympathetic Westerners, the apartment also was a repository of the unanswered hopes and demands of scores of plain Russian citizens. To the KGB, all these items, from scrolls to medals to zayavlenie, were fair game to be confiscated and held as "evidence" against Sakharov in any future criminal prosecution. Even the typewriters were supposed to be registered, for, under Soviet law, reproduction equipment of any kind other than pen and paper should be registered with the state.

When the telephone rang, Elena was having coffee with her 79-year-old mother, Ruf Grigorevna Bonner, a slip of a woman whose voice had sunk to a throaty baritone after decades of chain-smoking heavy Russian-style cigarettes with ready-made paper holders attached. With the two was Yelizaveta Konstantinovna Alexeyeva, a young Eurasian woman who had been virtually disowned by her own parents for falling in love with Alexei Semyenov, Elena's son by her first marriage. Lisa had lived with the Sakharovs for more than two years while waiting for permission from the state to emigrate from Russia to join Alexei, who had been allowed to leave for America in 1978. She was a lissome country girl with jet black hair and eyes and a gentle manner that concealed a stubborn resolution.

When Elena put down the receiver, the other two knew a crisis was at hand. Her hand flying, Elena desperately dialed some numbers on the apartment phone. Ever since 1974, the Sakharov telephone had been cut off from any international calls. But local and long-distance calls inside Russia had been possible despite the harassment of interrupted conversations and the whirs and clicks of recording devices tapped onto the line. Now the KGB's attention to detail on this arrest showed: even as Elena spun the dial, the telephone went dead. Quickly, Elena dispatched Lisa to run to any pay telephone that worked and try to get word to the foreign newsmen. Ruf Bonner "was to go as my bodyguard," Lisa said later. The women feared that the KGB would try to snatch the girl if they found her alone on the street.

They bundled up, took the elevator downstairs, and burst onto the sidewalk expecting the worst—a cordon of cops. To their astonishment, there wasn't a uniform or an agent in sight. They walked down the hill and over the small bridge that spans the Yauza, the little Moscow River tributary that meanders through the city northeast of the Kremlin. Two blocks from their building, they found a working public phone. Dropping a two-kopeck piece into the machine, Lisa made a call to a longtime close friend of Sakharov's. Then she called a Western correspondent. And then that phone went dead.

But it was enough. By the time a cordon of police and plainclothesmen assembled around the heavily built gray stone apartment building, the word was out. From their offices all over downtown Moscow, the Western press corps was streaming toward the apartment.

Correspondents rushed to the address and took up a vigil outside the guarded building. Burly uniformed police refused entrance to any foreigners and only allowed residents of the building inside. "There's been a robbery," lied one of the cops. When American television crews arrived, the police retreated inside. As night fell, Elena was escorted from the rear of the building by some agents and bundled into a battered police van whose windows were incongruously covered by small, neatly hemmed tan curtains. The van took Elena to her husband while we raced back to our offices to file fragmentary reports.

Elena's destination turned out to be Moscow's main international airport, Sheremetyevo, north of the city, where she was delivered to the police headquarters station. Andrei Dmitrievich walked out of the building and, for the first time, she knew he was safe. Then, they were driven to Domodedyevo, the sprawling airport to the east that handled hundreds of flights daily to the remote interior. They were put aboard a special jet and flown to Gorky, a city two hundred fifty miles east of the capital and closed to foreigners. This was to be the place of exile.

II

IF Andrei Sakharov had not existed, someone likely would have had to invent him as a way of illuminating in vulnerable human terms the transcendental cruelties of our atomic age. For the contradictions of his life up to the moment of his arrest were nightmarish.

As a patriotic young scientist, he made crucial contributions that put thermonuclear weapons in the hands of Soviet leaders. But as he matured and his knowledge of the world grew, he came to see Russia's rulers as expansionist despots, immeasurably strengthened by the weapons he had helped perfect. Where once he viewed the

United States and the West as adversaries of his long-suffering nation, he had come to sense that it was his own country's leaders who were more dangerous and perhaps only the United States possessed the power—and hopefully the resolve—to hold them in check. Once, the totalitarian essence of Soviet rule had not concerned him; now, he demanded democratic reform, political pluralism, and personal freedoms never tolerated by the Communist regime.

In a simply stated, yet complex and almost mystical vision of man's fate in the nuclear age, Sakharov had come to believe that genuine guarantees of human freedom were not simply desirable, but indispensable if the species was to have any chance of avoiding an inevitable plunge into devastating atomic warfare. Control of these ghastly weapons demanded the full interplay of every level of a society, so that every facet of its concerns—and its humanity—could be brought to bear on the struggle to subdue the instinct to destruction. Totalitarian rule stunted political maturity by demanding passivity from the people. The leadership's easy and unchallenged use of force to solve internal political questions posed immense dangers when such a regime was confronted by external problems. Beyond all this, denial of freedom throttled the dialogue, so vital to any society, over the nature and implications of the vast power it possessed—and how to wield it. From reflecting on the course of his own life, Sakharov well knew how impenetrable and formidable state power could be in brushing aside moral issues. He had come to realize that these moral questions—rather than matters of weapons and hardware—must be the starting point for any nation's leadership debates over the nuclear arsenal. Sakharov had been preoccupied for years with defining and giving voice to his views; the effort had carried him to the most anguished corners of human experience and the long journey had transformed him.

Andrei Sakharov was born on May 22, 1921, the first of two sons of a prominent Moscow physics teacher, Dmitri Ivanovich Sakharov. He grew up in a communal apartment in the historic city which the Bolsheviks recently had made their capital. Most of the flat's occupants were relatives of one degree or another, and this seems to have significantly strengthened the tall, dreamy child's sense of well-being and personal isolation from the tumultuous world the Communists were intently rebuilding in the war-ravaged country. The focal point of this large and intelligent clan was Sakharov's paternal grandmother, Babushka Maria Petrovna Sakharova, who was 59 when Andrei was born. Of mixed Polish–Russian descent, she had borne and raised five children, most of whom lived in Moscow and were part of the daily scene of the little boy's life. "Our home preserved the traditional atmosphere of a numerous and close-knit family—respect for hard work and ability, mutual aid, love for literature and science,"* Sakharov reminisced fondly from exile. But even then, the family was not immune to the cruelties of the new age. The émigré Soviet demographer who calls himself by the pseudonym Maksudov has carefully studied the Sakharov and Bonner families and found that the strife of the Revolution, and subsequent Civil War, is reflected in their family trees.

"Seven members of the family took part in World War I, while [later] five persons—four men and a woman—participated in the Civil War. Three of these fought with Kolchak, and one was mobilized by Hetaman Semenov but then [was] transferred to the Red Army. Four members of the family died of typhus and famine during the Civil War." Sakharov himself has said nothing of this aspect of his childhood; as with so many Russians, the notion of sacrifice and loss beyond normal endurance is simply part of the fabric of life.

As a well-known author of sixteen books popularizing science or teaching physics, Dmitri Sakharov pursued a rewarding career regardless of the new politics of the country. He was an excellent classical pianist and Andrei Dmitrievch Sakharov recalled hearing his father happily fill their home with the works of Beethoven, Chopin, Grieg, and Scriabin.

"Without evident social dislocation," observed Maksudov in his study of the families, "without emigration, change to physical labor, or insurmountable difficulties in obtaining higher education, this family of the Moscow-Russian intelligentsia became Soviet intelligentsia. Most probably, the process wasn't entirely smooth. Some members of the family must have found it hard to adjust; the lawyers and soldiers had to change jobs. But outwardly, these changes are not very noticeable."

The marriages of collateral relatives of the future Nobel Peace laureate brought other ethnic groups into the essentially Russian family tree: Armenians, Jews, Poles. (Many years later, the KGB

---

*Alexander Babyonyshev, *On Sakharov*, p. xi.

would circulate rumors that Sakharov in fact was not a Russian at all, but a Jew who had changed his surname from Tsukerman, or Sugarman, to the Russian version of the same name. This was one way the political police sought to explain the physicist's deviance to the narod. Moscow's Jewish activists regarded this effort as being in the anti-Semitic tradition of most Central European police forces.)

In many respects, Sakharov's childhood was idyllic. "Family influences were especially strong in my case, because I received my early schooling at home and then had difficulty relating to my own age group," he commented later. But the idyll was not to last. Having emerged by the close of the 1920s as first among party equals, Josef Stalin was about to begin the destruction of all opposition to his rule. In December 1929, the prelude to the Terror began, with Stalin's demand that forced collectivization of agriculture begin immediately, accompanied by the liquidation of landed peasants, the kulaks. The country was warned that foreign spies and turncoat collaborators were conspiring to undermine the state, and a wave of denunciations and espionage arrests began.

In 1930, before Andrei Sakharov had reached his tenth birthday, a talented uncle, Ivan Sakharov, was arrested by the secret police on suspicion of espionage. Ivan, an assistant director of the new Soviet state bank, had had the misfortune to have a close friend who went abroad as part of an official Soviet delegation—and defected. In the witch hunt that followed, the uncle was arrested and sent into internal exile. He worked for years as a draftsman and hydrologist on the Moscow–Volga Canal, and once escaped from his banishment long enough to attend his mother's funeral in 1941. Eventually, he was to die in a Gulag prison hospital in Krasnoyarsk during the war.

Ivan Sakharov's punishment was just the start for the family. By the time the terror-filled decade had run its course, four other immediate relatives were imprisoned: Uncle Vladimir in 1935, Uncle Konstantin in 1938, and Uncle Gennadi in 1941; Aunt Tatiana was arrested as the wife of an enemy of the people in 1938. But she was lucky: like another woman who had married into the family and later was arrested as the wife of an enemy of the people, Tatiana survived and returned to the family in 1943. The others died in prison.

Looking back on this grim chapter, demographer Maksudov commented: "In the 1930s, like all families in the country, the [Sakharov] family was chopped a fearsome blow. Nine members were repressed in the Terror. Ivan Sakharov [had] the longest camp experience. He died in prison after thirteen years of exile and imprisonment. Those men who were arrested between 1935 and 1938 died more quickly— in one to three years. Not one of the imprisoned male members of the family lived to be released, but both women who were arrested lived through their terms of five and eight years, respectively. . . . They were charged with espionage and sabotage, contact with enemy peoples, Trotskyism, etc. The targets of repression belonged to the Soviet intelligentsia proper. These were young, energetic people who had taken part in the war (four of the five who had fought in the Civil War were arrested), who had been educated in Soviet institutes, and who held leadership jobs. It's quite clear that their arrests threw not only their own lives into disarray, but also those of their relatives who remained free.

"Imagine the sleepless nights . . . how much suffering they must have endured for their near and dear who were in jail. . . . The Terror dealt a shattering blow to the older generation. It carried away a third of the men born before the Revolution and was the cause of death for two-thirds of the men who died between 1920 and 1943."

The young Andrei Dmitrievich and his immediate family came through all this tragedy safely. Andrei's thoughts delved deep in the austere riches of math and physics, subjects at which he proved remarkably gifted. The phenomenon of science's attraction as a refuge from the complexities of politics or repression is well known.

Whatever his later brilliance, Sakharov's high school years moved at a normal pace, and he was graduated with honors in 1938 and followed his father's footsteps into physics. With a group of other gifted Soviet youngsters, he moved into university-level studies.

When the Germans smashed across the Russian border early on the morning of June 22, 1941, panic swept Moscow. In the war's early months, Sakharov's classes were evacuated to the remote desert city of Ashkhabad, the capital of Soviet Turkmenia, then—as now—the most backward of all the USSR's fifteen republics. Its population of nomadic Moslem tribes tended scrawny sheep in the wastes of the Kara-Kum desert, seemingly more a part of the era of spears and shields than of Stuka and panzer. The changed locale did not interrupt his studies and Sakharov was graduated with honors in physics. In 1942, he and other promising new scientists were detailed to a

large munitions factory on the banks of the Volga which manufactured artillery shells and other ordnance for the Red Army.

He arrived at a moment of supreme crisis. The motherland was
in mortal danger, with the Nazis battering at the gates of Leningrad
and pushing deeper into the vital innards of central Russia. The Red
Army was being thrown back on almost every battle line. One of
the military's greatest problems was obtaining an adequate supply
of reliable artillery shells. In Sakharov's factory, teams of young
women peered at each casing under a bright light, searching for
flaws that could cause the shell to burst in gun barrel or at the
muzzle. The work was exhausting, time-consuming, and inaccurate.
Sakharov began analyzing the problem. Shortly, he hit upon a solution that allowed the inspection process to be mechanized, greatly
speeding production and quality. He received the first of what
would become a lifelong flood of citations, all of them marking him
as a man with prodigious powers of concentration and analysis.

With the war ended, he got married, returned to Moscow, and
enrolled in graduate studies at the Lebedev Physics Institute, perhaps the most prestigious of all the physics institutes in the country
and the match for intellectual talent of the best physics research
facilities in the world. Soon his wife, Klavdia, gave birth to the
young couple's first child, Tatiana, named after the aunt who had
been arrested seven years earlier.

But the cozy, sophisticated life of a Moscow professional which
Sakharov himself had enjoyed while growing up was to be denied
his own children. For the young physicist was about to join a titanic
scientific-engineering effort that would cloak his next twenty years
in the deepest secrecy. Instead of comfortable quarters and access to
the best that Soviet society and culture could offer to residents of
the capital, Sakharov and his family would spend most of the next
decade living in remote regions of the country on the job. He was
to be barred from ever talking about his work, and sometimes he
would seem almost phantomlike, coming and going without warning and living apart from his family despite his love for them.

As Sakharov was to find out to his own dismay many years later,
those lost moments could never be regained. He learned too late that
family ties never forged could not be created two decades later. That
was to be one burden of the post-war years. The other was that, with
the power of his intellect, Sakharov helped vault his backward motherland into the forefront of the nuclear age.

7

Sakharov and the Bomb

He was, as they say, a crystal of morality among our scientists.

—NIKITA S. KHRUSHCHEV

I

THE event that permanently altered Sakharov's life and joined his fate with our own occurred thousands of miles east of Moscow, when a single B-29 bomber wheeled in the clear air over Hiroshima, Japan, on the morning of August 6, 1945, and released an atomic bomb. The fireball burst two thousand feet over the ground and in the combined explosion, shock wave, and firestorm that followed, two-thirds of the city either vaporized or was burned to ashes. About one hundred thousand Japanese died.

News of the stupendous new weapon reached Moscow the same day, and twenty-four hours later Stalin launched the Soviet Union on a crash program to catch up and, if somehow possible, overtake the Americans. A second atomic bomb devastated Nagasaki and, within the next week, Japan capitulated. The collapse came so quickly that Stalin's long-planned revenge for the historic humbling of Russia by the Japanese in the Russo-Japanese War of 1904–1905 almost fell through. Soviet troops had been sent into battle against the Asian aggressors only a few weeks before the two atom bombs ended the war. That had been enough time to allow Stalin to claim the Kurile Islands and reclaim the southern half of oil-rich Sakhalin

Island as war reparations. But it had been a very close thing. The dictator knew that, with its fleets of long-range bombers and naval aircraft carriers operating for months far from home shores, capitalist America could dictate Washington's demands to any other nation in the world, and back them up with the ultimate threat of the atomic bomb. American scientists had put their rulers in an invulnerable position.

So even the Soviet victory over the Nazis was not enough to safeguard the USSR against its adversaries. Warfare had abruptly entered a whole new dimension and the motherland must not be left behind. The task ahead was enormous. But Stalin had the man for the job: secret police chief Lavrenti Beria. Only he commanded enough resources in the country and the vast organizational network that would be needed to build the bomb. For over the years of the Terror, the slave labor system had swallowed up millions of Russians, including thousands of scientists and engineers whose skills would be crucial to the effort.

As early as 1940, Soviet physicists under the leadership of the great theoretician Igor Kurchatov in Leningrad had concluded that a chain reaction could be achieved. But the war intervened and, despite the State Defense Committee's approval of high priority for nuclear weapons research, the Uranium Institute, set up to construct an atomic bomb, never possessed enough high-grade uranium, carbon, and other materials to attempt the feat. Little more than theoretical work had been accomplished by the time of the Hiroshima blast. Now, the slave labor resources of the nation were bent to the effort.

The first Soviet chain reaction went critical on Christmas Day 1946, and an important new date was established: a nuclear explosion in time to celebrate Stalin's seventieth birthday on December 21, 1949. Vast new settlements for the mining, separation, and enrichment of uranium were thrown up in the remote wastes of Central Asia and in the Urals at a place later called Kyshtym. Imprisoned scientists were joined by "contract" physicists who worked in nominally "free" institutes that functioned parallel to the prison institutes. The effort leaped ahead, aided by Moscow's espionage efforts, which now began to pay off. Vital information on plutonium diffusion, trigger mechanics, and other arcane subjects flowed out of the American weapons effort. When expatriate German physicist Klaus Fuchs finally was arrested by British counterspies in 1949, he confessed that he had been passing atomic secrets to the Russians since 1941. A Congressional investigation later estimated that the information may have saved the Soviets eighteen months.

This fevered world of spies and slave labor camps was unknown to Sakharov. His own scientific life was directed at defending his doctoral candidate's thesis (Soviet academic steps are more numerous and the path to full doctorate more complex than in most Western nations). The thesis was accepted in 1947, and a theoretical article, "The Generation of the Hard Component of Cosmic Rays," was published in a Soviet scientific journal. The fact that Sakharov's name was appearing in the relatively public forum of scientific journals is a sign that he had not yet joined the nuclear weapons program. The next year, two more theoretical articles by Sakharov were published: "The Excitation of a Gas-Discharge Plasma" and "The Interaction between Electron and Positron in Pair Production." An outsider could have concluded that this new scientist was making plausible progress in his chosen field of nuclear physics. It was just then that Sakharov went underground.

In mid-1948, his longtime mentor, physicist Igor Tamm, was charged with an entirely new task: he was to leapfrog the atomic bomb project and instead spearhead a visionary and daring attempt to surpass the United States totally by designing and building a much different kind of weapon—the hydrogen bomb. Tamm tapped his prodigy, Sakharov, and some other young Soviet nuclear physicists and plunged in. Instantly, Sakharov's name disappeared from public view. He was not to be heard from again for almost a decade. The cloak of secrecy was profound. Dissident Soviet scientist Boris Altschuler describes some of this in his brief memoir.*

"Get ready, we'll soon be going away," Tamm tells Sakharov and the others.

"Where and why?"

"I don't know myself," Tamm is said to have replied.

Not every Soviet scientist signed on to the nuclear armaments program. For example, Pyotr Kapitsa, a future winner of the Nobel Prize in physics, flatly refused to engage in weapons research. Stalin had him arrested. Kapitsa spent seven years under house arrest until the dictator died and then emerged to resume his research into the atom, his conscience untroubled. For his part, Sakharov has made

*On Sakharov, p. 132.

clear in *Sakharov Speaks* that he was not assailed by doubts of any sort when he first joined Tamm's team. "I had no doubts as to the vital importance of creating a Soviet superweapon—for our country and for the balance of power throughout the world. Carried away by the immensity of the task, I worked very strenuously and became the author or co-author of several key ideas." Sakharov is known in the West as the father of the Soviet H-bomb, a description he has rejected on the grounds that the collective nature of the effort makes it impossible to single out any individual. But there can be no doubt that it was the young physicist's ingenious mind that carried the Soviet effort past numerous problems at a rate that later shocked American analysts who had calculated that the USSR was several years behind the United States in thermonuclear research.

In 1950–51, Sakharov and Tamm took up the question of controlled nuclear fusion and together outlined the principles of achieving a controlled fusion reaction that could duplicate the energy of the stars and supply mankind with unlimited power by using hydrogen as a nuclear fuel. The two physicists proposed the magnetic confinement of superheated gaseous plasma in a doughnut-shaped ring surrounded by powerful electromagnets. Sakharov suggested inducing an electric current into the plasma confined inside this doughnut chamber that would set up another magnetic field and further confine the plasma. He theorized that this eventually would lead to the extreme temperatures required to start and maintain a controlled fusion reaction. The device was called the "tokamak," which means magnetic toroidal (or doughnut-shaped) chamber in Russian. The principles of his proposal were revealed to atomic physicists some years later at a series of international symposiums —and remain today among the most promising lines of research into controlled fusion. In the United States, for example, private and government grants in tokamak research total tens of millions of dollars, with much more to come throughout the 1980s.

The first Soviet atom bomb was exploded in August 1949, in plenty of time for Stalin's seventieth birthday, but this was the last nuclear advance the aging dictator was to see. When he died in March 1953, the hydrogen bomb project had not yet achieved its goal. In fact, America technically had beaten the Russians: on November 1, 1952, a vast fireball rent the southwest Pacific. But the American experiment used a "device" that weighed many tons. For all its immense power, the test did not yet give the United States an operational hydrogen weapon. Meanwhile, the USSR was rapidly closing the gap. On August 12, 1953, the Soviet Union detonated a hydrogen bomb device of its own—a massive and convincing demonstration that Soviet science could outstrip the mighty Americans regardless of the ravages of World War II and the backward state of the Soviet economy. The visionary dictator had departed the scene but no internal development could deter the thermonuclear weapons effort. Even the protracted and bitter fight for Kremlin supremacy, which lasted more than four years and was not resolved until Khrushchev finally bested the anti-party group in 1957, did not intervene.

The power of the new weapon was far beyond the human imagination. For example, the U.S. bomb exploded at Bikini in 1954 had a force equal to fifteen megatons, or fifteen million tons of TNT. This made it seven hundred fifty times more powerful than "Thin Man," the Hiroshima bomb, which had a force of twenty thousand tons of dynamite. As Khrushchev makes clear in his memoirs, the stupendous size of the H-bomb had a dizzying effect on the Kremlin. "I was overwhelmed by the idea [of the bomb]. . . . It was a terrifying weapon. It gave us an opportunity to exert moral pressure on those who were conducting aggressive policies against the Soviet Union. We developed and tested the hydrogen bomb not in preparation for an attack, but for defense of our country against those who might attack us."*

By the end of 1953, virtually every award and honor available within the USSR had been showered upon the young physicist who had helped so much to place this weapon in the hands of the leaders. At the age of 32, Sakharov was elected a full member of the Soviet Academy of Sciences, an unprecedented honor (collaborator Tamm, in contrast, had waited twenty years for full membership in the academy, receiving it the same year as Sakharov). He was awarded a coveted degree as a doctor of physical and mathematical sciences, received the Order of Lenin and the Stalin Prize, and was made a Hero of Socialist Labor. There were huge bonuses, and his already privileged status as a physicist became truly exalted. The family was given large new quarters and joined the special group of privileged Soviet citizens. The Sakharovs enjoyed vacations at well-appointed Black Sea spas, received special food parcels and clothing

---

*Khrushchev Remembers, The Last Testament, p. 71.

allowances, and had the use of an Academy car. There was a *dacha*, country house, in the exclusive party retreat village of Zhukovka outside Moscow, and access to the best health and medical facilities the country had to offer.

In time, his bonus would amount to more than one hundred twenty thousand rubles—even after long overdue currency reform cut the value of the ruble, it was more money than even senior party members would ever see in their own lifetimes. But, outside of a tiny handful of other weapons physicists and engineers, Sakharov's name was unknown. He was a national defense resource and, as such, spent his life secluded from the rest of the country. Only another scientist with a long memory would have recalled the papers by a promising young physicist that had appeared in the late 1940s and realized that the man somehow had been taken into the arms program.

Because of his vital importance to the country's military strength, extraordinary precautions were taken to safeguard his life. Sakharov was guarded around the clock and seldom allowed out of sight of his guards, even when he swam or skied. For security reasons, he could never speak of his work to anyone who lacked his own ultra-high security clearance—including his wife. He could never speak with a foreigner and never communicate in any way with anyone outside the territory of the USSR. Beginning about 1960, his family was given a comfortable apartment in Moscow, and moved there. Meanwhile, Sakharov spent most of his time at the weapons laboratories in the Urals or Central Asia.

The effect on Sakharov's personal life was profound: the excitement and challenges of the work remained beyond the reach of his immediate family and relatives. His reserved manner deepened into one of remote silence that shielded a gentle, almost childlike personality. He adored sweets, disliked pomposity, cared little for the privileges of his new status. He forgot things, delighted in stargazing, dreamed about achieving new insights into the formation of the universe itself. He enjoyed games and theories of games and probability and, like many scientists, spent much spare time devising number games. Despite the work and the separation, he retained a special air that others as unlike him as Khrushchev understood to be humanitarian and compassionate. In 1949, when Sakharov's wife gave birth to a second child and second daughter, they chose a name that bore unmistakably wistful connotations for a man engaged in devising the most powerful weapons mankind has ever known. Her name was Lyubov, the Russian word for "love."

Russia was stunned when Khrushchev denounced Stalin's crimes during his famous Secret Speech in 1956. Rehabilitation of political victims, which had begun slowly after Stalin's death, quickened, giving substance to the new leader's move. Dismemberment of the Gulag where millions had died ushered in a remarkable era of Soviet history. It didn't matter that Khrushchev had plotted the new policy as a way of consolidating his power and eliminating political enemies. The thaw that ever afterward would bear his name enveloped the country; the ferment that suddenly bubbled up within Moscow's intelligentsia also spread quickly to other intellectual centers, including those of the secret world of nuclear weapons development.

For Sakharov, the winds of change mirrored changes that were occurring within his view of his very special world and its morality. Over the years of his weapons work, Sakharov has said, he saw virtually every aspect of the program. As time passed, he became increasingly disturbed by the immense resources devoted to nuclear armaments; here was the kind of internal migration that had beset J. Robert Oppenheimer, the American physicist who perhaps most resembles Sakharov in doubting the very weapons he helped perfect. "I noticed that the control levers were in the hands of people who, though talented in their own way, were cynical," Sakharov wrote in his introduction to *Sakharov Speaks*. As his doubts grew, so did his striving for understanding of the world beyond the invisible empire of the atom.

In 1955, Sakharov obliquely raised his concerns with Soviet marshal M. I. Nedelin, a crusty former World War II artillery commander whom Khrushchev had chosen to build the country's strategic rocket forces. The young physicist suggested to the senior officer that it would be a catastrophe if thermonuclear weapons were ever used. Nedelin, who five years later was killed when an experimental rocket he wanted to observe blew up on the test pad, told Sakharov that the country's leaders could make up their own minds when it came to nuclear weapons. This was Sakharov's first known attempt to modify the regime's enthusiasm for the new arsenal it was amassing. Despite the rebuff, he continued working with the weapons program and in 1956 received a second award as a Hero of Socialist Labor and won a Lenin Prize—the highest distinction in the country. The next year, a son, named Dmitri after Sakharov's father, was born. The physicist authored an article on the dangers of nuclear testing that was published in a propaganda magazine, *The Soviet Union*, and reprinted in a number of foreign journals.

This kind of propaganda was useful to the state, but it also indicated Sakharov's strengthening resolve to speak his mind. He has written that in 1957 he became strongly influenced by the work of Linus Pauling, Albert Schweitzer, and other disarmament advocates, and that he felt himself "responsible for the problem of radioactive contamination from nuclear explosions."*

The Western scientists' concerns dated from the so-called "Bravo" hydrogen bomb test of 1954 at Bikini. The bomb detonated with a greater force than the scientists had calculated, and wind shifts that had not been predicted carried the fallout beyond the quarantine area. A Japanese fishing vessel, *The Lucky Dragon*, sailed unknowingly through the clouds of radioactivity. Shortly thereafter, the crew fell ill, and one eventually died from radiation poisoning.

The mishap helped forge the anti-nuclear movement in the West. The accident was reported in the Soviet press as one more example of American nuclear crime, the bombings of Hiroshima and Nagasaki having been the first. (Soviet school histories of World War II such as our children used in their four years of Moscow public education routinely described the Pacific war as having been ended by great feats of arms by the Soviet forces, while the Americans heinously sneak-attacked defenseless Japanese cities with their atom bombs.) Soviet propagandists knew they could have a field day with the *Lucky Dragon* tragedy because no such incident, if it ever occurred in Moscow's own weapons testing program, would have to be publicly acknowledged.

When the USSR launched its crash nuclear weapons program in the late 1940s, little was known about the hazards of storing the lethally radioactive wastes produced by manufacturing weapons-grade uranium. One of the fabrication facilities for atom bombs was the isolated site called Kyshtym, deep in the Ural Mountains in the vicinity of Sverdlovsk, the city over which Francis Gary Powers would be shot down in his U-2 in May 1960. The Kyshtym complex produced nuclear weapons and nuclear wastes. In late 1957, accord-

*Sakharov Speaks, p. 32.

ing to exiled Soviet biologist Zhores Medvedev in *Nuclear Disaster in the Urals,* sloppily stored and long-neglected wastes without warning suddenly heated and detonated, sending tons of intensely radioactive debris high into the air. It had been a heat discharge, somewhat akin to a kettle blowing its top. This was not an atomic explosion. But, within hours, strong winds spread toxic clouds of radioactive material far downwind. A mass evacuation began, but the fallout reached many places before either word of the disaster or rescuers and decontamination forces could get there. Victims of the mysterious catastrophe streamed into area hospitals.

There is no known account of how many Russians may have died of acute radiation poisoning—or even if anyone in fact did expire from the fallout. But anyone who had received more than about four thousand rads (a unit of radiation exposure) was doomed. Within the first few hours of exposure, these victims would be seized by vomiting and diarrhea that could not be controlled by any medicine. Profound mental depression would deepen into falling blood pressure, shock, convulsions, and coma. Within three days, the first Kyshtym disaster deaths would have been counted.

Russians who received between eighteen hundred and thirty-eight hundred rads would take longer to die—about ten days. Radiation fallout would kill the fast-growing cells of these victims' intestinal tracts, making digestion of any nutrients impossible. High fevers, diarrhea and other symptoms of gastric failure, and a reduced response to infection marked the fatal decline. The third group of early fatalities would have been those receiving between two hundred and one thousand rads, enough to destroy the bone marrow's production of red and white blood cells. From the third to the seventh weeks after exposure, they would be in grave danger from infections that their weakened bodies could not repel. Death would have come to some in this aftermath.

In the months and years afterward, many others who had survived the nuclear accident without apparent side effects would experience unaccountable strange maladies. In some cases these could take decades to emerge. Men and women alike might be made sterile by the radiation, sometimes for months, sometimes for the rest of their lives. Years later, there probably would be a higher incidence of blinding eye cataracts than elsewhere in the Soviet Union. The same would be true for leukemia and other forms of cancer. Finally, it was possible that genetic abnormalities and physical deformities would emerge to be passed inexorably from parents to children and their children for centuries. Unlike a flood, a fire, or even a war, this catastrophe would be locked within the genetic material of the cells themselves.

The Soviets have never acknowledged that anything like the Kyshtym accident has ever occurred—hardly a surprise in a nation where airplanes don't crash, trains don't derail, and coal mines don't blow up. Despite the fact that Medvedev's assertions initially were met with skepticism by a number of Western scientists, there is substantial reason to believe he was right. In recent years, some analysts in the West have begun defending him, in part because émigrés during the 1970s brought consistent descriptions of a vast area in the southern Urals that is closed to normal travel and where people are forbidden to live. Numerous other details, such as reports of periodic expeditions into the area by heavily suited squads that sound much like radiation decontamination units, lead to the strong suspicion that Medvedev's critics are wrong.

The Kyshtym disaster, or the probability of it, must be described, however. I believe it had a profound impact on Sakharov's development as a champion of human freedoms. My own belief is that he and other Soviet physicists learned early of the nuclear accident— either by credible gossip from their colleagues within the relatively small group of men engaged in the nuclear arms programs or be- cause, more logically, they were called upon for advice in the storage of atomic wastes so that the accident would never be repeated. Even in the tightly controlled world of police state military research, it is almost inconceivable that Sakharov and other key men in the nuclear programs would not have been consulted in the aftermath of Kyshtym. However elliptical the inquiries might have been, it would not have taken a man with the intellect of Sakharov very long to guess what had happened. At the same time, it is not surprising that Sakharov has never alluded to Kyshtym in his writings and recollections. He has refused to discuss the substance of the Soviet nuclear weapons program in any way that could be construed by the KGB as a violation of national security secrets. "I have never infringed state secrecy, and any talk of this is slander," Sakharov has asserted.* The Soviets many times have accused Sakharov of being duped by the West, plied with favors in return for military secrets; these accusations are secret police fabrications.

Prior to 1957, there is no strong evidence of substantial activism

*On Sakharov, p. 250.

on the part of the Soviet scientific community against the weapons programs and tests. This is easily attributable to the fact that Stalin was alive until 1953 and the Terror went unrepudiated for three more years after his death. In addition, aside from the highly likely event of individual radiation accidents in the manufacture of weapons-grade plutonium and weapons fabrication, it was not until the 1957 Kyshtym incident that Soviet scientists had the kind of wide experience with radiation poisoning that their American contemporaries had had after Hiroshima and Nagasaki—which sharpened fears of nuclear holocaust among U.S. nuclear scientists.

In part, I believe, the Urals disaster helps explain the peculiar vehemence with which Sakharov addresses the dangers of long-term genetic damage from weapons test fallout. The flavor of his anguish comes through most strongly in the introduction to *Sakharov Speaks:*

"As is known, the absorption of the radioactive products of nuclear explosions by the billions of people inhabiting the earth leads to an increase in the incidence of several diseases and birth defects, of so-called subthreshold biological effects—for example, because of damage to DNA molecules, the bearers of heredity. When the radioactive products of an explosion get into the atmosphere, each megaton of the nuclear explosion means thousands of unknown victims. And each series of tests of a nuclear weapon involves tens of megatons; i.e., tens of thousands of victims."

There is a genuine note of urgency detectable in the way the physicist describes his subsequent attempts—and repeated failures—to persuade the leaders to suspend their testing. He was joined by Tamm and Igor Kurchatov, the senior Soviet scientist who had accompanied Khrushchev to England in 1956 and who delivered a series of papers on nuclear fusion that included Sakharov's tokamak proposals. At one point, Kurchatov flew to Yalta in a fruitless attempt to talk the vacationing Khrushchev out of a new series of H-bomb tests. Although this struggle by the senior nuclear scientists of the USSR mirrored similar struggles in the United States, the conditions surrounding the Soviets' efforts were vastly different. While Western media delved into the question of health issues (much tougher reporting emerged in the post-Vietnam, post-Watergate era) and nuclear opponents spoke out and demonstrated mounting concerns that reflected the apprehensions of many more who were less vocal, ordinary Soviet citizens were told almost nothing about the dangers of nuclear testing, and did not even comprehend that such bombs were being exploded on Soviet soil. The relative ignorance and powerlessness of Russian masses in the face of nuclear testing must have sharpened Sakharov's concern about the consequences for a nation when its leaders starve the populace of information. As his views developed, he spoke out vehemently against the deliberate policies of the regime in keeping information from the masses. Sakharov's craving for cessation of the test series is tinged with rage, a very foreign emotion for so restrained and gentle a man.

The United States and the Soviet Union agreed to a one-year test moratorium in 1958 which actually lasted until mid-1961. Then, Khrushchev ordered up a massive demonstration of Soviet might to intimidate President Kennedy during a tense new showdown over the status of West Berlin. Sakharov desperately tried to head off the test, sending a note to Khrushchev during a meeting of scientists with Khrushchev and others in the Kremlin. The exchanges that followed between the two men and their own recollections of the dialogue make clear that their differences were irreconcilable. Different ethics, experience, and outlook divided the privileged and idealistic physicist and the immensely tough Soviet premier whose instincts remained largely those of a shrewd peasant with his own survival as a powerful leader uppermost in mind.

"To resume tests after a three-year moratorium would undermine the talks on banning tests and on disarmament, and would lead to a new round in the armaments race—especially in the sphere of intercontinental missiles and anti-missile defense," Sakharov wrote to Khrushchev.

In his memoirs, Khrushchev recalled: "[Sakharov] was devoted to the idea that science should bring peace and prosperity to the world, that it should help preserve and improve the conditions for human life. He hated the thought that science might be used to destroy life, to contaminate the atmosphere, to kill people slowly by radioactive poisoning. However, he went too far in thinking that he had the right to decide whether the bomb he had developed could ever be used in the future. . . .

"This conflict between Sakharov and me left a lasting imprint on us both. I took it as evidence that he didn't fully understand what was in the best interests of the state, and therefore from that moment on I was somewhat on my guard with him."

Khrushchev recollected that a petition was discussed and rejected and then, in a remarkable passage, he describes the ensuing gigantic explosion, which equaled fifty-seven million tons of TNT, nearly

15 percent greater than Soviet scientists had estimated: "The bomb made an immensely powerful blast. The world had never seen such an explosion before. . . . It was colossal, just incredible! Our experts later explained to me that if you took into account the shock wave and the radioactive contamination of the air, then the bomb produced as much destruction as 100 million tons of TNT."

Khrushchev ruefully noted that his advisers made clear to him that such a bomb was too big to be used safely against much of Central Europe because its fallout would poison ally East Germany as well as parts of Western Russia. "However, we would not jeopardize ourselves or our allies if we dropped the bomb on England, Spain, France, or the United States," he wrote.*

One year later, Sakharov attempted to persuade the Ministry of Medium Machine Building to forego "a routine test explosion that was actually useless from the technical point of view. The explosion was to be powerful, so that the number of anticipated victims was colossal. Realizing the unjustifiable criminal nature of this plan, I made desperate efforts to stop it. This went on for several weeks—weeks that for me were full of tension." The night before the shot, he telephoned the minister and threatened to resign if the test were carried out. The minister was unimpressed. Preparations continued and another attempt to postpone the experiment also failed. "The feeling of impotence and fright that seized me on that day has remained in my memory ever since, and it has worked much change in me as I moved toward my present attitude," Sakharov concluded.

Later that year, he suggested to senior officials that the USSR consider reviving an earlier U.S. proposal for banning tests in the atmosphere, oceans, and space, thus eliminating fallout contamination and allowing for a measure of seismographic monitoring. The partial test ban treaty was agreed to by Kennedy and Khrushchev and signed in 1963 in Moscow. It remains in force today, and Sakharov has said, "It is possible that my initiative was of help in this historic act."**

II

SIMULTANEOUS with these efforts, a second and equally remarkable battle was under way within the Soviet scientific community for

*Khrushchev Remembers, The Last Testament, p. 71.
**Sakharov Speaks, p. 34.

control of the science of genetics. Although genetics nominally was unrelated to atomic physics, the coming of the nuclear age had forced a close tie between the two disciplines because of the power of radiation to alter genetic structure. Inevitably, the struggle over the future of Soviet genetics involved Sakharov. His influence within the scientific community was so great that it proved decisive.

Ever since genetics emerged in the early nineteenth century as a new discipline, Russians have been among the leaders in studying biological inheritance. As a science that delved into the inherited nature of life on earth, genetics turned out to be especially vulnerable not only to fundamentalist religious attack, but also to political subversion. For a number of reasons, this proved especially true in post-revolutionary Russia. When the Bolsheviks came to power, they brought with them the ideological conviction that, in building a new social order, it also was possible to build a New Soviet Man. Like the know-nothing Red Guards of Mao's China two generations later, the peasant zealots of the new "science" of communism were eager to destroy while making their own indelible mark on human history. Stalin's murderous collectivization had ruined the nation's agriculture and, as output declined and the specter of chronic starvation grew, the search for a miracle recovery grew frantic. The stage was set for an assault that would shatter classic Russian genetics and send the fledgling Soviet Union firmly back to the dark ages of biological research.

The man who engineered this bizarre feat was a provincial agronomist named Trofim Lysenko, who surfaced in the mid-1930s claiming that his revolutionary methods of handling grain seed had brought enormous harvest yields. Lysenko claimed that some protein-rich, but slow-growing wheat varieties could be transformed into fast-growing strains by subjecting them to unusual environmental conditions. He claimed that in one generation, his "vernalization" techniques could induce winter wheat, normally planted in the fall to be harvested the next summer, to mature in a single season. He also said he could change fast-maturing spring wheat into high-protein winter wheat by exposing the seeds to frigid winter conditions. His claims ran directly opposite to Mendelian genetics, but they were backed by falsified harvest figures.

Much like the fraudulent Stakhanovite movement that appeared at about the same time, Lysenkoism swept forward. Lysenko's assertion that a living organism could be dramatically changed by environment independent of inheritance was powerfully seductive to the regime. By the end of the decade, Mendelian genetics was routed and the USSR became a scientific laughingstock to the rest of the world. But in Stalin's Russia, the consequences of failing to agree with the new crackpot orthodoxy could be grim. Biologists who opposed Lysenko were purged from their positions; by the late 1940s, a number of scientists, including one of the world's most influential plant geneticists, Nikolai Vavilov, were imprisoned because they refused to submit to the new theories. In a crowning perversion, Lysenko was made director of the Soviet Genetics Institute in 1940 and showered with awards, including membership in the Academy of Sciences.

When Stalin died, Lysenko managed to ingratiate himself with Khrushchev and continued riding high. But the atomic age caught up with him in a way that was not lacking in its own grim irony. By the mid-1950s, even the world of Soviet genetics had learned that radiation exposure could alter the cells' genetic codes, creating mutations—a ghastly, instant cause and effect somewhat analogous to Lysenkoist principles. There was an urgent need for the Soviets to probe this genetic danger. Lysenko, who preached that chromosomes were irrelevant to heredity, stood in the way. Sakharov was drawn into the effort to resume rational study of genetics. Because of his prestige, it was relatively easy to get audiences with the senior Kremlin leaders. In 1958, for example, he spoke about the crisis in Soviet biology with Mikhail Suslov, the gaunt, bespectacled party theoretician who was to serve as chief Soviet ideologue for nearly thirty years after the death of Stalin. The results were inconclusive, but Sakharov persisted, haunted by "the complete defenselessness of descendants with regard to our actions."*

The issue came up anew at an election to the Academy of Sciences in the early 1960s, when Academician Lysenko sought to have two colleagues admitted as full members. The two received provisional approval within the biology section of the research institute which Lysenko controlled, and then were blackballed by the full membership of the Academy after Sakharov and some other physicists argued forcefully against Lysenkoism. Khrushchev was infuriated but caught off guard. The next year, when the Academy stubbornly refused again to admit the two Lysenkoists to membership, Khrushchev in retaliation launched a plot to liquidate the

*On Sakharov, p. 184.

Academy of Sciences. But before he could carry it off, he was overthrown. Within a year, Lysenko had disappeared from the scene. Classic Mendelian genetics reappeared as an acceptable science, but the Lysenkoists hung on stubbornly through the succeeding decade. Meanwhile, Soviet biological research resumed along lines that the rest of the scientific world could understand.

The fight over Lysenko and his immense power moved Sakharov toward greater awareness of political questions; inevitably, his interest and new sensitivity came to be centered on the nature of a system that gave its leaders absolute power to decree which science was acceptable and which was not. The physicist's evolution as a man of political action with interests far beyond the borders of quantum physics continued.

The arrival of the Brezhnev leadership in October 1964 accelerated this process, for the Kremlin's new team soon made clear that the Khrushchev "Thaw" was over. The regime's crudest opening blow was the arrest of writers Andrei Sinyavsky and Yuri Daniel in 1965 on charges of crimes against the state for having their suppressed works published abroad without official permission. After a kangaroo trial in 1966, Sinyavsky was sentenced to the maximum punishment of seven years in labor camp. Daniel received a five-year sentence.

The vise was given another turn when the state quietly proposed a new law: Article 190-1 of the Russian Federation's criminal code, which set a three-year labor camp sentence for "circulation of fabrications known to be false which defame the Soviet state and social system." "One hundred ninety-prime," as it quickly became known, was intended to take its place beside the earlier and harsher Article 70, anti-Soviet agitation and propaganda, under which Sinyavsky and Daniel had been sentenced. This had proved an embarrassment to the Brezhnev leadership because the state's prosecutors had fumbled Article 70's requirement that it be shown that the writers deliberately intended to undermine Soviet power. If the scientists who had won the Lysenko fight believed that their victory heralded a more lenient, reasonable set of leaders, the promulgation of the new law indicated otherwise. In alarm, Tamm and Sakharov joined with nineteen other prominent scientists and artists to warn the figurehead parliament, the Supreme Soviet, that the new measure violated "socialist democracy." In a sign of what would become the new leaders' policy, the twenty-one intellectuals were ignored.

Sandwiched between the writers' arrests and the adoption of the new measure to expand "legal" methods of dealing with artistic and political dissent came yet another confrontation. This one involved the status of Stalin himself. Having been decimated by the Terror, Moscow's intelligentsia were especially sensitive to whispers of a rehabilitation for the denounced and disgraced dictator. Just such rumors had begun to circulate in the capital before the March 1966 party congress. The 23rd Congress, as the first Brezhnev-run national party conference since he and Premier Alexei Kosygin had come to power, had enhanced symbolic value which would add impact to any restoration of Stalin's place in the Soviet firmament. The smallest change in his status would send shock waves across Russia and throughout the Communist world.

Sakharov, Kapitsa, and Tamm, joining with a group of liberal-minded artists, attacked the rumored rehabilitation as a blow that would damage the party and the country. Most Western Communists would be repelled by any rehabilitation. Brezhnev backed down: Stalin remained interred at the foot of the Kremlin wall instead of being returned to the Lenin Mausoleum from which Khrushchev had had him removed at the beginning of the decade. But a stone bust atop a pedestal appeared at the Stalin grave site, an appropriate sign of the careful way the new leaders would seek throughout the Brezhnev era to improve the dictator's image, yet avoid a serious fight with the disaffected intelligentsia.

In looking back later on these formative months of the mid-1960s, Sakharov singled out his opposition to "one hundred ninety-prime" as of special significance: "Thus, for the first time my own fate became interwined with the fate of that group of people—a group that was small but very weighty on the moral (and, I daresay, the historical) plane—who subsequently came to be called 'dissenters.' "

Early in 1967, Sakharov and a Soviet journalist named Ernst Henry prepared an article on the role of scientists in society. They aimed to have it published by *Literaturnaya Gazeta*, the well-read literary weekly, in hopes of sparking the nation's intelligentsia to begin a serious discussion about reducing the threat of thermonuclear war. The Central Committee refused to authorize publication. In the exchange, Sakharov told Henry that the partial test ban treaty of 1963 came about in part because of efforts by Western as well as Soviet scientists. "This was an undeniable confirmation of the effectiveness of scientists and intellectuals in trying to solve the most important political problems," Sakharov declared.*

While much of the conversation was devoted to the destabilizing disadvantages of an anti-ballistic missile system (later banned by the Salt I treaty), Sakharov bluntly clarified for Henry the two subjects that haunt him—nuclear devastation and the individual's over-whelming moral responsibility to prevent it.

"If Clausewitz's formula were applied across the board in our day and age (i.e., war), we would be dealing not with the 'continuation of politics by other means' but with the total self-destruction of civilization. . . . The destruction of hundreds of millions of people, the genetic deformation of future generations, the destruction of cities and industry, transport, communication, agriculture, and the educational system, the outbreak of famine and epidemics, the rise of a savage and uncontrollable hatred of scientists and 'intellectuals' on the part of civilization's surviving victims, rampant superstition, ferocious nationalism, and the destruction of the material and infor-mational basis of civilization—all this would throw humanity centu-ries back, to the age of barbarism, and bring it to the brink of self-destruction. This is a gloomy prognosis, but we can't just brush the facts aside."

The two men talked of what American scientists could do to help extricate their country from the Vietnam War. "The historic re-sponsibility of American scientists and intellectuals at this critical juncture in world history is very great," Sakharov said in a typical passage that sounded patronizing but in fact was a way to talk indirectly to Soviet scientists through *Literaturnaya*'s columns. "If they deny their active or passive support to the war machine, if they can help explain to the American people how much more important the preservation of peace is than any or all American domestic problems, the war machine will begin to lose its power and more favorable circumstances will emerge. . . . The role of scientists and progressive intellectuals, their ways of thinking and acting, will be enormously enhanced throughout the world. . . . Scientists . . . must become aware of their power as one of the most important bulwarks of the idea of peaceful coexistence."**

Although never officially published, this exchange quickly turned up in the pages of one of the most unique samizdat journals of the

*Sakharov Speaks, p. 36.
**Stephen F. Cohen (ed.), *An End to Silence*, pp. 228–34.

period, Roy Medvedev's *Political Diary*. Sakharov has disclaimed any role in getting the article into samizdat, but it was a milestone in the steady and now irreversible course the physicist was to take over the next decade. *Political Diary* apparently was circulated to no more than a handful of senior party apparatchiks and disaffected Moscow intellectuals. But the underground journal was vivid, authoritative, and wide-ranging. Despite the Brezhnev chill and its own almost invisible circulation, the contents of *Political Diary* available to the West provide a very special insight into the nature and range of debate under way within Russia after Khrushchev departed from power. Stalin's crimes, socialist morality, guilt, and retribution all figured in the journal. Although Sakharov and Roy and Zhores Medvedev (identical twins) later would have a philosophical falling out over political reform questions, the brothers were crucial to his emergence as a human rights activist.

While his scientific work continued (three articles published in 1967 with such titles as "Quark-Muon Currents and the Violation of CP Invariance" and "Vacuum Quantum Fluctuations in Curved Space and the Theory of Gravitation"), Sakharov at the age of 46 had become a social and political thinker with an increasingly trenchant voice. From the moment that senior Soviet scientists became concerned about fallout dangers from atomic weapons tests, Sakharov's steady metamorphosis may have been inevitable. But as the Brezhnev era unfolded, with its mounting pressure on dissent, most other scientists, as celebrated and privileged as Sakharov, fell silent. Only he remained courageous enough to speak out—and suffer the consequences.

In May 1968, Moscow's flourishing network of typescript samizdat publishing suddenly caught fire when a new series of twelve linked essays began circulating under Sakharov's authorship.

"Progress, Coexistence, and Intellectual Freedom"* dealt with world ills: the threat of nuclear war, hunger, racism and overpopulation, environmental pollution, totalitarianism. Sakharov blamed the Americans for instigating the Vietnam War, and he blamed the Soviets for the Arab–Israeli confrontation. He called for a fundamental, extra-national dedication to the cause of peace.

"International affairs must be completely permeated with scientific methodology and a democratic spirit, with a fearless weighing

*Published as a book in the U.S. in 1968. See bibliography.

of all facts, views, and theories, with maximum publicity of ultimate and intermediate goals, and with a consistency of principles."

The work combined general principles of international conduct —"All people have the right to decide their own fate with a free expression of will"—and toughly worded denunciations of unacceptable aspects of the Soviet system—"The crippling censorship of Soviet artistic and political literature has again been intensified. . . . Wide indignation has been aroused by the recent decree . . . amending the Criminal Code in direct contravention of the civil rights proclaimed by our Constitution." He declared it "imperative, of course" that the state make public all evidence of Stalin era crimes "including the archives of the NKVD, and conduct nationwide investigations" that would identify all the criminals and, inevitably, lead to their punishment.

At the conclusion, he proposed a four-part "plan for cooperation" that depended for success on a series of international developments which, if they occurred, could not fail to transform the world. He optimistically foresaw by 1980 the demise of one-party communism and its replacement by multi-party systems, and a parallel "victory of the leftist reformist wing of the bourgeoisie, which will begin to implement a program of rapprochement with socialism, i.e., social progress, peaceful coexistence, and collaboration with socialism on a world scale and changes in the structure of ownership." These changes would bring the two superpowers together to "solve the problem of saving the poorer half of the world." A world government would come into existence by the year 2000.

Some years later in a rueful retrospective, Sakharov found the essay's ideas neither original nor profound. "Nonetheless, its basic ideas are dear to me. In it I clearly formulated the theses . . . that the rapprochement of the socialist and capitalist systems, accompanied by democratization, demilitarization, and social and technological progress, is the only alternative to the ruin of mankind."*

Within a few weeks, "Progress, Coexistence, and Intellectual Freedom" had been smuggled to the West, where it became a sensation. Soviet reaction was swift: the next month, Sakharov's top secret clearance was revoked and he was permanently banned from weapons work and reassigned to the Lebedev Physics Institute. But from the state's point of view, the damage had already been done.

*Sakharov Speaks, p. 37.

By mid-1969, millions of copies of "Progress" were in circulation abroad in more than a score of foreign languages. Renegade Sakharov had become a world figure.

The transformation from carefully concealed scientist to controversial social critic and defender of the downtrodden permanently overturned Sakharov's life. The framework of privilege remained— the limousine, dacha, special vacation, and health care facilities. But access was cut off to the inner world of the state, where powerful technocrats and their advisers advanced their ideas through the Central Committee maze to the interior chambers of the Politburo. Like an angel who had fallen, Sakharov was shunned and ostracized.

These rapid changes in his status took place at a time of intense private strain, for his wife of two decades, Klavdia, was gravely ill with cancer. Her death in 1968 left him a widower with two daughters—Tatiana, 24, and Lyubov, just 20—and a young son, Dmitri, born in 1957. The oldest daughter had married the year before, and now Sakharov was a grandfather with a granddaughter named Marina. However, father and offspring were not close. The children had hardly known him when they were young; when his moral migration began in the early 1960s, they had not participated. Now, with their mother dead and their father deeply immersed in the troubling political problems of perfect strangers, family cohesion crumbled, never to be restored. After his second marriage, these offspring faded from his life. The emotional center for him shifted to his new wife and her children, whom he came to consider his own.

8

Elena Georgevna Bonner

After all, Papa died in prison. That remains with me always, in my dreams, somewhere on the edge of dreaming . . . almost always. . . .

—ELENA G. BONNER

I

In the autumn of 1970, provincial authorities in the city of Kaluga about one hundred miles southwest of Moscow staged the criminal trial of two samizdat activists named Vail and Pimenov. Since it was a political matter, a verdict of guilty was a foregone conclusion. Even so, a small group of activists went down by elektrichka from Moscow to Kaluga, whose principal claim to Soviet attention was that the reclusive mathematician and space travel visionary Konstantin Tsiolkovsky had lived, studied, and died there. A cavernous museum to honor Tsiolkovsky, filled with replicas of the first sputnik and other Soviet space triumphs, had been built on a bluff above the Oka River, which ran through the city. The visitors, some of whom were mathematicians and physicists with a deep interest in celestial physics, paid no attention to the museum. Instead, they gathered outside the People's Courthouse in a gesture of support for the two activists. Under intense police scrutiny, they passed the day talking and making each other's acquaintance. Sakharov was among them.

So was a raw-boned, middle-aged woman with a swarthy, animated round face. She wore her long, graying hair drawn up in a no-nonsense bun, and her voice carried the pithy, distinctive tang of a person who has experienced enough of the world to have strong opinions of it. A chain-smoker, her thick-lensed glasses gave her grayish-amber eyes a startled, questioning expression that seemed somewhat out of character for someone so forthright and self-assured. The effect was accentuated by the pupil of her right eye: it was not a symmetrical black dot, but a jagged, dark opening, which increased the impression that she was in a state of constant surprise. The misshapen pupil was the result of a wound during the war and further damage later from glaucoma. Where the famous physicist and political critic was extraordinarily shy and retiring, this imposing woman was brash and passionate, someone who looked as if she had made up her mind. Where Sakharov tended to ghost through a crowd and arrive at the front with little effort, this woman was capable of pushing and shoving her way to the front of any line. As she waved her hands, puffed her cigarettes, and delivered her forthright views, she left the indelible impression that she could take care of herself. She did not cut a romantic figure and she was not there for romantic reasons.

Her name was Elena Georgevna Bonner, and she had been drawn into the tiny human rights movement out of a love of literature and a requirement for finding out truth. There was an inner drive in this woman to assert a personal stake in the fate of her nation and to exercise her individual rights. She responded to these impulses with a kind of grand, fated passion that outsiders believe only Russians have in their nature. In fact, she was not a Russian at all, but half Armenian and half Jewish, the offspring of people thrown together in the 1920s by furious currents of history that cut down millions— and in time caught up with her family as well. A pediatrician and mother of two, she had labored energetically and restlessly to help others and to fulfill what the state taught were the promises of the Revolution. Hers had been a life of adventure, pain, and intense sorrow. At the age of 47, divorced from her first husband and living with her children and her aged mother in a small Moscow apartment, she was an independent, hardy soul who appeared to be utterly self-sufficient. To an outsider who did not know or could not see the deep currents of emotion that welled inside her, it would seem unlikely that Elena Bonner would fall in love again, much less with anyone as withdrawn and mysterious as Andrei Sakharov.

Sakharov was 49 now; he had been outside the establishment for nearly two years and his journey through the new world of dissent continued at a brisk pace. He had taken up the study of the universe as his scientific pursuit, but it was the earthly realms that demanded most of his energy. The diverse and intense group of would-be political reformers, human rights protesters, and nationalist and religious activists who dared speak out included many tough-minded people who fascinated and attracted him. He sought discussions on every side, read much in the underground press, and worked to hone his ideas about the political, moral, and ethical life of his country.

Among his most important friends were Roy Medvedev, editor of *Political Diary*, and physicist Valentin Turchin,* who assisted Medvedev with the journal. Together the three men had seized on the start of a new decade, the sixth year of the Brezhnev era, as an opportunity to suggest anew from the sidelines a course of evolutionary change for the country. Their ambitious program of political reform foresaw an eventual end to totalitarian government. The Manifesto, as it came to be called, was boldly addressed to Brezhnev, Premier Alexei Kosygin, and President Nikolai Podgorny on "a question having great significance." As the trio analyzed their country's situation, they saw the vast natural and human resources of the motherland being squandered and the country falling farther and farther behind the United States, especially in such crucial advanced scientific and engineering areas as computer technology. The tract, which began circulating in Moscow's underground press within the intelligentsia, underscored their sense of themselves as a kind of loyal opposition:

"Is it really true that the socialist system provides poorer possibility than the capitalist for the development of productive force and that in economic competition socialism can't beat capitalism?

"Of course not!"

The real problem, they wrote,** was the Stalinist past, which had not been repudiated, and the survival of the dictator's bureaucratic system, which had not been fully reformed. They offered the "respected comrades" a fifteen-point reform program and warned that there was "no way out of the difficulties facing the country except

*Turchin later helped found an Amnesty International chapter in Moscow and was forced out of the country in 1977.
**Stephen F. Cohen (ed.), *An End to Silence*, pp. 317–27.

a course toward democratization carried out by the party. . . . A move to the right will not solve any problems." Among their proposed reform measures, which "could be carried out in four or five years," were such favorites of the era as an end to jamming foreign radio broadcasts, establishment of an independent court system, ending the internal passport system, public instead of party and state control of the media, "gradual introduction" of contested elections, and reduction of the secrecy surrounding the leadership. Despite the regime's increased pressure on all forms of dissent, and the throttling of Eastern bloc apostasy with the August 1968 invasion of Czechoslovakia, Sakharov continued to hope that the leaders would see the value of reform once it was called to their attention. This was an old Russian tradition—refusing to believe the system couldn't be made to work. Alexei Nikitin had harbored similar hopes.

Wrapped up as he was in matters of the universe and men's lives, there hardly seemed room for romance in his existence. Yet to the utter astonishment of both Sakharov and Elena Bonner, the Kaluga visit became unforgettable. When the day was over, he went back to Moscow—seemingly half-smitten already. And she knew something extraordinary had befallen her.

They began seeing each other. By the summer of 1971, Elena's children, Tatiana and Alexei, felt sufficiently curious about their mother's friend that they decided to visit Sakharov at his vacation dacha in the hamlet of Arsaul on the Black Sea. Tatiana, or Tanya, then just 21, had been married the previous December to Efrem Yankelevich, the son of a physician she had met and fallen in love with some years before. Even though they were plugged into the world of underground polemics and Efrem especially kept in touch with the growing selection of suppressed literary works, the young couple had only a shadowy idea of who Sakharov was. That he was a principal designer of the hydrogen bomb and had received the state's highest awards and prizes seemed barely within the realm of fact. Their lack of firm knowledge about him was testimony to the effectiveness of the state's security policies. Their first meeting with the physicist hardly augured well for the future.

Efrem recalled years later how, shortly after they were introduced, he attempted to break the ice by drawing Sakharov into a quick discussion of some contemporary novels that had attracted much comment in Moscow's intellectual circles. "I don't read much," Sakharov said mildly. The conversation died there. The next morning, Sakharov launched into a lengthy discourse on gravitational wave theory, which seemed to Efrem interesting, if somewhat arcane. There wasn't much Efrem could offer on his side of the subject. Sakharov's daughter, Lyubov, who also was staying at the dacha, was perfectly friendly, but remained somewhat aloof and abstracted like her father. She tried to be pleasant, but her life-style made her remote. Tanya could not help contrasting the way Lyuba carefully offered Efrem a single egg for breakfast with her own family's raucous joy over the same meal—any meal!—when everything on the table seemed somehow fit for a feast and everyone plunged in with gusto. Efrem was surprised to find that, while Sakharov liked the seaside, he didn't particularly seem to enjoy swimming. And—utterly out of character for a Russian intellectual —his game of chess was indifferent. The young peoples' verdict at the time: "He was mysterious."

Perhaps. But it didn't matter. At the end of the summer, Elena told her children: "We love each other." That sealed it. When they returned to Moscow and autumn arrived with the blustery weather that makes Russian families relish anew their stuffy, superheated flats, Sakharov began going to the Bonner apartment. After a while, he was a permanent member of the household. Later in the fall, he moved in for good. Soon, they were married and the hustle and bustle of life intensified as the human rights movements expanded throughout the first half of the 1970s. What with all the inhabitants of the apartment, there hardly seemed room for the meetings, discussions, meals, typing sessions, and endless stream of visitors besieging the family. But, somehow, everyone was accommodated.

The apartment consisted of two high-ceilinged rooms, kitchen and bathroom arranged in a line along a narrow entrance hall that led straight in from the eighth floor landing. The front hall was crowded with a large coat rack against one wall that fairly groaned under the weight of outer garments. A clutter of boots, shoes, and worn cloth slippers, which Russians wear when at home, jammed the entrance. The younger newlyweds, Tanya and Efrem, already occupied the front study–bedroom, which was equipped with a thinly mattressed double bed that served as a kind of couch during the day, several tall, glass-fronted bookcases, and some rickety side chairs. There were two small desks piled high with books and papers, and lamps with precariously leaning shades. Since the young people were eager to find their own apartment, it was decided that they should not be dislodged from the best room in the flat.

Fifteen-year-old Alexei, or Alyosha, as he was known, and his grandmother, Ruf Grigorevna Bonner, then 71, lived in the second room amid a similar collection of dusty, varnished furniture. The single beds served as couches during the day. Elena and Andrei Dmitrievich roomed in the kitchen, their narrow bed against the wall across from the stove. The palletlike bed served as a banquette during meals when the small, square table was pulled close. The kitchen also contained a small refrigerator, a small gas cook stove, and a sink and cupboard filled with mismatched dishes and flatware. A narrow balcony opened to the west off the kitchen and was useful for storing extra food and other odds and ends. In the summertime, efforts were made there to grow flowers in small boxes.

Amid all the comings and goings, Sakharov spent several hours a day in a peaceful corner of the jammed household, reading or thinking about the universe. Despite his humanitarian work, he could never put his scientific studies aside for good—nor did he ever want to. Quiet by nature, his scholarly pursuits hardly disturbed the lively ways of the family he had married into or the unusual woman who now was his wife.

Elena's volatile, ruminative, tough mind held loose dominion over the apartment and its occupants. In my acquaintance, few people have ever seemed so dissimilar in their exterior manners and interior mental and emotional patterns as Sakharov and his wife. Here truly was a case of opposites attracting.

More than a decade after they first met and fell in love, my wife and I spent many hours at the Chkalova Street apartment, talking to Elena. These visits invariably were tinged with sadness and strain, since they began after Sakharov had been exiled to Gorky in January 1980. There was hardly anything left of the earlier life they had led together. Tanya and Efrem had moved out of the apartment a short time after Elena was married. Then, after it became clear that the authorities would harass them as a way of getting at Sakharov, the young couple emigrated to the United States, settling in the Boston suburb of Newton. Alyosha had gone to the United States as well, leaving behind his former wife and their daughter, who had not wished to accompany him. His fiancée, Lisa Alexeyeva, had become a ward of the family and lived in the Sakharov home. Elena was dividing her time between Moscow and Gorky, which meant journeys sitting up all night on the unyielding wooden benches of third-class "hard car" trains under the watchful eye of the KGB from the moment she walked out the door of their exile apartment until she reached the Moscow flat, where Ruf Bonner and Lisa greeted her. She made these trips once or twice a month, stayed for a week or ten days, then returned to her husband.

Arrival in the capital really marked the beginning of her journey, for she had an endless round of tasks to achieve during each visit. The principal demand, as well as the most frustrating as time passed, was the burden of trying to keep her husband's plight before the world's eyes. She accomplished this by holding press conferences for the foreign correspondents to outline his views, demand answers from the regime which never came, and elicit the concern and interest of foreign diplomats in both her husband and the general situation of the human rights movement. As the months rolled by, with no change in Sakharov's status and no sign that the regime had any inclination to restore him to Moscow, the number of outsiders who responded to her arrival in Moscow tailed off sharply. The drama waned. American compassion centered on the hostages at the Teheran embassy. Pensive times. Yet her humor never totally deserted her. When she thought back to their first year together, she would grin. "The Kitchen Academic—we lived right here in this tiny room!"

Eliza and I stopped by on a regular basis, in part because we regretted not having known Sakharov better, in part because these were three innocent people caught in a situation from which there seemed no escape. Elena's tough, caring attitude toward friends and family and the love and admiration she had for her husband were palpable. She riveted our attention.

II

ELENA Georgevna Bonner was born on February 15, 1923, to Ruf Grigorevna Bonner and Georgyi Alikhanov, an Armenian who with his parents had fled the Turkish massacre of Armenians in 1915 and started a new life in the Georgian city of Tbilisi. Alikhanov's real name was Gevork Alikhanyan, but he followed the custom of many of his countrymen and Russianized it. Then he joined a band of Armenian revolutionaries gathering around Anastas Mikoyan* to work for the overthrow of the czarist regime that had protected them from the Turks. Alikhanov's fortunes prospered after the Revolution: he was a founder of the Armenian Communist Party and, in 1920–21, at the age of 24, served as an Armenian party chief in the ancient capital of Yerevan. But that same year, he was purged from the leadership and brought to Moscow. The move changed his life, for in the sophisticated capital, he met Ruf Bonner, then a slim-waisted 21-year-old with immense dark eyes and smouldering beauty. Born into a Jewish family in the eastern Siberian exile town of Chita, Ruf had come to the capital to attend university. Like her future spouse, she was an enthusiastic Bolshevik. And like many party marriages of that experimental and initially exciting time, theirs was dominated by party work. They were fired with revolutionary zeal: the country must be changed!

Ruf's Jewish roots paralleled the so-called *raznochintsi*, a special class of nineteenth century Russian intellectuals who possessed brains and ideals, but no titles or hereditary lands. There were fourteen separate official rankings or categories of humans in nineteenth century Russia, each with its own rights, responsibilities, tax rates, and so forth. The raznochintsi belonged to none of them. This shortcoming consigned them to such jobs as teachers and minor bureaucrats and established their position in the rigid czarist-era hierarchy as "people who lived between heaven and hell." They were shut out of the ruling structure; their intellectual attainments would never be matched by any privilege or power. In part because of this, and in part because by nature they were attracted to reformist egalitarian ideas, the raznochintsi were among the most disaffected of all the czar's subjects. They were sympathetic to the Decembrists, the nobility whose idealistic but doomed revolt in St. Petersburg in 1825 had claimed the imaginations and affections of Russian liberals ever since. The Decembrists were sent into exile, many of them to the Chita region of the Far East. Over the years, they were joined by the raznochintsi, who later were sympathetic with the far more successful revolution of 1905. This was where Ruf Bonner's family had honed its ideals.

---

*One of the most durable members of the Soviet leadership, serving Stalin, Khrushchev, and Brezhnev.

The family's identification with the long, determined quest for a just society survived virtually intact through the upheavals of war, revolution, famine, and terror that moved across the empire in the twentieth century. It was a legacy that could not be ignored by the present-day family members. Like all Soviet families, they were confronted daily by the shearing contradictions between family values based on personal morality and the disturbing reality of Soviet values. For "those who think differently," as political dissidents were known, there was no choice. But most Soviet families were not equal to the struggle—they gave in to the state.

During one of the long conversations Eliza and I had with Elena, she offered an example that richly illustrated this part of their lives. She recalled how, shortly after Sakharov had come to live with them, he had fallen into a long debate with Alyosha over whether the youth should join the Komsomol at school. Alyosha then was 16 and in his ninth year (equivalent to a high school junior in the United States). "Andrei was teaching him conformism—that sometimes, a situation arises when a person must live in a certain way to achieve something. After all, a person has to get an education. And it's a pity for a gifted boy not to get the best. And so forth," she recounted.

"The conversation went on for several days. It ended as I sat reading nearby. Andrei said: 'I'm not going to talk to Alyosha about this anymore.' I asked why, and he explained: 'Alyosha taught me a good lesson. He said to me, 'Why can you, Andrei Dmitrich,* think you can allow yourself to be honest, but not me?'' "

Relating this conversation, Elena raised another question: "What about our grown-ups? Do they know nothing about this fraud? They know everything. The only thing Alyosha didn't know was that unless you take part you won't be given an apartment, you won't get permission to travel abroad. That he didn't know, but all the rest he knew. By the ninth class, he knew all the rest, and he'd already made his choice, and he said to my Sakharov: 'Andrei Dmitrich, you allow yourself to be honest, why do you deprive me of this right?'

"So in this case, a young man made the choice between conformism and nonconformism. Ninety-nine percent of Soviet youth are not stupider than Alyosha, but they join the Komsomol though it

*The patronymic "-ovich" is usually shortened in conversation.

is meaningless—they do anything they must to assure themselves a Soviet career . . . [so] life is doublethink—Orwell! To say they are all idiots isn't possible. They are intelligent; they don't understand less well than a 16-year-old. They understand more than Alyosha. They make a conscious choice."

The matter of choice had a special meaning to the family. According to a clan legend, the family's unusual name of Bonner came about under suitably unusual circumstances. It is said that, during a forced passage into Siberian exile more than a century ago, an obscure Jewish outcast whose real name is lost to time fell in with a Polish count who, likely with a touch of irony, called himself "Bonheur"—French for good luck. For some money and perhaps the dazzling notion of a nobleman's title, the anonymous antecedent traded names and identification papers with the Pole. Prince became pauper—and soon escaped from exile. Pauper became—Bonner. Over the years, various Jewish families such as the Bronshteins and Rubensteins intermarried with the Bonners, but the descendants on Ruf's side have proudly and almost defiantly kept their happenstance family name.

Apocryphal or not, the tale gives a sense of the optimistic, iconoclastic spirit that seems to have been passed down from generation to generation. Ruf Bonner was in this mold: she wasn't much interested in housework or in dandling infant children on her knee. After her marriage, she spent months away from Moscow, working in various public health and literacy campaigns that took her to remote regions of the new nation where infant mortality was an epidemic and barely one person in a hundred could read and write. Even her first pregnancy did not dampen her enthusiasm for these arduous humanitarian journeys. One of the tours took Ruf to the small oasis city of Merv, in Turkmenia, where most Moslems bitterly opposed the arrival of the Reds. On the day she went into labor, she was taken to the hospital that served the Russians in the Moslem town. That night, she gave birth to Elena Georgevna. A few hours later, nurses rushed in and warned her that marauders were reported heading for the hospital. Ruf forced herself from bed, wrapped the baby in a sheet, and took refuge with friends. The next morning, she learned that raiding Moslem warriors of the Basmachi rebellion had swept down on the hospital and slaughtered everyone who had remained behind. Then the warriors faded away into the wastelands across the Afghan border. Ruf made her way back to Moscow and continued serving the party, now as a propagandist.

Her husband, Georgyi Alikhanov, was a tempestuous, headstrong revolutionary whom Stalin once called "a large-toothed pike." Ruf remembered him as "the kind of fish you wouldn't put in an aquarium. He was one of those who couldn't be obedient or submissive and, as a result, he often rose to the top, then fell down. That's what they said of him. He wasn't compatible with control." Whatever shortcomings he may have had, they were not important to his daughter Elena. She turned wistful one day as she described him: with his flashing dark eyes, thick dark hair, prominent nose, dramatic moustache, and intensely romantic good looks, the swashbuckling Alikhanov was the center of his young daughter's universe. "Papa wasn't a nationalist, but a very active, idealistic Communist. He had studied with Mikoyan and he always took a socialist position."

Like Stalin and Mikoyan, Alikhanov had attended religious seminary and, despite his revolutionary's inclination for action, Elena remembered him as an educated man who loved poetry and quoted it easily in the best traditions of his people. He spoke excellent German and French as well as Russian and Armenian. "I was my father's daughter, no doubt. People said that. He was always home on Sundays . . . in fact, I think he was home more than my mother, because she was working as a propagandist in the Moscow City Committee and studying at the same time. On Sundays, we read poems together and he always said to me, 'What a beautiful girl you are!' My spiritual contact with my papa was through poetry."

The family moved to the Soviet Far East for several years, then went to Leningrad, where Ruf gave birth to a son, Igor, in 1927. They returned to Moscow around the end of the 1920s, and Alikhanov began working in the Third International, the Comintern, formed by Lenin to promote world revolution. Hundreds of future Communist figures flocked to Moscow to steep themselves in ideological and strategic doctrine. The family lived at No. 9 Gorky Street, barely three blocks from the Kremlin. Now the Luxe Hotel, the building is one of the most famous in Moscow, having once been home to dozens of foreign revolutionaries. As a young girl, Elena played parlor games with the likes of Tito, Togliatti, and Leopold Trepper, the famous double agent whose Red Orchestra penetrated the Nazi high command during World War II. One of her warmest memories was of her times with Jako Valter, a cousin of Tito's.

The Comintern was a place of intense excitement and intrigue, where wily revolutionaries hardened by repression at the hands of foreign kings and prime ministers plotted the spread of communism across the face of the globe. To Elena, it was a place where idealism reigned. "That generation was completely sincere in their beliefs," she said. "There was no speculation, no corruption . . . they all had a completely sincere desire to change things in the world. In our Comintern house, Russians and foreigners lived and worked together; we helped them with their Russian language and their social obligations. All believed then . . . absolutely. Everyone was wrapped up in romantic revolutionaryism." She paused. "But now it's clear we should have tied ourselves to humanism."

Georgyi Alikhanov was being groomed for a high position by Sergei Kirov, who after Lenin's death had lined up with Stalin and was rewarded with the job of Leningrad party boss. During their years in Leningrad, the Alikhanov–Bonner family had lived in the same building as Kirov, and the regional chieftain apparently was impressed with the Armenian. Toward the close of the 1920s, Kirov supported Stalin against the so-called Right Opposition of Nikolai Bukharin and others. A ruthless and ambitious man, his career prospered. By the early 1930s, Kirov had gained immense power in his own right and perhaps was readying a challenge to the dictator— in which Alikhanov might have figured. However, before the Armenian could take up his post, Stalin struck: Kirov was assassinated on December 1, 1934, in a plot likely engineered by Stalin himself. The dictator promptly turned the tables further, calling the slaying proof of an anti-Stalinist conspiracy. Within months, hundreds of senior Leningrad party men were tortured and shot, and the organization was destroyed. The Terror was born.

"My father was very upset, but he never spoke of anything to do with the Kirov murder," Elena recalled. At first, the purge seemed to her somewhat remote, like the bitter strife between Huguenots and Catholics in sixteenth century France, when individual persecution gradually escalated to full-scale massacres. The difference was that the Huguenots had arms and could fight back. In Stalin's domain, the persecuted were defenseless. One day, she noticed a newspaper article that reported a new law: the death penalty had been extended to include children as young as 12 years of age. "My Mama didn't notice it, but I saw it and I realized it was a law by which they could kill their own children. Very bad people, romantic revolutionaries." As the months passed, fear expanded until it governed life. Yet life went on: 1935, then 1936 passed and the family continued its busy rounds in the service of the party. Now on the threshold of adolescence, Elena went off to school every day and banished the horror from her mind. "There were already many arrests in the Comintern by 1937, but we had survived that long and we thought it wouldn't happen."

But it did. On Thursday, May 27, 1937, "Papa went to work as usual, and I went to school as usual. But he never returned." Georgyi Alikhanov simply disappeared, as though he had never existed.

No word from the secret police. Elena's mother desperately sought an audience with Mikoyan, who now was high up in the leadership. "Ruf! Ruf! Get out of here—leave now!" he whispered. But where could they hide? And how could they simply abandon husband and father?

The frantic family sent five-ruble notes to prisons around Moscow in hopes of getting a receipt for "Prisoner Alikhanov." No answer. Then they were told to apply to Lefortovo Prison. "We all knew what that meant—he had been shot. But it's such a haunting, strange feeling, not knowing, even now, what happened to him. We never have officially heard that my father was killed."

With their hopes extinguished, they went to Leningrad, moving in with Babushka Tatiana Bonner, a bookkeeper. Obscurity was no protection. A short time later, they awakened early one morning to pounding on the door. Before they could collect their wits, the secret police stormed in, searched the apartment, and seized Matvei Bonner, Elena's 41-year-old uncle who had been living with them. A forestry engineer, he had survived the murderous trench warfare of World War I and had been a loyal Red Army volunteer during the Civil War. He was executed by the NKVD. A short time later, his wife was arrested.

And on December 29, 1937, the police came for Georgyi Alikhanov's spouse—the wife of an enemy of the people. Like her husband, Ruf Bonner vanished without a trace. Suddenly, Elena, 14, and Igor, 10, were "orphans of 1937," in author Ilya Ehrenburg's phrase. It was to be two years before they found out that their mother was alive, a forced laborer in a camp near Karaganda, some fifteen hundred miles to the east in Kazakhstan.

Meanwhile, the children's fate hung in the balance because the secret police now were sending the children of purge victims off to state-run orphanages, where they were given complete new identities so that they could never again trace their parents or relatives. Elena was hauled before the authorities and expelled from the Komsomol organization at her school. The wheels seemed to be grinding toward the obliteration of the family. Were she and Igor about to be seized and charged with anti-state crimes? Desperate, Elena went to Moscow and put her case before the Central Committee of the Komsomol. Just at that moment, an intervention unexpectedly stalled the national campaign that was taking shape against the country's children. In remarks carried by the central press, Stalin was quoted as saying that children should not be made to answer for the sins of their parents. With this reprieve, Elena made her way back to Leningrad.

III

"IN 1940, I was a young girl and I read poetry. One of my friends became a poet and he wrote: '*The smoke from Pompeii, the martyrs,/- The destruction of Rotterdam,/The pygmies prophesy all of our life with their own hands. . . .*' In general, it was a generation that wrote very depressed verses."

In June 1941, Elena Bonner was an 18-year-old university student in Leningrad, majoring in philology and pursuing a strong interest in medicine as a volunteer orderly in the military reserve nursing corps. "There was a slogan: 'Girls of our country, develop a second defense role!' I was very Soviet and a conscientious person. And I went ahead and did this. Young girls were supposed to go off and marry someone in the Far East to help the population. Fortunately, I didn't do that! But the attitude was completely typical of my youth."

When Hitler's armies stormed east that month, the "orphans of '37" loyally flocked to military service to save the motherland—and their supreme leader. Such was the mystical power of Stalin. But what choice did they have? Like hundreds of thousands of other Leningraders, Elena was mobilized to repel the German attack on the cradle of the Revolution. She joined the medical corps and was sent to the front. Hitler demanded that the city be wiped from the face of the earth. By July, the Wermacht was nearing the approaches to the city; on September 8, Leningrad was surrounded and cut off from the rest of the country. The siege had begun. It was to last nine hundred days. On October 26, a German bomb fell near Elena's front-line medical unit. A fragment from the explosion hit her under the left arm, sliced into her body below the shoulder, and ploughed out across her back. She was carried to the rear, critically wounded.

"We all felt we would die in the war. There wasn't much difference between men and women of my generation on this feeling. A poet, Georgyi Suvorov, said that if anyone of us lives through this it will be a miracle. But if we die, there is nothing to regret, for we have lived like humans for mankind. We believed there was a reason for our deaths . . . that we had to die."

It was not to be. Elena was evacuated from the city and a long recuperation followed. The wound proved to be a blessing in disguise, for, by the time she returned to the war months later, starvation, shelling, and the most bitter winter in memory had killed hundreds of thousands of Leningraders.

In 1943, she was assigned as a senior nurse on trains evacuating wounded troops to Sverdlovsk in the southern Urals, far behind the lines. The nursing detachment had its own unit of the Komsomol, and Elena, now a lieutenant, became the "Komsorg," or chief organizer. This position of authority probably saved her from serious trouble when one day she tried to help some captured German soldiers. It happened that the medical evacuation train pulled into a siding somewhere in central Russia. Across the platform stood another train, this one crammed with grimy, defeated German prisoners of war. Probably they were heading east to the horrors of the Gulag. Seeing the crisply uniformed nurses, the Germans began begging for cigarettes and soap.

Elena walked over to the POW train and gave some smokes to the Germans—not the rough camp tobacco of the Soviet enlisted troops, but the finer papirosi, with their cured leaf and attached stiff paper holders that were supplied to officers. She made no attempt to hide her actions; once these men had been enemy, now they were defeated humans.

She was brought before a Komsomol disciplinary tribunal for aiding the enemy. But she defended herself and, in view of her post as a leader, was exonerated.

Although Soviet forces throughout central Russia were immeasurably stronger now, the medical trains operated close to the front lines, and were never safe from aerial attack. Elena was tending wounded when a flight of German fighters appeared. They dived to strafe, and the train burst into flame. Amid the cries for help and the shrieks of the newly wounded, she and other nurses frantically struggled to get the men to safety in the ditches along the tracks. Elena was in the burning car when the planes returned and opened fire again. A shell fragment struck her in the face.

For months she lay near death; when she started to improve, doctors predicted she would lose her sight within eighteen months. Miraculously, Elena recovered. By the spring of 1945, she was back with a front-line medical team and rolled into Potsdam with the Soviet cohort as the Third Reich collapsed. She even remembered meeting some GIs at a series of dances the Americans organized in the first few weeks after the defeat of Germany—when the two great powers were still on speaking terms. "I wasn't a usual Soviet person," she said once, "because I already knew many foreigners from the years of life in the Comintern." Her meetings with the Americans contributed to this special feeling of internationalism and psychological contact with the world outside the USSR.

After the war, she spent a long time in a naval hospital being treated for her eyesight, the start of a lifelong fight to save her vision. She finally was mustered out of the service as a war invalid, Class II, entitling her to a pension and preferential medical care, vacation sanitariums, and other benefits. Unlike her younger brother, who became a career naval officer, Elena craved civilian life and humanitarian work. She entered medical school and looked forward to the new post-war country they would build.

"Under Stalin, everything was understood. It was a different world from the world of today. It was fully understood that to be openly against the system was impossible. But more than that, at the front, I always had the sense that, if we won the war, we wouldn't live this way. Emancipation would come. This was a widespread feeling, especially among young officers. Like me, these officers had joined the army after high school or one or two years at university. These were the people who waged the war, not the generals. These young officers who fought with the soldiers—these were the people who strategically decided the war. Our lieutenants were our real heroes, not the generals. And among these people, my army friends, this sense was very strong. It showed in even small things.

"I sat one day mending my stockings. We were in a kind of railroad car; everyone was sitting around talking. And one young guy said, "When the war ends, you won't have to do that kind of work.'

"I answered: 'So quickly?'

" 'Well, not right away of course, but soon.'

"Yes, the war will end, I thought. We'll win after all. Fascism won't exist. . . . And look now: thirty-seven more years of Soviet fascism. And so the question arises, a very strange question for me: should we really have won the war after all? We had to. We had to drive the Fascists out. But to this day, I keep asking myself the question—should we have won? I don't know. Our victory gave substance to this fraud of a patriotic upbringing. Since now we have won."

9

Elena Bonner
and the State

*The Russians are . . . perfectly normal. . . .
They want a rug and they want to save up for
a car.*

—ELENA BONNER

I

In May 1954, Elena Bonner received a telegram from Anastas
Mikoyan, inviting her to meet with him in Moscow. Elena was a
pediatrician in Leningrad now, a married woman of 31, with a doctor
husband, Ivan Semenov, and 3-year-old daughter, Tanya. Although
Stalin had died more than a year earlier, and his secret police chief,
Lavrenti Beria, had been executed, bringing an end to the Terror,
millions of Russians remained in slave labor camps or in exile com-
munities across the country. Elena's mother was still in exile for the
crime of being the wife of an enemy of the people; the mass amnesty
and rehabilitation were still two years off.

Curious to see what her father's old friend wanted after sixteen
years of stony silence, Elena went down to the capital. Spring had
come to Moscow, softening its decrepit grays and browns with new
foliage. Lilacs bloomed in the parks and byways.

The Razina Street address where Elena was to meet Mikoyan was
in the Kitaiski Gorod, or Chinese City section of old Moscow east
of the Kremlin. This was one of the oldest lanes in the city, a narrow
curve of cobble that led east from St. Basil's Church in the middle

of Red Square down a steep hill to the bottom of Nogina Square, the ancient depression below the fortress walls where the city's Jews established their main synagogue and where the Communist party's Central Committee had its headquarters. Not far away stood the former club where, for decades before Stalin's rise, Moscow's Armenian community met to sing, dance, and declaim their national poetry through long nights of ethnic joy. Stalin had destroyed the club in his drive to extirpate national identities. The neighborhood was full of memories—most of the recent ones unpleasant. Even the Georgians had suffered under the dictator. The only solace (as they told us in Tbilisi a generation after the tyrant's death) was that he had killed more of the hated Great Russians than of his own countrymen.

By 1954, Mikoyan had been in leadership positions for nearly thirty years. He had been a member of the Politburo for nineteen years, was head of foreign trade for the USSR, and was deeply involved in supporting Khrushchev in his behind-the-scenes struggle with Georgyi Malenkov for Kremlin supremacy. At 58, "Antanas," as close friends affectionately called him, was a polished world traveler whose survival had brought him a remarkable reputation as a wily tactician with Westernized ways. Moscow abounded with Mikoyan tales that somehow missed what must have been the ruthless side of his personality. Few Russians we talked with later seemed to remember that the conspirators who ousted Khrushchev in 1964 had sent Mikoyan down to the leader's sumptuous Black Sea vacation compound to fetch the leader back to Moscow where he would be denounced and thrown from power. Instead, most people remembered the innocuous fable that Mikoyan had founded the Soviet ice cream industry after being introduced to it during an early trip to the United States. Upon his return to Russia, Mikoyan was said to have convinced Stalin that, even though ice cream was a sinful capitalist invention, this was less important than the fact that it could be made in a way that used milk otherwise unfit for consumption. By the late 1970s you could order any flavor of Soviet ice cream you wanted—as long as it was vanilla. And as any patriotic Russian would tell you, firm in his ignorance of Howard Johnson's twenty-eight flavors and related glories of bourgeois decadence, "Ours is really tastier than yours. Try some, and surely you'll agree!"

When Elena was ushered into Mikoyan's office, the powerful and practiced survivor stood, wrapped her in a huge embrace, and kissed her warmly. Always a smooth dresser, he looked positively svelte in contrast to the unkempt, baggy-suited Russians who peopled the place. As they embraced, Elena was surprised to see how much younger than his 58 years he looked. She peered at him closely and believed she had found the answer: he seemed to have dyed his hair.

Mikoyan began reminiscing about his life with Georgyi Alikhanov. As the conversation developed, Elena realized with a surge of emotion that the new regime was exploring ways to rehabilitate Stalin's victims. Here was a remarkable opportunity. But there also was something peculiar about the man's interest in the fate of her father. Hadn't Mikoyan lived near the pinnacle long enough to extract the information he needed from the leadership archives? After all, Elena's father was not some obscure *muzhik*, peasant, revolutionary, but an important figure in the foundation of the state. It should have been relatively simple for Mikoyan to trace the truth. Nevertheless, he now wanted to learn from Elena exactly how her father had died. But she, a teenager away at school when her father was taken, could be of no help. She knew only that Papa apparently had been executed in Lefortovo shortly after he was arrested—and even Mikoyan knew that much.

He looked at her gravely. "I want you to know that we weren't able to do anything to help," he said. "We were powerless." Should she admire or despise him? Was this how he had survived—by avoiding blame? The conversation wandered to less painful topics, then turned to her present situation. She explained the demands made by family and profession and the harsh living conditions in Leningrad, which were not helped by the low pay she was earning.

"How much would that be?" he asked in a solicitous tone.

"Six hundred rubles a month."

"What!" Mikoyan exclaimed in shocked surprise. "I don't understand. Why so little?"

It was Elena's turn to be shocked. "Antanas, all doctors receive that!" How could a member of the Politburo not know something like this? His ignorance of everyday life in his own country stunned her. The Soviet leadership was as out of touch with Soviet reality as the czars had been. Where could such monumental indifference lead the country in the years to come? For starters, she concluded that the state now had little use for pediatrics—the emphasis, as always, was on industrial resources and rebuilding the country's productive capacities. But what of the campaigns against infant mortality that her mother had led twenty years earlier? Elena's analysis of the Kremlin's interest in matters of public health was remarkably similar to the views that Anatoli Koryagin was to offer about psychiatry so many years later.

After this inconclusive and awkward encounter, Mikoyan continued to meet with Elena periodically over the next decade to check on her life and offer help when it was needed. In time, as he aged and her activism took shape, the distance between them grew and she assumed he was displeased with her. But despite their increasing political differences, Mikoyan's emotional tie to her family continued. More than once, he intervened to help the daughter of his old comrade.

In the summer of 1965, for example, Elena's eyesight took a turn for the worse. An operation was necessary to preserve her vision, but in the entire country only one man could perform it, a Professor Krasnov. Elena arranged a consultation with Krasnov, who warned her that she must be operated on very soon. A few days might mean the difference between vision and blindness. However, he couldn't help her, Krasnov briskly informed her. He only performed surgery in the Kremlin clinic for the leaders and their families—and it would take her two years to finagle entrance to that most privileged hospital. She would have to find someone else to do the delicate operation, and he had no suggestions. Distraught, Elena telephoned the dismal news to her mother and then returned to her pediatric job.

Two hours later, Ruf called back. "A Kremlin car will pick you up today. Everything is arranged." Elena was furious at the prospect of special favors. But when a Kremlin car arrived that night, she reluctantly agreed to go. Krasnov operated on her the next day, and her sight was saved. Ruf had called Mikoyan and he had informed the Kremlin hospital watchdogs that surgery must be performed to save the eyesight of his "niece."

II

FOR Elena, life in Leningrad as a working mother was filled with numerous demands and rewards. But like millions of her countrymen, Elena already had survived a murderous purge and a murderous war and, in truth, she found post-war Russia a trifle dull when measured against the adventures to which she had become accustomed. She hungered for genuine humane service. She also was eager to see something more of the mysterious world beyond Soviet territory than what was afforded in the one tantalizing episode in Potsdam a decade earlier.

An opportunity unexpectedly presented itself from an unlikely place: Iraq. There, the pro-Western and British-dominated monarchy was ousted in 1958 and replaced by a self-proclaimed republic. Always quick to seek leverage in the rapidly changing post-war mosaic of emerging Arab nationalism, the Kremlin launched economic and humanitarian aid programs to strengthen the new leadership of Abdul Karim Kassem. As Khrushchev recollected, "Our support of the Iraqi revolution under the leadership of Kassem further enhanced our prestige in the Arab world."[*]

Elena went to Baghdad as part of a medical team of twenty-six members. Not surprising in one so dedicated to the notion of public service, her views on the intent of the mission did not conform with those of Khrushchev: "We weren't furthering Soviet power in any way," she said. "Soviet power didn't do anything to cause a change in the government of Iraq."

Elena's two years in Iraq delivered surprises about foreign reality, and about her own countrymen as well. Perhaps the most puzzling aspect for a person who had lived under Soviet conditions was the jarring way in which the contradictions of Iraqi society were so openly revealed. The apparent jumble of lives in Baghdad was very different from the carefully maintained illusion of uniformity that the regime at home had achieved. In Moscow, privilege and wealth surely existed, but were carefully concealed from the masses. Elena's awareness of the opulent life of Soviet leaders came chiefly through her contact with benefactor Mikoyan.

"I can't say that Iraq was the West; it really was eastern. But it was very different. I was amazed by the beggars and the wealthy, by the freedom and the lack of rights. Both sides existed there, but in general it seemed to me that, despite the illiteracy and poverty, much culture existed there as well. It was a discovery for me."

Her eagerness to penetrate and understand the exotic Middle East and her openness to the life she found there set her aside from her colleagues.

[*]*Khrushchev Remembers*, p. 385.

"The Levant astounded me, rich and peaceful. We traveled there to swim when we had three free days. A bit like the bourgeois, we took a room in a hotel, walked about on the beach. But my astonishment in general was of another sort. These sacrifices of revolution —the poor, the Kurds (who continued fighting against the new government), an unending war, demonstrations, assassination attempts—these all were enthusiasms of the Soviet Union. This was the time when Khrushchev went to the West and, in Iraq, lots and lots of children were named Khrushchev. Not Saliat, not Abdul, but Khrushchev. All the boys were Khrushchevs. What enthusiasm for the Soviet Union! This was peculiar. Somehow, it became clear to me that, once again, I was seeing theater. So there was lots that was good and lots that was bad there, but the lighting was all the same —theatrical, false.

"The attitude of Soviet officials also astonished me. I'm not speaking now of the twenty doctors—doctors after all are a special caste, although they, too, can be very different one from another. There were lots of Soviet officials there, and their relationship to the Arabs, to the Iraqis, indicated no understanding or internationalism of a normal sort. They behaved worse than colonialists in Kipling's time. That one of these *chinovniki*, senior bureaucrats, could say such rude things to our faces about some Arab or dark-skinned person! It was all irrational to me; these insults were worse than swear words. I felt it strongly, as I always felt about anti-Semitism here—not for myself, but generally that it was awful that humans behaved so insultingly. The effect probably was greater on me because I grew up in Comintern, in conditions of real internationalism."

Upon her return to Russia two years later, as she passed through passport control and customs searches, Elena was concerned to find that the Green Hats, the KGB border guards, treated the physicians as if they were criminals trying to smuggle contraband. Where was their sense of achievement about the humanitarian experimental society? As the days passed, she found herself sinking into depression, a phenomenon that repeated itself whenever she returned from travel abroad. Whatever joy she may have felt about the homecoming was dissipated by the aura of suspicion that pervaded life in Russia. "I've gone abroad many times, and each time I come back, I feel depressed. Each time I feel that I need medication to get me out of my depressed state. It's like a distinct fall in barometric pressure.

"I arrive, leave the airport, and, very soon, travel somewhere on the elektrichka and go out on the train platform to have a smoke. Without fail, some Russian citizen, some old gal, comes up to me to say, 'What are you doing smoking?' They just have to say something to me. There I am, standing quietly on the platform, not bothering anyone, and I think to myself, 'Why does it have to be like this in our country?' In every other country in the world, a fellow can smoke or not smoke—it doesn't matter to the next guy. A fellow can sleep or not sleep with or without whomever he wishes. But in our country, no! Everyone—not necessarily the KGB, not the police, but we ourselves—butts into everybody else's business . . . the Great Russian People! It's really interesting to me to know if this was the way it was before the Revolution, or if it's just nowadays that we are raised with the sense of social obligation to keep track of everyone else."

Russians like to tell foreigners that there is no Russian word for "privacy." Elena offered another way of describing the phenomenon: "I'll tell you a proverb from the eighteenth century: 'My neighbor's cow has just taken a deep breath.' "

Many of Elena's friends in pre-war Leningrad had been poets and authors and she had always harbored an interest in writing. She was now inspired to take up the pen and recount her observations and adventures in Iraq. But when she began submitting her work to various Soviet publications, Elena experienced another aspect of Soviet literary life: state censors were as ready to butt in as anyone else. They took a magnifying glass to every sentence. An essay, "Notes of a Doctor," was published in the Leningrad literary journal, *Neva*, only after heavy censorship. While telling of her duties and the demands of teaching and healing in a Third World setting, she also had described the nature of the religious strife between Shi'ite and Sunni Moslems. But the censors' attitude was that "such matters are not the business of a Soviet physician." The paragraphs landed in the wastebasket. Finding a new outlet for her energies, she soon was a regular contributor to the national youth magazine, *Yunost*. There were short stories, brief accounts of life abroad, and helpful tales of people dealing with their problems. Although Elena was not to know of it for years, one of her most enthusiastic readers was a young Buryat-Russian girl named Yelizaveta Alexeyeva.

Elena's move toward writing coincided with the sudden emergence in the late 1950s of a new generation of Soviet writers, poets, and artists. After decades of conformity under Stalin, the country was stirring with hope and experimental daring as the Khrushchev Thaw took hold and long-repressed creative urges came to life. Yevgeny Yevtushenko, Bella Akhmadulina, Andrei Voznesensky, Bulat Okudzhava, and others of the Youth Movement gave readings in Leningrad to packed houses and concert halls. Every new issue of *Novy Mir*, New World, promised new sensations. The literary awakening continued into the 1960s, bringing young novelists and short-story writers like Vasili Aksyonov and Vladimir Voinovich to prominence. Aksyonov in particular struck a chord in disaffected Soviet youth with his gritty tales of life on the assembly lines and in the jerry-built concrete walk-ups of the new cities. They were derisively called "Khrushchev houses"—badly prefabricated apartment houses of no more than five stories to circumvent a widely heralded law that required elevators in every building of six floors or more.

The sense of pushing out the narrow limits of what the state would accept as legitimate self-expression continued to grow. A Picasso exhibit ignited Leningrad's intelligentsia with its genius. Russians fought to get into the exhibit hall, stayed for hours, fought to stay after the hall closed, and then fought with each other over what it was supposed to mean. Although the artists were generally a decade younger than Elena, making her feel at the outer limits of the generation, she identified completely with their aspirations. "It seemed to me that other generations would never have related in the same way," she mused.

One aspect of the Thaw included an attempt to document Stalin's crimes—a massive effort. Commissions were set up to probe into whatever records could be found of trials, hearings, and illegal charges. During this period, Elena was sent to Armenia to seek information about her father's early party career, which had been suppressed during the Terror. She spent several painful months at the party archives in Yerevan, the capital, poring over long-hidden records. When the research was finished, she realized she could not bear the strain of writing about her papa. "It would simply be too hard." Instead, she chose to write an account of another figure of the earlier era, a man named Karganov. His fate had been similar to her father's; the paths of many of the early Bolsheviks had led to the same destination—Stalin's firing squads.

Elena could not prevent herself from thinking that "we were somehow responsible for what our parents had done and what had been done to them. We wanted to defend them, and I thought it would be easier to do this through the party—to correct the record and make things better." Inexplicable as it may seem to an outsider, this reasoning led her to join the party.

Meanwhile, Elena's marriage to Ivan Semenov had begun to turn sour. When their son Alyosha contracted rheumatic fever in 1962, she moved to Moscow with the children in search of better medical care and a new life.

During the Thaw, the capital was a feast for the intellectually freewheeling Bonner family. Soon Elena was drawn from the edge of the scene into the midst of the artistic and political ferment. When Khrushchev's dismissal from power was announced in October 1964, Elena "took it as a very serious thing." She kept Tanya home from school, fearing that there might be demonstrations or disorders in support of the fallen leader. But the capital was mired in indifference. "I thought it couldn't be possible for the country to be so dead, but it was. Internal conditions for us are always somewhere between hope and hopelessness!

"Now I think our Khrushchev generally was a weak man with good points, but he couldn't manage. They removed him quickly; seven years [1957–64] is a short time in our stable sort of system. Then came these people. I generally don't understand governmental affairs. Brezhnev seemed to me such an unimportant figure. I thought he was only temporary. And how many years has it been already? Almost like Stalin! When Khrushchev fell I thought: "That's our theater again.' The next day in the newspapers, not a bit of truth: 'voluntarism, blah, blah, blah.' Just twaddle. Not a bit of truth. For all that Secret Speech at the 20th Party Congress, we knew nothing about Khrushchev. It's not for nothing that this anecdote exists:

" 'Grandma, was Lenin good?'

" 'Good.'

" 'And Stalin—good?'

" 'Bad.'

" 'And Khrushchev—good?'

" 'Bad.'

" 'And Brezhnev—good?'

" 'He'll die soon and we'll find out!'

"And that's it. He'll die and we'll find out. Theater . . . nothing but theater."

III

WHEN the 1965–66 Sinyavsky–Daniel persecution signaled the new orthodoxy of the Brezhnev leadership and literary and political dissent moved into samizdat, Elena made the transition as well. Before long, she and others were spending their nights secretly reading suppressed works, and then passing them on to friends. The movement was giving birth to itself. As repressions spread, with searches, threats, and jailings, a group of Moscow intellectuals began keeping an archive of the regime's actions. Elena was drawn into this unprecedented effort and, in 1968, the "Chronicle of Current Events" was launched. From the beginning, this journal aimed to describe in a low-key, dispassionate way all human rights matters throughout the country. Although the samizdat phenomenon had its roots in the staunch anti-Soviet nationalist movement of Catholic Lithuania, the Moscow-based Chronicle established a standard of reliable, nonpolemical news gathering that found an audience abroad. The Chronicle reported arrests, trials, imprisonments, appeals, medical abuses, religious repression, hunger strikes, forced breakups of families, exiles, and beatings. As the years passed, smuggling of the Chronicle to the West continued despite the regime's efforts to extinguish it. The Chronicle's painstakingly assembled issues slowly sharpened foreign understanding of the struggle for individual rights in the Soviet Union and the regime's tactics in combating the activists.

Elena later became active in the effort to produce and distribute the journal. "The Chronicle appeared and I was one of the circle of people who read it, then I became one of the people who, as [underground troubadour Alexander] Galich sang, 'Erika is keeping four copies' [a pun on a typewriter brand name]. Then there were more copies, and then I began to keep many copies here. At first, I only read the writings of others and then I started to write reports myself . . . and so forth. Among my friends, there were many who were a lot more active than I."

The Chronicle's debut coincided with the Soviet invasion of Czechoslovakia, an event that stunned the world. The invasion also triggered a series of public protests by activists in Moscow and elsewhere that drew wide foreign press coverage. The drama and meaning of these demonstrations were enhanced in the United States and Britain when it was revealed that one of the activists was

Pavel Litvinov, grandson of Maksim Litvinov. Litvinov, a Jew, had been Stalin's commissar of foreign affairs throughout the 1930s until his dismissal prior to Stalin's signing of the Non-Aggression Pact with Hitler in 1939. Maksim Litvinov had later served as Soviet ambassador to America during World War II. His ties to Britain were familial: his wife, Ivy, an accomplished short-story writer whose work appeared in the *New Yorker*, was English.

But several months before the August 1968 invasion of Czecho-slovakia, Elena was given permission to travel to France to visit some maternal relatives. In Paris, she watched with amazement as French youth rose up against their elders in the summer upheavals that eventually sent de Gaulle into retirement. After the dulling mass conformity of her own society, she felt herself reeling in the face of the open contentiousness and contumely. The turmoil between the generations in France seemed to her, at first, to swamp the City of Light itself.

"I arrived in Paris when there was dirt everywhere. It was June and slogans were still up all over the Sorbonne. In some regions, city blocks were breast-deep in trash." Public services were bogged down and the polemics of protest rang in the streets.

Through her relatives, she began meeting some of the well-to-do French whose handsome, privileged children seemed dedicated to the cause of a new order. But as she learned more, Elena began to feel that these suave young Frenchmen and their companions were in fact romancing each other with furious talk of revolution that carried little real conviction. Among Elena's relatives was a young Parisian woman who "owned an elegant castle and drove a fancy car, but went around in clothing so ragged that I thought I should buy her a dress. But then, I understood this was a way of life: a chateau, a car, and torn jeans." She came to view their brave speeches and revolutionary plotting as deluded play-acting. The upheavals in France reminded her sharply of the cynicism of Soviet life where people could adopt a role to suit their needs.

"This happens in the [Soviet] emigration. Ten dissidents leave here, and [miraculously] a hundred arrive in the West. They talk confidently about the human rights movement, very knowledge-ably, but here in Moscow they don't take part in the movement at all. Lots of Soviets go abroad on business trips, or go as official tourists, artists, and so forth. Here they are the archetypal confor-mists because the one thing that matters to them is the right to travel.

And when they get to the West, they declare: 'I left because I didn't have artistic freedom,' though the same people don't talk about freedom here. Or they say, 'I didn't have religious freedom, or ... or ... or. ...' 1968 in France made the same sort of impression on me—they were like chameleons who had easily changed their colors. But it was all very superficial; they were the same bourgeoisie. Those girls in their torn jeans would never give up their castles. They knew that in ten years they would inherit the castles and they would want to use them. But all the same, these people were thrilled with the revolution."

When the Warsaw Pact crushed the Czech Spring in August, Elena watched the events for hours on French television. At first, she was convinced that there would be mass demonstrations in Russia against the Brezhnev leadership; once again, she was astonished and sick at heart that nothing occurred. "From the 22nd of August, it was as if I were not alive. I felt as though it couldn't be true, as though mankind had to hit its head against a wall it was so awful. And then I saw how people of the French left and the not very far left reacted. There was a certain disenchantment with [their own] revolution, and a sincere sorrow for the Czechs. Czechoslovakia cured me forever of any revolutionary romanticism. What was the real reason we went into Czechoslovakia with tanks? Not, as we said, because of threats that the West Germans might go in themselves. No. The reason was freedom of speech; that's the only reason we went in with tanks."

At the end of September, Elena returned to Moscow to find much of the Soviet intelligentsia in deep depression. Warsaw Pact tanks in Prague had dispelled their remaining illusions about greater freedoms. The Brezhnev doctrine of intervention to protect "socialist gains" in Eastern Europe guaranteed trouble for activists at home. Despite arrests, however, an extraordinary string of public protests continued in the aftermath of the Czech crisis. Many friends of Pavel Litvinov publicly supported him. Vladimir Bukovsky, Alexander Ginsberg, Yuri Orlov, and dozens of other activists raised their voices. When Soviet Army general Petro Grigorenko, a Ukrainian patriot and increasingly active spokesman for dispossessed Crimean Tatars, was arrested in May 1969 in the Central Asian capital of Tashkent, dozens of Tatars demonstrated there and in Moscow. Grigorenko was a much-decorated hero of World War II, with a staunch and passionate character. His advocacy further mobilized the disaffected intelligentsia against the regime.

Meanwhile, the anxiety of Soviet Jews over their own fate and that of Israel had escalated since the 1967 six-day Arab–Israeli war. Although the USSR had been the first major power to recognize the state of Israel in 1948, Moscow had armed the Arabs and twice encouraged its clients to make war on Israel. Soviet Jews saw the 1967 conflict as a David vs. Goliath contest and, for the first time in their lives, many openly identified with the embattled Jewish homeland. Moscow broke diplomatic relations with Israel and official anti-Semitism inside the country burgeoned in the aftermath of Israel's victory. The practice increased of denying Jews faculty positions and top-level jobs for which they were qualified. University doors were closed to more and more Jewish children, forcing them into lower-ranked institutes. Facing such an uncertain future, the impulse to emigrate took grip. But in the Soviet Union, a nation of guarded borders, voluntary emigration does not exist. As the pressure to find a route out of the USSR rose, a small group of conspirators began plotting how to hijack a plane and flee the country.

On June 15, 1970, a small Aeroflot liner was boarding for a regional flight from Smolny Airport, Leningrad. Suddenly the KGB appeared and seized a dozen passengers waiting in the line. On the same day, there were other arrests in Kharkov, Riga, and Leningrad itself. This was the Leningrad hijacking plot, an activist plan to hijack a plane to Sweden to dramatize the bar to Jewish emigration.

A principal figure in the plot was Eduard (Edik) Kuznetsov, a volatile and charismatic man who had spent most of the 1960s in prison for organizing poetry readings in Mayakovsky Square. Elena Bonner had made his acquaintance and had sent him books during one of his prison terms (a practice since sharply restricted). When Kuznetsov was paroled to a town outside Moscow, he would slip into the capital and visit the Bonners, an additional presence in their already crowded flat. "The life in our apartment then would be incomprehensible to Americans," Elena said. "Alyosha and I lived in the front bedroom. In the next room, Mama and Tanya, and in the kitchen there was forever someone else. Edik might come; he had to spend the night secretly. I'd put up a cot in my room, and we'd all lie down to bed, each with his own book. I was reading something, there next to me was Lyosha reading Victor Hugo on the death penalty, and Edik over there, reading Nabokov.

"Lyosha would say, 'Edik, listen to this,' and he read out loud and, like any 13-year-old boy, was very upset about the death penalty, problems of morality, human sympathy, unhappiness. Edik would say, 'Lyosha, stop, I'm not interested in the problem of the death penalty.' And after the hijacking attempt, the death penalty hung over Kuznetsov."

Now, acting on instinct, Elena flew to Smolny Airport and traded a pack of American cigarettes for information from an airport baggage handler who had witnessed the incident. The next day from Moscow she called Western correspondents with further details. Later, when Kuznetsov's ailing mother was unable to help organize a defense for him, Elena shouldered the burden. Police investigators soon came to believe she was his aunt. Eventually, Elena attended his trial and provided a detailed transcript from memory, as the activists always tried to do at political trials.

"If the affair was shut up, these people would simply perish," she said. "It was purely this concrete wish to help them." Even though she helped Kuznetsov, Elena faulted him for leading younger, naive activists into the plot. She believed that, as a camp veteran, Kuznetsov was far more savvy about the dangers of massive state retaliation and should have steered the other conspirators away from it. "He's responsible for the fact that they went to jail. To this day, I consider it inadmissible what happened to these people." Despite her anger, she helped Kuznetsov. How could she explain this?

"There's this irrational reflex, and I can't say that I always act just the way I say. Say some guy comes running down the street and people are running after him and catch him. I automatically forget that perhaps this guy stole someone's purse. I fear that they'll catch him, and beat or kill him, and I'm on his side. It's quite natural, although if I saw him stealing the purse and could get him, I'd punch him in the face."

Her thoughts turned to the general question of imprisonment. "The most I want from our government is political amnesty. What our people want and don't want doesn't matter to me. I'm also a member of this people, according to my biography. I went to war together with our people; I spent four years in the trenches with them. Let the people themselves figure out what they need. I only need to see these people freed. I have always said that, as soon as political amnesty is granted, I will sit back and rejoice. That's all.

"My whole life, I have helped people in prison, from 1937 or 1938 right on. When Edik was arrested, that was only the first official time. But I had many friends who were dissenters. They always came to me; all these labor camp veterans were sent here by friends. I would make calls for them and try to help in other ways. I leave world questions and philosophy to others. Material help is what I can offer."

IV

IN the autumn of 1970, Elena made the trip to Kaluga that changed her life. Recalling the dizziness that seemed to envelop her and Sakharov as they fell in love, she told how they once had gone to the central telegraph office on Gorky Street to send telegrams to Brezhnev supporting endangered dissident friends. To their acute embarrassment, one of the telegraph clerks in the cavernous, noisy building mistook them for husband and wife. "But imagine," Elena declared with a snort of enjoyment, "it turned out to be a forecast from Central Telegraph!" On another occasion, she was late for a group meeting that included Sakharov and, when she arrived, Andrei Tverdokhlebov* demanded good-naturedly, "Elena, why did you disrupt us by coming so late? Andrei Dmitrich has done nothing but look out the window the whole time!"

To everyone's delight, Sakharov turned bright red.

Not long after, they married, an event that many of their friends had considered a foregone conclusion—ever since Kaluga. The marriage joined two of the most tireless activists in the Soviet Union. Throughout the 1970s, Elena and Andrei Dmitrievich worked at the center of Soviet political dissent. As circumstances and inclination dictated, separately or together, they composed and signed petitions, letters, and protests and issued public statements on behalf of scores of activists, as well as numerous groups of abused, repressed, or persecuted citizens. They attended political trials, remonstrated with the police, denounced the KGB, and made exhausting journeys to remote labor camps, prisons, courtrooms, and exile villages. In aid of dozens of incarcerated activists, they collected and distributed food, clothing, medical supplies, and books.

In 1973, Elena was interrogated four times by the KGB, an ordeal

---

*Co-founder that year with Sakharov and Valeri Chalidze of the Moscow Committee for Human Rights, Tverdokhlebov was imprisoned in 1975, and later left the USSR.

that left her drained and apprehensive about the future for herself and Sakharov. The questioning focused on her role in the smuggling of Kuznetsov's prison diaries out to the West. Elena accepted responsibility but, in an attempt to shield others, stonewalled the KGB on all other questions.

Meanwhile, she had contracted glaucoma. When Soviet physicians were unable to treat her properly, she asked for permission to go to Italy for treatment. Emigration authorities ignored her request. She and Sakharov pondered what to do. Their discussions centered on a hunger strike and they made preparations by laying in a large supply of Borzhomi mineral water on which they would subsist if they were forced to fast. At the last minute, the authorities backed down. Elena was allowed to travel to Italy, where doctors operated and told her she must return in two years for additional treatment. With time still remaining on her exit visa, she traveled to Oslo to accept Sakharov's Nobel Peace Prize and deliver his Nobel Lecture in December 1975. The address marked the apogee of international attention to Sakharov's views.

Calling the speech "Peace, Progress, and Human Rights," a deliberate echo of his first and most famous essay of seven years before, Sakharov opened by declaring his conviction that "international trust, mutual understanding, disarmament, and international security are inconceivable without an open society with freedom of information, freedom of conscience, the right to publish, and the right to travel and choose the country in which one wishes to live." He rejected Marxist dialectics, and affirmed his belief in "the original and decisive significance of civic and political rights in shaping the destiny of mankind."

He said that nuclear weapons confront mankind with the supreme danger of total annihilation, exacerbated by the political and economic polarization of the world into camps of have and have-not nations, with the superpowers vying for influence. Faced with a hostile world largely of their own making, the great powers had to comprehend that their only sane path was disarmament. And that hinged on forging trust between the superpowers beyond anything so far imagined. Sakharov counseled continued détente and, as the starting point for genuine trust, outlined an agenda of unprecedented mutual disclosures by Moscow and Washington of their strategic arsenals and deployments. He renewed his view that the democratization of the Soviet system was essential to world peace, and he called for an amnesty of all Soviet political prisoners. Sa-kharov then named one hundred thirty prisoners of conscience "known to me" and begged forgiveness from those he had not mentioned.

"Every single name, mentioned as well as unmentioned, repre-sents a hard and heroic destiny, years of suffering, years of strug-gling for human dignity." In order to be worthy of the judgment of the universe, he declared, all mankind must take up the struggle for human dignity: "We should not minimize our sacred endeavors in this world, where, like faint glimmers in the dark, we have emerged for a moment from the nothingness of dark unconscious-ness into a material existence. We must make good the demands of reason and create a life worthy of ourselves and of the goals we only dimly perceive."*

Five years later, the woman who had delivered Sakharov's vault-ing call to conscience and action sat in the study of her Moscow apartment and organized private care packages of food and books for friends in Poland. It was December 1980 and, as the national political crisis over Solidarity deepened, food lines in Poland had lengthened. She informed us matter-of-factly that, in addition to small numbers of books, the Poles and Soviet authorities allowed private care packages of up to two kilograms of sugar, two of rice, and two of cereals to be sent monthly without customs duty.

On this dark, blustery afternoon, Elena sat cross-legged on the wide daybed. With her hair gathered into its usual bun, an old brownish-gray wool shawl pulled around her shoulders, and a slow-burning filter-tipped "Capitol" brand cigarette sending its acrid smoke curling across her swarthy features, she looked like an Indian squaw.

"We [Soviets] aren't in the habit of sending personal aid to for-eigners in trouble," she said as she and Lisa Alexeyeva sorted through small piles of books in the study. "The state does such things here, and it is not a personal tradition with us." In this case, however, the intended recipients were Polish friends of Elena's mother who had been imprisoned in the Magadan camps during the Terror. "Now we've come full circle," she said. "Exile again for us."

She began ruminating anew on the events of her life. "All my childhood and youth, I was a real Soviet. No one forced me to join

*Alarm and Hope, pp. 4–18.

the army; I joined up myself. No one forced me to build kolkhoz associations [during the post-war reconstruction]—Tanya was still a nursing infant and I a student. I need not have gone. But I went, of my own accord! I worked many years. I really tried. In the medical newspaper, I wrote about my own problems in medical organization. Some of these articles caused a stir, gave rise to major study. This was all a personal attempt to somehow make this country and this government better—to improve this socialism.

"I was not an anti-Soviet person. And I'm not anti-Soviet now. Soviet power means nothing to me. When some correspondent asks me how I feel about the 26th Party Congress, I don't feel anything about it. It doesn't affect me. It's less interesting to me than the moon. Why must I proceed from an ideology when I don't have one? Concrete human concerns can and must move me, or I will be a corpse.

"The Social Revolutionaries [SRs] had a slogan: 'You must fight for your rights.' I liked this slogan a great deal even as a young girl, when SRs and Mensheviks came to visit grandmother. And I liked the SRs best of all. I was still a child, only 10 years old. What a romantic! How many years of my life I gave to Soviet power!

"Further, don't think I was angry with the government because my mother and father were arrested. But that did result in a kind of split point of view that remains somewhere in my soul. After all, Papa died in prison—that remains with me always, in my dreams, somewhere on the edge of dreams. . . . But along with that, I also felt for a long time the desire to straighten out the Soviet system. That was my wish. For a long time, even after I saw Iraq, after I saw the capitalist world, I thought that our world was correct, it just needed straightening out. . . . It was as though there were two impulses within me: the knowledge that my father had helped to set up this system which had turned out badly, and that I was responsible for what my father had done and I should correct it. This was all a variation on revolutionary romanticism.

"I'm not an original thinker or philosopher. That's outside my sphere of interest and my intellectual possibilities. [But] above all, I am for a moral beginning for our human rights movement. That's the one reality we have—for truth.

"Of course, our society is very cynical. One day at the polyclinic of the Academy of Sciences, I met a woman, the wife of an academic. Basically, I know little of these people and have seldom spent time in those circles. But I happened to have known this woman since childhood. She was the daughter of a writer and lived in an apartment house filled with writers, where I spent time off and on. And she started to talk to me in whispers on the staircase at the polyclinic: 'How upset we all are! My husband nearly had a heart attack when he heard about the exile of Sakharov. We feel great sympathy for you.'

"And I said to her, 'There's an excellent cure for your secret suffering and for that heart attack. It is for your husband to write a letter—I can dictate the essence for you—that he's opposed to Sakharov's exile. The heart attack will clear up immediately. It's true. That's the only way to stop worrying!' "

Elena gave a snort of derision. "There's her husband, an intelligent scientist. There's [another] physicist who's often here. He tells me how they're always asking him in whispers at conferences and academy meetings, 'How's Andrei Dmitrich? How are things in Gorky?' 'Oh, how we worry about him!' Et cetera. Of course, people are cynical. If these were simple people, then perhaps a tenth or a half of them would believe what's said on TV. But of six hundred academics, no one believes anything he hears, not anything. Or else they are moral cretins. But they are not cretins, they are intelligent people, much brighter than me, brighter some than Sakharov perhaps.

"Sakharov possesses a spiritual quality of an extremely rare sort, a spiritual honesty which is entirely his own. In this lies his special nature. When he was involved in atomic bomb work, his conscience began to torture him with the idea that this work was not right. But it was not Sakharov alone who made the hydrogen bomb. Two-thirds of the Academy was involved in that work. One hundred out of two hundred worked on one or another atomic bomb. Does that mean that not one of them had a conscience? Not at all!

"But they aren't honest. Sakharov doesn't let his conscience weigh him down; he doesn't let it threaten him. He believes that only by speaking the truth can one save the world. And what he believes, he says.

"In every way, Sakharov is above reproach, so blameless that it's even amusing. He has never been a drinker; he never in his life had a mistress. He's just that breed of man—virtuous. Once upon a time, there was such a group of Russian aristocratic intelligentsia, and he's a descendant of that small group. He's not of that group of Russian intellectuals who harbored anti-Semitism in their souls. He's of an entirely special category."

By way of illustrating this difference, Elena said, "It's not true that the heart of the Russian people is with the Poles. I was standing in line at the milk store in Gorky not long ago. The milk line included many old men, pensioners waiting for the milk to be delivered to the store. Two of them standing ahead of me started talking about Poland. [They were] septuagenarians, but an energetic pair. By their language, they were working-class people. Workers on pension, earning maybe one hundred twenty rubles a month, well-dressed by Soviet standards.

"One said to the other, 'Those Poles go on striking and striking and we have to feed them.' That's how the average Soviet thinks.

"In their hearts, the Russian people don't think about the Poles, they think about where to buy a rug. A rug. The Russians are a perfectly normal nation. They want a rug and they want to save up for a car."

"And do they want law and order?" I asked.

"They do want law and order," Elena said. "They don't concern themselves with intellectual questions. In the broad sense of the word, our people don't need freedom of speech, or freedom of travel. In the broad sense, our people want to travel abroad only to buy a decent jacket, not because the Louvre is in Paris. When I was in Baghdad, it cost twenty pounds to rent a car for a day and visit Babylon. There was room for four in the car. I said to my friends, other doctors, let's go when we have two free days together. They said I was out of my mind—for five pounds, it wasn't worth it. So I went alone. They were interested only in the bazaar, in things."

"So this is the New Soviet Man?"

Elena laughed. "This is no new man. All over the world, people want to live better. Every nation has its own level of life. So the American can own a house not with six bedrooms, but eight. And the yard around his house is not this size, but bigger. You don't want higher taxes or inflation. And the average Russian also would like to become wealthy, but according to his own norms. Ours are different from American ones, that's all.

"All the dissident freedoms and religious rebirth—these are not interesting to the New Soviet Man, either, even if he goes to church. No one's really interested in these movements—either here or in America. It's just talk.

"But most of our people try to believe in our theater. It's easier that way. They try to believe that the situation in America is hopeless, that unemployment is terrible, and that here it's really better. If you look at our TV for ten days, you'll see how everything here is good and in the U.S. it is bad: in America, there are earthquakes, blizzards, floods, airplane crashes, crime, daily highway deaths, narcotics addiction, alcoholism, unemployment, demonstrations against this and that, military bases and parachute training for attack. Why do they show us how your troops train and not ours? We don't have such soldiers, no military preparing itself. We're peaceful. Life here is good.

"Half of any program shows how we fulfill our plans, overfulfill them. Or it shows happy children. Every day for five or six hours, someone sings or dances on TV. Then there is the exploitation of the theme of health and welfare. We have adequate housing; in America, there are people without housing. . . . These things are forever being shown our people. It is very difficult for Soviets to get any idea of the truth of things outside.

"I respect my Sakharov when he says that place must be everybody's concern, that it's not possible to destroy the West and preserve ourselves. But we teach our people the opposite. We've got to teach that we are all one . . . that there's only one little earth turning about in space."

10

Ruf Grigorevna Bonner: The Genealogy of Repression

> . . . *If you maintained your spiritual integrity, that already was quite a feat under the conditions in which we lived.*
>
> —RUF G. BONNER

I

WHEN the regime selected the city of Gorky as the place of exile for Andrei Sakharov, the choice illuminated a series of ironies as rich and symmetrical as any that can be found in fiction. Gorky is an ancient place, famed as a citadel of Great Russian resistance to the invading Volga Tatars. In the modern era, Sakharov, heir to a family of Russian intellectuals, had supported the Tatars in their fruitless struggle to regain ancestral lands in the lush Crimea, lands from which the state had deported them during World War II.

For most of its seven centuries of existence, the city had been called Nizhny Novgorod, or Lower New City. In 1932, Stalin renamed the city to honor Maksim Gorky, author of *The Lower Depths* and other Realist works. Although a sympathetic Bolshevik, Gorky had broken with Lenin shortly after the Revolution, accusing him of dictatorial ways. He was quickly silenced by the new regime's censors. Later, Gorky reconciled his idealism to the brutal tactics of Russia's new rulers and became a personal friend of Stalin's. He was a founder and first president of the Soviet Writers Union, which gained power over all authors. Over the years, he helped define the new artistic school called Socialist Realism, the cage in which Stalin imprisoned the country's creative artistic energies. Gorky died in 1936 while undergoing medical treatment. Some Western historians believe that Stalin ordered Gorky killed; it was not the first time the dictator was suspected of having used medical treatment as a cover for homicide by poison or knife. Gorky's real name was Alexei Maksimovich Peshkov; he had adopted a pen name that he felt was more fitting to the world in which he found himself. In Russian, the word "gorky" means "bitter."

At about the time Stalin renamed Nizhny Novgorod, Henry Ford was building a truck factory there as part of his effort to get along with the Communists, and perhaps turn a profit as well. A number of unemployed Americans who sought jobs beyond Depression-era Detroit traveled to the USSR and helped build the factory and start up its assembly lines. This was the origin of the famed Gorky Auto Factory, one of the mainstays of the minuscule Soviet motor vehicle industry. Several years later when the Terror began, it did not help that most of the immigrants had renounced allegiance to capitalist America and had become Soviet citizens. Many were imprisoned as foreign spies and saboteurs.

Some of the American expatriates survived and, in the mid-1970s, a number of these now-elderly retirees joined the small chorus of Soviet voices demanding the right to emigrate. They wanted to return to America and Andrei Sakharov added his name to their list of supporters. Many of these would-be emigrants and former Gorky workers clustered in Moscow and petitioned for permission to travel to their homeland. They were treated like all other truth seekers and petitioners: Soviet authorities ignored them. The retirees kept company with each other, had some limited contacts with American correspondents, and nostalgically went to a Moscow movie theater that ran a weekly series of Hollywood films of the 1920s, '30s, and '40s. The Soviets had received some of the films as part of wartime U.S. aid and had captured others from the Germans. The reels were not in very good shape, but they were precious artifacts from Hollywood's golden age of black-and-white romantic comedies. The moviehouse is located in an enormous apartment building that Stalin himself helped design on the banks of the Moscow River near the Kremlin. As the years passed, the theater became a mecca for the former Americans. If you were elderly and had been cut off from your homeland for the past fifty years, you could go to the movies in Moscow and see for yourself how life had been in the States. The name of the moviehouse is "The Illusion."

There was yet another thread linking the fates of Sakharov and the city of Gorky: during the Terror, Sakharov's mother-in-law, Ruf Grigorevna Bonner, had been exiled to the Gorky region after surviving eight years in slave labor camps in Soviet Central Asia, where she had been sent because she was the wife of an enemy of the people. It had taken about forty years for family history to circle back on itself. In almost any other country on earth, such dreadful symmetry could comfortably be interpreted as random coincidence. But in Soviet Russia, the pattern was so deeply ingrained that no one considered it coincidental. Suffering and repression at the hands of the country's leaders moved from generation to generation; earlier tribulation earned no reprieve for those who came later. Ruf Bonner knew all about these imperatives of Soviet history. They terrified her.

And on March 4, 1980, six weeks after her son-in-law was sent into exile, history paid Ruf Bonner another visit. Without warning, the organs threw a police guard around the apartment where Ruf and Lisa Alexeyeva lived in Moscow. Two burly uniformed cops with pistols, billy clubs, and walkie-talkies took up positions outside the door to No. 68 Chkalova. They turned away nearly all visitors, allowing only a handful of family friends—and no activists—to bring food to the two women. The sudden move sent Ruf into a state of shock. Overwhelmed by a sense of vulnerability for both Lisa and herself, she was unable to cross the threshold of her home to pass between the two policemen.

Not long before the siege began at No. 68 Chkalova, Lisa Alexeyeva had been denounced by the regime as an immoral woman who had broken up Alyosha's marriage. But was this what the police guard was all about? In an eerie departure from its customary methods of dealing with Sakharov, Soviet propaganda refused to offer a word of explanation for the police barrier. Speculation grew among foreign diplomats and journalists that the organs were mounting a drive to expel Sakharov from the Academy of Sciences at the Academy's annual spring session that month. Some Westerners believed that the police stakeout was aimed at heading off any attempt by the physicist's family to organize a resistance to the regime's suspected move. In a system where the state has boundless power, it might seem unusual that the party would have any trouble punishing Sakharov if it wished.

However, the issue of party control of the Academy was not clear-cut. Some Westerners thought that, despite such bizarre—and, at times, lethal—political episodes as the Lysenko affair, the Academy of Sciences had regained a slim margin of independence from ideology and party control in the years since Stalin's death. Soviet science watchers at the American embassy reasoned that, if the approximately three hundred fifty voting members of the Academy capitulated and ousted Sakharov, they would make themselves more vulnerable to similar control. In the foreigners' eyes, the other academicians had a vested interest in preserving the status quo. Therefore, some analysts viewed the police guard as an outward sign of a struggle that would soon emerge from the Academy's hallowed chambers. Most Soviet dissidents, however, felt that the Academy would do as it was told; the guard meant that authorities were worried about the reaction of foreign scientists if Sakharov were expelled and his counterattacks reached the West via the family remaining in Moscow.

All these complicated speculations meant nothing to Ruf Bonner. In psychological terms, she was as firmly barricaded inside the flat as if the KGB had sealed the door.

Toward the end of the second week under siege, some mutual friends told me that the two women had made an important observation about their guards. Each morning at about 6 A.M., the policemen went off duty and their replacements did not arrive until about 7:30. The friends suggested that it might be possible for me to see the women during that unguarded window of time. It would be essential to avoid telegraphing any attempt to the organs ahead of time. Since Eliza and I had been regular visitors to the family, I had no doubt that, if I could get to the door of No. 68 without interference, Lisa and Ruf would let me in.

Eliza and I talked over the situation and decided that I should attempt to see them on Sunday morning. On Saturday night, I made one simple preparation: I parked the office car out toward the edge of the compound where we lived, deliberately putting it in easy view of the two KGB booths that monitor activity in "K-7," as Westerners call the sprawling Kutuzovsky area.

The next morning I got up early. "Where are you going so early?" Eliza asked with elaborate clarity, for the benefit of the microphones known to be buried in the walls of our four-room flat.

"It's a great day for skiing," I replied with equal clarity. It wasn't much of a ruse and I felt foolish togged out in my ancient Nordic corduroy knickers and long woolen socks. I hadn't been skiing all winter. But we do what we can. I took my cross-country skis downstairs, threw them over my shoulder, and walked out to the car. With what I hoped was a nonchalant wave to the cops, who had nothing else of interest to look at on an early Sunday morning, I slung the skis into the wagon and drove away. The goons in the butka gestured derisively and put in a call to the Department of Comings and Goings: "Going skiing."

I drove around the Ring Road, hung a U-turn near the Chkalova apartment building, pulled into a narrow side street, parked, locked, and slipped into the building. Taking the elevator to the ninth floor, I walked quietly down one floor. The time was 6:15 A.M.—as predicted, no cops. A quick knock, a moment's wait, and then the sound of the door chain being withdrawn. Lisa peered out. Her face broke into a surprised grin. "Come in!"

In minutes, fresh coffee grounds were boiling à la Russe in a battered pipkin on the gas stove and Ruf, Lisa, and I were enjoying our first cigarettes of the day. But there was nothing pleasant about the conversation. As we talked, I began to think that there was another explanation for the police guard. The ultimate target, of course, would always remain Sakharov. Although banished, he had defied the regime and found ways to issue a series of statements denouncing his exile that were published in the West. As a result, Ruf and Lisa had been warned to cut off contacts with Westerners. The police blockade bluntly drove home this warning. But as the minutes passed and I understood their situation better, I could see that Ruf also was an important target of opportunity for the KGB. There was ample reason to reach this conclusion. Earlier that year, Ruf had asked the Soviet government for permission to spend several months in the United States visiting her grandchildren, Alyosha and Tatiana. The authorities had granted it, assuring Ruf that she could go to America on a personal visit and return. This was a rare privilege, but, in view of the fact that Elena had been granted several trips abroad, the notion of a trip for Ruf was not remarkable. The organs could only gain by removing a staunch member of the Bonner clan from the scene, thus reducing the emotional and psychological support for Elena and Sakharov. However, there was a catch.

Lisa Alexeyeva also had requested exit permission so that she could join Alyosha in America and marry him. The answer to Lisa had been: *nyet!* Repeatedly, our Russian friends had told us that one of the strengths of the regime lay in its very unpredictability. The arbitrary way in which Lisa's request had been denied seemed to confirm this. The sole purpose of refusing appeared to be to inflict pain. This was easy for the regime.

To complicate matters, Ruf had vowed not to leave the USSR without Lisa. So the two women were locked in their own struggle with the authorities. In such confrontations, the organs operate with the same assiduous attention to detail that is applied to keeping the proletariat in check: they divide to conquer. Forcing Ruf to give in was another purpose of the police guard, which she sensed but had no way of escaping.

"This repression is aimed at liquidating all information about Andrei Dmitrich, breaking friendships and family ties, and achieving the deepest isolation," Ruf said in a gloomy, depressed voice as Lisa poured out coffee. "In the end, the organs intend to send Lisa and me into exile as well. That is what will happen to both of us. They want to take the apartment from me and prevent my daughter from ever coming to Moscow again." The police, she said, had frightened away a number of Old Bolshevik friends from her own years in the camps and exile. "These are people who either defended the Soviet Union from Nazi fascism or went through repression because of their beliefs," Ruf said. "But they are old now and afraid to come anymore—and they did so much to preserve this country. For myself, I don't even have the right to receive mail anymore. All communications have been broken with my family. I have received no photographs of my great-grandchildren [in America] and no word from my grandchildren. They call this 'humanism.' " She spat out the last words.

I left the apartment at about 7:15. Again, no cops. The next day, I filed the story of the siege and the *Post* used it in the editions of the following day. And one day after that, the police disappeared. Although it is flattering to think so, there was no sign of a connection between the two events. The Academy of Sciences never voted on Sakharov's membership, and there never was another police blockade of the Moscow apartment. The entire episode remained a mystery and the only thing that was clear was the unpredictable power of the state. Ruf realized that she had virtually no choice: either she went to America by herself, or she forfeited all hope of seeing her grandchildren again. Lisa's fate was a separate question, and the state had no intention of deciding this in conjunction with its offer of safe passage for Ruf Grigorevna.

In the end, the organs won. A few months later, urged by Elena and Lisa, Ruf left the USSR for America. Lisa remained behind.

II

RUF Grigorevna Bonner had devoted herself to the causes of the Revolution, and her good deeds had been repaid with evil. This is not what history is supposed to teach, and few people are adequately armored against such an outcome.

More than a year after the police siege in Moscow, Eliza and I talked with Ruf at length about what had befallen her. At first, she was reluctant to speak; by nature, she is self-effacing and at her age not especially eager to relive painful moments. But as we proceeded, her judgments emerged, pithy and poignant. The setting for these interviews was as different from Moscow—or eastern Siberia, where Ruf was born on August 18, 1900—as could be imagined. We sat in a cozy living room on a quiet, tree-shaded side street in the suburban Boston community of Newton, Massachusetts. This was home for Ruf's granddaughter, Tanya, and Efrem Yankelevich; for their two small children, Matvei and Anya; and for Alyosha Semenov, Tanya's brother.

"I was born a contemporary of the century," Ruf began, "and spent my childhood and youth among influences which affected me throughout my life. From childhood, I was used to such concepts as exile, arrest, prison term, search—these were a part of our daily existence, long before the Revolution."

For those who live in the West, the word Siberia conjures up a vision of labor camps and privation. Gorky called Siberia the "land of death and chains." While Ruf's recollections reinforced this, she explained an important, if overlooked, part of Siberia's reality: as a frontier and exile depository for innovative social thinkers and their sympathizers, eastern Siberia also was an exciting, adventurous laboratory where ideas had a chance to flourish far from the crushing power of authorities at the Center—Moscow. Over the decades, Siberia spawned a special feeling of independence and individual fortitude.

The high cultural level of the region could be explained "first as a result of the influence of the exiles and the people condemned to hard labor there under the czars. In addition, government administrators were different from their counterparts in central Russia. Few would take such [Siberian] jobs voluntarily. Mostly, they took them after falling into disfavor—and so it was for the governors-general of almost all the administrative regions of that part of the country. A great many cultured and high-ranking members of the court ended up in the border regions. So, of course, they were more liberal than other governors and, of course, they helped make possible the greater cultural development of those eastern regions. Any village in which the exiled Decembrists lived became noticeably more cultured. The workers and the peasants became more educated as a result of the influence of those people. Eastern Siberia differs completely from central Russia. It has richer land, richer people, and, as I have said, a much higher cultural level. But in central Russia, I met with illiteracy, backwardness, a sense of hopelessness.

"This breakdown already had begun before the Revolution. Soviet power merely finished off the process. That's why I'm one of those who feels that culture, education, and knowledge serve to raise not only the cultural but also the material level of a population. If in place of vodka there appeared books; if in the place of beer halls, schools—that would be a major step. That's why I was persuaded and worked in the cultural area and liked it."

After the Soviets came to power, after the Civil War and the first severe famine under Communist rule, Ruf dedicated herself to bringing culture to the impoverished hinterlands.

"Until 1937, all my work generally was in the establishment of culture for the narod: there were libraries and clubs, mobile libraries and film shows, new educational departments to teach the working class right in their factories. It was a whole system for educating and promoting culture for those who had no exposure to culture, who lived to all intents and purposes without culture.

"I had seen the basic needs of the people. Those scourges of the people—alcoholism and other problems which ruined the lives of the poor—derived from their lack of culture." Beyond that, the idealistic youth of Ruf's era "had been brought up in the tradition that culture gives rise to a sense of responsibility and a corresponding development of self-knowledge. Without culture, the establishment of a humane and ordered society is not possible. I shared that point of view. I was never drawn toward agriculture or management or political organization. My penchant was for cultural things, and I liked this field."

Nurtured by the humanistic preachings of Tolstoy, Turgenev, and other Russian classicists, she at first saw the Revolution as the salvation of the nation. Then came the Civil War. "I was witness at one and the same time to both the Red Army and the White. Where I lived, we were in the middle of the action. One day, the region might belong to the Whites and the next day to our side. We saw the cruelty and injustice of both armies. I can't place greater blame on one side or the other. The Civil War was even crueler than most wars. Most wars take place between two states which hold to some sort of code and principles, some kind of organization and structure. But this war, like most civil wars, was not organized and, therefore, was more awful and cruel—and I saw the cruelty of both sides in the Soviet Far East."

One of the cruelties was the formation of a battalion of Jewish conscripts by the White Army general Hetaman Semyenov, a warlord supported by the Japanese who, together with the United States, Great Britain, and other outsiders, sent military detachments into Russia on the side of the Whites. Semyenov was notorious for his brutality. "He sent Jewish boys out as the vanguard and placed the trained and armed troops behind them. Most of this Jewish battalion had never carried arms. They were used as cannon fodder, sent to certain death. It was a guaranteed death for Jews, a form of pogrom. A huge number died." Ruf's own brother Matvei served for a year in this Jewish battalion. Miraculously, he escaped with his life—only to be executed under Stalin in 1937.

But it was the Japanese whom the Russians feared most. "They were a different race, from a different culture, and they were particularly hated because of the War of 1905 [the Russo–Japanese War, which the Russians lost]. The Japanese were well-armed, well-dressed, and completely supplied with their own horses, housekeeping materials, cooking utensils, and foodstuffs. They even had their own teahouses. Obviously, this was completely alien to the Russian spirit and way of life, and our fear lasted right up through the last war." Ruf recalled how astonished the Russians had been when Japanese occupiers shamelessly bathed right on the street, dipping the water from rain barrels set up for the purpose. The sight of all those naked Oriental bodies repelled the Russians.

Through the 1930s, until 1937, Ruf continued working for the new

Soviet state. "Then, in 1937, they arrested my husband in Moscow. It was May 1937. And in December 1937 they took me. Although I was held in prison a long time before my camp term, the sentence was absolutely standard. At that time, Stalin wished to liquidate a certain layer of society and he established a group of people who in secret arrived at sentences to achieve this. For instance, my husband was arrested and shot as an enemy of the people. Then, as a member of his family, I could receive three, five, or eight years of strict regime labor camp—whether I was guilty of any crime or not. My sentence was eight years' hard labor in a camp."

In the slave camp in Akmolinsk oblast, a southern region of Kazakhstan, the Russians farmed and mined coal and copper and the Kazakhs pursued semi-nomadic shepherding. "We didn't have the right to correspond. My family didn't know how I was, nor I they." The closed camp was reserved for wives of traitors. Food was slop; beds were lice-filled mats laid on wooden frames in barracks that lacked running water or sanitation. The women made bricks from the clay of Kazakhstan, and, when the brick supply was sufficient, worked as hod carriers and masons, building military barracks. Then they were put to work extending the agricultural canal system in the vicinity of Karaganda in central Kazakhstan. "We dug with shovels, without any machinery." Later, Ruf was assigned to a crew that built stoves for barracks.

After about four years, the camp regime became even more harsh. The slop that was called food deteriorated even further. "We knew from experience that, when things got worse, something unpleasant had happened. This time we didn't know for quite a while exactly what had occurred. But no matter how hard they tried to shut people off from the outside, in a camp rumors eventually start to get out. Some driver comes in, perhaps bringing guests to see the camp administrator. A work brigade marches past, and the driver happens to be chatting with the guard about the military situation. The brigade returns to the barracks and within moments the word spreads from barrack to barrack that a war is going on."

Ruf's brigade was sent to lay track in a crash project to transport the autumn harvest west to European Russia and the troops. That first year of the war, there was an enormous harvest, but no way to move it from the region. "So we were brought in to lay about one hundred kilometers [sixty-two miles] of track. We dug the track bed, but they didn't bring in the rails and the whole harvest froze.

You had to go only a few kilometers to see great piles of vegetables frozen like stones and covered with snow. That was the first year."

The following year, the rails arrived and the spur line was finished. Then the women built a vegetable-processing factory, a textile factory, and an arms plant. Months and years drifted away in a haze of work, hunger, and sickness until Ruf's labor camp sentence ended in 1946. She was transferred to exile. She was barred from large cities but was able to live in outlying hamlets, first near Leningrad and later near Gorky.

When Stalin died in the spring of 1953, Ruf was in exile in a provincial village. She was astounded by the villagers' reaction to the news of his death. "It was a miserably poor, destroyed, poverty-stricken village—yet they felt sorry for him! Though it seems strange, the villagers sympathized with him. Incomprehensible, that sort of mass psychosis. In this farm village, I heard nothing about the ruinous waste wrought by Stalin. They looked at the story and pictures in the newspaper and they said, 'Poor thing, he's surrounded by comrades and party officials at his burial, but not one member of his family to mourn him.' Poor thing! They felt sorry for him because there was no one to cry over him, only officialdom. These people magnified and glorified this man.

"And, of course, they were afraid things would get worse. And sure enough, that May there was a devaluation of the currency." So far as the peasants were concerned, this had no direct effect on their economy because, under Stalin, farm peasants were paid not in money but in barter items, such as firewood, flour, and potatoes. As a result, even septuagenarians who could barely walk were forced to continue working since they had no pensions or other means to buy food. Elsewhere, the devaluation destroyed the salary Soviet workers had received for the past ten years. "The idea of a good salary was gone. So they felt vindicated in their conviction that the death of Stalin would bring only trouble."

But for those in prison or exile, economic matters meant nothing when compared to the promise of freedom that accompanied the dictator's death. By the end of 1954, some months after Elena had met Mikoyan, Ruf was released from exile and rehabilitated. "I did not have a job again, but was given a pension. My working life had come to an end."

What was the meaning of such an ordeal?

"After that, I thought a lot about the history I had seen. Long before 1937, in the first period of Soviet power, throughout the cultural activities in which I took part, the old Russian intelligentsia either emigrated or died in prison, exile, or forced labor. In other words, they were repressed or lived on into this new epoch, hidden away and making certain compromises. Very few lived fully, or entered fully into the new Soviet period. So there was the problem of creating a *new* Soviet intelligentsia. These were people of my generation or a little younger, born in 1900–10. I can say from my own experience that, by 1936, they had developed into a real and loyal Soviet intelligentsia. But, here again, Soviet power miscalculated.

"These were thoughtful, honest people. Most of them were economists and historians, and they began to study history accurately and honestly, and they began to criticize the government. They created 'schools of thought' of their own, but they were completely loyal to the government. I know a whole group who were instructed to write up the history of the Russian Communist Party or the Social Democratic movement. Conscientiously and honestly, they wrote what they understood to have happened. And each and every one of them was destroyed—to the very last person.

"So, on the one hand, a young, new Soviet intelligentsia was founded. And, on the other, within the party, the more intelligent a man was, the more cultured, the more it was that puzzling questions occurred to him. Such a man was not suspicious of the new system, but asking questions of it. These people weren't dissidents in the modern sense, but a sort of splinter party. They didn't undermine the system. Basically, they supported it, but they habitually criticized it, suggested different corrections—sometimes economic, sometimes political.

"Stalin quickly understood that this movement which he himself had created wouldn't do. So all of them were destroyed. It wasn't a matter of a few unusual arrests. It was a matter of wiping out a whole layer of society—party leaders, the cultural founders of the Revolution, academics, professors, teachers, and students. A whole great group was scraped off the face of the Russian earth."

"Then what kind of a society was it that Stalin founded?" we asked.

Ruf regarded us with a cool expression. "What he founded, I don't know. What he destroyed, that I know. I saw with my own eyes."

She paused, arranging her thoughts. "Let me think. . . .

"He founded a strong apparatus of control, even stronger than that of the old regime. It's true that, under the old system, there were camps and prison traditions, but they allowed a man to preserve his life. In Stalin's camps, only a miracle could save an individual's life. Miracles saved the lives of the strongest, the cleverest, the best workers. So it is difficult for me to say what he created. The others, a mass of people, were melted down like a column of steel.

"Stalin founded a great power, built on the bones of the imprisoned, on the bones of destroyed agriculture, on forced labor, on norms that could never be fulfilled. He founded a great power. And he founded a party of a new type. Although, more accurately, it should be called a government of a new type."

Who was responsible for the tyranny? Like millions of her countrymen, Ruf had spent years struggling with this burden.

"Nowadays, the question arises as to whether our generation is responsible for what happened. I have been thinking about this for a long time. And I think that, in Russia, there is no one generation that can look at itself and say it is responsible for what happened. After all, some form of catastrophe has visited Russia in practically every generation. What is the cause for this? Why is it? I don't know, but I don't think the point is to place blame for what happened in the past, but to look ahead to the future. Now there are new generations, no longer mine, but the one after mine, and the one after that. Two generations who are active. And they are asking the party what they are responsible for. In my opinion, we are responsible in some measure, and so also is the generation before mine. However, it is difficult to judge who is more to blame, who less.

"Then there is the question of collective versus personal responsibility. On the one hand, if your whole generation is guilty, then, from one point of view, you must be guilty also. However, if you look at it from the point of view of your own personal life, and if you did not betray anyone or ascribe false guilt to anyone under the system in which we lived, well, if you maintained your spiritual integrity, that already was quite a feat under the conditions in which we lived.

"You can say that a mass of people who took part in certain activities contributed to a horrendous sin against the country. But, at the same time, you may personally have saved the lives of ten or twenty people. So, are you then guilty for the catastrophe? You can't judge it that way. So, as I think it over, I can say we were both guilty and not guilty."

"Perhaps this is over for good and can't happen again," Eliza suggested.

"Well, it's hardly likely to happen again in such a form—such wild outbreak and reaction. Scarcely likely to repeat itself in the same way. How many millions of people died under Stalin and in the war? That won't happen again. But maybe in a different form. Wars go on and on, keep breaking out over and over again. Afghanistan was to have taken just a few days [to install a new Marxist regime], and how long has it been . . . several years already. Now that it's a matter of partisan warfare, it will drag on for ages. And look at Poland. How long can that go on? There are too many conflicts, because the free world makes too many mistakes."

"Perhaps we don't understand our own freedom well enough," I offered.

"Don't understand it or don't defend it? I can't say because I'm not a student of these things. But I have the impression that there is too little understanding. Too much naiveté. And, particularly in your country, the one country which has never been invaded, has never had enemies on its territory. You don't know what that is. But Russia, on the other hand, knows from the time of the Tatars, three hundred years under their yoke. And then years under the yoke of Stalin.

"So for us, there was some kind of preparation. You've had no preparation at all. You're used to freedom. You greet each other: 'How you doing?' 'Well, thank you.' A sense of well-being, of confidence. The way you think seems like a sign of strength, because you're strong. You can be honest, confident, optimistic. But what if, in fact, it's just ignorance, lack of experience."

III

BY the close of the 1950s, Ruf was living in Moscow. The Chkalova apartment was a gift from the Khrushchev regime to make partial amends for her suffering. For tens of thousands of Terror victims, an apartment was the sole reparation for imprisonment. Ruf's pension was adequate and, although she never again would hold a job, she was ready to reenter the life of her country, her family, and her era. But it was not that simple. The camp survivors found that, during their years in the archipelago, an immense gulf had opened between them and the rest of their countrymen.

"A different tragedy took place," she said. "Most of my generation who had been in the camps immediately came into conflict with their children. Their children had come back from the army as young lions, victors. And we were returning from the camps, from death. Almost all the women of my age found that their children were completely alien, beings from another world. Some were invalids, wounded in the war, but they were victors. They were on top.

"On the other hand, we had achieved nothing. And by that time, our children thought that our generation, with its political mistakes, had brought destruction upon their generation. And maybe they were right. The actions of our generation had led to war. In other words, we had been the murderers of our own children. You can look at it that way. True or false, you can judge it that way if you want to."

We asked if such things were discussed openly between rehabilitated parents and their victorious children.

"Oh, no. Some pondered the idea, and conflicts often erupted between the generations. On the one hand, they knew that we had suffered a great deal, and they loved us and sincerely felt for us. But, on the other hand, they belonged to a different age. They were winners, with an entirely different sense of things. They were completely different. . . . And the former prisoners and I? We had crawled out of the camps.

"At the time they couldn't imagine the camps and didn't want to know about them. And I couldn't bring myself to describe what it was like. Only later could a person begin to talk about it, and then only with one's nearest and dearest and it wasn't all that easy. This was the time of victory. The camps were frightening and behind us. Besides, the children knew something about horrors. They had been through the war. They'd seen things. They were adequately educated in these kinds of things. And they could judge for themselves without needing details.

"At first, some of my old friends who had never been arrested came round to see me. Most of them were very sympathetic. Some felt uncomfortable, especially those who were the most honest, whose thinking had progressed during the years of my absence. Some of them candidly expressed their feelings, but these were very few. Most of them came two or three times to express their sympathy, and to see if they could help. But the ties of the past no longer existed, and, after a while, they didn't come back. In fact, they'd had their own bad times and sufferings. The whole time of the Terror they had shivered, glancing over their shoulders, wondering if and when they might be taken. It is a terrible situation. You are not guilty, but all the same, you are waiting for punishment. All those seventeen years I spent in camp and exile, they were at home, expecting punishment.

"People who live through such times become emotionally deformed. It is very difficult to withstand such an atmosphere—there is nervous anticipation and fear all the time. Who knows what he might say or be overheard saying? Something innocent he said might betray him. Several people told me it would have been better if they had been in the camps, with friends and relatives. So when I returned, I was completely isolated in a psychological way. I had no common language except with my campmates."

It also seemed to Ruf as if the children were better able to deal rationally with the changes stirring Russia after Stalin's death. "When they came home from the war, they quickly saw the shortcomings of the system and began to take a stand. They understood this before we did; while we were still in the camps this change in attitude was setting in. They understood better than their parents that the Thaw and the new liberalism under Khrushchev were not really changing the system. And so, young people from our children's generation began to take our places in prison even before all of us had been fully rehabilitated and sent home.

"This was really quite natural. The older folks, shut off for years in the camps, were kept somewhat infantile. But those who had taken part in the flow of events were better able to respond to them. Take me, for example," she said with a self-deprecatory grin. "After a time, I began to understand that the Thaw had been a deception . . . if not an outright deception, it had slid off somewhere and disappeared. Once my views on the Thaw changed and came closer to the younger generation's, then I could be their helper—and not the other way around, as it had been at the start of my rehabilitation." Many camp survivors had grappled successfully with this problem, but not all. "The rest remained infantile, unable to think over their experiences or look accurately at what had happened. These were the tragic members of my generation.

"A great influence on me, of course, was my children's disagreement with the current situation, and then, of course, my family's connection with Andrei Sakharov. By that time, my family had reached a thoroughly realistic position. Now it's called a dissident position. so, let us call it that. And by this time, I, too, had become a part of it—comprehending, sympathetic. But my movement in that direction was a process that took many years.

"To revamp one's thinking, to rebuild yourself after seventeen years—almost a quarter of a century without literature, newspapers, social contacts, nothing—well, like it or not, you become like one tossed out of the flow of life. It takes a very long time to reattach one's self. Most of my generation held onto their old ideas, preserved their antediluvian attitudes. Despite their sufferings, they were not able to analyze what they had seen. It was a kind of sclerosis—not merely physical, but spiritual.

"Here's an example: I have a childhood friend who, like me, sat for seventeen years. She had a son, and he sat for seventeen years. This was not on his father's account, but on his own account, because he criticized the government. And my friend couldn't understand or support her son. Now, how could that happen? I don't know. They carry the old ideas right into the grave. I've lost almost all my old friends as a result of this condition. In contrast, I have two or three close friends who live in Poland. They were friends before the camps, and we have seen each other since. We have maintained our friendship to this day because we have continued our interest in world events. For the others, such an interest does not exist. For them, the world has stopped.

"They hid themselves under the covers, took the position that nothing had changed, that it was all as it should have been. 'We suffered, yes. But it was just that some mistakes were made, that's all. . . .' They kept up their belief and hope during their time in the camps; they thought it was all for the best and that's how they've continued to think. Even when it meant watching your own son sit for seventeen years after you'd already sat seventeen! Sclerosis. Inability to move forward. Blind belief always supports you."

"You don't think of yourself as a dissident?" I asked.

"Me? No! What sort of a dissident am I? I just happened to have landed in dissident surroundings and, to the extent that I can, I try

to help in human and personal ways. I don't get up and speak
. . . I help out in a private way. After all, they're my children!"

Many Westerners believe that the Terror died with Stalin and can
never return. But Soviets who lived through it are not so sanguine.
No one recognizes better than Soviets themselves that the apparatus
has never been fully disbanded. Ruf explained how this worked in
the lives of friends who ended their friendship with her. "It was a
self-defense mechanism with them. 'If I don't touch you, then you
won't touch me, right?' Not many dared do otherwise, because most
were frightened for family and friends. A general fear. An unreal
fear that can tie us hand and foot. Perhaps, an unbelievable fear.

"There were those who were close to me. But many were afraid
to visit me, and now, even to write to me. And not without reason.
The organs might call them at work and say, 'You are keeping
forbidden contacts and for this you'll be thrown out of work.' The
organs threaten them.

"There was an old, experienced teacher, for instance, a longtime
friend. They asked him, 'Why are you making contact with a member of Sakharov's family?' And here I am, a woman who herself was
repressed, and now a member of Sakharov's family. The teacher said
to me, 'What do I do?'

"So I said to him, 'There's nothing to do. Just stop seeing me.
What else is there for you to do? Do without me.'

"For me, there was nothing left to be afraid of. Yet, even I was
afraid. I had a son, and I was afraid for him—from the moment
Sakharov appeared in our lives. I, who had been through the camps
also, was afraid again. So I understand the power of fear . . . so I
can't judge others if I myself was afraid."

Ruf's son was in the Soviet merchant marine. Although he had
earned two college-level degrees and had served for twenty years,
he had never captained his own ship. That honor is reserved for
members of the Communist party, and Ruf's son had steadfastly
refused to join the party.

"He was interested in nothing but the sea. He said in a very
straight fashion that there was no point in his having any contact
with my family because he couldn't live without the sea. 'On dry
land, I'd be a goner,' he'd say."

The one thing essential to his seafaring life was his international
passport, a rare possession for a Soviet citizen. Since there was
constant police surveillance of the Sakharov apartment, Ruf feared

her son would be detected if he tried to visit her there in Moscow. He would be stripped of the passport and his seafaring days would be over. "I wouldn't let my son come to my home. I wouldn't let him cross my threshold."

In 1976, Ruf's son died at sea at the age of 49. His body was brought to Moscow for interment and fellow mariners paid their respects to his mother. "Our apartment building was so crowded with people that no one could get through," Ruf said. "The KGB couldn't figure out what was going on. Not knowing about my son, they couldn't figure out why all these officers were coming to see Sakharov! But when the KGB found out they were coming to me, they calmed down." Her face creased in a rueful grin. There was a long silence.

"So my son never came to visit me. It was as simple as that. We set up secret, private meetings—just the two of us. I had to set up secret meetings with my own son.

"No one can ever know his own strength," Ruf said after another long pause. "Never. If anyone had ever told me before 1937 what I would live through . . . I would never have believed that, somehow, I would endure and endure."

11

The Battle for Lisa

*I don't regret those years. In fact, now it seems
too little time that I was with them.*

—LISA ALEXEYEVA

I

ON Thanksgiving Day 1981, twenty-eight people, Russians and Americans, gathered around a long table in the dining room of a very old house on a Vermont hillside. Like Russia itself, this was a region of early frosts and late thaws, immense woodpiles, and cozy, superheated kitchens. But there also were specific New England touches so different from the Russian experience that they could not escape attention: one-room schoolhouses, white-steepled churches that swelled with organ music and worshippers of a Sunday, columned town meeting halls where people argued and voted their consciences in full view of their fellow citizens. Generations of ancestors lay peacefully nearby in stonewalled cemeteries where the worn white headstones somehow had tilted just enough to catch the distant slant of autumn sunset. The long, flat rays fell on these stones; they glowed softly red in the faint autumn light.

Despite modern American technology, which questions the purpose of anything so venerable, these artifacts possess uncommon strength, offering refreshment and continuity to the region's rock-ribbed inhabitants. This place, where *Mayflower* is the ship not the moving van, abides as a storehouse of New World tradition.

The Russians, presided over by a huge man with a white beard, felt at home. Beyond the broad front door with its heavy, hand-forged strap hinges, the land lay bare, brown, and sere, showing the "weatherbeaten face" that Pilgrim Father William Bradford described in 1620 and which no one has ever described better. The Russian patriarch, a man of letters named Lev Kopelev, thought the countryside resembled the Ural Mountains, where he had often traveled in his early manhood. But, in all his long life, Kopelev had hardly imagined that he would be spending this particular day in such surroundings—nor had we.

It had come about this way: Lev and his wife, Raisa (Raya) Orlova, our first friends in Moscow, were expelled from Russia at the end of 1980 as part of the crackdown against political activists. They settled in West Germany where, for a number of reasons, they were celebrities. Lev was fluent in German and a world-renowned scholar of German literature. His staunch defense of Alexander Solzhenitsyn and other renegade and oppressed Soviet writers was well known across the Continent. During World War II, Kopelev had become enraged when his Red Army unit, fighting its way toward Berlin, raped German civilians and pillaged their villages. His anger over Soviet barbarity cost him ten years' imprisonment for treason; his memoirs describing this had been published in Europe and sold well. In addition, interviews with Lev by Klaus Bednarz of Westdeutscher Rundfunk radio–television and other enterprising West German correspondents in Moscow had become an institution in the Federal Republic. Germans queued for the autograph of this exile and mobbed his lectures, which dealt with how Russian and German writers viewed each other's culture and society. Raya, his wife, also gave lectures about modern American literature, her specialty. She yearned to see the country whose contemporary writers she knew far better than did most Americans; her opportunity came when the Kopelevs accepted an offer from Columbia University to travel and lecture in the United States during the fall 1981 semester. Shortly thereafter, they called us in Vermont, where I had just settled in with my family to write this book.

"We want to spend our first Thanksgiving in freedom with you in New England," Raya said. We were overjoyed, for we had only returned from Moscow a few months earlier and were still feeling the heavy magnetism of that country. Beyond that, we would have the chance to return the hospitality the Kopelevs had fearlessly showered on us during our four years in Moscow. And so they had come to spend Thanksgiving week with us—Lev, Raya, and seven of their close friends and relatives who had emigrated or been forced into exile and who also were our friends. The first night set the tone.

After driving north together from Connecticut, we arrived at our darkened farmhouse on a dirt road that winds between two steep hills beneath the brow of the Pomfret Highlands near Woodstock, Vermont. We lit a fire in the cold stove, brewed up some tea, and sat down to table in the country kitchen. As steam curled from the teacups and the wind tossed and howled outside, Lev leaned back in a baronial chair at the end of the table. The room was in shadow.

"Ahhh . . . this is so incredible," he sighed. Raya's face was wreathed in smiles. Ours were, too. We clasped hands around the table.

In an instant, we were transported back to their steamy kitchen on Red Army Street, where we had passed so many hours together, arguing, explaining, analyzing. Even their stubborn philodendron tendril that made its way from a pot atop the dish cabinet along a string toward the ceiling light fixture seemed to materialize in the semi-darkness. Tricks of the mind. The heavier gravity of Moscow had pulled these things from memory. We savored our feelings.

We had last seen Lev and Raya at their departure from Sheremetyevo Airport the previous December. Airport customs inspectors had spent hours deciding which of the few personal possessions the elderly couple wanted to take with them into exile carried the greatest sentimental value and therefore should be confiscated. For a time, Lev's heavy gnarled walking stick, an inseparable companion, was in jeopardy. Then the authorities' interest fastened on a small wooden cigarette box that contained some dirt. It had no economic value, of course.

But the sharp-eyed customs men knew that, of all the possessions the Kopelevs wanted to take West, this one had value beyond measure. "Not allowed!" they barked, and the box was seized. Triumphantly, they sent Lev into exile without the pinch of Russian soil that, like all Russian exiles down through history, he wanted sprinkled on his grave when he died in banishment.

After the Kopelevs were aboard the Aeroflot plane bound for Vienna, I went back to the office and filed a story for the *Post* describing what the customs men had done and why. The paper carried it on an inside page in the next day's editions, which had a circulation of about six hundred thousand. The story also was picked up by the Los Angeles Times–Washington Post News Service, which has about five hundred client papers in the U.S. and abroad, and thus reaches millions of additional readers.

Anthony Austin, the veteran Moscow correspondent of *The New York Times*, had been at Sheremetyevo Airport as well and was outraged by the seizure of the wooden cigarette box. He also wrote a story about the Kopelevs' departure, which subsequently won him an in-house publisher's award, and was carried in the paper the next day and transmitted by the *Times*'s news service to its hundreds of foreign and domestic clients, with their additional millions of readers. While we continued on our news-gathering rounds in Moscow, moving on to other stories, our reports of this seemingly minor but telling official cruelty at the airport circulated in the world community beyond Soviet borders. Now, Lev leaned forward in his chair in our Vermont kitchen to tell us that the story had a sequel.

A few weeks after he and Raya had settled in West Germany, a small envelope had arrived in the mail, sent by some unknown Western European. Lev opened it, unsure of what to expect. Inside was a pinch of Russian earth.

Within the next few months other foreigners Lev had never met wrote of their distress over the customs incident. These strangers, traveling in Russia, had brought back something for a Soviet exile, they explained. Each letter contained a pinch of Russian soil. One person, Lev told us with a huge smile, had even visited their former apartment house on Red Army Street and had sent earth from the modest flower and shrub garden beside the entrance. His benefactors had vowed that, when the end finally came, this Soviet exile would sleep in peace.

Now, months later, the last Thursday of November arrived—American Thanksgiving. We dressed for the occasion and drove a few miles north to the 150-year-old farmhouse of Eliza's parents, Celina and Edmund Kellogg, who were waiting to welcome the Russians along with their own burgeoning Yankee family. The moment was at hand: a stuffed and steaming turkey, endless side dishes, homemade pies, sparkling cider, and wine and beer awaited. Most of the seven ages of man were drawn up around the fifteen-foot mahogany table: the oldest, an 84-year-old matriarch; the youngest, a 6-year-old girl with barrettes in her hair and an angelic expression.

The Russians and the Americans bowed their heads and Bradford's timeless account of the Pilgrims' arrival in the New World, which has always seemed to me to summarize the hopes that forged America, was read for all to hear:

"Being thus arrived in a good harbor and brought safe to land, they fell upon their knees and blessed the God of heaven who had brought them over the vast and furious ocean, and delivered them from all the perils and miseries thereof, again to set their feet on the firm and stable earth, their proper element. . . ."

The room was silent as the brief, magisterial passage ended. Heads bowed, Lev and Raya seemed sunk in their own thoughts, in the grip of intense strain. Whatever joy there had been since they arrived in Vermont was being swept aside by a grim sequence of events that was now unfolding in the Soviet Union.

Five thousand miles away, Andrei Sakharov and Elena Bonner, the Kopelevs' closest friends, were locked in a new fight with the state. Their goal was to force the authorities to issue an emigration visa so their son's fiancée, Lisa Alexeyeva, could leave the Soviet Union to live with Alyosha in the United States. The Sakharovs' weapon in this struggle was the hunger strike. While we and millions of other Americans pulled up our chairs around mountains of food and blessed our freedom, the physicist and his wife were putting their lives on the line to gain freedom for Lisa.

II

THE notion of voluntary starvation as a weapon in a political showdown with the Soviet state initially appalled Elena Bonner. She had often expressed her typically forthright views about this question. Ruf Bonner recalled that arguments in the house over the pros and cons of hunger strikes went back to the time when Eduard Kuznetsov had talked passionately of his own plans to begin a hunger strike. Elena had been furious with him. Kuznetsov went ahead but she never reconciled herself to his act. Whenever starvation was mentioned as a possible tactic against the regime, Elena would not hesitate: "I hate it! I cannot imagine how people can take such a route. It is completely unnatural."

The dynamics of political fasting were complex, even in an open society. Success depended almost entirely on access to public opinion or some other form of humanitarian intervention to force concessions from the authorities. In most countries, the confrontation would become dramatic news, but that was no guarantee a fast could force concessions. For example, ten Irish nationalists died of starvation in the Maze Prison in 1981 in a vain effort to force their British jailers to grant them "political" status. The British had refused to yield.

The outcome of fasting to win a confrontation with a closed totalitarian state such as the USSR was even less certain. Over the years, there had been many hunger strikes by Soviet political prisoners to protest brutality, illegal punishments, and sadistic privation in the strict regime labor camps of the Perm region. In almost every case, news of the strikes had been kept within the confines of the camps and only seeped out months later, long after the fasts had ended. Intense suffering frequently won only minuscule victories— if any at all. Such fasts underscored the strong resolve of political prisoners to insist on their rights, even in labor camp. But in reality the gains were small. And there was always the risk of falling short, capitulating without wringing any concessions from the state. It was easy to predict failure.

But the Sakharovs had almost no recourse other than to put their own lives in jeopardy. Their living conditions in Gorky approximated imprisonment. They were quartered in a four-room, ground-floor flat in a raw twelve-story skyscraper in a windswept new area of the city. Although large by Soviet standards, the flat was located in a building where KGB and Interior Ministry bureaucrats lived. It was said in Gorky that the Sakharov apartment had been used as a transit flat, or "safe house," for KGB agents en route to or from sensitive assignments. The apartment house, No. 213 Prospekt Gagarina, was in the city's Shcherbinki election district where Yuri Andropov, the bespectacled KGB chief who would maneuver himself into the supreme leadership after Brezhnev's death in 1982, ran unopposed for a seat in the Supreme Soviet, the rubberstamp parliament.

A police guard was maintained around the clock at the entrance to Sakharov's apartment. For a while Ruf and Lisa were able to visit from Moscow, but of Gorky's 1.2 million inhabitants, only two persons, fellow scientists, were allowed to visit the Sakharovs. One of these men, Mark Kovner, was a Jew who had applied to emigrate and had been refused for many years. A district police station was located in the building next door, and nearly all who tried to see the couple or even approached their building were intercepted and hauled off to the police station for extensive questioning. There was no telephone, but the organs had bugged the apartment and overheard every conversation.

Prospekt Gagarina was a broad, ugly boulevard named after the first man in space, Yuri Gagarin. The Sakharov apartment also overlooked the Oka River, the same tributary of the Moscow River that flowed through the city of Kaluga south of the capital where Elena and Andrei Dmitrievich had met and fallen in love. The view was quintessential Soviet-style cityscape: sprawling, badly built brick and concrete apartment blocks set well back from broad boulevards; trees and bushes in no particular pattern along the verges of the streets; grass, never mown, at waist height. People wandered the streets in restless hordes, their string bags at the ready. They queued for apples, queued for carrots, queued for ice cream. When tank trucks of *kvass*, the rootbeerlike national drink, pulled up on the sidewalks during the hot summer days, people queued for that, too. The queues of Gorky defined life.

A stiff wind whipped across the Shcherbinki district much of the time. Dust swirled in spring and summer; rain and snow fell in autumn and winter. At a post and telephone exchange nearby, the couple was allowed to make only local calls. Most mail sent to them never arrived, although the authorities permitted them to exchange brief telegrams almost daily with Lisa in Moscow. When they went shopping or took a walk, agents followed closely and broke up almost every casual encounter. When he left the apartment, Sakharov always carried a briefcase containing his personal papers and scientific research. He was certain the police would steal his work if they ever found the opportunity. Jamming gear was trained on the apartment, blocking out all radio reception. But the Sakharovs discovered that they could elude the interference by taking a portable shortwave radio into a nearby park and strolling with it there.

Soviet scientists blandly told their Western colleagues that Sakharov had full access to physics institutes and libraries in Gorky. This was a lie. Sakharov was barred from those places and he seldom received bulletins or information from the Academy of Sciences. In vain, Sakharov assailed this. Nevertheless, he continued his research into the nature of the universe. In time, some of these papers were smuggled out of Gorky and published in the West.

Western scientists marveled that he was able to continue his work.

Surveillance extended to their old Moscow friends. On one occasion, a doughty old friend who had never been a political activist painstakingly planned a trip to Gorky. She carefully purchased an airplane ticket and bought one of Sakharov's favorite delicacies, a chocolate waffle cake, as a present. The flight to Gorky was uneventful and, when she landed, she hailed a cab and gave the driver the Sakharov address. After a short distance, police stopped the cab. "We've been waiting fifteen minutes for you," admonished the policeman.

The woman was taken to a police station and interrogated by a tall, well-dressed agent.

"Why did you come to see Sakharov?"

"To spend some time and bring him this chocolate waffle cake."

"I can't believe that a 70-year-old woman would come all the way from Moscow just to give someone a cake."

"I'm very sorry for you," Sakharov's friend replied resolutely. "You don't know the meaning of love. People honor men of genius. They honor and love Sakharov."

"It's a mystery to me why you would come only to give him a cake," the agent repeated. "How do you want to go back home?"

"I don't want to," said the woman. "I also want to see Elena Georgievna. She's not under the terms of exile. I'll take the cake to her."

"You'll be able to see her in Moscow. Do you want to take the train or the plane back?"

"I'd like to see a little of Gorky first," the old woman said.

"I'll drive you around myself."

"I'd rather go on two feet."

"You can see it from the windows of my car."

"You can send me out on a plane or a train," the woman replied. She accepted the agent's offer to deliver the cake and wrote out a note wishing the Sakharovs well.

"You can't say we've been unpleasant to you," the agent said smugly.

"No," she agreed. "You've only stopped me from doing what I wanted."

"You've spoiled our Sunday," the man said after the return ticket had been bought and the plane was boarding.

"And you've spoiled mine." She returned to Moscow. The next

day, a telegram arrived from Elena: "We're sadly eating the cake without you," it said.

"This isn't exile and it isn't exactly prison," the friend told us later as she described her trip. "It's called house arrest in any other country."

That was not the end of this woman's efforts to make contact with Sakharov. During the first summer of exile, her son took the train to Gorky and with great care cased the setup. He discovered that every apartment had a small balcony at the rear of the building, out of sight of the guards at the entrance or the police station nearby. The young man passed behind the building, vaulted over the first-floor balcony railing, and tapped on the Sakharovs' window. Astonished, the Sakharovs let him in and the night passed in a swirl of excited conversation which the police did not bother to interrupt.

There had been other penetrations of the barriers around Sakharov. For example, just six weeks after he was exiled, the physicist gave me a comprehensive interview in an exchange of written questions and answers. His views were blunt and grim.

"We enter the 1980s under very difficult conditions," he wrote in answer to my first written question. "Exploiting a period of general aggravation of the international situation, the authorities have made a mighty attempt to eliminate any display of dissidence both in Moscow and in the provinces. . . . Religious persecutions have been intensified, the number of permissions for emigration has been cut back sharply, the persecutions against Crimean Tatars have been increased. The action against me is part of a widespread campaign against dissidents. Its specific cause probably was my statement about events in Afghanistan; I think it was being prepared for a long time."

He was not hopeful that any fundamental change would occur in Soviet society in the foreseeable future. "International security, the preservation of world peace, the welfare and the spiritual freedom of the people of our country demand changes in the structure of our society in the direction of greater pluralism in economic, ideological, and cultural areas. They demand greater openness in society—the free exchange of information and free choice of residency.

"I think it unlikely that such changes will take place in the near future. Our totalitarian society, with its caste and bureaucratic structure, its complete lack of freedom of expression or democratic mechanisms for decision-making, is extraordinarily inert. It can rot and petrify for years without any attempt at change—thus creating an even greater threat to the world."

Sakharov had written about twenty-five hundred words in answer to my questions; the *Post* used them all. The physicist specifically mentioned twenty-eight other activists who had been imprisoned over the years, and then he had this to say about Americans:

"Turning especially to Americans—among whom my children and grandchildren now live—I think first of all of the democratic traditions of the American people, of their steadfastness and love of life. The latest events in Iran, Afghanistan, and other parts of the world have posed a serious challenge above all to America. The Americans, their government, and their president have honorably answered this challenge. Let the rest follow their lead."

Other important interviews soon followed. Sakharov realized that he still could reach out and touch the outside world. But, as the first year passed, the novelty of piercing the barrier subsided among the outsiders.

Elena's train travels to and from Moscow were the sole link between Gorky and the world. They were never easy. Ruf and Lisa, who made the trip a number of times, found them nightmares. Each time, Ruf was so exhausted that she took to her bed as soon as she had arrived either in Moscow or Gorky. "And I didn't have to deal with any kind of complications," Ruf said. "I'd be put on the train carefully and met at the other end. Still, it was very hard. The cars were always crowded and uncomfortable. The bags wouldn't fit. People would be cross and anxious. Frozen or wet food would start to drip and make a mess. Milk products would drip, then eggs would break. God only knows what couldn't make a mess!"

Occasionally, there was some comic relief. Ruf recounted the tribulations of a Gorky engineer with whom she once shared a compartment on her return journey to Moscow. The hapless man had important official business to accomplish for his factory: he was to deliver a major report to the supercilious bureaucrats of the ministry which supposedly managed his industry. But the report was small change compared to the real purpose of his trip. He was hauling a mountain of money, string bags, and extensive food and clothing shopping lists that all his friends expected him to fulfill. "This is the custom in our factory," he announced with an unhappy shake of his head.

"Anyone who is sent to Moscow goes with a list of things to buy for all the others and with a packet of money from each to spend. I have to give a speech at the ministry, but all I can think about is how I'm going to carry out all the errands I have listed in my briefcase—the thirty net shopping bags, the thirty packets of money, the thirty lists of things to buy. As soon as I arrive in Moscow, I race off to see two relatives who live there. They call their friends and relatives and I hand out my thirty lists, sacks, and packets of money so they can do the shopping for me.

"Then I rush off to the ministry to give my speech—completely unprepared! And no time at all to get ready. After that, I'll have the evening free, as I don't have to return to Gorky until the next day. I'll spend the whole night running from store to store until they all close. Then comes the nightmare of figuring out what goes to whom and who gets what change. That takes me a whole week, during which I won't be able to get any work done. The next time, a guy from a different department will get sent on the business trip and it will be his turn to cope with all this. So, from the point of view of business, these business trips are a complete loss. They are focused entirely on shopping.

"In Moscow, I'm scolded for not doing a good job, or perhaps they accept the speech, unprepared as it is. But my head is totally occupied with my shopping. The people who ought to be handling these things are my wife or my mother—but here I am, saddled with them!"

As the months dragged by, the trips became harder for Elena to endure. Although she steeled herself, they took their toll. "It was hard on her physically and emotionally," Lisa recalled months later. "She was always worrying. When she was in Gorky, Elena would worry about what was happening in Moscow. When she got to Moscow, she'd worry about what was happening in Gorky. Two years of this and, of course, her physical condition had been affected, weakened. She was not as strong as she once was." In mid-1980, the authorities suddenly barred Lisa from going to Gorky. Ruf had already departed to the United States to see her grandchildren, and so the full burden of carrying food and clothing from Moscow to the undersupplied provincial city fell to Elena. It was not until May 1981 that Lisa returned to Gorky. She accomplished this by slipping aboard a train and taking the same route as had the son of the Sakharovs' old friend: over the balcony and into the apartment. After several days with the Sakharovs, she left without interference;

this encouraged her to make another trip in August with Elena, which also went off successfully. But, by then, Elena was approaching exhaustion, and there was no guarantee how long the organs would allow her trips to continue. Both she and Sakharov were warned several times to break off all foreign contact. They ignored the warnings, but they could not forget them. Time was passing, their situation seemed to be deteriorating, and Lisa Alexeyeva was no closer to getting permission to leave the country than she had been three years earlier. At any moment, the state might strike decisively at them, completely shutting off all contact with the outside world.

Meanwhile, Alyosha, Tanya, and Efrem had been at work in America to try to strengthen the legal ties between Alyosha and Lisa in hopes of improving her chance of receiving a visa. They determined that a proxy marriage would help. Most states in the U.S. do not recognize proxy marriages. But the state of Montana does. In late spring of 1981, in a Montana courthouse eight thousand miles from Moscow, Alyosha married Lisa by proxy.

My wife happened to be in the Sakharov apartment on Chkalova when Associated Press bureau chief Tom Kent arrived with the news that Alyosha and Lisa were man and wife—in the eyes of the state of Montana. Proclaiming that the marriage was "just a formality," Elena nevertheless embraced her proxy daughter-in-law and gave her a kiss. She told Eliza sternly that there were no tears in her eyes because this was a joyful moment. But despite the proxy marriage, when Lisa reapplied for an exit visa, she was refused.

As the summer of 1981 wore on with no further change in Lisa's situation, a confrontation with the authorities seemed inevitable. With a showdown, Sakharov's exile would burst anew on the conscience of the world. In time, some activists would criticize the physicist for concentrating his immense power on a purely personal matter instead of devoting his efforts to political prisoners. But a struggle on behalf of one individual could serve to dramatize the plight of others. Lisa was not a political activist; she was a woman in love—punished because she had given her heart to the stepson of a man the state feared.

Lisa recalled that Andrei Dmitrievich first mentioned fasting in the spring of 1981. "The idea that a hunger strike might be a worthwhile step to take was already in his mind—he thought he might accomplish something that way." Time passed, and he worked to convince Elena that a fast was the step they should take, and the only right one as well. "Agreement between them was essential," Lisa said. "In August, they talked about the hunger strike as something that might someday be necessary; it was not something definite. Of course, she was worried about him risking his life."

In September, Elena returned to Moscow and contracted influenza, with the result that her eyes became inflamed. Her general health was weakening due to the stress and the medicine necessary for her eye condition, which had affected her heart, not an auspicious sign if a fast was planned. Returning to Gorky, Elena continued her recuperation. Near the end of October, Elena reappeared in Moscow and announced to Lisa that they were going ahead with it.

"It was announced to me as accomplished fact: this was to be done. They asked me not to question them or try to get them to change their minds. I was not to doubt their wisdom, but to believe in them. If they had decided this was the right thing to do, that meant the hunger strike was their only remaining course of action. Elena persuaded me that it was essential. I was terribly frightened for them, but I could only accept their decision. Once they'd agreed they were going to carry it out, that was that. If I'd tried to quarrel, make things difficult, I would have added psychologically to their burden."

Protest by fasting was not new to Sakharov. He had fasted at least once before, in the mid-1970s on behalf of imprisoned dissident Vladimir Bukovsky. That time, Elena was in a Moscow hospital, under treatment for her eyes. Only Ruf was in the flat when Sakharov announced he would eat no more. "All of a sudden, he refused to eat his dinner. I'd prepared supper and he said, 'I'm not going to have any, thanks,' " Ruf recalled.

" 'Why, don't you feel well?'

" 'From today on, I'm just not going to eat.'

" 'What do you mean, not eat!'

" 'I'm going to fast.'

" 'But why fast! For what purpose? What's happened?' "

Sakharov stated that he was going on a hunger strike for Bukovsky. Ruf poured tea and sat with him. "You can't imagine how awful that was. I was alone; he'd already had a heart attack with some attendant paralysis, and here he was, going on a hunger strike. I was terrified and insisted we call a doctor. I didn't dare call one from the Academy, so I got my own doctor and she categorically refused to let him take such a course. He had developed an irregular heartbeat. He was behaving like a crazy man, someone gone out of his mind. The next day, he also ate nothing. There was nothing in the house in preparation for this step, such as mineral water. Nothing."

The following day, a friend came by and Ruf told him what was going on. The friend, Boris Altschuler, went out and stocked up on Borzhomi, a tangy mineral water favorite of Russians, which contains salts to help counter the effect of fasting. Sakharov drank Borzhomi during the strike, which lasted eleven days. As it turned out, he had carefully timed his Bukovsky protest to coincide with the 1974 visit to Moscow of President Nixon. Sakharov wanted maximum foreign press coverage and he got it. Bukovsky later was swapped for Luis Corvalan, a Chilean Communist imprisoned by the Pinochet regime.

Now the fast planned on behalf of Lisa was timed to coincide with a visit by Leonid Brezhnev to Bonn. West German chancellor Helmut Schmidt was a leading spokesman for détente with the Kremlin and his coalition government had backed the Soviet human rights movement, so one of the goals of political rapprochement was to ease Sovet emigration restrictions. There was a framework in place for maximum impact of the Sakharovs' fast. As word of the Sakharovs' decision spread through Moscow, friends and activists who had supported the family visited the apartment to try to convince Lisa to dissuade the couple. But she had given her word.

"All their friends and acquaintances were appalled at the decision and tried somehow to influence them against it. They were all worried, of course, about what the strike might do to Elena Georgevna and Andrei Dmitrievich, how they'd come out of it. This effort to persuade them added to the difficulty they faced. And I was trying to convince the friends that the decision was the right one, while all the time I myself was worrying about it no less than they. To tell the friends that the strike was necessary . . . inescapable . . . was terribly hard for me."

III

LIKE so much else in the saga of the Sakharov family, the notion that Yelizaveta Konstantinovna Alexeyeva would become the center of yet another international drama involving the physicist seemed wildly improbable four years earlier when she had entered their lives. As Lisa herself said some years later, "An ordinary romance during my student years changed my life."

More than anyone who had come into the orbit of the Sakharov and Bonner families in the post-war period, Lisa was uniquely Soviet—the daughter of a military bureaucrat. She was born on November 20, 1955, in East Germany, where her father was attached to the immense Soviet garrison army whose dual function is to help protect the East Germans from NATO invaders and to protect the Eastern bloc's Russian overlords from an East German uprising.

Konstantin Alexandrovich Alexeyev was a Buryat Mongol from the Buryat Autonomous Soviet Socialist Republic, a huge territory lying east of Lake Baikal, the world's deepest lake, which holds one-fifth of all the fresh water on earth. He grew up in the western part of Buryatia, where Buryats had been Russianized for several generations, changing their names and giving up their nomadic ways and native tongue for the customs and language of the dominant race. Neither Lisa's father nor his parents could speak Buryat. Her great-grandparents knew the language, but "only great-grandmother used it—to swear at people." Lisa's father served in the Soviet Army during the Great Patriotic War and made military engineering his career. His wife, Yekaterina, was a Russian from Mariinsk in western Siberia, much younger than her husband.

They lived in a succession of military towns in Byelorussia where Lisa's father helped run factories administered by the Soviet military, but staffed by civilians. The couple had two daughters; the younger, Lisa, grew into a tall, slim, quiet girl with exotic, Eurasian features. In the early 1960s, the family moved to Bronnitsa, a small city outside Moscow. Bronnitsa had been an important Moscow River shipping center in medieval times, but the modern era of rail and air transport had left it something of a backwater. With a population of about twenty-five thousand, Bronnitsa was the site of two military factories and several other industrial enterprises. During her childhood, Lisa remembered that "life was generally prosperous. Recently, the food situation has been poor. The atmosphere has changed. Life has become anxious, troubled. But, before, it was peaceful, untroubled."

Most residents lived in small houses with electricity but no running water, gas, or central heating. The largest residential building in the city was a four-story brick "Khrushchev" apartment house with eighty flats, running water, bathrooms, central heating, and gas stoves. Occupancy was reserved for the privileged of Bronnitsa: the Alexeyevs and other military families lived there. Later, they moved to a house owned by the factory where Lisa's father worked. "It was a duplex, but, in our case, two families lived on each side, one on each floor. It was called a Finnish house; I don't know why. The Finns probably wouldn't recognize it."

Good in mathematics like her father, Lisa graduated with high marks from the local school at age 17, and was accepted by the mathematics branch of one of the country's best teachers' colleges, the Lenin Pedagogical Institute in Moscow. That same year, party leaders decreed that entrance requirements for rural applicants would be lowered as a way of raising the educational level in the countryside. The graduates then would be returned to the hinterlands where they would institute better teaching methods. "The idea was a good and useful one, but it didn't last long," Lisa said. At the same time that the central authorities were redressing the shortage of rural teachers, they began to realize that there was a sudden shortage of city mathematics teachers. Closer inspection revealed that would-be math pedagogues in Moscow were deserting the blackboard for the new and better-paid calling of computer programmer. So the planners reversed their goals, since it was more important to have good mathematics teachers in Moscow than in the countryside. More stringent entrance requirements were reestablished and the institute was told to restrict its math entrants to students who already possessed a Moscow *propusk*, permit. The emphasis on improving rural educational levels faded. Students from the hinterlands again became rare at the institute, especially in mathematics. In common with nearly all her classmates, city or country, Lisa was already cynical about what the society insisted was indispensable for a promising future.

"I enrolled in the Komsomol at the earliest possible age, 14." This was the required first step toward party membership. "And I was very pleased about it. We belonged to the first generation that looked on these matters in a cynical way. We understood that this step, which we could take on our own, would allow us to live better later on. I understood this. But belonging to the Komsomol was also a form of socializing, as we young people saw it. We'd get together, talk about interesting things. But, mainly, people joined the Komsomol so as not to be different, so as to avoid complications later on. Only a few didn't join. I was in no way different from the other students. I was a Komsomol member like everyone else, but political views neither united nor divided us. There simply were no political views."

While at the institute, Lisa lived in an enormous dormitory near the sprawling national fairgrounds on Moscow's north side. Like most of her new friends, Lisa's studies took up the bare minimum of her time; Moscow was such a big place and there was much to explore. The atmosphere in the dorm was relaxed, but the institute imposed a strict routine of political instruction, Komsomol meetings, and departmental sessions where political ideas were discussed. Privately declaring politics nonsense, Lisa and most of her classmates skipped these excruciatingly dull meetings whenever they could. It was easy not to go. "Of course, the senior faculty threatened to punish us, but no one paid much attention. So until something really bad occurred, such as being called in for an official dressing down for cutting every political class, we didn't bother to attend."

Lisa had a roommate who was five years older and graduated from the institute several years ahead of her, but kept in touch despite being sent to western Siberia to teach. Living conditions were crude and unyielding there, the roommate wrote, and she was deeply moved by the psychological suffering and depression she found. In later letters, she said she had met a man and fallen in love. Two children were born in rapid succession, and then both babies fell ill. Medical care was backward and both children died. When the local authorities showed obvious indifference to her suffering, Lisa's friend questioned why medical care was so poor. Soon, grave doubts assailed her about the goals of Soviet society. By the time she returned from Siberia, her hair was turning white. She was 28 years old.

"When I was young and growing up as a member of the first post-war generation," this woman told Lisa, "I was very proud to be a citizen of the Soviet Union and no other country. But now, I know that life here is shit. If I found the chance, I would leave and never miss this place!"

"Through her, I began to understand," Lisa said. "My views weren't altered by samizdat or anything 'political,' but my friend's sense of the country's intentions and her bitter life experience, the fact that out of her sufferings came her understanding, this was real to me personally and could be proven true. I knew something about dissidents, but my knowledge was not direct, personal information about their activities or views, and so it didn't affect me in the same way as my friend's life did."

Occasionally, the students listened to the BBC World Service's Russian language broadcasts. "We weren't listening for something special, nor did I read the papers with the idea of looking for something, as I did later. It was fashionable to listen seriously to the radio, but this took a lot of time away from other pursuits that were more important to us—like music and dancing!" There was one commentator in particular whom Lisa enjoyed, an émigré Russian named Anatoli Goldberg, whose smooth voice somehow penetrated the noise from the regime's electronic jammers. Through Goldberg of the BBC, Lisa first heard of Andrei Sakharov. Within a year or so, she had met the scientist's stepson.

Because of poor grades, Lisa had been forced to repeat her third year at the institute, and as a result she was with students who were a year younger. One of her new classmates was a tall, bespectacled young man with dark eyes, dark complexion, and a quiet manner. He preferred dark clothes that accentuated both his remote ways and his good looks. His class performance showed him to be a talented mathematician. At 21, Alyosha Semenov already was married, the father of a small daughter, and estranged from his wife. His biography was no different from that of millions of other young Soviets. Teenage marriage and divorce are common in the USSR; about one in three Soviet marriages ends within the first year.

As a child, Alyosha had been seriously ill with rheumatic fever, but he had grown into a rangy man with his mother's coloration and none of her outspokenness. Like Lisa, his quiet manner concealed a strong, passionate personality. They became good friends and, in the spring of 1977, lovers. "At that time, I was scarcely interested in Sakharov's social activity and in Alyosha's family ties. And I certainly didn't imagine that Andrei Dmitrievich's activities could have any influence on our fates."

Alyosha took care not to involve Lisa with the life of his family. He knew the authorities would leap to interfere in the usual crude ways: visits to her professors, pressure from the Komsomol, frightening KGB interviews with her parents. For Lisa, Alyosha's family remained remote, inhabiting a world she knew little about. She met

Tanya and Efrem only once, when Alyosha brought her to the apartment in 1977. Lisa met her future father-in-law at the same time —in an elevator. "We greeted each other, but I had the impression he didn't see me. Of course, he had a lot on his mind, a lot of worries. But, generally, he seemed the typical absent-minded professor. I also thought him older than he was. Later, I realized I was mistaken, that in fact his face was quite young."

Elena was not at home on this occasion, and it was not until much later that she learned of Lisa's involvement with her son. By that time, Elena was being denounced by the media for breaking up Alyosha's marriage, as though she had connived against her son's first wife out of sheer malice.

"As usual," Elena told the family with a laugh, "I'm the last to know what's going on, but all the pine cones are thrown at me!" Not long after, Tanya and Efrem left Russia for the States, so they left little impression on Lisa.

On March 1, 1978, with official promises that Lisa would be allowed to join him soon, Alyosha departed for America. The promises were lies. The authorities had no intention of allowing her to leave the country. On the contrary, they were interested in punishing Lisa for her love affair with the son of such notorious anti-regime activists.

Enamored as she was, Lisa never took into account the possible dangers from the state. "I didn't make any plans or think about how our relationship might develop in the future," she said later. "I did not understand why Alyosha's parents insisted that he leave, but I had no reason not to trust him or them—either at the time, or later. But after several years of life in the Sakharov family, when my fate no longer depended on me, but began to depend on the KGB, I understood that if he had not left, he would have become a hostage to Sakharov's public activity the same way I did."

She was called before academic administrators and criticized for poor grades; the Komsomol organization joined in, sanctimoniously accusing her of immoral behavior. She threatened to sue them for slander. "I wanted to frighten them if I could, but, most of all, not to give in." When the teaching assignments for those to graduate were posted, all Moscow-area students except Lisa had jobs in the capital. She was assigned to Magadan, in the extreme northeastern tip of Siberia between the Sea of Okhotsk, the Chukchi Sea, and the Bering Strait. Magadan had been the heart of the Gulag, a place of death camps set in mountainous isolation or grim tundra. Lisa protested and was told that, if she refused to accept the assignment, she would be expelled. She vowed never to go to Magadan.

By the end of the final term, her studies had collapsed; she longed only for Alyosha, who could never return. There were stiff practice teaching sessions. She did badly, was absent a great deal, and flunked the training. The authorities had triumphed: Lisa was dismissed from the institute just before graduation. "It was shameful to have worked six years, to have almost completed my studies, and then to get thrown out. Later, however, it didn't matter. I realized there wasn't much that was useful to learn anyway. Whether I had the piece of paper or not didn't matter all that much."

Meanwhile, the only way she could be reunited with Alyosha was by applying for an exit visa. "Like most Soviets, I had never been abroad on my own and the Jewish and German emigration which had begun early in the 1970s affected none of my friends." With her decision made, Lisa announced to her parents that she wanted to leave the Soviet Union. Stunned, fearful, and scandalized, they ordered her out of their lives. Alone now and with no place to live, Lisa turned to Elena, a woman she barely knew. "At first, it was hard for us to get used to each other. But, eventually, Elena Georgevna made it clear to me that I was a member of the family. And after that, everything took its natural course." And so Lisa moved into the Chkalova apartment.

Between the summer of 1978 and the autumn of 1981, she applied numerous times to OVIR (Otdel Vis I Registratsii), the emigration department of the Interior Ministry, for an exit visa. Each time, she was refused.

"Soviet authorities publicly assert that there are only four reasons for which Soviet citizens may be refused an exit visa: possession of state secrets, military service, a prison sentence, and objections by dependent parents. Had this been true, I would have left Russia in 1978. Unfortunately, there are no written laws regarding emigration. There are [only] rules of the game to which all people who seek exit visas must subject themselves."

For more than a year, Lisa tried unsuccessfully to obtain written approval from her parents to emigrate. "My parents refused outright to sign anything that might assist my departure. My father is a sincere and straightforward person and the thought of my leaving was horrifying to him and my mother. Like the majority of Soviet citizens, they believed what Soviet propaganda kept persuading them to believe about the horrors of Western life and the sanctity of love for the socialist motherland."

In the spring of 1979, the KGB told Lisa's mother that Alyosha no longer loved her daughter, news that quickly made its way to Lisa. Depressed and unable to find out the truth, Lisa took an overdose of tranquilizers. When she saw that Lisa seemed unusually withdrawn and lethargic, Elena rushed her to a hospital. While she was recuperating, Lisa's distraught father appeared at the hospital. The KGB seized the moment and moved to have her pronounced mentally incompetent. This could have cleared the way for a stay in a Soviet psycho-prison, but Lisa's doctors, risking their careers, defied the secret police and ruled that there was no basis for further treatment, especially of the kind the KGB had in mind. Lisa was not suffering from derangement, the doctors said; she had acted out of desperation.

Two and a half years later, it was the Sakharovs' turn to act out of desperation. In a letter to Leonid Brezhnev, Sakharov denounced the treatment of Lisa in unusually harsh terms. "This is blatant hostage-taking by the KGB for revenge and pressure on me." The hunger strike was set to begin in Gorky on November 22, 1981.

IV

ON Monday night, November 21, Andrei Dmitrievich and Elena Georgevna shared what would be their last meal together for an unknown number of days to come. Sakharov was 60 years of age and suffered from chronic heart problems that restricted blood circulation, making his extremities cold and clammy and increasing the paleness of his face. He was under general medical care, and he took his blood pressure almost daily using a portable apparatus friends had bought in the West. Elena, 58, had suffered a variety of circulatory episodes in recent years and had not fully recovered from her severe bout with flu. In traditional Russian style, their final supper before the fast was not large, consisting of leftovers, bread, cheese, and butter. They had tea, which Sakharov preferred piping hot. He liked to sip it from the saucer while holding a piece of apple in his teeth. Later that night when they prepared for bed, the only certainty was that they would see the strike through together.

The next morning, they arose, weighed themselves, drank some Borzhomi to replenish body salts, and spent the rest of the day in their usual pursuits. Sakharov devoted several hours to theoretical work; Elena wrote letters to friends. They listened to the radio for dispatches from the West, but since they could not leave the apartment for fear of being arrested, because of their hunger strike, and separated, they could not escape the special jamming and thus heard little. They exercised regularly, pacing vigorously back and forth on the narrow balcony to keep circulation up and maintain strength. Consulting a book that described the effects of fasting, they compared their own symptoms with interest. They kept to this daily routine as long as they were in the apartment.

Within a few days, the Sakharovs were losing weight rapidly as their bodies burned fat to provide the necessary protein. Although their resolve did not flag, they were increasingly listless. The hunger pangs slowly diminished, to be replaced by feelings of dullness and slight depression. The mineral water salts helped relieve some of the effects of starvation, but soon their livers would be raided for carbohydrates, and then muscle tissue would be assimilated as a source of protein to burn after their body fat had been used up. The possible loss of muscle constituted one of their fast's gravest dangers, since both husband and wife already had weak hearts. Elena's blood pressure declined and, soon, she found that walking around the apartment was a wearying chore that made her dizzy.

For the first few days, brief telegrams of encouragement from Lisa reached the Sakharovs. But the KGB soon put a stop to this. Toward the end of the first week, a letter was smuggled out of the apartment from Andrei Dmitrievich. It quickly made its way to the West. The hunger strike, wrote Sakharov, "is a struggle for the right of anyone to come and go from this country. It is a defense of my rights and honor. No change in our health or empty words will change our minds, only the departure of Lisa. We will continue the hunger strike until the problem is solved."

In a postscript, Sakharov thanked American physicist Sydney Drell for his support, adding: "A tragic end will signify a murder agreed to by the KGB and [abetted] by the complete silence of my colleagues in the Academy of Sciences." The letter stated that he had lost about seventeen pounds and Elena nearly fifteen. His blood pressure, he reported, was also dropping.

The day after Sakharov's letter began its hidden journey to the

West, two visiting French scientists appealed to Anatoli P. Alexandrov, president of the Soviet Academy of Sciences to intervene on behalf of the physicist. "It's the government's business," Alexandrov told them curtly. But outside Russia, public condemnation of the Kremlin was rising. Several European governments joined the protest, passing resolutions pressing Brezhnev to guarantee an exit visa for Lisa. Western scientific groups warned that a complete rupture of international exchanges could result unless a humane solution was found. Despite the barriers to the outside world, the drama was gathering force. Once again, Sakharov was succeeding against all the odds at rallying foreign concern against the Moscow authorities.

Meanwhile, thanks to its eavesdropping equipment, the KGB knew that the couple's condition was deteriorating at an alarming rate. Each day weakened them further, yet they seemed prepared to die before abandoning their attempt to get Lisa out of the country. With the rest of the world now looking on, could the Kremlin dare let the Sakharovs die? Or would the state be forced to capitulate?

As the confrontation continued, it almost seemed as if Lisa, the object of it all, had been overlooked. She was apparently helpless in Moscow, powerless to aid the Sakharovs in making a breakthrough. As the days passed, her anxiety mounted. Although Western governments had reacted, she felt that their responses could never be strong enough to force the Kremlin to relent. At the same time, it seemed perfectly plausible to her that the regime would be pleased to see the Sakharovs die. She detected no concern on the part of the Academy of Sciences to protect Sakharov. And with communication now cut off between her and the Gorky apartment, she was left to imagine the worst.

Two paths lay open: to wait for events to run their course or to intervene as best she could. Deciding on the latter, Lisa demanded a meeting with Academy President Alexandrov to plead with him to help Sakharov. Alexandrov refused to meet, stiffly informing her through a secretary that there was nothing more he could do. When she persisted, Lisa was informed that, if she wanted action, she should go to Gorky and speak with Sakharov himself. Several more days of stalemate passed. Lisa searched frantically for a positive sign from the authorities. As she combed through her recollections of her conversations with the Academy, she suddenly thought she could see a clear sign: hadn't Alexandrov recommended that she go to Gorky herself? Was this a veiled hint from the authorities that they would allow her to see the Sakharovs? And, if so, should she try? Lisa pondered what to do.

Then, on December 4, thirteen days after the hunger strike had begun, the state took action to limit its losses. In Gorky, the secret police battered open the Sakharovs' locked door, hauled the weakened physicist and his wife outside, and drove them off to separate city hospitals where they were registered under aliases. In Moscow, the Soviet press agency, Tass, announced that "medical assistance is being administered to [the Sakharovs] to prevent any complications in the state of their health." The government newspaper, *Izvestia*, quickly denounced Lisa and charged that Sakharov aimed to wreck détente with his fast. The paper published a letter purportedly from Lisa's parents: "Our daughter is being intensively brainwashed in an anti-Soviet spirit by Sakharov, Bonner, and company, with the aim of forcing her to leave the Soviet Union," they wrote.

In Gorky, doctors and KGB agents informed Sakharov that Elena had capitulated, ending her hunger strike. He refused to believe them and continued his fast. Meanwhile, in the other hospital where she was being held, white-coated personnel wheeled a cart of gleaming equipment into Elena's room and arranged it by her bedside. There were intravenous tubes, needles, restraints for legs and arms, and other apparatus. "This is the way we start," one of the aides said, indicating a surgical steel forceps with which to pry jaws apart. It all looked like medieval torture gear. Before the technicians left, Elena was told that her husband was dying. Furious, she vowed never to give up the fast until Lisa was free.

But even as the KGB was attempting to take control in Gorky, Alexandrov's casual suggestion that Lisa talk to Sakharov herself was having its impact on the crisis. The forced hospitalization made clear to Lisa that the lives of her benefactors were in jeopardy. Perhaps if she did go to Gorky something good would come of it for the Sakharovs and herself. Lisa headed for the train station with friends. But, as she was waiting on the platform, two KGB men appeared, hustled her into a car, and drove off. Her friends went to a telephone and news of the apparent abduction soon reached foreign reporters and was on the wires to the West.

The agents released Lisa on the outskirts of Moscow with a warning not to attempt the trip to Gorky again. She made her way back to the center of the city by subway and bus. At the apartment she recounted the details of her conversations with Alexandrov to the foreign correspondents, and it seemed clear that Academy president Alexandrov was guilty of tormenting Sakharov through Lisa. More headlines, more world criticism of Soviet science. The Academy's careful pose of neutrality, so important to deflecting the Sakharov controversy when Soviet scientists in the future would seek wider scientific exchanges abroad, was in jeopardy. The U.S. Congress passed a resolution supporting the Sakharovs and the Reagan White House issued its own statement of support. The KGB's intervention and Alexandrov's suggestion had raised new problems for the regime.

On December 7, with the Sakharovs' fast in its sixteenth day, Lisa went to KGB headquarters at Lyubyanka Prison and requested to see any agent acquainted with the Sakharov case. After waiting in a small reception room off the side entrance to the downtown complex, she was taken through silent corridors to a nondescript room inside the bastion and presented to a man who introduced himself as Alexander V. Baranov. He was about 50 and looked vaguely familiar. Curious, Lisa studied him, certain she had seen him before. Baranov was a man of jarring contrasts: he carried himself with a certain European-style dignity, spoke with a refined Moscow accent, and maintained a pleasant self-confidence without being overbearing. Yet there was a disconcerting asymmetry to his face. The left eye was noticeably larger than the right and, while the rest of Baranov's face was mobile and expressive, this eye had a fixed stare that gave the left side of his face the appearance of a predator. Lisa thought at first that the eye was artificial, but then could see that its pupil dilated and contracted with the light; the fixed stare was genuine. As she looked at the man, she suddenly placed him. "Oh, I know you!" she burst out. Baranov looked uncomfortable: he was the agent who had come to the Chkalova apartment on that January day nearly two years earlier to oversee Elena's departure into exile with Sakharov.

Before the conversation had progressed much farther, Baranov broke it off and informed Lisa that they would see someone else. He led her upstairs to the office of an entirely different sort of agent: a man called Sergei Ivanovich Sokolov. Baranov informed her that Sokolov was a key boss in the KGB's Moscow office, the most important metropolitan secret police bureau in the country. Of middle age, Sokolov was a brusque, crude bureaucrat who had elbowed his way up the KGB command chain. Despite his barely suppressed rage, Lisa realized that, if he was willing to see her, this meant that the authorities themselves were struggling to find a way to resolve the hunger strike. Something had happened to force this upon them, but she could only guess at the circumstance.

Unknown to Lisa, Elena's medical condition was deteriorating rapidly. Even though she was hospitalized, Elena continued to refuse food or other nourishment. Her blood pressure had steadily dropped and the doctors feared she soon would be in a coma. Then it wouldn't matter whether or not the medical staff could force her jaws open with their special equipment. The KGB must find a way out, but could Lisa be made to bend?

Sokolov launched into a denunciation of the Sakharovs. As he repeated the state's formula diatribe, Lisa understood his intention. "They didn't know how to bring the strike to an end—or how to move without losing face. Although I didn't know it, Andrei Dmitrievich and Elena Georgevna were in a life-threatening condition. Now the KGB hoped that I could help them find a dignified way out."

Lisa regarded Sokolov steadily, trying not to betray her apprehension. She hadn't foreseen such an encounter, but there was no escaping the significance of this moment. She might never get to see this man again, or find him groping so aimlessly for a solution. "It all depends on you, not me," Lisa said evenly. "It is you who must do something." What else could she say to them? "Let me go!" Sokolov's face boiled with rage—but then he surprised her. "The question of your traveling to Gorky will be decided tomorrow!" he blustered. Then he abruptly dismissed her without further explanation. She hadn't asked to go to Gorky; why had Sokolov raised this possibility?

Tantalized by this hopeful but tentative sign, Lisa returned to the apartment. Accompanied by several long-time friends of the family, she waited in vain through the night and the next day for any word from Lyubyanka. It was as though she had never talked with Baranov and Sokolov. Her apprehension intensified. The strike was in its seventeenth day with no end in sight and no word from Gorky. She called Alexandrov. This time, he spoke to her and his words chilled her soul. "Sakharov's condition is poor," he said. "I am expecting a decision on this problem today or tomorrow." On this ominous note, he hung up.

On Wednesday, December 9, the eighteenth day of the strike,

there was a knock at the door of the Chkalova flat. A KGB messenger stood outside. Lisa was summoned back to Lyubyanka. Baranov greeted her in the reception room and then took her to another office. Sokolov, the senior man, was nowhere to be seen. She knew the state's methods well enough to realize that this meant some decision had been taken and underlings like Baranov would handle it from now on. She braced herself.

"Sakharov has agreed to end his hunger strike," Baranov said. "And you are allowed to leave the country." She sat impassively, not believing she had heard him right. He said again, "The decision has been made to let you go." Relieved yet suspicious, she looked at him without speaking. Baranov told her more: he said that when Sakharov was informed the previous day that Lisa would be given an exit visa he had agreed to end the hunger strike. The way Baranov described the sequence, it sounded right to Lisa. But this was the KGB speaking and only a fool would trust what they said unless there was further proof—such as word from Sakharov himself, or an exit visa and international passport that would carry her through the phalanx of Green Hat KGB border guards at Sheremetyevo Airport.

Although Baranov assured her that everything would be worked out in detail, he offered no further information, telling her she must wait for the situation to be fully resolved. Lisa left, knowing that the only way she could attempt to hold the organs to their word was to nail them publicly in the world press. From a pay phone, she began calling correspondents to report Baranov's announcement that she would be allowed to leave the country and that the hunger strike was over. Later she held a press conference at the apartment and described her conversation with the KGB man in detail. Even after this, Lisa and the family's friends had no certainty that the organs were telling the truth. They passed the night in tense conversation, making brave, but uncertain, reassurances to each other that the state wouldn't dare reverse itself now.

The next day, Baranov summoned Lisa again; he had something more to say. Wearily, she made her third trip to the secret police headquarters. Before the conversation could begin, Baranov's phone rang. It was Academician Alexandrov calling. Lisa was motioned to the phone and Alexandrov vigorously reassured her that Sakharov had indeed ended his fast. While the couple's condition was serious, he said, they were no longer in danger. The crisis had been resolved and soon she would be free to leave the USSR and there would be no reprisals against anyone.

As she put the phone down, Lisa allowed herself for the first time to believe that the authorities were telling her the truth. Elena and Andrei Dmitrievich really had won!

But here she was in Baranov's Lyubyanka office, not far from basement cells where uncounted numbers of Russians had been tortured and executed. There still was such a long way to go before everyone was safe. And when Baranov greeted her, she knew that trouble was coming. "Lisa," he began, rudely ignoring the correct, formal term of address, Yelizaveta Konstantinovna, which custom dictated and which he had carefully used in their previous encounters. In substituting the familiar short form of her name, which only her closest friends and relatives were privileged to use, Baranov adopted a KGB tactic of demeaning an adversary in an insultingly suggestive way, as though Lisa were a child or a woman too stupid or foolish to discern right from wrong. Before she could object, he launched into a lecture of her "duties" as a Soviet woman and patriot. "Your departure depends entirely upon you—and your behavior," he declared. "I will lay down the conditions of your leaving: you will end your contacts with foreign correspondents; you will conduct yourself in a quiet manner that does not disgrace the Soviet state; you will—"

"——I am Yelizaveta Konstantinovna to you!" she interrupted, her relief suddenly erupting into fury. "You liar! You're all liars! Andrei Dmitrievich is probably already dead! You've shown me no proof that I will leave! This is all just a sham to calm things down! Elena Georgevna may be dead, too! I can't accept the KGB's word without some positive proof they are alive! When I know for sure they have ended their strike, then we can all stop worrying about their condition at your hands!"

While Baranov remonstrated and tried to continue laying down conditions for her departure, Lisa stormed out of his office. At the apartment she called another press conference and told the journalists how the KGB was seeking to cut her contacts with them, using the threat of preventing her departure. No sooner had the correspondents left than a KGB messenger arrived. He informed Lisa that OVIR emigration officials would have her international passport ready to be picked up the next day. The KGB, it seemed, had only wanted to intimidate her one last time.

The next day, Lisa went to the emigration bureau. Here, dozens of privileged Russians and anxious Soviet Jews waited long hours while bureaucrats in a rabbit warren of offices reluctantly issued temporary travel permissions to a handful of citizens each day and permanent exit visas to the despised but declining number of Jews. Among the travel applicants might be a high party official leading a formal delegation, a senior scientist planning a visit to an increasingly rare conference in the West, or a KGB officer with a list of musicians or dancers who had been cleared at the last minute for a concert tour abroad. There also might be families of Jews hoping to find new lives in Israel or America, or Armenians from Yerevan dreaming of joining relatives in California. It didn't matter who was in line—tension hung over the OVIR office. In the Brezhnev era, the emigration department had become a notorious center of corruption, with officials trading freedom for immense bribes and cutting the KGB in on their operations. There had been some personnel shuffles from time to time, but Interior Minister Nikolai Schelekov, a longtime Brezhnev crony who lived in the same building as the Kremlin leader, successfully blocked any meaningful cleanup. Lisa's special situation cut through the deliberate delaying tactics of OVIR clerks. She quickly picked up the precious passport.

A short time later, Baranov informed her that she was free to go to Gorky "if you like." Lisa dashed for a ticket office, and spent three hours in line waiting to get her tickets. Then there was a complication: the ticket agent had oversold the train. The tickets had to be returned and exchanged. It was not until 2 A.M. the following morning that Lisa and Natalya Viktorevna Hesse, a longtime friend of Elena's from Leningrad, boarded a Gorky-bound train. To their alarm, "the train stood for another three hours at the gate. Three more hours of nerves on edge." At last, the unexplained delays were over and they rolled out of the station toward Gorky.

They reached the exile city without further trouble, but, once there, they faced a new problem: locating Elena and Andrei. There were many hospitals serving the city's million inhabitants, and the couple could be in any one of them. The odds against finding them were much higher than either woman could have figured, for Lisa and Natalya Viktorevna did not know that the Sakharovs had originally been sent to separate hospitals or that, now reunited in one hospital suite, they were registered under pseudonyms. Oblivious of these complications, the two travelers huddled and "by guesswork" decided to try a regional hospital called Semashko. At the reception desk, their inquiries were met with indifference. "There are no such patients on the list," the clerk said coldly. Although she was certain the request would be refused, Lisa asked the woman to call a senior physician just to make sure. To her astonishment, the bureaucrat "obediently picked up the phone." As Lisa and Natalya Viktorevna watched, the receptionist penciled in "Sakharov" and "Bonner" next to two unfamiliar last names. With spirits soaring, the two women were ushered through the hospital's corridors.

They reached a door and peered in. Sakharov, haggard and gray-faced, was sitting listlessly in an armchair next to his bed while a nurse bent over him, taking his blood pressure. Without a moment's hesitation, the two women walked in. Transfixed, the physicist struggled to his feet and hobbled toward them, dragging the blood pressure machine with him. "Lisa! Natasha!" Another flurry and, amid sobs of anguish and relief, Elena Bonner came in from her adjoining room, her face a pale gray, lips blue, and eyes sunken deep in their sockets, her hardy voice pinched by her ordeal to a high, strange treble. Fear, grief, joy, triumph, longing, and regret mingled in the reunion. It was the last time all three could be together.

Almost immediately doctors appeared, demanding that the visit come to an end. The patients' strength must be conserved. Elena shooed the medical staff from the room and Lisa had three more hours with the Sakharovs. Then, through the pain of her final goodbye, she heard Andrei Dmitrievich say: "Be happy together."

The two women returned to Moscow. The next week was a confusion of errands, appointments, arrangements, and leave-taking as Lisa readied herself for departure. On Lisa's last night in Moscow, Elena arrived at the apartment, and so did Lisa's parents. There was an awkward meeting as the older antagonists confronted each other and groped for some understanding while the young woman they all loved watched them apprehensively. And then, in what appeared to Lisa to be a miraculous exercise of willpower, her father and Elena seemed to set aside their resentment and suspicion. Hesitantly, they began talking about the experience they most shared: wartime service. Soon, Lisa was aware that her father's fear and rejection, which had bordered on hatred, was mellowing. Elena, he now realized, had suffered defending the motherland. However painful and obscure Elena's motives might be, here was a woman who had shed her own blood for the country. Konstantin Alexeyev seemed to see Elena in a new way. There would never be friendship, but the blind antagonism had been blunted, and that was more than Lisa had ever hoped for.

Late that evening, with the final preparations completed, Elena and Lisa sat together in the kitchen. "We talked through the night. It was impossible to imagine that, in a few hours, we would kiss for a last time and that I would leave. We tried not to think about that. Over the last few years, we had been apart only a short time, and nearly every day when we were separated we exchanged telegrams telling each other our condition. It was only when I was with Elena Georgevna that I felt really alive; the rest of the time I counted the days until she arrived."

The next day, Lisa left the Soviet Union, flying to Paris aboard an Aeroflot flight. An enormous crowd of reporters dazed her with cameras, lights, and recording gear. After a few prepared words, she fled into seclusion with Tanya, Efrem, and Alyosha. She was in the West, and free. But like all the family, her heart would never be fully freed from Moscow or the man and woman who remained behind, banished.

"My departure means they [are] completely alone—without children, without assistance. Loneliness awaits Elena Georgevna in the Moscow apartment. In Gorky, both are in the power of the KGB: round-the-clock monitoring, policemen at the door, the same hateful apartment forced on them. Everything remains the same."

12

Soviet Reality:
Lessons for Living

*Every single time you speak the truth—that is
a heroic deed.*

—YEVGENY V.

I

SHAKING his head, Yevgeny adjusted his eyeglasses, polished them on his shirtfront, and returned them to their precarious position on his thin-bridged nose. A huge grin spread across his face as he peered from his bedroom window. From our vantage point on the daybed, Eliza and I watched his silent mirth with sympathetic delight.

The first summer hot spell of 1981 had turned Moscow into a dusty metropolis filled with sweaty Russians. We were sweating right along with them and drinking kvass, the rootbeerlike drink made from dried crusts of brown bread. Despite the unpromising nature of its principal ingredient, well-made kvass is a delicious thirst quencher.

On numerous occasions over the past year, Yevgeny V., or Zhenia, had been telling us about his life as a Communist party official, bureaucrat, family man, and practical patriot. He was a man who spent his days in pursuit of privilege while balancing carefully —and successfully—on the high wire between public conformity and private conscience. Of all the Russians we had met, Zhenia seemed among those most eager and able to explain the disturbing deceptions of Soviet reality. Now he reckoned that he had found a useful clue that would help foreign friends to understand these hidden absurdities.

With a theatrical sweep of his kvass glass, Zhenia commanded us: "Look at that building over there and all will be clear."

A fourteen-story apartment house was nearing completion in the dusty lot across from his own building. Construction had begun only the previous fall, meaning that the pace of work had been remarkably quick. Such speed was unmistakable evidence that the new building was a cooperative. More and more, Soviet middle managers had found ways to amass thousands of rubles, form cooperatives under the aegis of one institute or another, and build themselves expensive high-rise flats which could be bought and sold or passed down within a family. Senior party people, technocrats, or the security services had enough clout to wring honest work from the construction brigades. With the fourteenth floor of the building almost closed in, Mosstroi Kombinat No. 3, the construction enterprise, had hung a large sign from the tenth floor balconies facing Zhenia's window. In bold white cyrillic letters on the usual red background, the sign proclaimed: *THIS APARTMENT HOUSE WAS BUILT FROM CONSERVED MATERIALS.*

"How can a building be constructed from parts saved from other buildings?" Zhenia asked, his eyes gleaming. "Either the buildings from which this material came were constructed, or they weren't! Either the holes in those other buildings contained windows, or they were bricked up or boarded over or left open, in which case the building is not a building but an aboveground cave or a bird's nest. What about the bricks used to raise this fine new apartment house across the way? Where did they come from? Was another building reduced by one story to create a strategic reserve of bricks? Fourteen other buildings, each a single story shorter than the plan?

"If you are puzzled by failing to find answers to those questions, another answer suggests itself. This sign across the way is an outward confession that you can steal all the material you need for a fourteen-story building, so long as you call it 'conserved' bricks, mortar, and glass. And that raises questions of its own. For example, why are ten window frames being made by the window-frame factory if they are not to be used in a specific project? Who ordered

them from the frame factory? How did Gosplan [the central economic planning authority] allow such waste? There is only one
answer and it is this—the frames were built to be stolen.

"But no one will check something like this. You can stop a water
leak in a faucet or a pipe, and you can save electricity by turning
out the lights. But how can you conserve on glass for a building?
How can you economize on toilets? There is only one way: by
building flats without toilets! The whole idea is beyond comprehen-
sion. Therefore, we must look right past it. When people read such
a sign, they spit on it, figuratively speaking, because even though
they are indifferent to most of what they see, the sign degrades their
intelligence even further. They know they have read a lie perpe-
trated by the Soviet state about a fundamental fact—the creation of
an apartment building.

"People are so used to this kind of lie and it is so impossible to
escape these lies that after they have spat on the sign, they say, 'Well,
this apartment house surely was built from materials that were saved
from other projects. How clever we are under Soviet power.' This
encourages double consciousness. Inside their heads, people don't
support the party or the state itself, but they're afraid to say so, of
course.

"How do we get out of this situation? I don't know. The fact that
people see the truth and are afraid to speak it is our greatest tragedy.
Our history handles this lesson quite well. The truth seekers are
adrift in this society; they refuse to understand that, in a state such
as ours, the party's absolute control gives it control over reality in
a very direct way. Since there's no pluralism, there's no democracy.
In terms of everyday life, that means there can be no real dissent.
The system has complete power to affect every single person in the
society."

From time to time, Zhenia pointed out how the central newspapers, such as *Pravda*, Truth, resorted to sarcastic cautionary tales
in an effort (largely unsuccessful) to draw the line between acceptable deception, as demonstrated by the sign on the new apartment
house, and unacceptable lying that damaged the state.

For example, *Pravda* once printed a tale that rivaled the "saved
materials" sign in obscuring the margin between myth and reality.
This was the story of the Siversk tractor repair factory serving farms
in the Leningrad area, one of the poorest agricultural regions in the

USSR. The factory was crucial to raising productivity for the collective and state farms around the old imperial capital. When it was dedicated in the late 1970s, Siversk had a rated capacity of overhauling fourteen thousand large tractors a year. "It is not a factory, it is a beautiful piece of art," *Pravda* slyly reported, "the largest enterprise of an industrial branch that fully meets the needs of collective and state farms in the northwest regions of the nonblack earth zone [a northern agricultural zone of thin soils]." The paper reserved special praise for the senior officials who initially approved the project and saw that it was built and functioning, uncharacteristically, well ahead of schedule. The list of veteran administrators at the gala dedication was long, and "there are many, many others who helped achieve this triumph over difficulty," *Pravda* said.

There was only one real shortcoming about the repair facility, noted the official newspaper of the Central Committee—the Siversk factory didn't exist. Although it was on the region's official books as one of the most important recent achievements, the enterprise in fact was a collection of moldy, roofless buildings in a rubble-strewn industrial site hidden behind a solid fence, the paper reported. An elderly watchman presided over the useless hulks. He had a rifle, but his chief enemy seemed to have been solitude.

As *Pravda* unraveled the saga, it turned out that, from the moment work on the sprawling new facility got under way in 1974, officials of the Leningrad Oblast Construction Trust No. 49 had been plagued by delays. As the setbacks multiplied, the officials began papering over the truth, signing off on completion reports when nothing had been completed, meeting each stage of the complex construction with false accounts of progress. Fairly soon, unsuspecting senior bureaucrats and party men in Leningrad and Moscow were praising the locals for their remarkable progress. Almost before they realized it, the overseers were reporting that the new complex met every specification. To report otherwise might have brought a snooper, and the chiefs of Construction Trust No. 49 didn't need that.

When the factory was declared ready for installation of the expensive machine tools to recondition tractor engines, there was new trouble: the machine tool enterprise had never expected anything but the usual delays during construction of the tractor enterprise. Although the toolworks had accepted orders for repair machinery and had been paid in advance for some of it, the equipment had never been built—and the money was long since gone. However, the toolworks could not refuse to install the machines. There might be criticism from Leningrad headquarters or, worse, from the Center, Moscow. Careers could be ruined. Like any good shaggy dog, this one simply grew more hair.

The tool enterprise signed off on phantom delivery and installation reports, and forwarded the papers to Leningrad headquarters. Now the Siversk factory was ready for production. Meanwhile, an older repair factory—an actual one—was torn down because the more efficient new facility made it obsolete. The local environmental inspector signed a document saying that the new factory was nonpolluting. The fire inspector attested to the fact that it was no fire hazard. Other inspectors and building-code enforcers signed similar approvals. Later, they argued that they had acted in an exemplary manner: since the factory didn't exist, it couldn't pollute or pose a fire hazard. The deception was so complete, and senior officials' inertia so great, that N. V. Bosenko, the chairman of the State Committee of Agricultural Technical Means of the Russian Federation, recommended medals and prestigious state congratulations to dozens of officials. It took months for investigators to find out that the factory was a phantom.

As he laughed over this tale, Zhenia summarized what he called an important truth about Soviet reality: "A bear hunter in Siberia may have killed twenty bears at close range, choked them to death with his own hands. But his courage disappears straight into the ground when he faces the party. To face a bear is one thing. To face the party is something very different! The smart bear hunters know that. Their children learn from the beginning that the system is the enemy and they quickly find out exactly what they can do and what they can't do. So every single time you speak the truth, this is a heroic deed.

"The landscape of our country is filled with signs like the one on this new building that twist the mind of a reasonable man and make him settle for the unreal as a condition of sanity."

Zhenia offered another example of how reality and make-believe can clash in a system that rewards falsehood and penalizes truth. This episode, also reported by *Pravda*, was set in Minsk, the capital of Byelorussia, and involved the hapless managers of an electrical manufacturing plant who attempted to computerize their operation. In the early 1970s, the managers purchased a rare and costly "Minsk-32" computer, complete with typewriter-style console and terminal, printer, card-feed unit, and data-processing and storage components. Computers are still relatively rare in the Soviet civilian economy. Even at the Soviet Bank for Foreign Trade in the early 1980s, the abacus was the preferred instrument of computation in complex foreign currency transactions. So the factory chiefs were justifiably proud of their daring modernity, which probably helped them overlook a tiny cloud on the horizon: an institute in the western Siberian capital of Novosibirsk, hired to write thirty-one software programs to run the computer, was slightly behind in its delivery schedule. In fact, the Novosibirsk enterprise had unilaterally reduced the number of programs to twenty-six. When the time came to start up the computer, the software designers had completed only eight programs. "There were no objections to this," reproved *Pravda*, "though it is clear that an insufficiently used system does not justify itself economically. The factory managers wanted to claim as soon as possible that the system had been launched. They meant to say that progress is not alien to them." Soon there were other, far more serious problems than unfulfilled software orders.

The difficulty arose when the computer, as its first task, was ordered to identify workers whose output showed that they were goldbricking. The machine spewed out a list. When the list grew dangerously long, foremen began falsifying production reports—largely to protect themselves. The computer then was put to work scanning the overall production schedules to pinpoint assembly-line bottlenecks. But the men on the line enjoyed the bottlenecks, because each delay gave them time to relax for a smoke and some gossip. They fed more false data to the white-smocked technicians who ran the Minsk-32.

At first, the factory managers staunchly backed the computer's ability to identify problems. "Two months of experimental calculation reveals weak production discipline [that has] undermined information about fulfilling norms," they told the workers. "It is necessary to pay serious attention to the department of automated systems management." The Soviet Luddites had other ideas. When the computer sought accurate information on completion rates for some power plant generating equipment, production manager E. Voronyelsky told his superiors: "Construction of electric stations is such a complicated thing that it is completely impossible to keep a useful record." Sabotage of the electronic marvel moved forward on other fronts: foremen estabished two sets of books—one for the computer, and one for themselves. Double bookkeeping spread. Even the personnel department, strongly interested in worker performance, set up two different reporting systems.

With these countermeasures taking hold, the supervisors faced another problem: how to deal with the twenty-seven technicians who ran the computer. Before long, a solution was found; the electronic interlopers were sent to Coventry. "The [computer] section was psychologically separated from the collective with the silent agreement of the department managers," reported *Pravda*. This final move took the stuffing out of the men who had longed for a Minsk-32 in the first place. The chiefs knew it was time for a face-saving change of course, and they turned on their would-be electronic efficiency expert.

"Why do we need a computerized management system?" asked the chief engineer, Vladimir Vibrobov, who had spearheaded the drive to install the machine. "If the central department doesn't want to take our system and demands that documents be done manually, even they don't want to use the computer's work." The *Pravda* correspondent commented, "The department doesn't cope with the plan and the last thing they need is a computer system which makes their shortcomings so vivid. No responsible person in the department wanted to play any longer with progress."

Engineer Vibrobov knew what had to be done: "Byelo Russian State Power Construction Department sells computer," read the for-sale notice in the newspaper *Evening Minsk*. "We tried to catch up with fashion," mused Vibrobov. "We thought that, if the computer was a thinking machine, it would think for us. And all it brought us was trouble."

Zhenia summed up this saga in one word: "*Bardak,*" he said. "That used to mean a whorehouse, but now the word mostly means a mess. These messes come from the live-and-let-live psychology of our system, which works like this: one steals, the second watches, and the third is silent. The violence committed in this relationship is not only violence to reality, but it becomes criminal and moral violence as well.

"I've never lived in other countries, but I don't think that any other form of government in the world encourages people to steal so much from the state. Salaries are low, there is nothing to buy anyway, so everybody must steal. I think at least 10 percent of everything made in a factory or grown for market is stolen. And it begins with the smallest things. In candy factories, they steal chocolate and sugar, or the liqueur for the candy fillings. Not long ago, a woman worker in the Red October Candy Factory here in Moscow was caught with twenty bars of chocolate in her bag. They gave her a five-year sentence as a deterrent to others. But millions steal anyway. In tobacco factories, they steal cigarettes. In packing plants, they steal vegetables or canned goods, or jars of tomatoes. This is a normal order of business. In the Moskvich car factory, each worker probably steals the value of one car a year."

"Why?" we asked.

"Because he can steal a simple switch that costs twenty-seven kopecks and sell it for three rubles. People understand how to specialize in certain areas. A woman who works in a silk factory quickly learns how to steal silk thread and wrap it around herself under her dress. Or she puts it in her boot. Lenin had a saying: 'Socialism is accounting." But the fact is, when the state is in charge, no one is responsible, no one cares.

"An example might be found in a factory where there are many accidents. The party watchdogs add up the accidents and then call in the factory director. The party man has the power to dismiss the director. Instead, he gets a promise from the director that matters will be taken care of, and together they falsify the safety records. Now the factory director is in the same position as a man who takes a bribe. His problem is taken care of, but he has participated in a crime. And if the injured workers protest, they get a few weeks' extra vacation, and that buys them off. So everyone is linked in a chain of corruption which the party induced in the first place."

Zhenia's reflections reminded me of the situation Alexei Nikitin had tried to correct, and I asked him about the party's view of such "truth seekers." He didn't hesitate to answer.

"Perhaps one in ten of these people find the truthful answers to their petitions. But most don't, because, if a worker is unhappy, he complains against the director of his enterprise—a natural reaction. But since the director himself is a party member, he is in no danger, for the party will close ranks against the worker. And if the worker persists, then his little son will be thrown out of kindergarten, because the school is run by the factory which the director controls in the interests of the party. So the smart man bends and does nothing. The principled man takes his complaint higher and higher until he runs into trouble that overwhelms him. Then, perhaps, he also becomes smart. He has learned how to believe in our party reality."

II

ZHENIA V. grew up in the equivalent of middle-class comfort in Moscow and spent his life as a willing student of party reality. His father, Vladimir, was a bureaucrat in the vast Ministry of Trade, "a member of a technical group that prepares technical questions and never answers them. He was a paper–filling-out bureaucrat, a link in the great chains that bind the country together." Zhenia's mother, Olga, taught science in a technical institute, and his maternal grandmother helped raise him. Zhenia was evacuated from the capital during World War II and lived in Kazakhstan where he and his mother and babushka were taken in by a family of Moslem Kazakhs. When he returned to Moscow after the war, he did well in school and took the usual route designed to place him in the party: Young Octobrist, Young Pioneer, League of Young Communists. He studied at an economics institute, graduated toward the middle of his class, and spent the first few years of young adulthood on a major Komsomol project in Siberia. Here he earned a bundle of rubles and, more important, proved that he was a serious-minded young man with no intellectual pretensions. In the eyes of the party, this was distinctly in his favor. Members of the intelligentsia, in the same way they shunned military service, avoided working on the party's national Hero projects, such as the Bratsk High Dam or the Baikal–Amur Magistral, the new railroad being forged through the sparsely settled taiga of central Siberia to the Pacific Coast. Their refusal to participate in these demonstrations of Soviet power reinforced the regime's unsympathetic view of intellectuals as fundamentally disloyal citizens. A party man might be the intellectual superior of the intelligentsia, and he might even be fascinated by them, but no matter: he must not forget that the intelligentsia despised the party even though they feared its political police. So Zhenia steered clear of intellectuals and sniped at them when he could.

Similarly, Americans were feared as intellectually superior citizens of a technological behemoth. This made it important to jab at Americans whenever an opportunity presented itself. It didn't matter that Zhenia and his colleagues had never met an American. His friends' reaction when a Soviet spacecraft reached Venus ahead of the U.S. summarized their crude insecurity. "Ha, there'll be earwax all over Venus by the time John Glenn arrives!" the Russians crowed. Muzhik humor was uncivilized, but unfailingly nourishing. You always knew who the butt of the joke was.

Zhenia had no brothers and sisters, but there were two cousins on his father's side. Even though these relatives also lived in Moscow, Zhenia rarely mixed with them. Both cousins were heavy drinkers. Worse yet, they had become journalists. In Russia, this meant propagandists and, as Zhenia matured, he took a strong dislike to propaganda of every kind. He kept this potentially damaging quirk well hidden, but it was wise for him to steer clear of the cousins and they reciprocated—perhaps, he reflected occasionally, because he was an economist in a country whose economy seemed to have been invented by Gogol or Gogol's nearest Western relative, Jonathan Swift, the Irishman.

When he returned from Siberia in the early 1960s, Zhenia thought about trying for a postgraduate degree. But he met a young party woman named Masha and soon they were married. Instead of studies, Zhenia found himself looking for a job. His papa helped out, talking to his own circle of friends and party men. Zhenia was hired as a junior analyst at Gosplan, the vast state planning agency that seemed to be engaged in every economic decision in the Soviet Union, from determining the price of gold fillings to decreeing how many metal eyelets a man's shoe should have.

Zhenia was put in an office whose employees checked other bureaucrats' reports and wrote their own reports of those reviewed. The packet of forms then was sent along to another, more exalted level of the maze. Before long, Zhenia discovered that there were different degrees of report writing. Some offices were limited to filling out not more than ten or fifteen lines per report, while more important offices were authorized to fill out fifty or sixty lines before sending the papers onward. Success was measured by how many lines a bureaucrat had filled out. It was unclear what impact the reports themselves had, but there was no denying their fundamental importance as a source of employment in Soviet society. In fact, a

1983 state study revealed that eight hundred billion pieces of paper were filtering through the civilian sector at any moment, a discovery that helped explain why the Soviet economy was slowly running down. According to a story by my Moscow bureau successor, Dusko Doder, the new Kremlin leadership under Yuri Andropov was searching for ways to stem the tidal wave of form–filling-out, but no one in the upper echelons was sure how to proceed. Meanwhile, there was full employment for Zhenia and his colleagues.

Zhenia kept his head down and steadily advanced within Gosplan. More important, he advanced within the party, moving from candidate to full party membership. In 1964, when Khrushchev was replaced, Brezhnev became party secretary and Alexei Kosygin, premier. For a time, it looked as if Kosygin would force economic reforms on the system. But, by the late 1960s, Brezhnev and his conservative Politburo allies had thwarted the premier; there would be no major changes. The party would continue to involve itself in every economic decision at every level while opposing local initiative as a danger to its control. Zhenia was indifferent to all this.

"Thirty years ago, people may have believed in the party. That was just after Stalin died. We had suffered for a long time under Stalin and it helped us to believe there was some higher purpose to these sacrifices. But within the next ten years or so, belief in the party died. In general, people of my generation now stake their lives only on what their party careers can bring them. The ideology means nothing to anyone but Suslov.* Even he spends his time justifying the twists and turns as principled positions when everyone knows that our country is motivated by simple opportunism.

"There's another reason why party people no longer believe in the ideology, if they ever did. You can't really move ahead anywhere *without* the party. If you look at the middle management of this country, you will see that 99 percent of it is party while the party only accounts for about 6 percent of the entire population. Were we so smart as to choose right in each and every case, finding only the most brilliant managers and bureaucrats to run our country? Not at all! Membership in the Communist party of the Soviet Union is far more important than talent or brains. To move ahead, it helps to be talented, of course. But whenever there is advancement, the first

---

*Mikhail Suslov, 1902–82, Politburo member and chief party ideologue for over thirty years.

question is: 'Is he a party member?' If the answer is, 'No,' the chance for promotion is practically zero. The result is cynicism and a defensive psychology that demands, 'Who cares what we believe in?' The most important thing for anyone inside or outside the party is to learn how to get along with the organs of the party. And, of course, this is easier when you're inside. So it's natural for talented people to be discouraged from seeking leadership positions. Complete mediocrity rules this country at most levels."

Zhenia sketched for us the career of a young woman who might have been a female version of himself, although he claimed he had simply dreamed her up to help illuminate the system. He gave her the name of Ksenia. Her mother was a high school graduate who worked in the personnel office at party headquarters in an outlying region of the capital, preparing technical questions for job applicants. "Papa is a mindless bureaucrat who has risen above his modest education. In school, Ksenia gets low marks, mostly threes [Cs]. She knows she would never make it into an institute, but she doesn't want to work in a factory. She knows if she can get a party billet, she can get ahead. So she works hard as a Young Pioneer and becomes a Komsomol member. After graduation from school, she comes back as a senior leader for the Pioneers. This is the first real entry of the dossier that will get her into the party. There are certain other things over which she has no control; specifically, she better not be a Jew or even half-blooded. And there must be no relatives living abroad.

"After a year, she might be a Komsomol instructor, and then she is on an escalator that will move her up even if she does nothing more, because now she is chosen as a candidate member of the party. Frequently, the choice has nothing to do with talent. The word comes out from Moscow Center: find a woman with a proletarian background for such-and-such a raion. This happens especially in the countryside, and on kolkhozes it is common to find people of limited intelligence or energy, or even some old babushka, made a party member because there is a directive to add some women to make things look better. Otherwise, women would never be allowed to share in the privilege system the way they do. For our Ksenia, the Komsomol has its own schools of higher education, without significant exams or competition. She can attend for three years, study the party history, and get a degree in that. Now she is qualified to teach party history, a rote job that requires no thinking whatsoever. It's very hard to find a good humanities job in the Moscow area, but Ksenia knows the party will look out for her, and soon she has what she wants—a teaching position in a party classroom. Next, it is necessary to figure out where to live in Moscow.

"From the party point of view, some regions are better than others. There are industrial regions and intelligentsia regions. The industrial regions are the prestigious ones because these are the raions of the working class. Ksenia has no intention of joining the working class, but she must be able to claim solidarity with them. By the way, it's extremely prestigious to have a worker somewhere in the family tree—a son, a father, a brother. Even if only for two or three months one year a decade ago! So, our young woman lives in Zhdanovski, Proletarskii, or Baumanski raion. She'd better not live in Gagarinski raion, for that's where a number of scientific institutes with their Jews are located. She becomes an instructor and, pretty soon, she is a department leader.

"She wants to move up in the regional party committee and now she has reached a possible competitive point. There are many regional department heads and only two or three party secretaries. Perhaps Ksenia has realized that it is within her grasp to become a secretary, or chief, of a regional Komsomol organization. If she can achieve that, an elevated career is guaranteed. But the competition is stiff. She will have to be clever, and know instinctively which senior party men to heap with praise. She must be very tactful and diplomatic. And, of course, it doesn't hurt if she 'sleeps high'—takes a senior party man as a lover.

"For his part, the party man who makes love to Ksenia must himself be very, very careful. He'd better not 'heat up on women,' as the saying goes." Zhenia offered a wry smile. "We may have the same drives as the decadent bourgeoisie, but the party is very prudish, since it must appear to set the moral tone for the country. Despite the personal excesses of Brezhnev in collecting fine cars, or of Stalin in getting drunk every night, or of Khrushchev in guzzling vodka at state receptions and also getting drunk, our tradition is one of vigilant public modesty. We know Lenin had a mistress, but this is glossed over and we pay stern lip service to fidelity in marriage.

"So any affair must be extremely discreet: no tracks at all. No talking about it to anyone. No boasting. No love letters. They can be found and used against the chieftain if Ksenia gets angry and leaves him or he goes back to his wife. If he's careful, he can change wives, but he's got to keep it quiet. In short, this takes most of the fun out of an affair."

"Just like our New England Puritans," I suggested. "A party man can have a good time as long as he doesn't enjoy it."

"Yes, exactly like you," Zhenia laughed. "If he's an older man, he may get away with it because there is general sympathy for a man who gets rid of an old babushka and finds someone young and sweet." His tone was ironic, as if he wanted to reassure me of the human qualities of his seniors. "There are plenty of these marriages and they aren't frowned on, because all the old bulls want the same for themselves. And it's natural for parents to want this kind of marriage for their daughters—a life of material advantage at the side of an older man who won't be too demanding.

"But a young guy can't fool around. Four or five other ambitious young men are likely to want his job. And there is sympathy for a young wife who gets dumped by a young husband. In fact, the young man may have rivals who want to use his wife against him. So they may try to take her as a lover, at least for long enough to finish off her foolish husband who's out playing around with Ksenia.

"In general, Ksenia finds and pays court to a 'hairy arm' who protects her throughout her career. The same thing works for men as well. Maybe the best example to cite for you is that of Yuri Brezhnev, our leader's son. He never worked in the party organization. Yet he became first deputy minister of trade and drives a Mercedes. He certainly had a 'hairy arm!' "

"Where's the payoff?" I asked.

"Privileges! In a society of deficit, privilege is the key to the good life!"

Zhenia smiled and leaned forward, his eyes focused on some point in the distance. "Privilege is everywhere if you know how to look for it. "In a factory, the chief engineer and the director have cars and dachas. When one of these men retires, he generally keeps the dacha but loses the car. When he dies, the dacha goes back to the state. If he is a 'first face,' his privilege is at the top of his level of the party."

III

AT the age of 45, Zhenia had created a comfortable life for himself, his wife, Masha, and their son, Pavel. The family lived near Moscow

State University in a three-room apartment that was notable for the number of foreign items it contained. These included a secondhand Dutch-made phonograph (six hundred rules), East German lacquer-finished bookshelves (eight hundred fifty rubles plus unknown special favors for the manager of the furniture store), a Japanese transistor radio (eight hundred rubles), a West German table lighter (one hundred rubles), several American calendars, Polish glassware, and the internationally acclaimed Karsh of Ottawa photographic portrait of Ernest Hemingway with beard and bulky turtleneck. Like many of his countrymen, Zhenia had a passion for Jack London and Hemingway among the many American writers whose works he had read. He had an incomplete collection of these two in translation, and Pavel had inherited his father's love of the American authors. Father and son also shared a consuming interest in American jazz and maintained a large collection of Soviet records and some Eastern bloc recording artists. Zhenia and his son had listened to Willis Conover, the Voice of America's jazz expert, and they revered an eclectic group of American jazz musicians: Louis Armstrong, Miles Davis, Fats Waller, Ornette Coleman, Charlie Parker, Billie Holiday, Duke Ellington—and Bing Crosby. Their passion for jazz was the thing that first brought us together.

Alexei Kozlov, one of the most resourceful of Moscow's longtime jazz musicians, had taken me to a Moscow music school auditorium to hear a rehearsal by jazz groups for an upcoming competition. I was astounded by the technical prowess and smooth sophistication of the groups, whose music ran the gamut from blues to swing to modern with some interesting stops in between. The hunger for American jazz in Russia is a phenomenon for which the regime has never found an adequate answer, and probably never will, since the party has never repudiated the idea that jazz is decadent. Kozlov, a marvelously intense saxophonist in his late 40s, was a major figure in the endless skirmishing with party cultural watchdogs over jazz experimentation. He himself had played blues, rock, hard rock, cool jazz, swing, and perhaps half a dozen other styles in search of artistic self-expression and official approval. By the summer of 1980, his newest group, Arsenal, was playing a seamless fusion jazz that combined a driving percussion section with a strong wind group, highlighted by his own emotional and inventive sax solos. It had taken months, but Kozlov had brought his music past the censors and out on stage for showcasing during the Moscow Olympics. The night I saw Arsenal perform on the stage at the hulking Rossiya Hotel theater, the group demonstrated the kind of excitement and control that could have packed houses in the States. But Arsenal's Rossiya performance had not yet occurred when Kozlov and his woman friend, a lovely Tatar with exotic features, took me to the jazz school rehearsal.

While we were there, various musicians and afficionados shyly approached Kozlov to offer greetings or receive his advice, or simply to share delight at the rehearsals. Pavel V. was among them, and when he learned that I was an American, he couldn't contain himself. Within a few moments, he was nearly sitting in my lap, his narrow head and ragged, pageboy mane in my face as he whispered intense questions:

"Did you ever see Ellington? What does Conover look like? Gerry Mulligan . . . whatever happened to him? How about 'Billie Sings the Blues?' " The questions showered down on me, and when I couldn't answer most of them, exasperation set in. Pavel knew much more than I did about every aspect of American jazz, just as most Soviet scholars of American literature know their authors better than Americans do and Soviet propagandists know immense amounts about the United States Constitution—even if they don't understand it.

The one thing I had was records—not hundreds, but a few dozen, as eclectic a collection as that of Zhenia and his son: some Django Reinhardt, Erroll Garner, Count Basie, Ellington, Holiday, Basie, and the famous 1947 Louis Armstrong concert at Symphony Hall, Boston. Ingredients for a fast friendship were at hand. Pavel didn't hesitate.

There were some brief meetings in the most public place we could think of—Pushkin Square, one of the busiest spots in downtown Moscow. The small, tree-lined park is a three-block-long mall bounded by the Garden Ring inner circumferential road and two of Moscow's most important shopping streets, Gorky and Petrovka. On all but the coldest winter days the square bustles with pedestrians scurrying for food and clothing or movie and theater tickets. It is the traditional gathering place for lovers, friends, acquaintances, and news contacts. For these reasons, the square, like the Intourist and National Hotels farther down Gorky Street (the Fifth Avenue of Moscow), also is a popular hangout for KGB agents, schemers, and opportunists on the lookout for gullible foreigners. Dangling mouth-watering black-market prices, these sidewalk operators hunt for tourists and try to arrange illegal deals for money, furs, or artwork. Most of these sleazy figures from the demimonde work as informants or provocateurs for the organs. The statue of the great poet is ringed by park benches, and the plaza between the monument and the modernistic Rossiya movie theater to the north is crisscrossed with paths.

After a few meetings there to hand over some records, Pavel next called me from a pay phone near the Hotel Ukraina on Kutuzovsky Prospekt a few blocks from our compound. This was a customary place to meet as well, from which we could walk down along the river embankment. In large part because my knowledge was so limited, jazz soon was exhausted as a satisfactory topic between us. Pavel then moved to his other interest, American writers. Here I was better able to hold up my end of things. Then Pavel invited me to visit him at home. We talked about the possible consequences for him and his family. "It is not a problem," he said; so I went. The conversations focused on the life of students and student attitudes. There were other visits.

Some weeks later, and breaking all his own best rules, Zhenia made an unannounced midday appearance while we were sitting with Pavel in the kitchen of his apartment. I felt somewhat uncomfortable at first, as though I had been caught tempting his son with forbidden riches. Later, I guessed that Zhenia's arrival had been anything but accidental. And then, Zhenia apparently decided there would be no turning back. It was never precisely clear to me what motivated him to take the risk of making friends with an American correspondent and his family. Perhaps Zhenia wasn't sure himself. I think he simply gave in to a curiosity so intense it was irresistible. He had reached a certain career limit, had acquired most of what he and his family could enjoy in the way of material goods, and wasn't looking for much more. He also had learned a great deal about life in his country and had a desire to pass the knowledge on to someone. The fact that we were the recipients of this impulse was one of the hidden benefits that détente fostered inside Russia in the 1970s.

The relaxation of tensions, as the Russians call détente, brought more foreigners to Moscow in the 1970s than at any time since World War II, when circumstances were vastly different. As a result, for the first time in the history of Soviet power and in the history of the city, foreigners—and, more important, Westerners— were in Moscow as a large, permanent, peaceful presence. Joining them were increasing thousands of Western tourists. Despite the extraordinary effectiveness of the KGB-penetrated Intourist travel agency at thwarting uncontrolled contacts between tourists and ordinary Soviets, the sightseeing foreigners had a conditioning effect on Moscovites. All the state propaganda urgings to maintain vigilance against outsiders could not blunt the impact of seeing resident foreigners send their children to Soviet schools, shop in local markets, attend plays, movies, and theater, and, in many cases, converse in Russian with their fellow drama and music lovers. Not since Khrushchev's gala 1957 International Youth Festival, in which Soviet youth and teenagers from dozens of other countries literally danced together in the streets in a happening that is still revered, had there been such an intermingling of Soviets and outsiders as in the 1970s.

For many Soviets like Zhenia, the sudden, relatively easy access to foreigners caused profound yearnings. Psychological barriers of long duration slowly came down inside Moscow and we made friends with Zhenia—and he with us.

From his father-in-law, Zhenia had inherited a Moskvich auto, which the family used in summer as transportation to a rented dacha twenty-five miles south of the city. In most other seasons, the old car sat beneath a tarpaulin behind the apartment house, its innards worked on intermittently by a friend of Pavel's who knew where to get replacement parts. Although it was endless trouble, the car also was money in the bank—about five thousand rubles on the illegal used-car market if the family ever wanted to get rid of it. Neither Pavel nor Masha drove; Papa had the license in the family. Here was authentic Soviet-style privilege. Zhenia's dacha was owned by the widow of a Trade Ministry official who had been one of several "hairy arms" for Zhenia's father. The family rented two rooms in the house and shared kitchen and bath with the widow. The widow tended a small garden of lettuce and tomato plants but, during the two summers we visited, there was not enough sun to ripen the tomatoes. They were pickled for the winter. We got to know the dacha and its surroundings very well, for Zhenia invited us there on many summer weekends.

We had two cars in Moscow: a Volvo station wagon owned by the *Post* and our personal car, a small red Soviet-made Fiat 124 subcompact. Called a Zhiguli, about six hundred thousand of these cars, more than any other Soviet type, are manufactured annually at a giant auto factory that the Russians bought from the Italians and moved lock, stock, and barrel to a new city on the Volga named after Palmiro Togliatti, the Italian Communist leader. There are three kinds of Zhigulis: a low-priced, underpowered, four-door sedan; a low-priced, underpowered, four-door station wagon; and a four-door sedan with deluxe trim and a souped-up engine for the export trade. Resident foreigners could easily and quickly buy Zhigulis direct from the state for two thousand dollars, radio and heater included. The Soviet ruble price was more than double that, and the normal waiting time for a Soviet buyer was between five and seven years. This was because Moscow sold about a third to a half of each year's production abroad for hard currency, despite the immense demand for cars at home. These facts told all we needed to know about the value of the ruble and the regime's interest in satisfying citizens' demands for a higher living standard.

We took the Zhiguli on trips to the countryside in the belief that, despite its unmistakably foreign plates, it still was less conspicuous than the Volvo. Sunday mornings in June and July, we filled the car with picnic baskets, blankets, Frisbees, and kites, stuffed ourselves inside, and headed for the dacha belt south of Moscow. Once there, we would park the car in the woods several hundred yards from Zhenia's house in hopes this would confuse any sentinels. It probably confused no one, but, like most such precautions, however feeble they might be, we all felt somewhat better for having tried.

The grounds around the house went untended: grass grew to waist height and unpruned bushes and stubborn young saplings dotted the yard. No one thought to cut the grass, in part because lawnmowers are simply not part of Soviet life. As summer wore on, the oddly shaped wooden and brick houses of the dacha community almost seemed to disappear, melting harmoniously into the landscape, swallowed up by a sea of maturing field grass against a background of tall, aromatic pines. A wonderful sense of peaceful abandon took hold. After enduring years of Washington weekends shattered by the racket of rotary mowers running at full throttle over the postage-stamp lawns in the neighborhood where we lived, we found the relaxed Russian tradition a beguilingly sane summer life-style.

During the summer, Masha spent as much time as possible in the country, and Zhenia and Pavel came out on weekends, the car laden with food from downtown. Father and son took long walks in the forests nearby while Masha prepared soup, a meat dish, potatoes, and plates of salad, raw vegetables, and greens. Sometimes the men gathered wildflowers and brought them back. Occasionally, the family organized a picnic; the favorite spot was a small clearing in the woods beside a huge hayfield farmed by the local kolkhoz. There was always a small fire, and we often boiled potatoes in water drawn from a mossy pipe where a spring rose in the middle of the pine woods. One weekend, we discovered that an enormous haymow, perhaps fifteen feet high and twice as long, had appeared in the middle of the field during our absence. We spent the afternoon throwing each other off the mountain, and, to our surprise, no one showed up to remonstrate about the need to preserve the harvest for the gains of the Revolution—or the winter welfare of the cows.

On especially hot weekends, we went swimming in a branch of the Moscow River that ran through the countryside about a mile from the dacha. A walk down a country lane, across a series of paved roads and then around the perimeter of a fenced-off sanitarium, took us to the steep bank of the river. In one of those remarkable scenes of hardy Russian pleasure seeking, we would mingle with as many as five hundred bathers gathered on the bank. With their suety bodies painfully white from months of cloudy northern weather, courting couples, families, and adolescents sat or lay on towels on the trampled grass and soaked up June sun. The river at that point was sluggish, almost a millpond, with a slime-covered mud bottom. The slow-moving water was thick with algae, and tiny plants with leaves like brilliant green confetti floated on the surface. The river looked like a great cauldron of pea soup. No matter. The Russians had come to cool themselves: the river was jammed with people splashing through the viscous vegetation as though they were swimming in a sparkling new Olympic pool. Here, Zhenia continued his discourse on privilege and safety.

"In higher circles, this question is asked: 'Do you have a *kremlovka?*', a Kremlin privilege. These are for the higher bosses, and the first and most important part of this privilege is health care at special clinics, since health services are at a low level in our country. The second part of the privilege is to be able to order food from special stores where prices are much lower than in regular stores. In this food supply system, there are different levels. At the lowest, you might order up to a hundred rubles of food a month, equivalent to about two hundred fifty rubles in the regular markets. This is called a *paiok,* a food ration.

"From the level of regional party secretary and higher, there is slang to describe the food privileges: the *avozka,* or 'possible bag,' is the word applied to the amounts of food that can be ordered by these senior people. 'Do you have an avozka? 'Yes.' 'Oh-ho!' Envy and fear spring from the lips of the inferior questioner, who will be at some pains in the future to cultivate a friendship if the more powerful man is interested. If he is not interested, then our man, or our hypothetical Ksenia, will grovel or steer around this interestingly powerful, but possibly troublesome fellow. Avozka privileges may go to levels of one hundred to one hundred fifty to two hundred rubles. Maybe even Brezhnev has to pay for his groceries, but without any limit.

"These special food privileges are closely held. For example, in the Ministry of Trade, anyone who is a member of the 'colleagues,' the uppermost circle, has these advantages. 'Colleagues' would be the minister himself and perhaps eight or ten assistants and the main department heads. In some huge ministries, there may be twenty-five separate departments and twenty-five chiefs, but only twenty 'possible bags' in all. One department head gets the privilege and another, no less important, doesn't. It's very hard to say why this is so. Perhaps it depends on how you smile at the minister at the morning meetings. Sometimes the fight for privilege can end up in open combat. For example, when two ministries were merged some years ago, about forty department chiefs had to be fitted into twenty slots. A wild war broke out for spoils. All order disappeared and the new ministry had to start over again in deciding who would get what. One of the assistant ministers was a good man, a believer in the ideals of the party. He was an orderly person, he knew what had to be done, and he had the brains to see issues beyond tomorrow. But because the situation was so foreign to his hopes for the country, he proved unequal to the task of apportioning privilege. The reorganization backfired on him, and he wound up stripped of most of his own privileges. His misplaced idealism cost him everything but his job, and in the end he became the butt of jokes because he couldn't even hold onto his own advantages. This is one example of the lack of guarantees even though a person may be a senior party or government official.

"Since there is some variation in the way privilege is apportioned, a smart party man has an incentive to go after extras. He might strive to take on greater 'social responsibilities,' such as becoming the editor of the 'wall paper,' the factory newspaper that is plastered up in the cafeteria and corridors of the administration buildings. Or he could volunteer to bring political enlightenment to the workers on behalf of the party—dull work, but essential in the profile if one is to improve the packet of privilege.

"But where does this leave the country when it comes to economic output or industrial performance? On a daily basis, very little that the party deals with in a factory or production enterprise has any impact on these questions. And economic performance, after all, is far more important in determining our living standards than any political doctrine. This is one of many paradoxes, for, while the party is deeply involved in every economic decision, much of what the party does has no connection with improving production.

"After metals and gas and oil, forest and wood products are the most important in the nation," Zhenia said. "How can this country, with its vast northern forests, its unlimited riches of pine, birch, and larch—how can we have a paper shortage? How can there be a shortage of timber for shoring and making forms for concrete? To find the answer, we must analyze what happens the moment a tree is cut down. What happens then? What happens is that the tree is piled in the forest, along with tens of thousands of other felled trees. Instead of being hauled to a sawmill or a processing plant and put under a roof, the trees are left out unsheltered. Nine out of every ten trees cut down this year will rot! That is a true statistic. But, for obvious reasons, no one will ever read of it in the central press. A people's control commission might investigate if there is enough of a stink made about waste in some local raion, but here is what happens:

"The control commission arrives and looks around and estimates that two hundred thousand rubles of timber is lying outside, rotting. So this is a scandal and something certainly will be done about it. The commission files a detailed report and gives it to the local timber products director. The director now has a problem, because he should fire the foremen and any others responsible for these state losses. He has a plan that will solve the problem—he pockets the report! Then he growls at the commission, 'Settle down. This is not something to make a scandal over.' They quiet down, for what other choice do they have? After all, the director has better lines into the party than they do, since they are seen as troublemakers anyway. In a few months, the commission might come back with another report. But, what the hell, it's only a report, isn't it, and the director already has shown he knows how to take care of these things. So he pockets the new report. Now we have come almost full circle. The smart man bends and bows to the reality our party has created. He does nothing. The principled person takes his complaint higher in the party organization and, if there is no response, attempts to climb even higher. In the end, he will fall—or be pushed. Obviously, this is the worst possible outcome. Our Ksenia will never make this kind of mistake."

"What kind of mistake will she make?" I asked.

"Probably none," Zhenia replied. "She works in raion headquarters and has the opportunity to learn nearly everything about the failings of her colleagues. As the years pass, she uses this information intelligently and finally she reaches about as high as she can: she becomes regional Komsomol chief. Women used to have important roles in the party sixty and seventy years ago, but, aside from some unusual individuals in this or that regional organization, women have little meaning to the party today. In that respect, you can say it is safer to be a woman than a man, for, although their place is inferior, it is quite secure in party affairs. Women cannot rule, but they also face fewer risks.

"Ksenia will marry a party man, have a child shortly after, and, pretty soon, she will be consumed with the desire to make sure that her child has even more advantages than she had. Her most important gift to her child is to have that child go to one of the special schools in Moscow where there is advanced instruction in one subject, such as English or mathematics. English is especially good for a girl because it means she might become an Intourist guide or even part of a delegation going abroad. Math isn't so good because mathematics and the sciences are dominated completely by men and also happen to be matters of state security. Like all her countrymen, Ksenia knows nothing at all about military matters and doesn't want to know. Her greatest desire is for her child to have an opportunity to travel abroad, preferably to an English-speaking country like Britain, Canada, or the United States! This probably is impossible, since travel to those countries is at the very top of the state's list of rewards—something normally reserved for the 'first faces' and those around them. But no Soviet can be indifferent to the idea of foreign travel. It's a dream worth chasing."

IV

ZHENIA's mention of the privileges of a "first face" reminded me of a story told to me at a diplomatic party by a clever Soviet gossip. This tale involved Dmitri Polyansky, once a first deputy premier who was bounced from his post by Brezhnev in 1973. According to the gossip-monger, Polyansky was completely undone by his demotion, which had wrought havoc with his privileged existence. For months afterward, Polyansky telephoned senior Kremlin aides plaintively seeking to know why various articles were being removed from his Moscow apartment and country dacha. Polyansky's prime concern was with pillows. "Why were they taken from my beds here and in the country?" Polyansky was quoted as saying.

"Because they are not your pillows, comrade," was the answer. "They belong to the Central Committee."

"But this is very unfair," the demoted deputy premier retorted. "Where can I find pillows and pillowcases in Moscow? I don't know any stores that sell such things."

"Comrade, you'll just have to find out for yourself."

Another of the gossip's tales had to do with Khrushchev, sulking after he was ousted from power. Khrushchev apparently refused to return a set of ignition keys for a fast motorboat that some foreign dignitary had shortsightedly given him as a state gift shortly before the Soviet leader's forced retirement. According to the gossip, the Central Committee never succeeded in convincing the former chief of state that he should send his motorboat keys back to the Kremlin. However, technicians seemed to have no difficulty hot-wiring the ignition when they wanted to use the craft.

The purveyor of these amusingly malicious tidbits about the once high and mighty was none other than Viktor Louis, considered by Westerners in Moscow to be the most notorious Soviet go-between for the KGB in post-Stalinist Russia. Louis is a unique figure and a description of his luxurious life-style and how he uses it serves as counterpoint to Zhenia's gritty pursuit of privilege at the far more orthodox level of party minion.

Now in his 50s, Vitali Evgennevich Lui, a.k.a. Viktor Louis, got his start more than thirty years ago when he went to see Edmund Stevens, an American who has spent most of his life in Moscow working for a variety of American, British, and Italian news organizations. Louis said he had served time in the Gulag for befriending foreigners, had learned English, and wanted an interesting job that would allow him to perfect the language. Stevens, a man with a subtle grasp of Soviet ways who in 1950 won a Pulitzer Prize for his Moscow reporting, hired Louis as secretary–translator.

According to John Barron in *KGB: The Secret Work of Soviet Secret Agents,* Louis as a young man had a history of black-marketeering which may have landed him in prison and, in the late 1950s, began doing errands for the KGB's Second Chief Directorate, which deals with foreigners. Even in the 1950s, when there were only a handful of closely watched foreign newsmen in Moscow, a Soviet working for Westerners found himself exposed to a way of life that simply didn't exist for any but the most powerful Russians. The times dictated extreme discretion in dealing with foreigners, but it was possible to gain a glimpse of the material richness of Western life.

In the West, it turned out, there were such things as shoes that fit, raincoats that shed water, toothbrushes whose bristles stayed in place, umbrellas that opened and closed more than once without disintegrating, fragrant soap, perfume, toilet paper, and sanitary napkins. Beyond such crass material goods, there could be access to uncensored books and news from elsewhere in the world. Even if a person couldn't actually own these things or didn't dare be seen reading them, it was still possible to learn about them. There were photo magazines like *Life,* and catalogues from places like Sears Roebuck that contained more than a thousand pages of illustrations, prices, weights, and sizes—a treasure trove of information to wonder at.

Soon, Viktor Louis was married to an Englishwoman named Jennifer, who had come to the Soviet Union as a nanny and who stayed, eventually to preside over a house as fine as that of any member of the English gentry. By the early 1960s, Viktor was the only Soviet citizen allowed to work as an accredited correspondent for a "bourgeois" newspaper, as the Western free press is labeled. His credentials as a correspondent for the London *Evening News* gave him a strangely powerful hold over Soviet authorities: unlike his countrymen, who are denied the right to cross Soviet borders, Louis found it easy to obtain permission to travel abroad. He never lacked for funds to make lengthy journeys to far-flung places. Within a few years, he had logged thousands of miles of foreign travel and had become the only truly globe-girdling, jet-age, nondip-lomatic traveler the Soviet Union has ever produced. When I made his acquaintance in Moscow in the late 1970s, Viktor boasted that he had been to more than a hundred sovereign nations. His byline has appeared in numerous Western papers, including *The Washington Post,* and he has written a book arguing that Red China is about to break up because of ethnic animosity among the billion citizens of the People's Republic.

John Barron has labeled Louis a specialist in KGB disinformation. Viktor's stories from Moscow principally report Soviet diplomatic views, as well as some economic developments. Occasionally, he scores a minor beat when there is a realignment of some of the "first faces." But, aside from the sensation of a Soviet maintaining a byline in a Western newspaper, his copy is not notable either for spark or for insight. From these articles, it would be next to impossible to extrapolate the importance to the Soviets of a person like Louis. Although Soviet propagandists, diplomats, and trade and economic missions handle most contacts with the outside world, a need always exists in a closed society for a specialized "back channel" to conduct and control certain kinds of businesses in the gray world between the public sphere of government statecraft and the covert activities of espionage tradecraft. This is Viktor Louis's world.

In 1964, he leaked Khrushchev's ouster to Western correspond-ents. In 1967, Louis sought to get a pirated version of Svetlana Stalin's memoirs, *Twenty Letters to a Friend,* published in the West well ahead of the authorized edition, thus diffusing their eventual impact. The attempt failed. The next year, he was trying with equal lack of success to have Alexander Solzhenitsyn's *Cancer Ward* pub-lished in Europe. Publication just then could have aided the regime in its repression of the novelist and historian.

Pirating the work of others is nothing new to Viktor Louis. He does not shrink from boasting about his first major literary and financial windfall: his unauthorized translation into Russian of Lerner and Loewe's *My Fair Lady.* The musical was a sensation when it made its debut in Moscow more than twenty years ago and has been in repertory ever since. Louis receives a modest royalty payment in rubles for each performance, whereas the American authors, he told me with a smile, had not received so much as one kopeck. "Well, why should they?" he demanded in characteris-tically abrasive fashion when I pressed him on the point at a cocktail party. "There was no copyright agreement in force between us [the United States and the USSR] then." If he ever has to pay royalties, Louis would face a complication: he lifted several songs from the Lerner and Loewe movie *GiGi* and grafted them onto *My Fair Lady*.

"They sound much better in *My Fair Lady*," he said sarcastically. "And besides, what Russian audience will know the difference?"

But, as a librettist, Viktor Louis earned only rubles—worthless if one's taste runs to Western goods. For those things, a Russian needs hard currency, just like any capitalist, and access to stores where they are sold. Enter Viktor and Jennifer Louis, best-selling publishers and authors. Since there is no up-to-date Moscow telephone directory and Soviet information operators are more interested in finding out the identity of the person asking for a foreigner's phone number than in providing the number, the Louises' handy *Information Moscow* pocket-sized telephone book is indispensable to the hundred or so embassies and more than two hundred capitalist businesses, banks, airlines, and news organizations headquartered in Moscow. The couple face no competitors. With an efficiency undreamed of elsewhere in Russia, their office staff keeps close track of the comings and goings of the foreigners.

"Is this Mr. Klose?" the pleasant voice would say. "This is *Information Moscow*. Will you be in the city through the end of the year? Wonderful! Now . . . you are married aren't you? Excellent! In our next edition, we are going to list wives' names, too. Would she like her name mentioned? What is your wife's name, please? How many copies of the Spring/Summer edition would you like? Please pay by Series D ruble coupon [a form of hard-currency certificate] or by transfer from the Soviet Bank for Foreign Trade. You will be billed."

The constant turnover of foreigners assures a steady demand for the phone book, which includes the complete Diplomatic List, lists of hotels, restaurants, theaters, churches, and other public facilities, and a directory of the Western firms that struggle against exorbitant Soviet rents to maintain Moscow offices in the faint hope that the USSR someday will emerge as an important market for capitalists. The book is printed in England and shows signs of genuine prosperity. Amid a spate of come-ons from the Socialist countries ("Visit Berlin—Get to Know the German Democratic Republic"), the twice-yearly issues include an increasing number of expensive full-page, four-color ads for Air France, American Express, Japan Air Lines, and other Western firms eager for patronage from the small group of resident foreigners with hard-currency bank accounts. Viktor and Jennifer also have branched out to publish a hardbacked *The Complete Guide to the Soviet Union* and several variations on the basic *Information Moscow*, such as an expanded "companion volume" called *U.S. Information Moscow*, which sells for $9.95. The basic Louis directory costs the hard-currency equivalent of five rubles, about $7.50 for the 320-page pocket-sized guide. Thousands of copies have been sold over the years. In a country where a dollar brings six times the official exchange rate on the black-market, Viktor and Jennifer Louis are wealthy.

With their three sons, the couple live in a large country house in the fashionable writers' retreat of Peredelkino outside Moscow. The spacious, rebuilt dacha, tucked behind a sturdy wooden fence, has an above ground swimming pool and a floodlit tennis court that is used as an ice rink in winter. The house is crammed with priceless pre-revolutionary antique furniture, icons, sculpture, bas reliefs, and rare books.

Viktor is nearly six feet tall, tall for a Russian, and wears good English worsteds, conservative ties, ascots, Harris tweeds, and handmade loafers. His thick dark hair is graying at the temples and he is paunchy; his round face and generous mouth glow with the effects of a rich diet. Frequently, he wears steel-rimmed glasses which do nothing to soften the impression of a shrewd, restless intelligence behind his watchful, pale blue eyes. He cultivates a supercilious and blasé manner that some in Moscow find entertainingly roguish and others find offensive.

Once, at a reception, I was talking with a Swedish diplomat about a pending international symposium to delve into the fate of Raoul Wallenberg, the wartime Swedish hero arrested by the Soviets in Budapest in 1944 while he was engaged in rescuing Hungarian Jews. The Kremlin has maintained that Wallenberg fell ill and died in Soviet custody before he could be repatriated after the war. But there have been persistent rumors as recently as the mid-1970s that the diplomat survived and that the Soviets planned to keep him imprisoned until his death rather than admit their wrongdoing. The Swedish diplomat was earnestly telling me that several Soviet prison-camp survivors now living in the West believed that Wallenberg was still alive. Viktor Louis strolled up.

"Émigrés lying for a few pieces of silver!" Louis burst in.

The diplomat flushed with rage. "What an incredible statement!" he fumed as Louis smiled broadly.

Visitors to the Louis dacha, shamelessly escorted around by Louis himself, are frequently stunned by the opulence of the couple's fine antiques and expensive furnishings. Even to my eye, untrained in the finer points of iconography, the religious artifacts are remarkable: extraordinary wooden statues and altar pieces, crucifixes, and, of course, many superb icons. Guiding me with studied insouciance one afternoon, Viktor laid part of his good fortune indirectly at the feet of the man about whom he clearly enjoys telling malicious stories—Nikita Khrushchev.

"After the Revolution, hundreds of churches in Siberia were simply boarded up and abandoned," he explained. "They weren't desecrated the way the churches of Moscow and other cities have been. In the late 1950s, Khrushchev became outraged that the Siberian churches had been spared. So Young Pioneers, organized into special parties, led torchlight processions to the churches, pried open their doors, and the religious artifacts—the artwork of hundreds of years—were torn out of the churches, thrown into a pile in the village square, and burned. They had bonfires all over Siberia. You could get very fine icons at very reasonable prices in those years. This is no longer true, of course!"

His tale of desecration made me think of the large Russian Orthodox church near the diplomatic food store, which was used as an electric manufacturing plant, and the church near the courthouse on the Yauza Canal in central Moscow where Anatoli Scharansky was convicted of treason, which was used as a cabbage and potato warehouse. But the most powerful and disturbing religious defilement I ever saw was of a cemetery that lay in a grove of trees on a bluff overlooking the Moscow River on the southern rim of the city. While strolling nearby during a picnic outing with some friends, we wandered into the shade to discover that the cemetery had been attacked recently by earth-moving equipment. The cast-iron fences that Russians put around each burial plot and the headstones with their niches for photographs of the deceased had been knocked over and the ground bulldozed into deep furrows and pits. The corners of moldy caskets stuck out of the raw soil at odd angles.

The Louises also own dozens of superbly executed bronze busts of Russian princes and czars going back to the earliest era of Muscovy, and an assemblage of carved wooden furniture, including a horse-drawn sleigh in the shape of a swan that would fetch high bids at any London or New York auction house. In this bizarre, non-Soviet setting, Viktor and Jennifer entertain an endless stream of guests drawn from the senior diplomatic lists and the famous and powerful who visit Moscow for business or pleasure. On these occasions, the long table in the dining room glistens with crystal, bone china, and heavy silver. The wines are very good and the food the equal of that of the best embassy kitchens in Moscow. Viktor's private splendor extends further to include two videotape players, an electric Scotch tape dispenser, portable telephones, and expensive hi-fi equipment. If guests are not sufficiently dazzled by this time, Viktor can offer further treasures. The last time I looked, he owned a spotlessly restored 1937 Bentley convertible, resplendent in British racing green; a 1977 Mercedes-Benz 450SL in gun-metal gray; a Volvo 264 limousine in two-tone gray; and a late model Oldsmobile station wagon.

Jennifer, a woman with plain features, who dresses sensibly in tweeds and walking shoes, seems an unlikely companion for this sybaritic Soviet. But she keeps herself busy in ways that manage to complement Viktor's interests in the foreign community. Her teaching at the Anglican Sunday school brings her into close contact with the British embassy and the Episcopal minister whose flock is likely to include some parishioners with domestic and spiritual troubles. There are always crumbs of gossip that gives clues as to who is in or out of favor with the ambassador, who has a reliable marriage, and who might be considered a philanderer. These crumbs have a certain value no matter what world capital a person may find himself in. In spring and summer, Jennifer issues gardening invitations to embassy wives and other members of the International Women's Club, whose activities have drawn her generous support and interest. "Come help me in the garden," she says, where premium-quality bulbs and perennials have been imported from Europe. The women, cooped up in small Moscow apartments, leap at the chance to dig in a garden, even someone else's, without worrying about the stares of Russians. Later, there is a civilized tea and careful chit-chat is exchanged.

Moved by a touch of malice of my own, I once described this household and its contents to an older Soviet journalist with whom I occasionally locked ideological horns. The Soviet propagandist, who of course would never be invited within ten miles of the dacha, at first feigned ignorance of the existence of such a Soviet entrepreneur. But, as I piled on detail after detail, his protestations of ignorance faded and he listened with ill-concealed disgust. His anger was intensified by the fact that he had recently vacated his own three-room apartment and given it to his grown children, while he himself was living in a one-room communal apartment with his beautiful new wife, a woman thirty years his junior. When I finished, the journalist's eyes glittered. "We've replaced one set of corrupt czars with another," he said.

13

Pilgrimage to a Funeral

So that there won't be a trace—sweep every-
thing clean,
Curse me and shame me and roar.
My finish line is the horizon, my ribbon, the
edge of the earth.
I must be first at the horizon.

—VLADIMIR VYSOTSKY*

I

EARLY one morning in the summer of 1980, Vladimir Vysotsky, the tempestuous man who wrote the lines above, died of a heart attack brought on by alcohol and exhaustion. More than any other single event during my stay in Russia, the dramatic funeral of Vysotsky four days later symbolized the unfulfilled mass yearning for truthful literature and speech that smolders beneath the surface of Soviet reality. His death and the events surrounding his burial made clear in simple, stark terms the impact of censorship on people's lives. The threads of this episode weave art, state, and daily life together in a dramatic way that helps illuminate part of Soviet society.

Vysotsky was 42 when he died. Some hours earlier, he had appeared on the stage of the avant-garde Taganka Theater playing the lead role in Bertolt Brecht's didactic *The Life of Galileo*, which deals

*From "The Horizon," a poem, translated by H. William Tjalsma, in *Metropol*, p. 172.

with the responsibilities a man of genius faces in a harsh society. *Galileo* was tailor-made for Vystosky, with his whiskey-roughened baritone and intensely personal, somewhat extravagant acting style. The most celebrated member of the Taganka repertory company, he was a sandy-haired, Soviet Marlon Brando, noted for his stormy temperament, cleverness, and self-indulgence, as well as his dedication to his art.

Vystosky's personality seemed in many ways a reflection of the Taganka company itself, which had become world famous because of the remarkable success of its director, Yuri Lyubimov, at challenging political orthodoxy and surviving. A blocky, dynamic man with an engaging manner, Lyubimov was a subtle master at mixing dull, socialist realist dramas that venerate the system with a few daring plays that defy the narrow strictures of acceptable themes. Lyubimov's principal triumphs during our Moscow years were an adaptation of Mikhail Bulgakov's surreal political allegory *The Master and Margarita* and a compelling dramatization of Yuri Trifonov's powerful novella of Stalinist-era betrayal and guilt, *The House on the Embankment*. Of the two plays, the latter was potentially the more troublesome to the censors, since it deals directly with the shadows of the Terror, a subject about which the less said the better in the Brezhnev era. But Lyubimov succeeded in producing the work on his stage anyway.

Although they acknowledged his courage, some of Moscow's intelligentsia displayed an ambiguous attitude toward Lyubimov. Many of these critics could not bring themselves to compromise with either the authorities or their own consciences, and, as a result, their works probably would never be seen by their countrymen. And so they looked with suspicion upon someone like Lyubimov, who could pick his way through the thicket of censors and cultural watchdogs to emerge with a production that staked out new ground even as it made concessions to the cultural authorities. Sometimes, exasperated with the dismally barren morality of state culture, the capital's intellectuals bleakly condemned Lyubimov's success, calling it "caviar theater," or "*beriozka* theater," a derogatory reference to the hard-currency luxury stores open only to foreigners. There is much to what they say.

The Master and Margarita and *The House on the Embankment* are performed only a few times a month and, even though the Taganka is usually packed, like most Moscow theaters, the total number of

Soviets who have seen these daring plays is minuscule when compared to the country's population of some two hundred seventy million. While provincial intelligentsia strive to keep abreast of the capital's latest developments, Soviet media offer little help in the way of frank discussion of the themes that make Lyubimov's experiments so extraordinary. The number of citizens able to see a Lyubimov production is further reduced by the fact that senior party men and officials of the KGB and other security organs flock to the Taganka as the most intellectually stimulating theater available in the capital. These cadres deem it important to keep abreast of unorthodox political expression—even productions like Taganka's that already have gone through censorship. The apparatchiki jostle for tickets with foreigners drawn to the Taganka by its notoriety, and ordinary Soviet citizens consequently dismiss the possibility of ever seeing one of these controversial productions. Although the adaptation of *The Master and Margarita* had been playing for several years by the time we arrived in Moscow, we came to know many artists, writers, actors, and scientists—highest caste of all—who had angled unsuccessfully for years for tickets. Lyubimov's Taganka is without doubt the most prestigious theater in the land, because here a questing Soviet can find the blend of politics, art, and thematic daring that stimulates thought, reflection, and feeling.

The director's success was reflected in the physical spread of his establishment. Originally housed in a cramped theater on the western edge of Taganka Square some blocks from the Kremlin in an old part of the city, the company has expanded into an angular, modern facility behind its first home. A dark, high-ceilinged arcade-like passage connects the two structures, creating a sense of hushed expectancy as the audience files toward their seats. The new auditorium, with a capacity of about seven hundred, stands beside the square, an irregularly shaped plaza about the size of a football field. The square itself is situated atop a small hill where nine streets converge, many of them narrow lanes that ascend from a surrounding neighborhood of crumbling pre-revolutionary buildings. These buildings of yellow and green stucco with white trim house offices, shops, apartments, and a hospital. Ramp roads connect the square to the traffic-clogged Ring Road, the main inner-city highway that circles the center of Moscow. The Ring passes beneath Taganka Hill and the square in two tunnels. Although vehicles rumble and clatter throughout the day, an air of old Moscow is preserved in the area, an impression enhanced by a handsome church which stands just off the square, making an informal and nostalgic axis with the theater complex and the small, battered kiosks where cigarettes, newspapers, and souvenirs are sold. This was Vysotsky's base, but his great popularity rested on other activities as well.

In films, he had gained an immense following as the hard-bitten detective hero of a series drawn from the best-selling crime procedural novels of Arkady and Zhores Viner. His rakish image was further enhanced by the fact that he was married to a French actress, Marina Vlady, who spent a fair amount of time abroad.

But the mainspring of his mass appeal stemmed from his third career: that of balladeer of the working man. Appealing to millions of Soviets, Vysotsky had composed and sung dozens of tough-guy blue-collar songs describing their lives in the nation's factories, beer parlors, and dormitories. Many of his songs were available on officially approved record albums, which sold out instantly whenever they appeared on the shelves of the main Melodia record shop in central Moscow or elsewhere. The songs of disillusion and lament, some based on his own experiences as a young man who had served time in Soviet penal camps, added to Vysotsky's reputation as an anti-establishment figure.

Far more important than these official recordings were numerous other songs of anger and emptiness which Vysotsky had recorded but which the authorities refused to clear for release on the ground that they were too negative and did nothing to uplift the lives of Soviets. Despite the authorities, these banned songs, taped during boozy evenings with friends in various Moscow salons, circulated widely in *magnitizdat*, the tape-recording equivalent of samizdat, which had taken hold in the early 1970s with the advent of cassette players, adding a rich new vein of comment and humor that flowed beneath the sterile surface of official art. Vysotsky occupied a unique position in the magnitizdat world as one of the USSR's three most revered modern underground troubadours. The others of this powerful trio were Bulat Okudzhava, a former Georgian school teacher, many of whose pacifist ballads could only be heard in magnitizdat; and Alexander Galich, whose glittering, brittle political songs had driven the regime to force Galich into exile abroad. Of the three singers, the scratchy, flawed underground tapes of Vysotsky tunes became the favorites in work camps and construction sites across the country. "You could hear them blaring out of the windows of dormitories in the middle of Siberia," one of Vysotsky's friends told me after the actor's death.

Here is a sample of his rough-and-ready romanticism, taken from the collection of Vysotsky songs and poems included in the *Metropol* almanac:

Write Me a Letter, Lads*

My first term was too much for me.
They'll slap on maybe a year or two more.
So write me a letter, lads.
How are things in that free world of yours?

What are you drinking out there?
There's nothing but snow here, nothing to drink.
So, lads, write me all about it.
Nothing happening here. What do you think?

I'd like a look at your ugly mugs!
It's really tough for me without you.
What's with Nadiukha there, who's she with?
Alone? Let her write me a letter, too.

Maybe only the Last Judgment is final!
A letter, for me, would be a lifeline.
Maybe they won't hand it over.
But a letter, lads, that'd be fine . . .

When Vysotsky died on July 24, 1980, the authorities were all too aware that the loss of the Taganka's most charismatic actor and the country's most popular bootleg balladeer could have enormous repercussions, made worse by the fact that the regime was opposed to the very things that gave the balladeer his power. So the party stifled news of Vysotsky's death. The regime could not be seen to honor such a voice. There was no obituary in the central press, no announcement on radio or television. But, before long, Vysotsky's black-bordered photograph was prominently displayed on a billboard at the entrance to the Taganka Theater. In Moscow, where word of mouth is far more reliable than official news, this was enough to ensure a groundswell of open, public emotion such as had not been seen since 1953 when Stalin's death brought waves of

*Translated by H. William Tjalsma, *Metropol*, p. 154.

grieving Soviet citizens pouring into Red Square. The theater company began planning a memorial service, and, while Vysotsky's wife, who was in Western Europe, arranged to fly back to Moscow, friends sought permission to bury his remains in the city, choosing not to have him cremated, which is the usual Soviet custom.

However, city officials, insisting that interment could not take place in any major Moscow cemetery, demanded that Vysotsky be buried in a provincial town—the farther away, the better. Lyubimov and a number of Vysotsky's friends balked; they argued that he deserved a final resting place in the capital where he had lived, worked, and gained his fame, where citizens in future years could visit the grave and honor him in Russian tradition with flowers and graveside recitations of his verses. Impossible, replied the authorities. The actor's friends began calling influential party people, urging them to avoid a damaging scandal. They warned that the Western press, many of whom had seen Vysotsky perform at the Taganka and on television, soon would learn about the controversy and report it, with inevitable damage to the regime. Moscow would be seen as brutal, fearful of homage to the memory of a balladeer. Still no resolution. Then, one of Vysotsky's closest friends had an inspired idea: he would appeal to Galina Brezhnev, the plump, passionate daughter of Leonid Ilyich Brezhnev, and he telephoned her.

Galina Brezhnev was as near to being a theater groupie as anyone of her exalted status could be. As a young woman, she was reputed to have married a circus juggler in the Ukraine despite her parents' objections. Now in her late forties or early fifties, she lived in Moscow, surrounded by a coterie of officially acceptable as well as some semi-official artists. She frequented the circus and knew many popular performing artists. Toward the close of her father's eighteen-year reign, she would be linked to a black-market jewelry scandal that centered on the world-famous Moscow Circus and a juggler with the improbable name of Boris the Gypsy. But, when she was asked to intercede on behalf of Vysotsky, that still lay ahead. Guardedly, Galina indicated that a solution might be found. More delay. Then, suddenly, the authorities relented. Burial of Vysotsky would be permitted in Moscow's Vagankovskoye Cemetery, one of the oldest and best known in the country, where such major literary figures as poet Sergei Yesenin were buried.

A large, walled expanse a few miles northwest of the Kremlin, the cemetery backed up to the Begovaya rail and subway stations, easily reachable by trolley and bus along heavily traveled routes from the city center. Perhaps because of Galina Brezhnev's intercession, the authorites now seemed eager to accommodate the mourners and designated a plot for Vysotsky just inside the main gate.

This seemed to eliminate the possibility that Vysotsky would suffer in death the fate that had befallen Khrushchev at Novodyevichy Cemetery. There, the regime, fearful of the emergence of a Khrushchev cult, maintained strict vigilance. Guards were stationed at a gate to the inner burial ground. Families visiting the graves of relatives were required to show their special permit before they could walk along the paths of the inner cemetery where massive granite and marble sculptures mark the grave sites of some of the Soviet era's most famous aircraft designers, propagandists, and party figures.

(One day, Eliza and I managed to get inside this closed area by accompanying friends who had an inner Novodyevichy permit. We spent long moments at Khrushchev's grave looking at the stunning bust of him that his family had commissioned from the sculptor Ernst Neizvestny, later exiled abroad. The sculpture protrays Khrushchev in interwoven halves of black and white marble, a haunting evocation of the warring personality that experienced raging frenzies followed by periods of cool calculation. The regime's continuing nervousness about the status of the man they had deposed was personified in the watchful presence of an informant, who hovered nearby until we left.)

With interment in Moscow assured, Vysotsky's supporters made plans for a memorial service at Taganka Theater at noon on July 28, after which burial would take place. Once again, beyond a notice posted on the theater billboard, no public announcement of the occasion was allowed.

Moscow at that time had been transformed by massive police precautions mounted by the regime for the 1980 Summer Olympics. As mentioned earlier, the uniformed police force had been quadrupled from the usual fifty thousand to two hundred thousand officers and patrolmen, plus unknown thousands of extra KGB. For weeks before the July 19 opening day, police had manned inspection barricades on the roads and highways leading into the capital, suspending the licenses of drivers for the tiniest infractions of the country's detailed safety regulations. My colleague Dan Fisher, Moscow bureau chief of *The Los Angeles Times*, reported that the police even sidelined one motorist after they found that the iodine of his first-aid kit had dried up. The streets were almost empty of private cars, nearly all daytime commercial traffic had vanished, and the sidewalks were similarly deserted. Service on many incoming suburban elektrichki had been suspended, effectively discouraging the flood of one million daily provincial shoppers. The regime meant to enjoy and display its Olympics without worrying that provincial peasants would strip the downtown stores of the merchandise so carefully stocked to demonstrate that Soviets lived very well indeed. City dwellers were delighted that the crowds had been dispersed. For the first time in their memories they could shop without competing with the provincials to get a place in line. Other millions of Muscovites and their children had been sent on extended summer vacations or business trips outside the capital; and for months, the authorities, working through party committees at the local block and apartment-house level, had compiled lists of alleged alcoholics, psychotics, and other unreliable citizens. For the duration of the Games these had been either removed to sanitoriums outside the city or pressured to take extended vacations away from town. Muscovites dryly called this a *chistka*, a purge.

The city itself sparkled. For more than four years, the regime had been refurbishing the capital's monuments, churches, and historic buildings to ensure that the first Olympics held in the Soviet Union would impress foreign visitors as no other such spectacle had. Road crews of women had patched thousands of potholes, and female paint crews had swarmed over much of downtown, splashing pigment on everything in sight while their male supervisors lounged on the sidewalks or headed for the beer bar. To the north, bulldozers had flattened hundreds of ramshackle, century-old, peasant cottages that lined the superhighway from Sheremetyevo Airport, the gateway for most foreign spectators. The ground had been seeded and grass grew where thousands of peasants had once lived. They had been dispersed from their longtime homes to the raw, concrete high-rises sprouting everywhere at the farthest edges of the city. Because the routes to Moscow from the west and south were seldom used by foreigners, the hamlets in those areas had been spared destruction. But crews had carefully replaced and repainted more than thirty miles of picket fences and the gingerbread façades of thousands of wooden izbas along the

Minsk Chaussee and other major roads to the distant western border. The crowning achievement in this careful, mendacious effort to showcase Moscow as a well-kept, prosperous world capital was the regilding and restoration of many of the city's long-abandoned and desecrated Russian Orthodox churches and cathedrals. As sophisticated Moscovites looked on with unconcealed contempt, dozens of churches, some of them previously used as cabbage warehouses or anti-religious museums, were painstakingly restored to the height of their pre-revolutionary beauty—on the outside. They shone forth in pastel green, azure, and yellow, or gaudy combinations of brown, red, white, and green in brilliant, mosaic-like patterns. And they were crowned with fresh gold so that the domes glowed for blocks with special luster against the somber brown and concrete facades of the rest of the city. One of the cleverest deceptions was the complete restoration of a dilapidated mosque near a new, covered Olympic stadium and pool complex off Prospekt Mira, Peace Street. Once an abandoned ruin tucked out of sight behind a large stucco apothecary and apartment house, the building was shored up, replastered, painted, and given bright new golden domes where once some of Moscow's ubiquitous crows had nested. With the face-lifting complete, the stucco apartment house hiding this glory was razed so that tourists traveling the busy boulevard could look out at an edifice certain to reassure them that religion is in good health in the USSR. Short of a close inspection, no tourist could imagine that most of these glittering holy places were nothing more than stage-craft. Since most of the refurbished churches would never open their doors and religious activists were routinely persecuted, the face-lifts sent a different kind of message to Soviets themselves: that Constitutional guarantees of freedom of religion were a sham. The feverish state-sponsored cleanup gave chilling force and meaning to this point.

By reducing the number of citizens on the streets, the authorities also narrowed the chance of unsupervised contacts between Soviets and the thousands of foreigners who had come to see the Games. Those courageous enough to wander in the direction of downtown faced roving squads of uniformed police or plainclothesmen who stopped pedestrians at random to check their documents and bundled them off to police stations if all was not in order. These physical steps were reinforced with massive psychological armoring of Moscovites against the dangers of Western tourists. Teachers told their pupils that American and other Western tourists would offer them contaminated gum, and police warned shop clerks and restaurant waitresses to stay vigilant; U.S. and West German agents posing as tourists might leave bombs behind tables and under sales counters.

Meanwhile, convoys of buses with police escorts sped teams of uniformed athletes or tourists through the empty city from heavily guarded stadium to cordoned-off hotel or Olympic Village and back again. From their bus windows, the tourists and athletes peered out at the empty streets for some clue to the nature of life there, nearly as remote from the vast, beflagged capital as if the scenery around them were a freshly painted and gilded stage set—which in almost every respect it was. For all the visitors could see of the real Moscow, the city might have been under martial law, partially evacuated because of a plague or some other great calamity.

Against the background of this security clamp-down, the word spread: the Taganka Theater would honor Vladimir Vysotsky at noon, Monday, July 28, with interment later that afternoon at Vagankovskoe. Like a brushfire, the news swept across the city. At 4 A.M. that day, as the brief night of northern summer turned to early dawn, ordinary citizens began lining up before the doors of the Taganka Theater to pay their last respects to their beloved troubadour.

II

SHORTLY after 10 A.M., my Soviet secretary, Regina, and I set out from Kutuzovsky compound for a drive across the city to the Taganka. Even though I had never met Vysotsky, his reputation was so great that we intended to pay our respects. Driving the office car was the *Post*'s longtime official chauffeur, Ivan Feodorvich Kare-zin, a cheerful peasant's son who had driven "Shtudebakers" during the war. He was a man who maintained a sheeplike respect for uniformed authority, and he had a weakness for vodka. Like all Soviets in the employ of foreigners, Ivan was required to report whatever he knew of our activities to the KGB at regular intervals.

When we reached the embankment below the Rossiya Hotel about a mile from the square, we could see that traffic had come to a halt and long lines of vehicles stretched back down the embankment boulevard toward us. The broad sidewalks along the embankment were awash with pedestrians, their dark bodies and heads undulating like a sea. Police were diverting traffic well short of Taganka Square. We moved slowly ahead, obeying the flashing batons and impatiently gesturing hands of the police and turned north. It looked as though we were going to have to detour completely around the square. But, at my insistence, Ivan ignored a policeman's furiously waving baton and darted into a narrow side street.

We found ourselves in a maze of crooked alleys and macadam lanes, and we headed generally uphill at a steady pace while pedestrians walked briskly past us. When we could go no farther, Ivan pulled the Volvo into the rear courtyard of a hospital. It was clear that Ivan's services would not be needed the rest of the day and I released him to go off on his own. A few nurses and convalescing patients observed my foreign clothes with mild curiosity that intensified when Regina and I scrambled out through a hole in the chain-link fence enclosing the courtyard. In the alleys beyond, men and women hurtled uphill around us—climbing over fences, over shed garages, and through bushes, using tree branches to surmount larger obstacles and drop from alley to alley. There was an electricity in the air that made me think of panicky police and the crowd surge before a riot. We finally emerged from the alleys and crossed to the edge of Taganka Square.

Thousands of silent people had congregated in the open expanse, with more constantly pressing in from side streets in every direction. Traffic, almost at a halt, ground slowly through the massed throng; dozens of police tried to open lanes for the heavy trucks and busses of a normal day in Moscow, but Soviet citizens flowed in behind the vehicles like a sea. Scores had climbed out on the metal roofs of nearby buildings; others clustered atop sidewalk kiosks, parked buses, and concrete palisade fences across from the theater, or perched in the trees lining one side of the square.

As the collective emotion of this vast gathering washed over me, I began to sense something curious: an aura of spontaneous sharing. These were people who normally came together in sullen queues and ticket lines—where the first and perhaps only instinct is to elbow a fellow human being out of the way. But now, I mingled with these thousands of Soviets and saw shy smiles of recognition of hundreds of faces—people signaling to each other as if to say: *"Here we are; isn't this something!"* As the day passed with Vysotsky's fans waiting quietly for nothing more than a glimpse of his casket, the sense of solidarity seemed to strengthen. Somewhere during the hours I spent at Taganka, it dawned on me that I was a spectator at a pilgrimage. I had never seen anything like it in Russia and I doubt that many others had.

As the sun mounted into a luminous midsummer sky that seemed to shimmer white, the crowd filled all the area of Taganka and snaked in long lines past the nearby Dormition church and down Taganka Hill. Many of the mourners carried roses, carnations, gladioli, or bunches of wildflowers gathered from the fields and verges. The people of the square were mostly the young men and women whose adulation had made Vysotsky such a public figure. But there were many hundreds of middle-aged and older men and women as well. In fact, every Soviet generation was represented, to the oldest pensioners. The women wore sundresses whose cheap dyes had faded to pastel, and many of the older women shaded their eyes from the blazing white light with kerchiefs. As the temperature rose, young men took off their shirts. Older men wore cheap open-necked sport shirts in bright colors, heavy gray or brown trousers, and porkpie hats made of synthetic or natural straw.

"He was a simple, straightforward voice," said an old pensioner beside me, clutching a small bouquet of roses. "He spoke for all of us." She tipped her head to include the rest who stood and milled in the square.

"He spoke to my son, and to me," murmured a man who had shielded his bald head with a boat-shaped paper hat fashioned from a copy of *Pravda*.

"But why are you here?" I asked.

"To say goodbye," the man replied. "We will miss Vysotsky very much. This is a sad moment. And what about you?"

"I'm an American journalist and I will be writing an article about this for my newspaper." I waited to see if the man felt endangered by that announcement.

He cast a quick glance at the mourners around us to check for snitches. The people nearby appeared indifferent, but, like most people, probably were eager to eavesdrop if they could. "What newspaper do you represent?" the man asked.

"*The Washington Post,*" I said, and then got in a question: "How did you hear about Vysotsky's death?"

"Through the Voice of America," he said, giving me a quick,

guarded inspection. "I've heard of your newspaper. It is the government paper, isn't it?" He nodded his head as if confirming his own answer. "Very authoritative."

"We don't have a 'government' paper in America. Nothing there like your *Izvestia.* "

"All the same, you are the most authoritative paper in your country, aren't you, speaking for the government?"

I had been down this road many times before and knew it was next to impossible for most Soviets to grasp the meaning of an 'independent' newspaper. So I changed the subject. "Where do you live? Are you from Moscow?"

Instead of answering, the man edged away a few paces.

I did the same—in the other direction. I continued working the crowd, and found that most were from Moscow. They had heard Vysotsky's voice singing his songs or had seen him on television or in films. Not one had seen the actor on the Taganka stage in a live performance. Even so, they wanted to honor him whether or not they were allowed inside the theater. Their fervor was very Russian, and sometimes surprised me with its intensity. One young woman, learning that I was a Western correspondent, grabbed my wrist in her excitement—a public gesture toward a stranger almost unheard of in strait-laced and watchful Soviet society. "You must write that he was the most important voice in the country for *our* generation," she commanded. Then she looked at me carefully. "Is he known in the West?"

"Only to a small group of people who specialize in contemporary Soviet culture," I said.

"That is very difficult to accept," she replied. "You are missing so much!"

Some time later, the doors of the theater opened, and suddenly there was purposeful stir and movement as the original lines of mourners surged forward to view Vysotsky.

The bier stood on the slight incline of the Taganka stage set for *Hamlet,* Vysotsky's best-known role. The actor's body was dressed in a dark suit and lay in an open coffin decorated in black and white satin. Huge floral arrangements and displays and more modest bouquets surrounded the casket. Here was a moment of proper tribute to the man. But the great haste with which the visitors were hustled through the theater offended some who had hoped to pause a few moments beside the body, according to custom. One woman, who had stood in line for five hours, complained, "They did this all wrong. They should have embalmed him and let him be viewed for three or four days, until all were satisfied." But this was a complaint from one of the more fortunate, since most of the thousands never got within fifty yards of the theater.

Several hours later, the public was barred and the theater filled with hundreds of Vysotsky's family and major figures from Moscow's compressed and contentious creative community. Vysotsky's wife, Marina Vlady, who had flown in from Paris with several relatives, sat in the front row, dressed in black. Lyubimov was present, along with many others who had helped defend Vysotsky against state censors and cultural watchdogs. A subtle political conflict developed between these mourners and a number of party and culture officials representing the system. Moscow culture chief Vitali Anturov rose to eulogize Vysotsky, extolling him as a fine actor who had brought special qualities to stage and screen, and who justified the state's faith in his artistic abilities. However, Anturov stubbornly avoided mention of why more than fifteen thousand Soviet citizens now waited in suffocating heat to pay their last respects. The state's principal representative said nothing about Vysotsky the balladeer. Anturov's purpose was to see that the image of Vysotsky was obscured, if that was at all possible. And so it fell to Lyubimov himself to redeem his charismatic star.

The audience tensed in anticipation as Lyubimov stood and addressed the theater. Vysotsky, he said, surely would be remembered as a talented actor and singer, but he was something more. "He was a bard, the keeper of our national lore, our pain, and our happiness as well." In a variation of what my friend had said of Vysotsky's appeal in working-class homes, Lyubimov recalled that, during a recent tour by the Taganka company of the vast Kamaz truck factory in central Russia, the troupe had heard Vysotsky's songs blaring from workers' dormitories along the street from the train station to the guesthouse. "This is what people will remember of Vladimir Vysotsky!" declared Lyubimov.

Outside, as hours passed and the cortege still had not departed for Vagankovskoe Cemetery, the crowd's mood of passive expectancy began to change. Mounted policemen and three busloads of fresh police reinforcements dressed in white blouses and ceremonial white cap covers in honor of the Olympics arrived and set to work clearing the rooftops and trees of spectators. Uncharacteristically,

the crowd spunkily objected to the police. When officers grabbed
the legs of youths and tried to haul them down from the trees, the
crowd jeered and booed. When police cleared the fencetops east of
the theater, the young spectators waited a few minutes, then climbed
back up again. Scuffles broke out in front of the theater when police
on foot tried to cordon off the sidewalk. *"Pozor! Pozor!* Shame!
Shame!" the crowd hooted. Mass excitement rippled through the
throng and then subsided as mounted police, their horses high-
stepping dangerously, pushed toward the theater entrance and easily cleared a path so the cortege could assemble.

Several large trucks drew up before the theater and workmen
began loading the huge floral arrangements into them. In Soviet
style, the hearse that would transport the immediate family and the
casket to the grave site was a gray and black bus. About mid-
afternoon, the police stopped all traffic around the square, and the
funeral party assembled. The trucks pulled out first, followed by a
number of buses. As the bus carrying Vysotsky's body moved away,
the crowd undulated and then, as if on signal, began to move slowly
toward the roadway that led down to the Ring. When the bus
accelerated, hundreds began to walk faster beside the bus, casting
flowers at it. *"Do svidaniya! Do svidaniya!"* they cried. Goodbye,
goodbye.

As the bus rolled onto the access road, several hundred people
who had been sitting on a knoll overlooking the ramp got to their
feet and swarmed after it, throwing flowers and bidding farewell.
Police whistled and bellowed as the mourners surged down onto the
Ring Road and became a long body of runners like an impromptu
marathon.

I suddenly spotted a lustrous Mercedes sedan nosing along near
me. Sitting in the front passenger seat was an interesting Soviet
source whom I had known for some time. As the car inched abreast
of me, I tapped on the tinted glass window and gestured for the man
to let me in. He had a few words with the driver, then quickly
motioned to me. Two women dressed in black and nearly buried in
flowers were huddled in the rear seat, crying and clinging to each
other. My Soviet friend, for that is what I consider him, whispered
that the women were related either to Vysotsky or to his wife. He
then introduced me to the driver, a young Middle Eastern business-
man who was well known as a party giver and companion of the
bored offspring of senior party and government leaders, the

"Golden Generation," who lived in circumstances not much different from those of Viktor Louis. This was the circle in which my Soviet friend liked best to circulate, performing favors for the relations of the mighty and maintaining contact with Westerners, chiefly Americans, who would present him with forbidden books in English. We inched out onto the Ring Road and, when the Olympic traffic police spotted the Mercedes and the letter "M" for "merchant" on the license plate, they waved us onward. We sped to Vagankovskoe in air-conditioned comfort.

In the much smaller confines of the cemetery, the mourners had formed themselves into a genuine Russian crowd—a mass of humans packed together like sardines. When the official mourners had assembled at graveside, the casket, now covered, was borne forward by the pallbearers and lowered into the ground, with several thousand looking on.

Later, my Soviet friend and I walked together back across the city. "There is Soviet truth," he said, "and then there is what happened here today. This was the most extraordinary event in recent memory. I was not in Moscow when Stalin died and have never seen anything like this in my life. For spontaneity—and unfortunately, for lasting meaning—this surpasses even the International Youth Festival."

That festival staged by Khrushchev in 1957 was the first major opening of Moscow to foreigners since World War II. The result was an extraordinary love-in; for about two weeks, crowds of Soviet and foreign teenagers congregated in the streets, and sang and danced together, and spent the nights in open discussion of the future of the Socialist movement. The sense of change engendered by the festival lingered for a long time, especially among Soviet youth, but when Khrushchev was dismissed the illusions of genuine change faded, to be replaced by the air of stolid endurance that permeates the USSR today.

Speaking again of Vysotsky's funeral, my friend said, "Clearly, the authorities had no idea that something of this magnitude could take place. Did you see how frightened and subdued the police looked? They didn't really know how to handle it. Can anyone who has never seen such a spontaneous gathering, who has never participated in a genuine demonstration or a confrontation, have any idea of what to do?"

One of the reasons I had such admiration for this Soviet friend was his ability to make just these kinds of statements. Like his countrymen in the square, he had certainly never seen such a spontaneous mass event. But he refused *not* to think about the implications of what had just happened. His mind reached out without hesitation to embrace what he sensed, but could not actually know, was the essence of life in free societies.

"The air of participation was so strong that the police might have been tempted to join in," he continued. "Although, in fact, I believe they really were more frightened of touching off something worse than anything else. Anyway, this is an example of how the powers can be out of touch and at the same time control everything.

"As a troubadour, Vysotsky was so remarkable because he spoke to the widest possible segment of the population. Unlike Galich, he was not so political that the politically indifferent or timid would simply ignore him. And because he was younger than Okudzhava, he had a wider following. But the authorities send Okudzhava on tour, even to the West. Having him outside helps mislead foreigners into thinking that the Soviet Union is a country where political satire is not extinguished. *This* is true beriozka theater.

"Another reason for his popularity is that Vysotsky sang about the camps, and, let's face it, plenty of people in this country, high and low alike, know something about the camps!" My friend gave a snort of derision. "In that, we have been quite democratic, I would say!"

When we reached the Barrikadny Metro station near the American embassy, it was clear that the heavy Olympic police patrols made it uncomfortable for him to be seen with me. We parted warmly. I took the subway four stops southeast to the Taganka station. By now it was close to 7 P.M. and with the sun well in the west—fat, red, and warm in the smog of Moscow—bright color and details were beginning to fade to grays, browns, and dusty greens.

The center of the square had returned to normal as pedestrians made their way through heavy vehicle traffic. But as I approached the theater, I could see that scores of Soviets were still milling about. The police also were there. Having discarded their good manners, they strode up and down, glowering at the knots of people clustered on the sidewalks. Other Moscovites paused to look at the photograph of the dead actor in front of the theater. The police were not happy with any of this.

At one of the aluminum-sided kiosks across from the Taganka, about a dozen people were bunched nervously together, much like reporters who compare notes after a speech. To my surprise, they all had notebooks or paper and were busy copying something that had been taped to the front of the closed-up kiosk. From the outer edge of the group, I couldn't make out what these people were copying. So I asked. "His verses," somebody muttered. My interest now as intent as theirs, I craned forward and hauled out my own notebook.

Just then, I felt someone shove against me from behind. I turned, instinctively angry, as a powerfully built policeman lunged for the taped sheet of paper. Just as suddenly, the hand of a narrow-shoul-dered young man in front of me shot forward. Tearing the verses from the policeman, he plunged away as the irate officer grabbed for his jacket. "Give me that!" Without a backward glance, the youth ducked into the group and out the other side with the policeman in hot pursuit.

"For shame! Bastard!" the Soviets yelled after the cop; then, disconsolately, they began dispersing. The poem was gone so quickly, I had no time to read it. Perhaps it was this one:

Ice Sheet*

An ice sheet on Earth, an ice sheet
All the year long!

An ice sheet on Earth, an ice sheet!
As if there's no spring, no summer,
The planet dressed in something slippery,
People falling slam onto the ice.

An ice sheet on Earth, an ice sheet,
All the year long!

Even when flying around the planet,
Not touching it with their feet—
If not one then the other will fall—
Ice sheet on the Earth, ice sheet!—
Boots trampling across it, trampling.

An ice sheet on Earth, an ice sheet,
All the year long!

*Translated by H. William Tjalsma, *Metropol*, p. 164.

As if there's no spring, no summer!
People falling slam onto the ice!
Ice sheet on the Earth, ice sheet!
Ice sheet all the year long.

14

Censorship Wars

Grass can grow up through pavement. But it's better for the world when grass grows naturally.

—VLADIMIR N.

I

O<small>N</small> November 18, 1980, at 11 A.M., a young Moscow author delivered a petition to the city's cultural authorities asking permission to establish a new literary club, Belles Lettres, that would be independent of the official Writers Union. The members would be a few dozen writers of experimental prose, who wanted to meet occasionally for discussions of their work and publish an uncensored, limited-circulation journal of their avant-garde writings.

In letters to the Moscow City Council and culture departments of the ruling Central Committee, the seven would-be organizers asserted that lack of an official outlet for experimental writing was weakening the vitality of Soviet literature. Many talented voices that could enrich the nation's cultural life were being ignored by hidebound Writers Union officials and publishing house editors, they said. They thought Belles Lettres could have an artistic impact similar to that generated when a group of experimental painters had set up an organization independent from the official Artists Union in 1974.

With the audacious and naive proposal delivered, the writers sat back to see what kind of response they would get. They didn't have long to wait.

About eight hours later, the principal petitioner, Yevgeny Popov, was driving with friends at dusk and talking about their hopes for the new club when a black Volga sedan cut in front of them, forcing their car to the curb. Three plainclothesmen leaped from the Volga and surrounded the writers' car. "One of these guys looks like the robber!" the agents shouted, ordering the men out. At a local police station, the writers were interrogated for several hours as suspects in a burglary. The KGB confiscated all their manuscripts, notes, and address books (permanently, as it turned out). The major find was a directory of two hundred pages listing names, addresses, and brief biographies of prospective members of Belles Lettres. With the surprise interception a complete success, the agents released the writers.

Over the next several days, the police ransacked the apartments of the seven original petitioners. Popov, who after being raided once had moved from his own apartment into seclusion with a sculptor friend, thought he had made an adroit move. But the police dragnet found him a second time. Empowered by their warrants, the police purported to be gathering evidence against a recently suppressed dissident political journal called *Poiski*, or *Searches*. Since most of the contributors to *Searches* already had been punished, some with severe prison sentences, the warrants were a pretext and meant to be perceived as such. Popov lost every story he had written in the previous fifteen years—as well as the typewriter on which he had written them.

Even as the secret police were harassing Popov and his colleagues, there were certain portents of cultural promise. A few weeks earlier, Soviet intellectuals had been heartened by an edition of the once-celebrated literary journal, *Novy Mir*, or *New World*, which they had generally scorned for nearly a decade. Under the leadership of Andrei Tvardovsky in the late 1950s and early 1960s, *Novy Mir* had published Solzhenitsyn and other major writers, spearheading the anti-Stalinist literary revolution that was such an important part of the Khrushchev Thaw. But in the less sympathetic Brezhnev era, Tvardovsky had been forced from his editorship and the journal had become a bastion of conformism. Without warning, however, the September 1980 edition had published some long-suppressed poems by Boris Pasternak, the officially disgraced novelist and poet who had died twenty years earlier and whose great work, *Doctor Zhivago*, is still unpublished in the Soviet Union, although it circulates privately in smuggled editions. (So great is the official enmity toward the novel that when the Hollywood movie version was shown by the American embassy some years ago, the Soviets made an official protest, which extended to complaints about the haunting "Lara's Theme" as well.) Then, as they were savoring the Pasternak poetry in *Novy Mir*, the intelligentsia received another special treat. The annual edition of the *Day of Poetry* appeared, carrying even more Pasternak poems and apparently flouting the usual censorship practices. The newly published poems included uncensored texts of "Gethsemane," "Mary Magdalene," "Christmas Star," and "Hamlet," from a cycle of twenty-four religious poems in the final section of *Zhivago*. Many Moscovites derided the sudden appearance of these long-banned works, saying, in the words of one, "It only proves the regime has the strength to deal with you after you're dead."

Nevertheless, to the young writers, these signs had seemed propitious for their request to form Belles Lettres and its uncensored journal. Consequently, when Eliza and I went to see some of them after the police searches, we found them shocked and extremely depressed.

"There was no politics in our plan," one of the writers insisted in an excited, exhausted voice as we sipped tea together. "I'm overwhelmed by this. It took them just eight hours to respond and this is the only way the regime seems to be able to answer us. We offered our open hand and they spat on it! We didn't want a confrontation with the authorities; we are only searching for a way to have an open dialogue on matters of art. We want a new form, a new corner, a new tongue."

The speaker was a man in his early thirties, demoralized by the run-in with the police, who asked me not to use his name, even though he was pleased to spell out his views for us. "We are the Czech generation," he said, meaning younger writers and artists who began working in the late 1960s at a time when the Soviet invasion of Czechoslovakia made clear which way the regime was headed on matters of politics and conformity. "We aren't dissidents. We know that the realities of life here are like the realities of the weather—harsh, cold, unpredictable. We've seen too many political games and all we want to do is to write. If the authorities eventually arrest us, it doesn't solve the problem."

What could explain the contradictions between the unexpected publication of the long-suppressed Pasternak poems and the stiff response to the young "Czech generation" writers? To Western eyes, the contradictions made little sense, perhaps explainable as a typical case of the Soviet left hand and right hand not communicating. But the simultaneous suppression of some writers and the slight rehabilitation of a major Soviet literary figure with a wide following both in the West and at home were perfectly consistent with the manipulation of the country's cultural life achieved during Brezhnev's long reign.

The subtlety of this control was dictated as much by external concerns that arose when Brezhnev turned to the West in the 1970s in pursuit of détente as by the usual doctrinal differences that occur within any complex ideology. Brezhnev's goals were easily identified and, to a large measure, shared by most Western capitalist governments: relaxing foreign political tensions, easing the arms race, and possibly marking the era as one of searching for peace after the decades of post–World War II tensions between East and West. Long before the Brezhnev leadership moved toward relaxation of tensions, as Russians call détente, it received some unexpected instruction about the consequences of its own impulse toward internal repression. The lesson took place in 1965–66 and involved two writers.

When Brezhnev came to power in 1964, one of his first tasks was to bring an end to the cultural ferment sparked by Khrushchev's de-Stalinization. Party members increasingly feared that, by revealing the party's widespread complicity in the dictator's crimes, the campaign against Stalin threatened to destroy their claim to moral authority over Soviet masses. To restore the party and instill confidence in its leadership, the new regime set out to muzzle the writers, whose voices were so instrumental in encouraging citizens to speak out. An example was required. The possibility of silencing Solzhenitsyn may have beckoned, but the time was not right to take on so protean a personality. The leaders settled instead on two lesser names, Yuri Daniel and Andrei Sinyavsky. These writers, unable to find publication inside the Soviet Union, had smuggled their work to the West for several years where it was published and both men were admired for inventive and thoughtful styles. They seemed perfect targets for the Brezhnev crackdown. The two men were arrested and, after well-publicized trials, imprisoned for crimes against the state. This was the leadership's well-aimed blow to halt the dangerous cultural thaw that threatened to fray party control. But, as has happened at other times in Russian history, the West unexpectedly imposed a degree of restraint on the country's new leaders. There were major protests in Western capitals; the Kremlin was ridiculed and condemned. The lesson was clear: Western interest in domestic Soviet policies ruled out reimposition of the kind of Stalinist tactics represented by the repression of Sinyavsky and Daniel.

The regime could not back down and rescind the sentences, but it would be many years before such stiff reprisals were again attempted against writers. Foreign outcry revealed to Moscow that the more liberal Khrushchev era had irreversibly altered Western perceptions of Soviet totalitarianism. Such behavior by the regime was no longer expected, or condoned, by Western capitals. If Moscow truly wanted to woo the Westerners, different tactics that avoided Western criticism must be found. The Kremlin could ignore this new Western perception only at risk to Brezhnev's longterm intention to improve the international image of the Soviet Union and ease the process of détente. The lessons of the Sinyavsky–Daniel trials would not be forgotten.

Détente, which marked the first half of the 1970s, required Moscow—out of simple self-interest—to project a more humanitarian image to the West. The Kremlin realized that there was political gain to be had for the Soviets if Moscow could help Western democratic leaders convince their skeptical electorates of the acceptability of trade and other important exchanges with a totalitarian superpower. Since the West seemed concerned with what happened to artists and writers, Soviet cultural authorities responded in their own way to Western interests. Some nonconformist art and literature was allowed. In a very limited sense, this had the effect of sporadically legitimizing Western concerns for freedom of self-expression.

Ever since the Sinyavsky–Daniel public relations debacle, the party has tolerated a certain amount of unofficial East–West trafficking by adventuresome Soviet authors. The regime stepped in harshly chiefly when a writer powerfully tapped into the country's fundamental—and unredressed—moral agonies. This was the case with the persecution and expulsion of Alexander Solzhenitsyn in 1974. Solzhenitsyn's power in the aftermath of the *Novy Mir* publication of "One Day in the Life of Ivan Denisovich," the great classic of the Thaw, was a phenomenon that transcended anything the country had experienced since the days of Stalin himself. Although the authorities came close to allowing publication of *Cancer Ward* before changing their minds, enough bootleg copies of the book had found their way into the country by the time we arrived more than a decade later so that most Moscow intellectuals were familiar with it. The *Gulag Archipelago* was less well-circulated, but revered by many whom we came to know. Solzhenitsyn's remarkable works had catapulted the messianic author onto another plane altogether. As one of our friends said, "They *had* to expel him because he had become a political figure in his own right and the party cannot tolerate anything like that."

The regime's most favored method of silencing writers immune to the blandishments of privilege was forced emigration abroad. This repression had its own special attraction: many Western countries greeted foreign exile as a humanitarian gesture by the Soviet regime. The Kremlin was perfectly willing to use Western abhorrence of Soviet labor camps and internal exile to its own public relations advantage. The most spectacular example was the sudden expulsion of Solzhenitsyn, but there have been dozens of others. The Association of American Publishers, in a tally completed in late summer of 1983, counted seventy-six Soviet authors—poets, novelists, essayists, historians, memoirists—forced into foreign exile since 1970 and another seventeen in internal exile or labor camps.

Tearful airport departures were common during our four years in Moscow. In our early months there, nearly a dozen writers and their families were expelled from the Soviet Union. To my American mind it seemed extraordinary that so harsh a government would, in effect, "reward" the writers by sending them west instead of east: the advantages of life in West Germany over life in a Siberian exile village seemed all too apparent when viewed from a Western perspective—and this was precisely the reaction anticipated by the regime. But my initial perception missed the wrenching tragedy that emigration meant for men and women who had devoted their lives to exploring Soviet existence in the motherland's rich language. Foreign exile would sever them from their roots.

I learned more about this when we became friends with Vasili Aksyonov, an ebullient, moustachioed man in his mid-40s with a streak of humor a yard wide. Restless, inventive, and driven, Aksyonov had spent all his life in the maze of Soviet literature, at times conforming, at times challenging the censors and cultural authorities. Like dozens of other writers and artists, Vasili's career encompassed a bewildering series of skirmishes with censors over a creative person's right to follow his own vision. These battles stood at the center of artistic expression in the Soviet Union and, as I came to understand the nature of the struggle, I also gained insight into why even an ostracized artist would abhor the notion of exile from his native land.

Tracing Aksyonov's history was the first step for me toward understanding. Trained as a physician, he had begun writing soon after completing medical school in the late 1950s. His tough, new style of blunt dialogue and his hard-bitten, youthful characters captivated his own generation. Aksyonov's first short stories were published in 1959 and *Colleagues,* a short novel, appeared the next year. In 1961, *A Ticket to the Stars* established Aksyonov as the most popular literary talent in the Soviet Union. He was at the cutting edge of a new wave of writers: Andrei Voznesensky, Bella Akhmadulina, Ilya Ehrenburg, Yevgeni Yevtushenko, and others who were exploring previously forbidden themes of estrangement and cynicism that reflected the country's exhaustion with Stalinist forms and the dismal industrial existence of tens of millions of citizens. A novella, *Oranges from Morocco,* appeared in 1963; *It's Time, My Love, It's Time* came the next year; and the best-seller *Halfway to the Moon* appeared two years later. Aksyonov was the J. D. Salinger of the Soviet Union, chronicler of the *stilyagi,* the fashion-conscious, rebellious Soviet youth of the Thaw who shocked the conservatives and cowed older generations by wearing their hair long, their pants tight, and their contempt and emptiness on their sleeves.

The characters and situations of his novels—and those of his fellow New Wave artists—challenged Socialist Realist dogma and, not surprisingly, Aksyonov had major difficulties with entrenched censors and controllers anxious to preserve Stalinist artistic conformity. In 1961, the apparatus struck back, targeting Aksyonov in a slashing propaganda campaign ordered by Khrushchev against the New Wave. The author was criticized for mindless modernism, for aping decadent Western literary themes offensive to "the spirit of Socialist realism," and for "an uncritical attitude toward Western culture." The diatribe continued the next year and went on through the spring of 1963. Denunciations poured in from around the country and were eagerly printed in *Pravda, Izvestia, Young Communist,* and other papers. The campaign even included an attack from Yuri Gagarin, the first man in space. In the end, Aksyonov capitulated, writing an apologetic article for *Pravda*.

But his penitence was short-lived. While he continued to produce short stories, novels, and screenplays, he also became politically active. He joined dozens of Writers Union members in a daring 1967 effort to discuss the ban on Solzhenitsyn's works, and the next year, along with twenty-three other officially acceptable writers, defended four activists who had recently been convicted of anti-Soviet agitation. Aksyonov was disciplined with a stiff reprimand. Even so, his official career prospered: in 1971, he was named to a special Writers Union auditing board, and, four years later, he was allowed to travel to the U.S., where he taught a seminar on Russian literature at UCLA. However, three years later, while he was in Paris on another trip, his career suddenly took a turn for the worse. In a *Le Monde* interview, Aksyonov complained that, although censors had rejected some of his work in the USSR, the Soviet All-Union Agency for Authors' Rights (VAAP) cynically was selling the same stories to French publishers. "Export wares," he declared. "Literature is not caviar and I am not a sturgeon." Upon his return to Russia, his reception was cold from the very officials who had sent him abroad to show that creativity flourishes in the Soviet Union. In Moscow once again, his frustration over the limitations on creativity within the country deepened. When we came to know him the following year, Aksyonov was involved in the challenge to the authorities that eventually would result in his expulsion from Russia.

This was the famous *Metropol* almanac, the collection of uncensored literature that surfaced in January 1979 as a direct attempt to break through the veil of official censorship.

Organized largely by Aksyonov, the *Metropol* effort involved twenty-three writers, from 66-year-old Semyon Lipkin, a founding member of the Soviet Writers Union, to two young men who were petitioning to join the union. The writers who contributed to *Metropol* condemned censorship and demanded that the collection, which included short stories, poems, criticism, and drama excerpts, be published without going through state censorship. Such an open challenge was unheard of in the USSR: no one in decades had seen anything quite like *Metropol*; it is likely that the episode will stand for many years as the most unusual and open censorship struggle, involving the greatest number of participants, in contemporary Soviet history.

"It would not be overly daring to assert that our culture suffers from something like a chronic ailment which might be defined either as 'hostility toward differentness' or simply 'fear of literature,' " Aksyonov and his four fellow editors wrote in a brief preface to *Metropol*. "The sickening inertia that exists in our literary journals and publishing houses has resulted in an exaggerated feeling of responsibility on everyone's part for each 'item' in our literature, which consequently is not only unable to be what it should be but is not even what it used to be. This universal sense of 'responsibility' produces a state of silent, stagnant fearfulness, a desire to trim every piece down to size. Works that do not fit established molds are condemned sometimes to many years of homeless wandering. Only the blind can fail to see that such writings are becoming more and more numerous each year, that they already constitute, as it were, a forbidden, untapped vein in our native world of letters."*

The collection drew its power in large part from the fact that the contributors included members of the accepted literary elite as well as writers from the politically suspect experimental fringes. Through Aksyonov, the principal editor, we came to know a number of the other contributors and from them learned additional lessons about the nature and meaning of Soviet censorship. Andrei Voznesensky, the poet, probably was the most luminous name among the twenty-three. He had recently won the nation's highest award, the Lenin Prize, for his poetry, and effortlessly attracted immense audiences whenever he gave readings. He was a sophisticated world traveler who did not shrink from being used as a cultural ambassador for the state. Like most of his colleagues, he had fought many skirmishes with the censors and, perhaps better than most, sensed the trouble his participation in *Metropol* might cause him. It is a measure of the frustration the writers shared that this resilient veteran joined the effort.

Others who added luster to the *kollektif*, collective, as the contributors half-seriously called themselves, included Bella Akhmadulina, the best female Soviet poet for the past fifteen years; Vladimir Vysotsky, the theater actor, movie star, and underground balladeer; Semyon Lipkin, widely known translator of Central

---

*Translated by George Saunders, *Metropol*, pp. xix–xx.

Asian epic poetry; and Fazil Iskander, an Abkhazian writer and poet with an increasing following among the cogniscenti.

Although the almanac, as the organizers called it, steered away from direct political themes, its two hundred fifty thousand words constituted a political challenge, since many of the stories, sketches, and poems already had been rejected by the censors at various publishing houses. A number of the stories violated the formal but unspoken rules of Soviet censorship by including explicit sexual references and descriptions that never appear in official Soviet literature. Other stories dealt with officially banned themes, such as the existence of an immortal soul; still others were sharply critical of official controls on the arts.

Metropol, which had been painstakingly produced in a few folio-sized originals, caused a sensation in Moscow's literary community and brought the organizers headlines in the West. Two precious copies already had been smuggled out of the country by the enterprising organizers. This was crucial to their strategy, for they hoped to increase the pressure on the authorities by being able to show that their work was publishable in the democratic West. A French publishing house intended a quick translation, and Ellendea and Carl Proffer's Ardis Press of Ann Arbor, Michigan, the preeminent publisher in America of banned Soviet literature and lost Czarist-era works, planned a facsimile edition. Reports of this activity flooded in from foreign radio broadcasts, sending the Moscow elite into delighted colloquies that helped relieve the leaden winter season.

The literary apparatus responded with ferocity. The state had no intention of giving in to the writers' demands. The authorities wanted only to punish them for their audacity, and the counterstrokes were sudden and swift. A number of the contributors were called in to the Writers Union and told to recant or lose their privileges, which included membership in the LitFond, the health and welfare arm of the union. Fazil Iskander, a short-story writer who helped edit the collection, was told that he was "only 20 percent guilty," implying that if he confessed his error he would face far less severe reprisal than Aksyonov. Aksyonov was accused by the media and the union leadership of organizing a "scandal" so that if he sought to emigrate he would have a warm reception from "Western anti-Sovieteers."

Meanwhile, authorities suddenly shelved plans to release a highly regarded new comedy film about the early years of flight in Russia.

The film had already previewed to rave reviews at the prestigious House of Film in central Moscow, and Goskino, the state movie distribution monopoly, had ordered hundreds of prints. Cancellation would cost the state millions of rubles. This was slight consolation for Aksyonov. Cancellation of the movie was a direct retaliation, to deny him a twelve thousand ruble payment (roughly equivalent to about eighteen thousand dollars, although without the ready buying power of the dollar) for his screenplay, and to ensure that his work would not be seen by the public.

Voznesensky unexpectedly found that a long-planned trip to the U.S. was in jeopardy, and Bella Akhmadulina was told that a number of poems previously accepted for publication now were unworthy of the public's interest. A planned reading tour, already a sellout in several provincial capitals, was scrubbed. Her husband, theatrical designer Boris Messerer, had designed the distinctive title page for the collection. Now, an exhibit of his drawings and sets scheduled to open in Czechoslovakia was yanked at the last minute.

In addition, long-scheduled translation projects were taken away from Semyon Lipkin and Inna Lisnyanskaya. This was only the first of many struggles with the authorities for this wonderful older couple, struggles that lasted nearly two years and continue today. Eliza and I were able to visit them on many occasions in their small, handsomely decorated apartment on Usiyevicha Ulitsa. They lived not far from Leningradsky Prospekt, the booming thoroughfare that carries traffic from the city center north to Sheremetyevo Airport and on to Leningrad. In this atmosphere we talked of their lives and their vicissitudes with the apparatus.

Semyon Israilovich Lipkin was uniquely qualified to judge his fellow writers. He had helped found the Writers Union in the heady years after the Revolution when Soviet youth genuinely dreamed of building a new society. He had served his country for decades, fought in the war at Stalingrad and Leningrad, and, on days when he needed food or medicine, he could display a chestful of ribbons for wounds and heroism that would quickly get him to the head of any waiting queue. He had spent years mastering the obscure languages of Central Asia, collecting, recording, and carefully translating the nomadic peoples' epics into Russian. His aim was to prevent the steady erosion of their exotic cultures against the spread of industrial life and urban settlement. For this he had won many state awards. Lipkin's deliberate manner of speech hid a sharp-witted intelligence that served him well in the frequently surreal episodes that can suddenly erupt in a Soviet citizen's life.

For example, he recalled for us what had befallen him during the battle for Stalingrad. Amid lethal German bombardment, Soviet counterattacks, and murderous hand-to-hand combat, the political commissars of Lipkin's unit suddenly decided to confer membership in the Communist party on the beleaguered survivors. Lipkin was appalled: "From childhood, I had believed in God. So I refused." The commissars were infuriated and demanded to know why Lipkin was insulting the party in this moment of supreme danger. "I always lose everything," he replied. During Stalin's reign, a person could be shot for losing his party card, he explained to us. In Stalingrad, there was instant recognition. Grins all around. *Here* was an excuse!

The same stubborn streak emerged during the attempts of Writers Union officials to persuade the Lipkins to abandon their *Metropol* colleagues. Feliks Kuznetsov, chief of the Moscow union, was the principal antagonist. "This entire scandal is anti-party, anti-Soviet," he declared.

"There is nothing in it which is anti-Soviet," Lipkin replied during this session. "It's all in the framework of what was laid out by the recent Party Congress . . . I forget which one."

"You've begun to take an anti-Soviet stand!" barked one of Kuznetsov's assistants.

"I'm not standing anywhere. You put me here."

"Just please write us a letter, say anything you please."

Next, it was Inna Lisnyanskaya's turn with Kuznetsov. He spent almost an hour trying to convince her to renounce the almanac and admit her error. "The whole time, I was trying to convince *him* to quiet down and understand that people in the West would hear about all this only if the Writers Union made a stink. 'Just publish ten thousand *Metropol*s, I told him, 'and no one will ever even know.' "

"You're being tricked, you and Lipkin," said Kuznetsov. "Aksyonov will leave the country, you'll be left behind here, and I won't publish your books!"

Having gotten nowhere, the officials tried another track. A publishing house official invited the Lipkins to come look at some illustrations for a book that would contain three of Lipkin's translated epics. The illustrations were beautiful; the editor said there would be a hundred thousand copies in the first printing. This was a handsome bribe.

"Look how beautiful they are," said the editor. "I'd like to go ahead of course, but, well, there's some trouble. You're part of *that thing* and . . . well, without a letter from you, I can't do anything."

"What sort of letter?"

"That you leave that thing."

Semyon Israilovich scrawled the letter: "*I helped with Metropol and I know it will be published with the help of State Publishing and the All-Union Agency for Authors' Rights.*"

"That's too little. You've got to say you were tricked into it, dragged into it, and now you reject them."

"No. I can't agree."

"Well, then I can't help you."

"That's all right."

"Go on vacation and think about it."

The Lipkins went on vacation and thought about it. They didn't budge. "I gave my word," Semyon Israilovich said by way of explanation. "They couldn't believe that a person has an imagination or personal honesty, or that a person would not want to live well. They can't understand why we did it."

Meanwhile, the apparatus concentrated its heaviest blows against the two kollektif members most vulnerable to reprisal. Yevgeny Popov, the Siberian writer, and his close friend, Viktor Yerofeyev, a critic and writer of experimental prose, had been waiting for months for provisional membership in the Writers Union. Membership meant that magazines and publishing houses would give serious consideration to their work instead of rejecting it out of hand because non-union status might mean political unreliability. Now, the union's hierarchy reversed itself and indicated that the two writers were unworthy of membership.

Six of the older contributors—Aksyonov, the Lipkins, Bella Akhmadulina, Iskander, and Andrei Bitov—threatened to resign from the union in protest if the two young writers were barred from membership. This move promised to increase the scandal over the almanac and deterred the apparatus from acting against the two writers. Negotiations about their fate began and continued through most of 1979. In October, a compromise was worked out by Kuznetsov and Sergei Mikhailkov, chairman of the larger Russian Federation Writers Union. Popov and Yerofeyev wrote a letter declaring that they were "deeply averse" to the kind of "propaganda fuss of no literary relevance" which had boiled up around *Metropol*. But when some hard-line Russian Federation Writers Union members failed to get the two writers to denounce the almanac itself as pornography and an insult to the state, the deal broke down. The authorities were in possession of the letter of repentance, but Popov and Yerofeyev were excluded from the union anyway.

At this point, the Lipkins followed through on their threat to resign from the union. They were immediately expelled from Lit-Fond, the health services arm of the union.

Inna recalled that, months after their resignation, they met a Writers Union official who seemed shocked to see them. "Why are *you* still here [in Russia]?"

"We're not emigrating," Semyou replied.

"You're *not!* Then why did you leave the Writers Union?"

"I can't live with other people's consciences . . . only with my own."

Semyon Israilovich had no illusions about what had become of the literary organization he had helped found. "No one must ever forget that the Writers Union now has only two functions: political and ideological. It has no creative function."

II

VASILI Aksyonov, *Metropol*'s principal editor and the man who had convinced the Lipkins to join the effort, reached his own decision about his future. He resigned from the Writers Union at the end of 1979. Akhmadulina, Bitov, and Iskander, who had vowed to resign, remained members. Bone-weary from months of conflict, Aksyonov sought permission to emigrate. "I already feel homesick," he told me one day, his head down between his shoulders like a battered prizefighter. His books were being pulled from the shelves of libraries and stores all over the country, and royalties were dwindling. Not only had the future receded, but in the peculiar way that can happen in the Soviet Union, it had almost ceased to exist for Aksyonov. "I have no place to go in this country. My career here has been finished. A writer cannot write without an audience."

We were sitting in the living room of the apartment where Aksyonov spent many days in his last year in Moscow. The building itself was an immense pile of gloomy, red-brown stone sprawled in a giant W-shape along the Moscow River a few blocks northeast of the Kremlin. Heavy wire-mesh awnings extended over the main entrances to guard pedestrians from chunks of stone that came loose during the harsh winters and tumbled from the facades. High above, a heavy spire squatted atop the center section of the building, reaching incongruously cathedral-like into the winter sky.

This was the Kotelnicheskaya apartment house, where some of the capital's richest, most prominent families live in high-ceilinged privilege. There are parquet floors, ornate woodwork, and smoothly operating elevators. The vast building, designed to the personal whim of Stalin, the ex-seminarian, is among the best examples of fascist-Gothic architecture to be found anywhere east of Berlin and west of Peking. There are seven such buildings in Moscow, all built at Stalin's command. We visited this huge *dom* at different times of day, but the scene at night was the most powerful, the most unvarying. The darkness cloaking the building seemed to clarify the designer's intentions for me. The structure welcomed darkness.

Within the wings of the W, the inner courtyard was quiet, a dark canyon through which a few Moscovites burdened with string bags moved soundlessly, disappearing homeward through dimly lit inner courtyard entrances. Lights glowed faintly in windows buried higher up in the beetling facade. A battered bread truck was usually parked at the service entrance of a ground-floor bread store. There, a delivery man in a fur hat and dirty smock threw empty wooden bread trays into the truck and a store attendant of impressive girth, with a small white cap pinned to her hair, groused at him. As we passed by, they gave us cool stares. The homey aroma of warm loaves never quite dispelled the building's false pomp. With its overblown stone decor, architectural confusion, and strange layout that turned it into an isolating maze, the apartment house was an unmistakable attempt at visual intimidation, the perfect physical symbol of a basic component of Soviet psychology.

Apartment No. 121 was the home of Maya Karmen, Aksyonov's long-time companion and widow of one of the USSR's most famous documentary cinematographers, Roman Karmen, who had died some months before; she was soon to become Aksyonov's wife. The apartment was a sumptuous place by anyone's reckoning, with its spacious hall that doubled as a foyer, two big rooms filled with imposing furniture, and a large, cozy kitchen paneled in wood. In the dining room, Aksyonov's collection of mugs, picked up during his travels abroad, sat atop a long shelf. A shortwave radio, digital clock, and color television stood in the corners. A portrait of Karl Marx with an Order of Lenin glued to his chest lent an irreverent touch. In most countries, a piece of sculpture like this would be a jest. Here, it was a statement.

During our visits, the telephone rang incessantly—with calls from friends, wanting news, wishing Maya and Vasili well. Always there was the possibility that the next call might be from the visa authorities, giving permission for them to leave. Similar nerve-wracking scenes had been played out in tens of thousands of homes during the great wave of Jewish emigration in the 1970s. But this was no consolation. The unpredictability of the state made each family's wait a nightmare. "This has been the hardest year of my life," Vasili said as we sat over tea. "There have been such critical changes in it. We have been suspended for so long, unable to expect anything from 'them.' The long months of goodbye, the tragic expressions in our friends' eyes. And it goes on and on and on."

The exit visas finally came and their situations eased. But then there was a flood of legal and official chores: trips to obscure bureaus, complex financial declarations to prove that Maya and Vasili owed nothing to the state . . . on and on.

As spring ripened, they spent weekends at their dacha in Peredelkino, the legendary village about fifteen miles west of Moscow where, for more than a century, Russia's writers had gone to relax in quiet forest groves. The Aksyonovs had bought their house from the family of a senior military man who had recently died. Like most of the other dachas, theirs was hidden behind a solid plank fence and a heavy gate. The house, at No. 17B Gorky Lane, had three rooms with a high, peaked roof and a small deck across the front. Every weekend for nearly three months the Aksyonovs produced a banquet there for any friends who cared to come. Dozens did. Of all ages, their presence brought parts of Vasili's past alive for me, and helped me to understand the forces that shaped him and much of the country's creative life as well. Vasili's attempts to explain Soviet reality to itself were rooted in the kind of experience with a native country that seldom befalls most Westerners.

One woman in particular caught my attention during these weekends. White-haired, about 70, she had a pension of fifty rubles a month and worked as a night guard at a city museum for another sixty rubles a month. Like millions of pensioners, she worked to eat. The woman had an interesting history. In 1937, at the age of 27, she was dispatched into the Gulag on a trumped-up charge. During a three-week journey with seventy-five other young women packed into a railroad cattlecar from the Butyrka Isolator in Moscow to slave labor camps in the Far East, she met Vasili Aksyonov's mother, Eugenia Ginsburg.

At the time, Eugenia Ginsburg was the wife of the Communist mayor of Kazan, a major provincial city on the Volga in the heart of Tartaria, four hundred fifty miles east of Moscow. Seeing what was coming, friends had begged Eugenia to change her identity and flee from Kazan with her two young sons. Ignoring the pleas, Eugenia stayed. Then one day, when Vasili was 4 years of age and his older brother, Alexei, was 10, there was a knock on the door. Eugenia had just disciplined the younger boy for some childish transgression and, when the rap of knuckles interrupted them, he was still in tears from her punishment. She answered the door—and eleven years passed before she saw Vasili again. The memory of his tear-stained face tortured her for years afterward.

Shortly after Eugenia was taken, Pavel Askyonov, Vasili's father and the mayor of the town, was arrested. He also disappeared into the Gulag. Vasili was sent to live with relatives elsewhere in Russia, and Alexei was sent to stay with other relatives in Leningrad. When the Wermacht besieged Leningrad after the June 1941 invasion, he was trapped there. It took the Russians nine hundred days to lift the siege, one day too long for Alexei Aksyonov. He was loaded aboard the first trainload of surviving children evacuated by the Red Army when they finally broke through, and there he died, at the age of 16. "My mother never forgot his face," said Vasili, who was to name his own son Alexei.

Eugenia Ginsburg wrote two volumes of memoirs of her life in the camps, *Journey into the Whirlwind* and *Within the Whirlwind*. Both have been published in the West, but not in the USSR. Devoid of polemics, they tell with stark simplicity how the cat-and-mouse game with her interrogators began and how it ended, with her confined to prison as "an enemy of the people" for having failed to denounce a superior. She tells of the years of privation and the astonishingly exalted meaning of even the simplest act of humanity in such an existence.

As with so many families that passed through the camps and

survived, her marriage did not. After they were released and rehabilitated, she and her husband lived apart. Eugenia Ginsburg spent her last years in Moscow. She died in 1977 and is buried in a cemetery on the eastern fringes of Moscow.

Meanwhile, the white-haired pensioner who had accompanied Eugenia Ginsburg on that fateful train journey in 1937 also had emerged from the camps. She was 45 then. Her family had disappeared without a trace. She returned to Moscow to the same apartment from which she had been seized eighteen years before. The same neighbors were still living next door, and they greeted her as if she had hardly been away. There are survivors like this everywhere in the Soviet Union and, for every one of them, there are one or two former neighbors who, to save their own skins, accused the victims of offenses against the state. In some cases, accuser and rehabilitated victim live across the same hallway, just as they did in 1937. One of the few links to any part of her life that the pensioner had was her friendship with Eugenia Ginsburg. She had searched for Eugenia and now maintained the friendship.

In 1955, Vasili was a young postgraduate medical student on a visit from Leningrad to Kazan. He was alseep one morning on a sofa bed, nursing a hangover, when his aunt answered a knock at the door. "She cried in horror, joy, surprise." The man standing there was Vasili's father. When Pavel Aksyonov was released during the rehabilitation after Stalin's death, he returned home to Kazan without notifying anyone ahead of time. "He had forgotten he could send a telegram," his son explained. Pavel Aksyonov settled again in Kazan, as a retiree. "It was a great pity and mistake that Khrushchev never again used these people," Vasili said one day. "They could have made a real contribution to the building of the state. Many were still willing despite what had happened."

Pavel Aksyonov spent part of his son's last summer in Russia at the Peredelkino dacha. Then 82, tall, spare, and vital, with lively eyes and the hammy instincts of a revivalist preacher—which, as an Old Bolshevik, he more or less was—the father was on hand one day when a visiting American brought to the house a Russian-language edition of a recent biography of Nikolai Bukharin, the leading liberal theorist of the Revolution, a man Lenin once had called "the darling of the party." Bright, sophisticated, and ruthless, Bukharin nevertheless made a mistake. He sided with Stalin to defeat Trotsky after Lenin's death in 1924. Within a few years Stalin had consolidated power and, a few years after that, Bukharin found himself the defendant at the centerpiece of the Great Purge, his own trial for treason. Stalin ordered him executed.

Now the old man grabbed the Bukharin book and peered intently at a section of photographs. "I knew him," he said, pointing at the picture of someone leaning close to Stalin. His finger rested on a photograph of Nikolai Yezhov, commissar of internal affairs who ran the purge for Stalin. He did his work so well that the Russian nickname for the purge, even today, is *yezhovschina.* In time, Yezhov himself was devoured by it. "He wasn't such a bad guy," said Pavel Aksyonov, whose own life had been shattered by the yezhovschina. "He knew a lot about people and how to talk with them."

That summer of 1980 was very wet and, between showers, we would sit on the deck of Vasili's dacha while formations of mosquitoes rose from the dense, damp foliage around the house to draw our blood. One afternoon, I found Maya alone and the house relatively quiet. We sipped fresh coffee and batted at the humming insects. Her mind was on a play, *The House on the Embankment,* adapted from a complex novella of the same name written by Yuri Trifonov in 1976. The novella deals with moral choice during the Terror. The play had premiered a few weeks before to rave reviews at the Taganka Theater and many of the intelligentsia had seen either the full preview rehearsal or the premiere. I had been fortunate enough to receive an invitation to the dress rehearsal; it was an extraordinary experience.

Trifonov, whose unexpected death in 1981 robbed the country of one of its most sophisticated and polished storytellers, was exploring the workings of time and moral complicity in his novella. The tale concerns a man, Glebov, who in his youth betrays his mentor and ultimately profits directly in his own career from the other's downfall. The play opens as Glebov, now a successful Moscow professor, accidentally happens upon a drunken derelict whom he suddenly recognizes from the house on the Moscow River embankment where they had both lived during Glebov's childhood. Appalled, he calls out, "Lev!" but the laborer ignores him, spits on the street in disgust, and passes by. In horror, Glebov realizes that the other man still has not forgiven him for the betrayal Glebov has been struggling all his life to forget. Despite the intervening years, his own shame and guilt are every bit as real and unbearable as at the moment of betrayal—and the other man will never forget. Here were themes that spoke to the soul of contemporary Soviet sensibilities.

The Taganka Theater's stage version of this story took place mostly behind a bizarre wall of glass panes stretched across the front of the stage. The glass front included small, hinged *fortochki*, or ventilation windows, such as every Russian house has, and several doors through which the characters moved back and forth. The glass was warped and dirty in a way that suggested the nature of the past. Microphones gave tinny, disembodied amplification to the voices from behind the wall, and the recollections of the main characters were dramatized by disturbing tableaux: a chorus of Young Pioneers in their red scarves and white shirts innocently singing songs idolizing Stalin from a ramp that carried the unmistakable suggestion of a gallows, and a group of darkened figures with illuminated, spectral heads recalling events from the past.

The night I attended, the audience was composed primarily of Moscow's artistic elite, many of whose parents had been imprisoned or executed in the Terror because of the kind of betrayal Trifonov described. Not a sound was to be heard from them throughout the first act. At intermission, people were nervous and guarded as we talked. But when the performance ended and the lights came up, the audience erupted into a standing ovation. Amid waves of emotional applause, Trifonov and director Yuri Lyubimov came to the stage, smiling as flowers from the audience cascaded over them. *The House on the Embankment* was the most exciting and compelling exploration of Soviet reality that had been seen in the capital in years.

"Why blame me for what happened?" shouts the young Glebov desperately in a passage that remains unforgettable. "Don't blame me—blame the times!"

"This is the way it was, certainly," Maya ruminated as we drank coffee. "Many people were caught in this. Now, it is very difficult to imagine, but it happened to millions."

Later that day, more than a dozen people gathered at the dacha for a feast of roast chicken, greens, potatoes, casserole, pickles, wine, vodka, dessert, and tea. They drifted in and out of the summerhouse to sit on the deck and discuss the play that had penetrated their lives. Inside, the feasting continued under the indifferent gaze of a large cat who lay on a windowsill near the table. The cat, an elderly tom with thick gray fur and quiet ways, lived part of the time under the dacha and the rest of the time with a neighboring family.

"It really is a homeless being," said Maya. "It looks after itself, has survived perhaps twenty years already, and always eats fully whatever it finds. This is a familiar approach to life, eating everything now because you don't know what tomorrow might bring. It is distinctive behavior. The cat has the personality of a zek."

Prisoners of the Gulag were called zeks. Survivors still call each other that in moments of communion obscure to Westerners. Pavel Aksyonov, a zek, stayed behind when his son finally left for the West. "Come visit us in the United States," Vasili said.

"No, I'm an old man, I won't," said the father, as if he had had enough of the strange place the world had become. He was an honored citizen of Kazan and, according to Vasili, when people there saw him on the street, walking with his beret pulled down on his head in the no-nonesense Russian style, they tipped their hats in respect to the Old Bolshevik. Some time ago, the father had received a commemorative scroll from the party, to which he still belonged, commending him for his many years of constructive service to the motherland. Nowhere among the fine words did the scroll mention his eighteen years of imprisonment. Those scrolls never do.

When Khrushchev personally attacked Vasili Aksyonov in 1961 for his daring new style, the Soviet premier said the young author was writing scandalously to avenge his father. Two decades later, when Aksyonov was in trouble over *Metropol*, Writers Union officials accused him of fomenting a scandal to avenge his mother.

A few days before he climbed aboard the jet that carried him to Paris together with Maya, now his wife, and her children by her first marriage, Aksyonov spent some time with me, ruminating about the unexpected course his life was taking. "In the West, I expect many changes for us; we will live under completely different conditions. But I don't think now that the writing changes. I already have been writing completely freely for many years. Merely my position will change. I became persona non grata here. In the West, I hope to be persona grata. I am acquainted with American, British, and German authors, and that stands for something.

"Of course, I will miss my friends. But I hope to be part of the literary world of the United States and Europe. It's a friendly world for me. It's enough for me to have a quiet place and pursue my writing. It's what I want."

III

AKSYONOV's departure on July 22, 1980, was the first that year of three crucial forced exiles abroad of Soviet writers. Together with the internal exile of Andrei Sakharov, the 1980 banishments permanently impoverished and intimidated Moscow's—and therefore the country's—intelligentsia for many years to come.

On November 12, 1980, Lev Kopelev and his wife, Raya Orlova, left for West Germany under circumstances already described. Their departure brought to an end one of Moscow's most unique institutions—the Kopelev apartment. There likely was no place in the country quite as exciting as that two-room apartment on Red Army Street where conversations—intensely intellectual, frequently funny, always lively—proceeded from midmorning to late at night in Russian, English, and German. The visitors to the Kopelevs were young Soviet poets, would-be novelists, historians, jazz musicians, literary critics, fledgling cinematographers, social researchers, physicists, and retirees. Some, like Lev himself, were elderly survivors of the camps. Some had been expelled from the Writers Union, or from scientific institutes because they had applied to emigrate. Some were simply friends risking their official positions by dropping in for tea and a chat. Jumbled into this mix were Western correspondents, European and American tourists, Western diplomats, occasional Western authors or their publishers, or the stray Soviet truth seeker with a complex complaint to which no one else cared to listen. The flat was a place of surprise, distraction, and continuous activity.

Although they had neither the fame of a Solzhenitsyn nor the worldwide moral stature of a Sakharov, Kopelev and his wife ranked close behind them in the context of life in the capital. Their home served as an intellectual switchboard where people from all over the country could plug in, cross-connect, and transfer ideas. In a nation where serendipitous unofficial free exchanges of ideas are frowned upon, the Kopelevs occupied a place of unusual significance and, for that reason alone, they were vulnerable to reprisal. They always knew the state could pressure them to leave by offering a Hobson's choice of "exile East or West—you choose." Lev had been ousted from the Writers Union in 1977 for attempting to defend Sakharov, and yet had continued speaking out on his behalf.

Once when I visited them in the spring of 1978, for example, Raya prophetically predicted their own banishment from Russia. It was the time when the regime had unexpectedly stripped virtuoso cellist Mstislav Rostropovich and his wife, soprano Galina Vishnevskaya, of their Soviet citizenship and denounced them as "ideological degenerates."

Rostropovich, the conductor of the Washington National Symphony, had been living outside Russia since 1974 and had spoken out repeatedly about the need for artistic freedom. Before going abroad, he had sheltered Solzhenitsyn during the period of harassment preceding the author's own exile. But the state, aware of the importance to the West of Rostropovich's art and his apparent freedom, had always winked at the musician's political activities. Then the blow fell and Moscovites were left to divine what the sudden move against Rostropovich might portend for their own situations.

"Rostropovich was on a musical level with Solzhenitsyn, but he was not the same kind of dissident," Raya said then. "When Rostropovich was in favor in Washington, the Soviets flirted with him, asking him to national receptions. For a while, they were content if he simply came home from time to time to demonstrate his loyalty. They wanted to keep him as a Soviet who occasionally worked abroad. But he made clear that he wanted conditions of freedom for himself and other illustrious musicians and that presented a choice of either changing the atmosphere in the country or forcing Rostropovich out. Of course, it was a lot easier to cut him off than to change the atmosphere. They obviously wanted to punish him by separating him from his friends. He had relatives here, many friends, a house. As they see it, in the West he has only his music. All of us, of course, face a possible similar fate. They could force us to leave and then cancel our citizenship."

On January 22, 1981, two months after they had gone into exile, Soviet authorities revealed that the Kopelevs had been secretly stripped of their citizenship.

Next to go was Vladimir Voinovich, the masterful satirist, who had not been published in Russia for years. His hilarious *The Life and Extraordinary Adventures of Private Ivan Chonkin* was a bootleg favorite in Moscow that has sold thousands of copies in the West. He had been reprimanded repeatedly for such irreverent accounts as *The Ivankiad* and hounded by the KGB, whose agents on one occasion gave him a drugged cigarette that made him sick for several days. His irreverence and courage were legendary. Once, Writers Union pooh-bahs asked for names for a proposed new committee that would recommend Soviet literary works for sale abroad. Voinovich suggested that, since their works had sold more copies in the West than all other Soviet authors combined, Sakharov and Solzhenitsyn should be appointed to run the committee.

Voinovich lived with his second wife, Irina, and their young daughter, Olga, in a pleasant apartment in an older building near the Kopelevs. More than most other writers we knew there, with the possible exception of the meticulous Roy Medvedev, Vladimir Voinovich had the air of a writer. His desk in the apartment's main room was heavy and old and he tried to set aside daily hours for writing. His major success, *Chonkin*, could be found in various foreign-language editions in a bookcase nearby. A handmade wooden miniature of the peasant soldier stood guard over the desk. The wooden version of Chonkin, whose wisdom, cunning, and stubbornness made him something of an alter ego to his creator, seemed to be reminding the author that his hero had more life left to live.*

The fact that Voinovich had been bottled up inside his own society for so long had only sharpened his sense of the freedom an artist must have. His views on this were blunt and decisive. For example, *Metropol*'s organizers barred contributions from several controversial figures, such as Lev Kopelev, saying they would serve as political lightning rods, jeopardizing the project's hopes of publication. Voinovich rejected that approach. "Once you already establish such conditions," he remarked one day, "then you don't have a free literature or a free challenge."

He applied for a one-year exit visa in April 1980 and received permission to go in December. A few days before his departure, we went to a farewell banquet hosted by Boris Messerer, the set designer, in his loft studio a few blocks from Red Square. The loft was on several levels, with wide steps leading dramatically up from the main studio area to a large platform that connected to a small kitchen near the entrance. Portions of backdrops, stage flies, and abstract designs on paper and particle board leaned against the walls. More than fifty friends who had been loyal to Voinovich during his long

---

*He did. Chonkin's adventures continue in *Pretender to the Throne* (Farrar, Straus and Giroux, 1981).

years of confrontation came for an evening of food, drink, reminis-
cence, and songs. Despite the candles, festive makeshift tables, platters of tasty home-cooked food, and overpowering Russian good
cheer, detectable tension settled over the gathering early on and
focused on his two children by a previous marriage, who were to
remain behind. Marina, then 21, and Pavel, 18, were clearly struggling to maintain their composure. The sense of impending loss was
deepened by the fact that most of the guests were close friends of
the Kopelevs and Aksyonovs. The talk around the banquet tables
centered on how the missing families were faring in the West. At
that moment, the prospect of life there seemed remote and almost
threatening, an impression reinforced by the Soviet Union's closed
borders, mail interceptions, and the difficulties in making or receiving international telephone calls.

The quietly somber mood lifted briefly when a well-known television actress began to sing satiric songs. Soon, the loft rang with
delighted laughter. Then, a man and woman began to sing a cap-
pella love songs and laments from the rich trove of Russia's romantic
past. Their voices, pure and throbbing, wove a melancholy spell.
Emotions were already near the surface, and Voinovich, who had
been conversing quietly with friends, suddenly stopped as if
stricken. He cast a tortured glance toward his older children, and
rushed from the room with a tearful oath. A stunned silence, and
then murmurs of sympathy passed through the gathering. Irina
Voinovich hurried to comfort her husband. In time, he returned,
red-eyed and subdued. Bulat Okudzhava, the balladeer, strummed
his battered guitar and began singing. Soon, this refrain brought a
peaceful new silence to the room:

> Each writes as he hears,
> Each hears just as he breathes,
> As he breathes, so he writes,
>   Not trying to please.
> So nature wanted it.
> Why is not our business.
> Why is not for us to judge.*

---

*Translated by Nina and Brennan Klose from a tape recording.

The instant of anguish transformed the evening from a leave-taking among old friends into a painful farewell echoing the tales of Russia's master storytellers. All understood the situation: he had no choice but to emigrate. "It hurts every one of us, right here," said a retired writer. She pointed to her heart.

The Way Out

I was alone in Moscow. Once again, it was summer, the same season in which I had arrived four years before. But now, in late June of 1981, there was no more time left for me; the Moscow assignment was coming to a close.

Eliza and the children had already flown off to America, and soon we would pick up our lives there. Eliza telephoned from Vermont one day, her voice tinny and ethereal as it came through over the office phone. As she talked, a strong summer breeze whipped Moscow's dust and grime through the small park beyond my office window. After we finished our conversation, I would walk there under the trees and hope to meet a young biologist with whom I had forged a friendship. Eliza, using the informal pseudonyms we had given various Russian friends in hopes of preserving their anonymity from the state ("The Fishes" had a tankful of guppies in their living room, "Mr. Remington" dreamed of owning an electric razor, etc.), said she already had spoken with various relatives of these Moscovites. We intended to keep our friendships going despite the fact that we might never again set foot in the Soviet capital. We knew that, whatever lay ahead, Russia would always be part of us. This was no less true for the children.

Each summer after the Moscow school year was over, Nina, Brennan, and Chandler had returned to America to be with their many relatives: grandparents and cousins of Eliza's Vermont clan and other kinfolk at the farm in Dutchess County, New York, where my brothers and sisters and I had grown up. But the children's experiences were now so radically different from those of my own childhood that I could not even begin to compare them.

Nina and Brennan had spent the entire four years in Soviet public schools and were fluent in Russian. Nina had studied music theory and flute twice a week at a nearby music school; Brennan had been part of a Young Pioneers club that built and flew model airplanes. Chandler had attended School No. 5 for almost two years and, to my American ear, his Russian seemed flawless. The children's classmates, or perhaps the classmates' parents, had little interest in fostering friendships with the sons and daughter of an American correspondent: it was too dangerous. But the children survived this particular isolation with little regret. We had many Soviet friends with children or grandchildren of ages close to those of our children, so daily life was not too solitary. The children felt more comfortable in Moscow's subways or on its clanking trolley cars than they did in any American city. They had spent as much time swimming in the Moscow River and kite-flying on its banks as anywhere else in the world. "The children miss Moscow," Eliza said before she hung up. Four years earlier, I would have laughed at such a statement. Now I knew this could be true.

I went looking for my young biologist. He was an innocuous, pleasant man who had nothing more serious on his mind than practicing his English on me, while I practiced my Russian on him. He never asked me for anything, which was unusual, and he liked to tell me small details of his personal life, such as the time he was working as a druzhinnik for his institute and was called to a disturbance in a beer bar. He arrived to find a drunken man dancing on the bar, while disgusted patrons made sarcastic remarks at the drunk. "Maybe I should take him into custody," he had suggested to the cashier. Groans of dismay greeted this tentative offer. "Don't you know that's the butcher?" several women said. "You arrest him and he'll get even—no meat for anyone."

I found Robert on a sagging wooden bench, staring with interest at a young woman who was sitting on a bench opposite. She had dark hair and a strong jaw. Some babushki were tending children and an old man, exhausted with age, sat slumped on another bench. A wonderfully commonplace Russian scene, I thought. The biologist stood up as I approached, shook my hand, and then escorted me away from the park. As we walked together, he shot a quick glance over his shoulder at the woman. Her face seemed blank and indifferent. Instantly, I recognized the situation. So it was not surprising when Robert, for that was the English name I had given this man, leaned toward me and said in a low voice, "She followed me here."

"Well . . . I'm sorry," I said, feeling weary and depressed.

"I can't see you anymore," Robert said. "I've been told at the institute that you're an evil man, dangerous, and I have been reprimanded for seeing you."

"Did they make you sign a protocol?"

"Not this time. But there can't be any 'next' time."

"It's all right, then," I said. "Not too serious. They couldn't think I'm all that dangerous or they would have done this a long time ago. Besides, I'm leaving the country soon anyway. After a few months, they'll forget all about it. You shouldn't have any more trouble." I spoke with more conviction than I felt.

Robert gave me a crestfallen look. "I wanted you to introduce me to your successor. But now I can't."

"Keep the telephone numbers I gave you and maybe you can risk trying a friendship with someone sometime in the future."

"I have something for you," he said. He reached into his valise and pulled out a large flat package and opened it for me. It was a photographic panorama of the Moscow skyline photographed from some high vantage point in the Kremlin. The gold domes of the fortress's churches gleamed in the foreground and farther away loomed the bulk of the Rossiya Hotel, the State Planning Committee, and other downtown landmarks.

"Thank you for taking the trouble to see me," Robert said as my throat worked. He gave me a warm handshake and walked away.

"Thank you," I said in a choked voice that he didn't seem to hear. "Goodbye." In a few moments, he was so far down the sidewalk that I couldn't pick him out in the crowd of pedestrians. I went back to the park; the young woman had vanished as well.

Ten days later, I flew out of Moscow for the United States. I'd been back to America four times during the four years, but this was completely different. I was very uncertain of my own feelings. At Kennedy Airport, the customs agent was a young woman. She looked at my declaration card. "What's it like in Russia?"

"Strange place. I loved it."

"You did, huh?"

"Yes."

"Well, welcome back home. Please open these two bags."

After a few days' reunion with the family in Dutchess County, Eliza and I went to Washington to complete arrangements with my editors for the sabbatical I needed to write this book. There, I discovered that behavior ingrained in Moscow dies slowly. I was at luncheon with the two *Post* correspondents who had preceded me in Moscow, Peter Osnos and Robert Kaiser. We were at the Federal City Club, where the tables are set well away from each other and privacy is no problem. The conversation turned to mutual Soviet friends. Halfway through the meal, the waiter came over with a slightly worried expression on his face.

"Is something wrong?" he asked.

Puzzled, we looked up. "No. . . ."

"Good," he said. "I just thought perhaps. . . ."

Then it dawned on us. Unconsciously, we had lowered our voices and our heads were almost under the table. It seemed that the only thing lacking was a "Soviet phrase book"—a child's magic slate— indispensable for "silent" conversations when who knows who might be listening.

Later that week, I telephoned an American whom I did not know to pass on a message from a mutual Soviet friend. My call reached the American in the middle of a business meeting.

"Yes?" he said, impatience in his voice.

"I have a message for you from . . . from. . . ." I suddenly realized I could remember only the pseudonym Eliza and I had used to protect our Soviet friend from reprisals. "From . . . the Little Beard!" I stammered helplessly.

"Who?" the American asked.

I tried again—and again could not conjure up the man's real name. It took us some time to figure out whom I was talking about.

From Washington, we planned to go to Vermont where we would live in the old farmhouse on a dirt road where we had spent most of the summers since the children were small.

It took a long time to start writing. When our belongings arrived from Moscow, unpacking them was a delight and also disquieting. The mementos were precious, such as a cracked teacup that an elderly friend had given us, or two battered metal holders for the teaglasses that Russians prefer. Each item reminded us that this extraordinary experience was over, and that there were people tucked away behind the Soviet Union's closed borders whom we would never see again. Occasionally, late at night, we could hear the children in their beds, speaking Russian in their sleep. Brennan came to breakfast one morning with a wistful expression. "I dreamed I was in Moscow," he said. "Confusing, isn't it?"

People were eager to know about our experiences, whether I thought the USSR could be trusted to uphold its end of a strategic arms agreement, or whether the nuclear freeze movement was the way to go. How did the Soviets view Reagan, and could détente ever resume? Where was the Soviet Union headed? Such questions made me think of conversations earlier that spring when the assignment was winding down. At such times, journalists customarily do something that most of us aren't very good at—gazing at a crystal ball. During my bout of prophecy, I had turned to Konstantin P., a teacher, whose passion was his country's history from the time of the Revolution to the present.

Konstantin's teaching chores were about to end for the year and his manner when I arrived at his apartment one afternoon was relaxed and professorial. In his small, book-lined study–bedroom at the rear of the apartment, the family dog, a pedigreed English spaniel, was stretched comfortably on the floor. Konstantin, a friend of many months, began stoking his pipe. He was unusual in one respect: he didn't mind talking about the future. Most Moscovites we knew, at every level of society, thought that questions about the future were a peculiarly Western invention and largely irrelevant to their own lives. They had little more to say about the future than this: "Things are bearable today. They might be worse tomorrow. Better not to ask."

Konstantin found such queries entertaining, but he answered them in a serious way. "In every generation," he said, "the system takes the most talented people, kills them, drives them to drink, or de-spirits them. This has happened with each generation since the Revolution.

"Today's leaders—Brezhnev and the men around him—are used to privilege and isolation from the rest of the country. They enjoy these things—travel abroad, eating and drinking well—as if they are the personal representatives of a world power. Love of power is a real stimulus for keeping the status quo. In order to go abroad, you have to have international power and prestige —that is the way these people think of these things. And since prestige is determined only by power, they jealously guard what they have. So, in a sense, we have arrived at the collective leadership that Khrushchev claimed he had created but in fact never did.

"This kind of leadership can achieve things it considers supremely important. We have always moved ruthlessly when important matters were at stake. The Czech invasion, for example. We do have a will to control in such situations."

"But doesn't a will to power mean a will to dominate—in this case, the world?" I asked.

Konstantin puffed away. "Certainly! Our leaders *do* want to dominate, just the way leaders of most countries have an urge to dominate. Fortunately, most countries are too small to do much dominating. Unfortunately, this cannot be said of us. But if you Americans worry about the Communists taking away your houses or your bank accounts—you've got it all wrong. The Soviet Union doesn't want to swallow the whole world. If the Soviet Union took France, where would our leaders go when they wanted to visit Paris? Paris would become like Kharkov, and that's no good!"

I laughed, but Konstantin did not think it funny. "This isn't a joke. I'm perfectly serious. For example, have you ever been to Latvia?"

"Yes. To Riga."

"What was your impression of Riga?"

"My impression was of an old Northern European city with a rich past that was slowly decaying right into the ground. It seemed haunted to me, even more than Leningrad."

"My point exactly. You see, I'm part Latvian on my mother's side, so I'm sensitive to this. As a Latvian, I know that Soviet power is slowly but surely ruining my native land. In another few decades, Riga will be destroyed. It will still be standing and exist as a city, but not as a Latvian city—as a Soviet city. Those are two very different things. And as a Russian on my father's side, I understand our capacity to ruin things. Riga doesn't have much time left. The thought makes me sad. But believe me when I say that our leaders don't want to 'take over the West' the way Margaret Thatcher says. We only want to terrorize the West and get what we want that way. The mistake most of your countrymen make is to think they can isolate us physically. That's not possible anymore. Our planes have very long ranges. You can't keep us in place the same way as in other times. Look at Afghanistan or Czechoslovakia. We can go where we please."

"So how do Western countries deal with the Kremlin?"

"Not by a grain embargo. Carter blundered there. He hurt his own farmers and, in the end, it meant nothing because Reagan has just lifted it. So Brezhnev says to us, 'Well, we ate before there was an embargo, we ate during the embargo, and now we will continue to eat. We are Soviets and we cannot be intimidated with corn.' Soviets can take pride in this—and they do. It was a propaganda disaster for you. Americans should say that the Soviets are dictators, that we invade other nations like Afghanistan, that we jail our own people for daring to think differently. That's the kind of psychological retaliation which forces the rest of the world to contemplate what the Soviet regime really is. But you can do what you want. You don't need a historian to tell you these things." He shrugged his shoulders in a way that made me laugh.

His pithy way of speaking comes through to me even now. The voice is fresh and, when I hear it, I can easily see him tamping his pipe, lighting up, preparing to speak. The mind's power to call up faces and inflections from across a vast distance of time and space seems to me as miraculous as a conjurer's trick. Yet our ability to comprehend life remains jagged, uneven, disturbing. There are no easy dreams of Russia.

Nothing I do can erase these Russian faces and voices from the eyes and ears of my mind. With no effort at all, I see Anatoli Koryagin, the psychiatrist, holding the photograph of his family under the dim light of a table lamp in a darkened Moscow apartment. Day and night, there is Alexei Nikitin, his voice strong, his face filled with earnest hope, bidding us goodbye in Donetsk.

Acknowledgments

I am indebted to many people, who helped me in many ways. This can only be a partial list.

At *The Washington Post:* Benjamin C. Bradlee, the executive editor, and Howard Simons, the managing editor, sent us to Moscow and generously gave me two years away from the paper to write this book. Bob and Hannah Kaiser, and Peter and Susan Osnos, our predecessors in Moscow, extended invaluable advice and friendship.

In Moscow, we were befriended by Kareemah and Michael Binyon, Candy and Dan Fisher, Linda and Gene Pell, and many other colleagues. Ann Garrels was a special friend to all five of us. Annette Delaume spent the first year in Moscow with us, officially a nanny, but always a member of our family.

Professor Harvey Fireside, Dr. Allan Wynn, and Peter Reddaway offered special assistance in dealing with the subject of Soviet psychiatric abuse. Dr. Fireside generously shared with me his translations of Anatoli Koryagin's accounts of his life and his criminal trial. These make up the bulk of Chapter 4.

My editor at W. W. Norton, Carol Houck Smith, who has worked with me before, suggested this project well before the Moscow assignment was over and shepherded me along the road to completion. She was tireless and resilient in finding the way.

Scores of Russians in their homes, as well as many who have emigrated to America, gave ceaselessly and bravely of their time, friendship, and insights in the effort to help me understand the fundamentals of life in their motherland. The family of Andrei

Dmitrievich Sakharov—Elena Georgevna Bonner, Ruf Grigorevna Bonner, Efrem and Tanya Yankelevich, and Lisa and Alexei Semenov—was extraordinarily patient and generous in this regard.

My mother, Virginia Taylor Klose, and Eliza's parents, Edmund and Celina Kellogg, gave us remarkable emotional and intellectual support throughout the Moscow sojourn and later in America. The same was true of our many siblings, especially Tibbie and Woody Klose, who with their children looked after us when we needed it most.

Finally, a special word of thanks to David Satter, who reached out a hand in Moscow, resumed our friendship from another time, and generously shared so much of his life in Russia with me.

Bibliography

Aksyonov, Vasily; Yerofeyev, Viktor; Iskander, Fazil; Bitov, Andrei; and Popov, Yevgeny (eds.). *Metropol: Literary Almanac.* New York: Norton, 1983.

Babyonyshev, Alexander (ed.). *On Sakharov.* New York: Knopf, 1982.

Barron, John. *KGB: The Secret Work of Soviet Secret Agents.* Pleasantville, N.Y.: Reader's Digest Press, 1974.

Block, Sidney; and Reddaway, Peter. *Russia's Political Hospitals.* London: Gollancz, 1977.

Bukovsky, Vladimir. *To Build a Castle: My Life as a Dissenter.* New York: Viking, 1979.

Carr, E. H. *The Russian Revolution from Lenin to Stalin.* New York: The Free Press, 1979.

Cohen, Stephen F. (ed.). *An End to Silence.* New York: Norton, 1982.

Fireside, Harvey. *Soviet Psychoprisons.* New York: Norton, 1979.

Ginzburg, Eugenia. *Journey into the Whirlwind.* New York: Harcourt, 1967.

———. *Within the Whirlwind.* New York: Harcourt, 1981.

Kaiser, Robert G. *Russia: The People and the Power.* New York: Atheneum, 1976.

Khrushchev, Nikita S. *Khrushchev Remembers.* Boston: Little, Brown, 1970.

———*Khrushchev Remembers: The Last Testament.* Boston: Little, Brown, 1974.

Kopelev, Lev. *To Be Preserved Forever.* Philadelphia: Lippincott, 1977.

Kuznetsov, Edward. *Prison Diaries.* New York: Stein, 1975.

Medvedev, Zhores A. *Nuclear Disaster in the Urals.* New York: Norton, 1979.

——— and Medvedev, Roy. *A Question of Madness: Repression by Psychiatry in the Soviet Union.* New York: Norton, 1979.

Podrabinek, Alexander. *Punitive Medicine*. Ann Arbor: Karoma, 1980.

Rubenstein, Joshua. *Soviet Dissidents*. Boston: Beacon, 1980.

Sakharov, Andrei D. *Alarm and Hope*. New York: Knopf, 1978.

——*My Country and the World*. New York: Vintage, 1975.

——*Progress, Coexistence, and Intellectual Freedom*. New York: Norton, 1968.

——*Sakharov Speaks*. New York: Knopf, 1974.

Shabad, Theodore. *Geography of the USSR*. New York: Columbia, 1951.

Smith, Hedrick. *The Russians*. New York: Quadrangle, 1976.

Troyat, Henri. *Catherine the Great*. New York: Dutton, 1980.

Voinovich, Vladimir. *In Plain Russian*. New York: Farrar, Straus and Giroux, 1979.

——.*The Ivankiad*. New York: Farrar, Straus and Giroux, 1977.

——.*The Life and Extraordinary Adventures of Private Ivan Chonkin*. New York: Farrar, Straus and Giroux, 1976.

Index